Benefits for Migrants Handbook

6th edition

Rebecca Walker, Timothy Lawrence and Michael Spencer

Child Poverty Action Gro···

CPAG promotes action for the prevention and relief of poverty among children and families with children. To achieve this, CPAG aims to: raise awareness of the causes, extent, nature and impact of poverty, and strategies for its eradication and prevention; bring about positive policy changes for families with children in poverty; and enable those eligible for income maintenance to have access to their full entitlement. If you are not already supporting us, please consider making a donation, or ask for details of our membership schemes, training courses and publications.

Published by Child Poverty Action Group
94 White Lion Street
London N1 9PF
Tel: 020 7837 7979
staff@cpag.org.uk
www.cpag.org.uk

A CIP record for this book is available from the British Library

ISBN: 978 1 906076 67 2

Child Poverty Action Group is a charity registered in England and Wales (registration number 294841) and in Scotland (registration number SC039339), and is a company limited by guarantee, registered in England (registration number 1993854). VAT number: 690 808117

Cover design by Devious Designs
Typeset by David Lewis XML Associates Ltd
Content management system by Konnectsoft www.konnectsoft.com
Printed by CPI Group (UK) Ltd, Croydon CR0 4YY

The authors

Rebecca Walker is a freelance trainer and and writer on welfare rights.

Timothy Lawrence is a solicitor specialising in immigration and asylum work at Southwark Law Centre in London.

Michael Spencer is CPAG's solicitor. Previously he was the solicitor for the Asylum Support Appeals Project.

Acknowledgements

The authors would like to thank everyone who has contributed to this book and all the authors of previous editions.

Thanks are particularly due this year to Les Allamby, Henri Krishna, Fiona Ripley, Sophie Wickham, everyone at the Asylum Support Appeals Project and Martin Williamson.

We would also like to thank Alison Key for editing and managing the production of the book, Katherine Dawson for compiling the index and Kathleen Armstrong for proofreading the text.

The law covered in this book was correct on 1 June 2014. It includes regulations laid and judgments delivered up to this date.

Contents

Abbreviations

AA	attendance allowance	IB	incapacity benefit
ACD	Asylum Casework Directorate	ICE	Independent Case Examiner
ARC	application registration card	IS	income support
ASAP	Asylum Support Appeals Project	JSA	jobseeker's allowance
ASU	Asylum Screening Unit	MA	maternity allowance
BIA	Border and Immigration Agency	MP	Member of Parliament
CA	carer's allowance	NAM	new asylum model
CAB	Citizens Advice Bureau	NASS	National Asylum Support Service
CJEU	Court of Justice of the European Union	NI	national insurance
		PC	pension credit
CRD	Case Resolution Directorate	PIP	personal independence payment
CTC	child tax credit	REA	reduced earnings allowance
DLA	disability living allowance	SAL	standard acknowledgement letter
DWP	Department for Work and Pensions	SAP	statutory adoption pay
EC	European Community	SDA	severe disablement allowance
ECJ	European Court of Justice	SMP	statutory maternity pay
EEA	European Economic Area	SPP	statutory paternity pay
EFTA	European Free Trade Association	SSP	statutory sick pay
ESA	employment and support allowance	TFEU	Treaty on the Functioning of the European Union
EU	European Union	UC	universal credit
FSU	Further Submissions Unit	UK	United Kingdom
HB	housing benefit	UKBA	UK Border Agency
HMCTS	HM Courts and Tribunals Service	UKVI	UK Visas and Immigration
HMRC	HM Revenue and Customs	WTC	working tax credit

Part 1

Introduction

Chapter 1

How to use this book

This chapter covers:
1. About this *Handbook* (below)
2. Checking the rules that affect you (p5)
3. Finding the relevant law (p6)

1. About this *Handbook*

This *Handbook* is designed to be used by migrants and their advisers wanting advice on entitlement to social security benefits and tax credits. By 'migrants' we mean people, including British citizens, who have come or returned to Great Britain from abroad and people who have left Great Britain temporarily or to live abroad.

The law determining benefit entitlement for migrants is complex and frequently changing. As a result, migrants are often refused benefits and tax credits to which they are entitled, or not paid for family members when they should be.

This *Handbook* explains the different requirements that must be satisfied in order to be entitled to benefits and tax credits, so that you can understand whether or not you satisfy them and effectively challenge incorrect decisions.

This *Handbook* covers the rules that are most likely to affect migrant claimants and their families, and the practical problems they are likely to face. It is not a complete guide to the benefit rules and should be used together with general guides, such as CPAG's *Welfare Benefits and Tax Credits Handbook*.

How this book is organised

The book is split into parts, and related chapters are grouped under these parts. For a description of the information covered in each part, see below. For the chapters included in each part, see the table of contents on pv.

Part 1 is an introduction to this *Handbook*.

Part 2 gives an overview of immigration law to help you identify your immigration status and understand the immigration terms that appear in the rest of this *Handbook*. **Note:** immigration law is complex and frequently changing. If you are unclear about your, or a member of your family's, immigration status, or the effects of claiming a benefit or tax credit, you should obtain advice from a specialist immigration adviser.

Part 3 covers the way your, and your family member's, immigration status affects your entitlement to benefits and tax credits. If you and all the people included in your claim are European Economic Area nationals, the rules in this part do not apply to you.

Part 4 covers the residence and presence requirements for all the benefits and tax credits.

Part 5 explains the way your entitlement to benefits and tax credits is affected if you, or a family member for whom you claim, go abroad.

Part 6 describes the way in which the European Union social security co-ordination rules and international agreements on social security can assist you either to satisfy entitlement conditions in the UK or to be paid UK benefits abroad.

Part 7 covers some issues that can be particularly problematic for migrants – delays, satisfying the national insurance number requirement and providing evidence to show you meet the immigration, residence and presence requirements.

Part 8 covers the main types of government support for people who have made an application for asylum in the UK.

Part 9 gives an overview of other possible sources of help that may be available to migrants.

Finding information

The two most efficient ways of finding information in this *Handbook* are to use the contents page or the index.

The contents shows the structure of the book and lists the parts, the chapters and the sections within each chapter.

The index contains entries in bold type, directing you to the general information on the subject or to the page(s) where the subject is covered more fully. Sub-entries under the bold headings are listed alphabetically and direct you to specific aspects of the subject.

Throughout this *Handbook* the text is referenced with the source of information given in footnotes which are at the end of each chapter. For more information on finding the relevant law, see p6.

2. **Checking the rules that affect you**

As the rules are complicated, it is helpful to approach them systematically.

If you are not a European Economic Area (EEA) national (see p39) or if anyone you could include in your claim is not an EEA national, work through the following steps.

- **Step one:** be clear about your immigration status. See Chapter 6 for help determining on what basis you are in the UK. If you are unsure about your immigration status, or that of anyone included in your claim, get specialist advice from your local law centre, Citizens Advice Bureau or other advice agency that gives immigration advice (see Appendix 2).
- **Step two:** check whether you are defined as a 'person subject to immigration control' (see Chapter 7). If you are not, your immigration status does not affect your benefit entitlement, but you must still satisfy any rules on residence and presence (see below). **Note:** your partner's immigration status may still affect your entitlement (see Step five below).
- **Step three:** if you are defined as a 'person subject to immigration control', check whether the particular benefit or tax credit is one that excludes 'people subject to immigration control' (see p63). If it is not, your immigration status does not affect your benefit entitlement but you must still satisfy any rules on residence and presence (see below).
- **Step four:** if the benefit you want to claim is one from which 'people subject to immigration control' are generally excluded, check whether you come into an exempt groups. These vary between the different benefits and tax credits (see p64). Even if you are in an exempt group, you must still satisfy all the other conditions of entitlement, including the residence and presence requirements (see below).
- **Step five:** if you cannot claim the benefit you want, but you have a partner who can, or if you can but have a partner or child who is subject to immigration control, check the rules on partners and children (see p71).
- **Step six:** if you or a member of your family have leave to enter or remain in the UK on condition that you do not have 'recourse to public funds', check whether any claim for benefits or tax credits could affect your/their immigration status (see p57).
- **Step seven:** if you are an asylum seeker or are dependent on an asylum seeker, you may be entitled to support that is available for asylum seekers (see Chapter 21).

If you are an EEA national, or you are not an EEA national and your immigration status does not exclude you from entitlement, work through the following steps.

- **Step one:** check the residence and presence requirements for the benefit or tax credit you want to claim (see Chapter 13).

- **Step two**: if you are required to be habitually resident, check whether you are exempt from or satisfy this requirement (see Chapter 11).
- **Step three**: if you are required to have a right to reside, check how this test operates for the benefit or tax credit you want to claim (p107) and check whether you have a right to reside (see Chapter 12).
- **Step four**: if you do not satisfy the residence and presence rules, the European Union (EU) social security co-ordination rules may assist you. The ways they may assist are explained for each benefit and tax credit in Chapter 13 and an overview of the way the rules operate and who they apply to is covered in Chapter 16.

If you are entitled to benefit and want to know if you can continue to be paid when you, or someone who is included in your claim, go abroad, see Chapter 14 for an overview of the rules and Chapter 15 for the specific rules for individual benefits and tax credits. If you are going to another EEA country, the EU co-ordination rules may assist. Chapter 15 covers the ways they may assist for each benefit and tax credit, and an explanation of the way the rules operate and who they apply to is covered in Chapter 16.

3. **Finding the relevant law**

The complexity of the rules that specifically affect migrants means that it can be useful to refer to the relevant law not only when you are challenging a decision, but also when you make your claim. In order to ensure that the decision maker makes the correct decision on your claim, it may be helpful to provide an accompanying letter, setting out the legal requirement that you must satisfy and the law confirming that you satisfy it, together with evidence that it applies to you. However, this does not guarantee that the correct decision will be made. If you are refused benefit when you believe you are entitled, you should challenge the decision. In any challenge, wherever possible, try to set out the relevant legal requirements and explain clearly how you meet them, citing the relevant law as appropriate.

This *Handbook* provides references to the law (both legislation and caselaw) and to guidance, to help you trace the source of the information given in the text.
- Find the information in the book relevant to the legal requirement you must satisfy and the text on how you satisfy it that applies to you.
- Find the footnote for that information and check the footnote text at the end of the chapter for the legal reference.
- Check Appendix 7 for an explanation of the abbreviations used in the references.
- See Appendices 2 and 4 for where to find the law and guidance online and for other useful sources of information.

- See Chapter 20 for information about providing evidence to show you satisfy legal requirements.

For a useful introduction to using legal sources, see CPAG's *Welfare Benefits and Tax Credits Handbook*.

Note: the law referred to in this *Handbook* applies in Great Britain. The equivalent law in Northern Ireland is very similar and, in most cases, has the same effect. Many of the differences are due to the fact that the legislation and the administrative and adjudicating bodies in Northern Ireland are named differently. However, in some cases the differences may be more significant.

Part 2

· ·

Immigration law

Chapter 2

· ·

Immigration and nationality law: overview

This chapter covers:
1. Immigration and nationality law (below)
2. The main types of immigration status (p13)
3. British nationality (p15)
4. Immigration and nationality applications (p16)
5. Appeals and other remedies (p18)
6. Deportation (p19)

---

1. Immigration and nationality law

The right to live, work and settle in the UK is regulated and controlled by a complex system of laws. These are amended frequently.

Sources of law

The main UK Acts of Parliament that are concerned with immigration and nationality law are:
*   Immigration Act 1971;
*   British Nationality Act 1981;
*   Immigration Act 1988;
*   Asylum and Immigration Appeals Act 1993;
*   Asylum and Immigration Act 1996;
*   Human Rights Act 1998;
*   Immigration and Asylum Act 1999;
*   Nationality, Immigration and Asylum Act 2002;
*   Asylum and Immigration (Treatment of Claimants, etc) Act 2004;
*   Immigration, Asylum and Nationality Act 2006;
*   UK Borders Act 2007;
*   Borders, Citizenship and Immigration Act 2009;
*   Immigration Act 2014.

These Acts are supplemented by;
* statutory instruments (regulations);
* the Immigration Rules;
* government policies.

You can find the original (as enacted) and revised versions of Acts of Parliament and statutory instruments at www.legislation.gov.uk, although more recent revisions may not be included.

The Immigration Rules and most government policies concerning immigration can be found on the Home Office UK Visas and Immigration website at www.gov.uk/government/organisations/uk-visas-and-immigration.

The UK has also signed various international treaties and conventions, which guarantee certain rights. These include the:
* European Convention for the Protection of Human Rights and Fundamental Freedoms 1950 (the 'European Convention on Human Rights'), incorporated, in part, into UK law by the Human Rights Act 1998;
* 1951 Convention Relating to the Status of Refugees and its 1967 Protocol, commonly referred to as 'the Refugee Convention';
* 1954 Convention Relating to the Status of Stateless Persons and the 1961 Convention on the Reduction of Statelessness;
* European Council Directive 2003/9/EC, laying down minimum standards for the reception of asylum seekers ('the Reception Directive');
* European Council Directive 2004/83/EC on minimum standards for the qualification and status of third-country nationals or stateless people as refugees or as people who otherwise need international protection, and the content of the protection granted ('the Qualification Directive');
* European Council Directive 2004/38/EC on the right of citizens of the European Union and their family members to move and reside freely within the territory of the member states ('the Citizens' Directive');
* 2005 Council of Europe Convention on Action Against Trafficking in Human Beings.

Caselaw of the tribunals and higher courts in the UK and Europe is also important in immigration and nationality law. Much of this can be accessed free of charge on the British and Irish Legal Information Institute website at www.bailii.org.

Relevant institutions

The **Home Secretary** (Secretary of State for the Home Department) is responsible for the **Home Office**. The department within the Home Office that deals with immigration control is currently called **UK Visas and Immigration (UKVI)**.

Immigration officers are generally responsible for processing people who arrive at the various UK ports of entry and for arresting, detaining and enforcing the removal of people from the UK. They have powers of search, entry, seizure and arrest of those suspected of having committed a criminal offence under immigration law, and may arrest and detain people who are liable to be detained in order to enforce their departure from the UK under immigration law.

Entry clearance officers stationed overseas are responsible for immigration control prior to entry to the UK, and now mainly operate behind commercial organisations responsible for the initial processing of applications. They decide whether to give **entry clearance** or **visas** to applicants under the Immigration Rules (see Chapter 3). They also decide whether to issue **family permits** (visas granted to family members of European Economic Area nationals – see Chapter 5).

Civil servants in UKVI are mainly responsible for deciding immigration and nationality applications made in the UK. Some applications made from outside the UK are also referred to civil servants in UKVI by visa officers stationed overseas.

HM Passport Office is the executive agency of the Home Office responsible for issuing UK passports and for administering the civil registration process in England and Wales – eg, births, deaths, marriages and civil partnerships.

Police officers are responsible for registering certain people who require leave to enter and remain in the UK, arresting people suspected of having committed a criminal offence under immigration law, and arresting and detaining people who are liable to be detained in order to enforce their departure from the UK under immigration law.

Judges of the **Immigration and Asylum Chambers of the First-tier Tribunal and the Upper Tribunal** are responsible for hearing and determining appeals against decisions made by entry clearance officers, immigration officers and the Secretary of State, applications for bail and most immigration-related judicial review applications.

Judges of the **Social Entitlement Chamber of the First-tier Tribunal** are responsible for determining appeals against decisions refusing asylum support.

Judges of the **Court of Appeal and UK Supreme Court** hear appeals from the Upper Tribunal, and judges of the **High Court** continue to decide applications for judicial review of certain types of decisions by the Home Secretary and her/his officers and the Upper Tribunal.

Cases may also be brought in the **Court of Justice of the European Union** if the matter concerns European Union law (which now includes asylum issues) and in the **European Court of Human Rights** if the matter concerns the European Convention on Human Rights.

2. **The main types of immigration status**

There are four main types of immigration status in the UK. You may be a person:
- with the right of abode. This includes British citizens (see p15);
- with leave to enter or remain (see Chapter 3);

- with a right to reside as a national of the European Economic Area (EEA) or as a family member of an EEA national (see Chapter 5);
- without status – eg, if you:
  - have entered the UK illegally;
  - previously had leave to enter or remain, but no longer have any such leave;
  - have made an asylum or human rights application when you sought to enter the UK – ie, at the port (see Chapter 4).

  If you are without status, you might be given temporary admission, temporary release or bail (see below).

Note: the term 'person subject to immigration control' is important for establishing someone's entitlement to social security benefits. It has a specific meaning that is explained on p55.

Temporary admission, temporary release and bail

If you make an application for leave to enter or remain at a port of entry or while in the UK at a time when you do not have leave, you may be given temporary admission to the UK until your application is decided. This includes applications for asylum or on human rights grounds. If you have been detained, you may be granted temporary release or bail. Temporary admission or temporary release may also be given if:

- you were refused leave in the UK, but you have remained; *or*
- you have remained in the UK after your limited leave to enter or remain expired;
- you entered the UK illegally and have subsequently come to the attention of the immigration authorities.

Temporary admission, temporary release and bail are best understood as alternatives to detention. This type of status may continue if you have been refused asylum or another type of application, including if you have made a new application or further submissions that you wish to be considered as a fresh asylum and/or human rights application (see p37).

If you were given temporary admission at a port of entry, you are considered to be 'lawfully present in the UK', unless and until that status is withdrawn from you. This can be significant in relation to the requirement to have lawfully resided in the UK for a specified period of time to become eligible for citizenship or for indefinite leave to remain on the grounds of long residence. It can also be relevant to your eligibility to claim benefits.

Temporary admission or release usually means you have conditions imposed on you. These can include a requirement to live at a specified address, to report to an immigration officer at a specified time and place, and not to engage in paid or unpaid employment. There are criminal penalties if you do not adhere to these conditions, and failing to do so can make it more likely that you will be detained.

If you have temporary admission, temporary release or bail, you should have been issued with a notice informing you of your status and any conditions that apply.

Note: in certain circumstances, UK Visas and Immigration must provide accommodation to people with, or applying for, temporary admission, temporary release and bail (see p344).

3. **British nationality**

You can acquire British nationality:

- at birth, depending on the date and place of your birth, and on the nationality/ citizenship, and immigration and/or marital status, of your parents; *or*
- on adoption; *or*
- by applying to the Home Secretary for naturalisation or registration; *or*
- as the result of legislative change.

Note: the examples given in this *Handbook* of how British citizenship may be acquired are basic. British nationality law is complex and there are many other routes that are not covered here.

There are six different forms of British nationality, only one of which (British citizenship) gives the right of abode in the UK (see below). A British national may be a:

- British citizen;
- British overseas territories citizen;
- British subject;
- British protected person;
- British national (overseas);
- British overseas citizen.

Some of the above forms of British nationality are rare and can no longer be acquired. In time, only British citizenship and British overseas territories citizenship will exist.

Multiple nationalities

Although some legal systems do not allow dual or multiple nationality or citizenship, UK law permits you to be a British national and a national of any number of other countries.

British nationals and the right of abode

'**The right of abode**' gives you the freedom to live in and to come to and go from the UK.

All full British citizens have the right of abode, but most people who have some other form of British nationality do not. Some Commonwealth citizens also have the right of abode, including people who are British nationals and not British citizens. However, it has not been possible to gain the right of abode since 1983 without also being a British citizen.

British nationals who do not have the right of abode generally require leave to enter or remain in the UK, but may have certain advantages over other foreign nationals in relation to applications for full British citizenship.

Acquiring British citizenship at birth

Most people, except children of diplomats or 'enemy aliens', born in the UK before 1 January 1983 automatically acquired British citizenship on that date.[1]

If you were born in the UK on or after 1 January 1983, you only acquired British citizenship if, at the time of your birth:

- your mother was a British citizen or was 'settled' in the UK – eg, she had indefinite leave to remain or permanent residence;[2] *or*
- your father was a British citizen or was 'settled' in the UK. If you were born before 1 July 2006, you could only gain citizenship from your father in this way if your parents were married, either at the time or subsequently. From 1 July 2006, this restriction has no longer applied. If you were born before this date and did not acquire British citizenship because your parents were not married, you may now be able to register as a British citizen.

From 1 January 1983, a child born overseas acquires British citizenship if either parent is a British citizen, unless that parent is her/himself a British citizen by descent – eg, because s/he was also born overseas.[3] The same policy as above applies to unmarried British fathers of children born abroad.

4. **Immigration and nationality applications**

Applying from outside the UK

You must obtain entry clearance before travelling to the UK to seek entry for most purposes.

Nationals of countries or territories listed in Appendix 1 of the Immigration Rules are known as 'visa nationals'. If you are a visa national, you must obtain a visa before travelling to the UK for any purpose (unless you are a refugee – see Chapter 4).

Nationals of all other countries ('non-visa nationals') may apply to an immigration officer at the port of arrival for entry for certain purposes, mainly for short-term visits. If you intend to stay for a longer period, you must usually obtain entry clearance before travelling.

Note: a European Economic Area (EEA) family permit is a visa issued to a non-EEA family member of an EEA national. However, it is not always necessary to obtain a family permit before being admitted to the UK. See p40 for more details.

An exempt vignette is issued to people, such as diplomats, who are exempt from the requirements of the Immigration Act 1971.

In most countries, you can apply for entry clearance online. In some countries, you must complete a printed application form. All applicants must attend a visa application centre in person. There is not a centre in every country in the world, so some applicants must travel to a different country to apply. Most applicants must have their fingerprints and facial image (known as 'biometric information') recorded at the visa application centre.

If you wish to apply for British nationality from outside the UK, you must usually send your application to UK Visas and Immigration (UKVI) in the UK.

Applying from within the UK

UKVI is responsible for processing applications made by people in the UK:
* for leave to remain in the UK, including for asylum;
* to extend their leave to remain or vary their leave to remain – ie, to change the type of leave or the conditions attached to it;
* for confirmation of their right to reside as an EEA national or the family member of an EEA national;
* for British nationality.

Some types of application can be made online from within the UK, but all applications must be supported by original documents.

A fee is charged for most in-country applications. Exceptions to this include an application:
* for leave to enter or remain for asylum reasons, including applications made under Article 3 of the European Convention on Human Rights for health reasons;
* for an extension of leave from someone who has had her/his asylum application rejected, but has been granted limited leave to enter or remain;
* from a child who is in the care of a local authority;
* for limited leave to enter or remain for certain purposes if UKVI accepts that the applicant is destitute.

Certain types of application must usually be made in person at a specified location. These include applications for asylum (except those made under Article 3 of the European Convention on Human Rights for health reasons) and further asylum and/or human rights submissions from someone who has previously applied for asylum unsuccessfully. Other types of application may also be made in person. A 'premium service' is available, with a shorter processing time (applications are sometimes dealt with on the same day), at an increased cost.

5. **Appeals and other remedies**

Appeals to the First-tier Tribunal

The First-tier Tribunal (Immigration and Asylum Chamber) is a judicial authority that is independent of the UK government.

You can appeal to the First-tier Tribunal against either an 'immigration decision' (see below) or a 'European Economic Area (EEA) decision' (see below). You can also apply to the First-tier Tribunal for bail from immigration detention.

Only the following are 'immigration decisions':[4]

- a decision by the Secretary of State that you can be removed from the UK where you have made a claim that you cannot be removed because of the Refugee Convention or because you are eligible for humanitarian protection;
- a decision by the Secretary of State to refuse a human rights claim you have made;
- a decision by the Secretary of State to revoke your leave to enter or remain as a refugee or as a person eligible for humanitarian protection.

'EEA decisions' are only decisions under the Immigration (European Economic Area) Regulations 2006 that concern:[5]

- a person's entitlement to be admitted to the UK;
- a person's entitlement to be issued with, have renewed or not to have revoked, a registration certificate, a residence card, a derivative residence card, a document certifying permanent residence or a permanent residence card;
- a person's removal from the UK; *or*
- the cancellation of a person's right to reside in the UK.

You can also appeal against a decision to deprive you of British citizenship.[6]

Appeals can only be made from within the UK against certain decisions and in certain circumstances, including if you have made a claim that your removal from the UK would be unlawful under the Refugee Convention or under the European Convention on Human Rights. The Secretary of State also has powers to prevent you from appealing from within the UK before you have been removed, or at all, if you have made an asylum and/or a human rights claim that is clearly unfounded, or if you failed to take an earlier opportunity to appeal.

In most cases, you must pay a fee when you appeal. This does not apply if you are appealing against a decision to remove you from the UK, if you are receiving legal aid, or if you are a child being supported by a local authority.

If you win your appeal, UK Visas and Immigration (UKVI) decides whether this means you must be granted leave or, in EEA law cases, whether your right to reside must be confirmed by issuing you with an appropriate document. Delays can occur while this is being considered (see p46).

Administrative review

If a decision has been made about you by UKVI that is not an 'immigration decision' or an 'EEA decision' (see p18), you may be able to apply to the Home Office for an administrative review. This is not carried out by an independent body. Examples of such decisions include a decision to refuse you entry clearance or to refuse you leave to enter or remain, or to remove you from the UK where you have not made an asylum, humanitarian protection or human rights claim.

Judicial review

If a decision has been made about you that does not carry a right to appeal, you may be able to challenge its lawfulness by applying for a judicial review to the Upper Tribunal or to the Administrative Court, depending on the nature of the decision. This includes a decision to uphold a refusal after an administrative review.

The Administrative Court also hears applications for bail from people in immigration detention if the grounds for bail cannot be considered by the First-tier Tribunal – ie, if the grounds relate to the lawfulness of the detention.

6. **Deportation**

'**Deportation**' is a procedure under which a person without the right of abode is removed from the UK and excluded from re-entering for as long as the deportation order remains in force. Deportation is most often used when someone has been convicted of a serious criminal offence. Deportation is not the same as '**administrative removal**', which is the procedure for removing someone who has entered the UK illegally or breached her/his conditions of leave – eg, by overstaying.

If you are being considered for deportation you may, whether or not you have leave to enter or remain, be detained, given temporary admission, or released or bailed with conditions. See p14 for further information.

Notes

3. British nationality
1 s11 BNA 1981
2 s1 BNA 1981
3 s2 BNA 1981

5. Appeals and other remedies
4 s82 NIAA 2002, as amended by the IA 2014
5 Reg 2(1) I(EEA) Regs
6 s40A BNA 1981

Chapter 3

. . . . .

Leave to enter or remain

This chapter covers:
1. Leave to enter or remain (below)
2. Time-limited leave (p23)
3. Indefinite leave (p23)
4. Employment (p24)
5. Recourse to public funds (p25)
6. Sponsorship (p26)

---

1. **Leave to enter or remain**

You are likely to require leave to enter or remain in the UK unless you have:
- the right of abode. This includes British citizens (see p15);
- a right to reside as a national of the European Economic Area (EEA), or as a family member of an EEA national (see p39).

The Immigration Rules set out the circumstances in which leave to enter or remain can be granted for various purposes, including for study, employment and business, family connections, long residence and asylum. They also stipulate the duration of the leave and any conditions attached to it, the circumstances in which leave will be refused, curtailed or revoked, and the criteria for deporting people whose presence in the UK is considered to be against the public interest – eg, if someone is a criminal.

Changes to the Immigration Rules must be notified to Parliament, but there does not need to be any debate before the changes take effect. A consolidated version is published on the UK Visas and Immigration (UKVI) website at www.gov.uk/government/organisations/uk-visas-and-immigration. The website also contains policy guidance that explains the Immigration Rules. The explanation given in the guidance is not always followed by tribunals and courts, but the guidance must usually be followed by UKVI decision makers and you can therefore rely on it if it is beneficial in your case.

Note: leave may also be granted outside the Immigration Rules (see p37).

. . . .

Conditions of your leave

Leave to enter or remain in the UK may be given subject to a limited number of conditions. If you breach the conditions attached to your leave, you may commit a criminal offence, your current leave could be curtailed or revoked, and future applications for leave could be refused. You could also be detained and removed from the UK.

The main conditions attached to leave granted under the Immigration Rules are:

- a restriction on the time you may remain in the UK (see p23);
- a requirement to register your residential address with the police;
- restrictions on your taking employment (see p24);
- a prohibition on your having recourse to 'public funds' (see p25).

Who is exempt from the usual conditions

Some people are exempt from some of the usual conditions attached to permission to enter and remain in the UK. The main categories of people who are exempt are seamen, aircrew, diplomats and members of the UK or visiting armed forces.[1]

EEA and Swiss nationals and their family members have separate rights and conditions of entry and residence in the UK (see Chapter 5).

Nationals of some other non-EEA states also have special rights to establish themselves or provide services in the UK for economic purposes under agreements of 'association'. The most notable of these has been an agreement between the European Community (EC) and Turkey (see below).

Turkish nationals

Turkish nationals can establish themselves in the UK for economic purposes under an agreement of 'association' between the EC (as it was at the date of the agreement) and Turkey.

This EC-Turkey association agreement of 12 September 1963 is known as the 'Ankara Agreement'. Its purpose was to promote a move towards abolishing the restrictions on people who wished to move between Turkey and the EC in order to establish themselves or provide services. This was to be achieved by prohibiting the introduction of new national restrictions that were less favourable than those in force on the 'relevant date'. In the case of the UK, this is 1 January 1973, the date the UK joined the EC. The Immigration Rules in effect on 1 January 1973 were less restrictive in certain respects than the current Immigration Rules. Turkish nationals can therefore have any relevant applications considered under these old, less restrictive, Immigration Rules.[2]

2. **Time-limited leave**

Leave may be granted for a limited period of time. Depending on the requirements in the Immigration Rules, you may be able to have it extended or varied (switched) to another category.

Note: any time-limited leave is automatically extended beyond the date it is due to expire if you make a valid application to extend or vary the leave before the expiry date. Your leave is extended until UK Visas and Immigration (UKVI) makes a decision on your application and, if this is refused, until any appeal rights are exhausted (see p46).[3] Leave is not extended if you appeal against a refusal of leave to remain and you did not have leave to enter or remain at the time you applied.

UKVI can take several years to process some applications – eg, those from people who have applied to extend leave given outside the Immigration Rules for human rights reasons. This can cause problems when you need to satisfy others that your leave has been extended in this way.

3. **Indefinite leave**

Indefinite leave to enter or remain in the UK is leave without a time restriction. Indefinite leave is sometimes referred to as 'settlement'.

There are no conditions (eg, on employment and claiming public funds – see p25) attached to indefinite leave.[4] However, you may still be classed as a 'person subject to immigration control' for benefit purposes and therefore restricted from claiming benefits if the leave was given on the basis of an undertaking by a sponsor that s/he would be responsible for your maintenance (see p59). Your sponsor may also be liable to repay any benefits claimed and may face criminal penalties (see p28). If you have been granted entry clearance or leave to enter on the basis of a maintenance undertaking, this is not stated on the document issued to you confirming this, and this may need to be checked with a decision maker. If you are in any doubt about whether the decision maker is correct, get specialist advice.

Indefinite leave can lapse if you are absent from the UK for too long (see p24). It can also be revoked (see p24).

If you have indefinite leave, you can leave the UK and return without your leave lapsing if:

- you wish to return to settle in the UK; *and*
- you have not been away from the UK for more than two years, unless there are special circumstances – eg, a previous long period of residence; *and*
- you did not receive any assistance from public funds towards the cost of leaving the UK. **Note:** 'public funds' in this context is the scheme that allows people to be reimbursed the costs of resettling in their country of origin. It does

not refer to the fact that you may have claimed benefits and other public funds while in the UK (see p25).[5]

Your indefinite leave may be revoked if:
- you become liable to deportation (see p19); *or*
- the leave was obtained by deception; *or*
- you cease to be a refugee for specified reasons, or if you were given indefinite leave as a result of the refugee status of another person, s/he ceases to be a refugee for one of these reasons.

Note: if you have been granted indefinite leave to enter the UK, your visa shows an 'expiry' or 'valid until' date. This is the date by which your entry clearance must be presented to enter the UK for the first time, after which you have indefinite leave and the date becomes irrelevant.[6]

---

4. **Employment**

Certain types of leave are granted with a condition prohibiting employment. For example, visitors are usually prohibited from working. Other types of leave limit the employment you may do to a certain number of hours in a week (eg, if you are given leave as a student), or for a specific period of employment or business activity. This may be described as 'authorised' work. If this applies to you, check the relevant government policy, published on the UK Visas and Immigration (UKVI) website.

If you have been given leave for specific employment (eg, under tiers two or three of the points-based system – see p28 – or, in the past, under a work permit) or a specific activity (such as self-employment, or as a writer, composer or artist), you can only work in the employment or undertake the activity for which you were given leave. If you wish to change employment, you must apply to UKVI for permission.

From 27 January 1997, employers have been required to check that all new employees have the right to work in the UK and can be prosecuted for employing a migrant who cannot lawfully work. The law on the employment of migrant workers has changed several times since this date and the checks an employer must make (or should have made) depend on the date the worker was first employed by the employer. The application of such checks might raise race discrimination issues. If you think you have been treated unfavourably by an employer or potential employer, get specialist advice.

5. **Recourse to public funds**

Leave to enter or remain for certain purposes is only granted if you can show that you and your dependants can, and will, be adequately maintained and accommodated without recourse to public funds. When leave is granted subject to a time limit, a condition prohibiting you from having recourse to public funds is usually imposed. This now includes most limited leave to enter or remain for family or private life reasons granted under Article 8 of the European Convention on Human Rights (see p33). If you have such a condition on your leave, it is stated on the document issued to you confirming the leave. If you breach this condition, you may commit a criminal offence, your current leave could be curtailed or revoked, and future applications for leave could be refused. You could also be detained and removed from the UK.

What are public funds

'Public funds' for the purposes of the Immigration Rules are:[7]
- attendance allowance;
- carer's allowance;
- child benefit;
- child tax credit;
- council tax benefit (now abolished);
- council tax reduction;
- disability living allowance;
- income-related employment and support allowance;
- housing benefit;
- income support;
- income-based jobseeker's allowance;
- pension credit;
- personal independence payment;
- severe disablement allowance;
- social fund payments;
- universal credit;
- working tax credit;
- housing and homelessness assistance.

Only the above are public funds; nothing else counts under the Immigration Rules, including other social security benefits, and education and National Health services.

Note: in certain cases, you can still claim benefits defined as public funds without breaching the condition not to have recourse to public funds. This applies if you come into one of the exempt groups who can claim these benefits, despite being a 'person subject to immigration control' (see p64).[8]

6. Sponsorship

Who is a sponsor

The Immigration Rules define a sponsor as the person in relation to whom you are seeking leave to enter or remain as a spouse, fiancé/e, civil partner, proposed civil partner, unmarried partner (including same-sex partner) or dependent relative.

The role of your sponsor is to maintain and support you in the UK. Parents must fulfil a similar role in the case of child applicants.[9] Support by third parties is permitted for some types of application,[10] but not for most applicants under the new Appendix FM of the Immigration Rules, under which most 'family' applications must now be made.

Financial requirements

In most cases, your sponsor must have a minimum annual income in order for you to be given leave to enter or remain as a family member.[11] The amount increases depending on the number of children in the family.

If your sponsor has savings in excess of a certain amount, these can be used to make up any shortfall in her/his annual income.

Your own income, savings and prospective income, and (in most cases) any support from a third party, are disregarded entirely.

Adequate maintenance

For leave to be granted under other parts of the Immigration Rules, including some family cases still, you must show that you can, and will, be maintained adequately without recourse to public funds. Whether or not there is adequate maintenance depends on the number of people who need maintaining and the income of the person or family unit concerned. The standard of adequacy currently required is that the income of the family as a whole must be equal to or greater than the amount an equivalent family would receive from income support (IS) if all the family members were entitled to have recourse to public funds. The use of this benchmark has been justified as necessary to prevent immigrant families or communities having a lower standard of living in the UK than the poorest British citizens.[12]

Note: support from third parties can be counted for some types of applications not made under Appendix FM of the Immigration Rules.[13]

Disability living allowance, attendance allowance and personal independence payment claimed by a sponsor can be included when establishing whether a family's income is the same or higher than the IS amount.[14] It is arguable that the same approach should be applied to industrial injuries disablement benefit and severe disablement allowance. You should obtain specialist advice if this might be an issue.

Adequate accommodation

In most cases, in order to be given leave to enter or remain as a family member, a certain standard and/or type of accommodation must be available to you.

There must be adequate accommodation for you and any dependants, without your having recourse to public funds and which the family owns or occupies exclusively.

For accommodation to be considered adequate, it must not be overcrowded or contravene public health regulations, and must also be 'adequate' in the broader sense of the word. For example, in one case the tribunal decided that a space described as a bedroom was not adequate in the broader sense for the children of an applicant seeking leave to enter to join his spouse because it was, in reality, little more than a corridor.[15]

The Housing Act 1985 contains statutory definitions of overcrowding in a 'dwelling house'. A 'dwelling house' includes both a privately owned house and one owned by a local authority. A house is overcrowded if two people aged 10 years or older of the opposite sex (other than husband and wife) have to sleep in the same room, or if the number of people sleeping in the house exceeds that permitted in the Act, which specifies the number of people for a given number of rooms or given floor area.

The Immigration Rules often require that the accommodation must be owned or occupied 'exclusively' by the family unit concerned. A separate bedroom for the exclusive use of the applicant and sponsor is sufficient to meet this requirement, so a family may live in shared accommodation, sharing other rooms (such as a kitchen and bathroom) with other occupants.[16]

If your circumstances change

If you needed to satisfy the maintenance and accommodation requirements under the Immigration Rules before your leave was granted, your leave may be curtailed and/or a further application refused if you or your sponsor do not continue to meet the requirements throughout the period of leave granted.[17]
Note: this only applies if your leave is subject to a time limit – ie, it does not apply if you have been granted indefinite leave to enter or remain (see p23). UK Visas and Immigration (UKVI) might discover that your circumstances have changed if, for example, you or your sponsor make a claim for social security benefits.

In addition, it appears that if you have been issued with a biometric residence permit (see p46), you must notify UKVI as soon as reasonably practicable if you know (or suspect) that a change in your circumstances means that you no longer qualify for leave under the Immigration Rules.[18] It is unclear whether this only applies to time-limited leave to remain or also to indefinite leave to remain.

If a change in your circumstances means you might not meet the requirements for the leave you have been granted, you should seek specialist advice urgently.

Maintenance undertakings

A sponsor may be asked to give a written undertaking to be responsible for your maintenance and accommodation or for your care for the period of leave granted and any further period of leave to remain that you may be granted while in the UK.[19] Undertakings are often requested for:
- dependent relatives, although not for children under 16 years coming for settlement;
- students relying on a private individual in the UK.

If you have been granted leave to enter or remain as a result of a maintenance undertaking, you are excluded from claiming benefits.[20] If you subsequently claim benefit while in the UK, your sponsor may be required to pay back the value of the benefit claimed.[21] This restriction applies until you have been in the UK for five years since the date of the undertaking or the date of entry. If your sponsor dies, the restriction lapses immediately.

A maintenance undertaking may be enforceable, even if it is not formally drafted and vice versa.[22] In one case, a formal declaration that a sponsor was able and willing to maintain and accommodate was held not to amount to an undertaking, as it did not include a promise to support.[23]

Sponsorship under the points-based system

For some categories in the Immigration Rules, points are awarded to someone applying for leave to enter or remain for having various attributes and levels of income and/or savings. This is different from points-based schemes in other countries, as all the categories in the Immigration Rules require applicants to have all the attributes for which points are notionally awarded and so, in reality, the UK system is a points-based system in name only.

There are five 'tiers' or categories of purpose under which leave may be granted under this system. These are:
- entrepreneurs, investors and exceptionally talented people – eg, scientists, engineers and artists;
- skilled workers with a job offer (usually only for occupations in which UKVI recognises there is a shortage of appropriately skilled workers available in the UK and European Economic Area labour market);
- students;
- youth mobility (previously called 'working holidays') and temporary workers – eg, for short-term creative or sporting events.

If you are applying under any tier, except highly skilled workers, you must usually be sponsored by an employer or educational institution. The sponsor must hold a certificate of sponsorship. This is a unique reference number that the sponsor issues to you to enable you to remain in the UK, as opposed to an actual certificate or document.

Sponsors must report to UKVI any significant changes in the sponsored person's circumstances, suspicions that s/he is breaching the conditions of her/his leave or significant changes in the sponsor's own circumstances – eg, if s/he stops trading or becomes insolvent.

Notes

1. Leave to enter or remain
1 s8 IA 1971
2 Art 41.1 Additional Protocol to the Agreement; *R (on the application of Veli Tum and Mehmet Dari) v Secretary of State for the Home Department*, C-16/05 [2007] ECR I-07415

2. Time-limited leave
3 The extension of leave while a right of appeal can be exercised only applies within the time limit for appealing and when an out-of-time appeal has been accepted.

3. Indefinite leave
4 s3(3)(a) IA 1971
5 paras 18-19 IR
6 See UKVI policy, 'Entry Clearance Guidance', ECB9.4, at www.gov.uk/government/publications/entry-clearance-vignettes-ecb09

5. Recourse to public funds
7 para 6 IR
8 Social Security (Immigration and Asylum) Consequential Amendments Regulations 2000, No.636, as amended by SI 2013/1474; para 6B IR

6. Sponsorship
9 para 297 and Appendix FM IR
10 *Mahad (previously referred to as AM) (Ethiopia) v Entry Clearance Officer* [2009] UKSC 16, 16 December 2009
11 Appendix FM IR

12 *KA (Pakistan)* [2006] UKAIT 065; approved in *AM (Ethiopia) and Ors and Another v Entry Clearance Officer* [2008] EWCA Civ 1082, 16 October 2008
13 *Mahad (previously referred to as AM) (Ethiopia) v Entry Clearance Officer* [2009] UKSC 16, 16 December 2009
14 *MK (Somalia) v Entry Clearance Officer* [2007] EWCA Civ 1521, 28 November 2007
15 *AS (Adequate Accommodation – Question of Fact) Pakistan* [2004] UKIAT 00006
16 Ch8, s1, annex F IDI. This includes information on the minimum size of a room and a table showing the maximum number of people allowed for any specific number of rooms.
17 paras 322(4)-23 IR
18 Reg 18 Immigration (Biometric Registration) Regulations 2008, No.3048
19 para 35 IR
20 s115(9)(c) IAA 1999
21 para 35 IR; ss78, 105 and 106 SSAA 1992
22 *R (Begum)* [2003] *The Times*, 4 December 2003
23 *Ahmed v SSWP* [2005] EWCA Civ 535

Chapter 4

Asylum and human rights

This chapter covers:
1. Asylum seekers (below)
2. Refugee leave and humanitarian protection (p32)
3. Stateless people (p33)
4. Leave for human rights and compassionate reasons (p33)
5. Fresh applications (p37)

1. Asylum seekers

Applying for asylum

Someone who has applied for recognition as a refugee or as a person requiring international protection in the UK is commonly called an 'asylum seeker'.

Asylum applications to UK Visas and Immigration (UKVI) can be made on one or more of the following grounds:

- under the Refugee Convention (see p12);
- under Article 3 of the Human Rights Convention (see p12). This prescribes that no one shall be subjected to torture or to inhuman or degrading treatment or punishment;
- under the Qualification Directive (see p12).

The most common other Human Rights Convention Article raised in immigration cases is Article 8, which protects a person's right to enjoy private and family life without unnecessary or disproportionate interference (see p33).

'Temporary protection' is a separate and specific category of leave introduced by the Qualification Directive. It is intended to be given to people following a declaration by the European Union (EU) Council in recognition of a mass influx of displaced people. There have been no declarations since the Directive came into force.

The definition of an asylum seeker for the purpose of support and accommodation (see p329) is limited to people who have applied under the Refugee Convention and/or Article 3 of the Human Rights Convention – ie, an application based only on Article 8 does not make someone an asylum seeker for asylum support purposes.[1] However, in certain situations, UKVI can provide accommodation to people who are subject to immigration control who are not asylum seekers (see p344).

An asylum seeker may apply for asylum at a port of entry before passing through passport control, or from inside the country, having entered the UK illegally or with leave for a different purpose under the Immigration Rules.

Note: if you delay making an in-country asylum application, your entitlement to asylum support may be affected (see p329).

If your asylum application is refused or withdrawn, and you have not successfully appealed, you may be able to make a fresh application (see p37).

Detention and removal

Many asylum seekers are given temporary admission while their asylum application is considered, but a significant number are detained while their application is 'fast-tracked' or if their application is considered to be 'manifestly unfounded'. They are detained in the expectation that their application will be considered quickly and they can then be quickly removed from the UK if it is refused. Other asylum seekers are detained waiting for removal to a third country (ie, not the UK or their country of nationality), which is deemed to be responsible for considering their application. The provisions for this have been agreed by international treaties between EU member states and other countries.

If you are a failed asylum seeker, you can be detained, provided the purpose of the detention is your removal from the UK and there is some prospect of that. Judges have decided that detention for several years for this purpose can be lawful, even if you pose no threat to society other than the risk that you might abscond.

Permission to work

If you are an asylum seeker who has not received a decision on your initial application for asylum after one year, and the delay was not your fault, you can apply to UKVI for permission to work.[2]

However, the work you can do is restricted to a short list of skilled occupations for which UKVI recognises there is a shortage of workers available in the UK, so, in practice, this is of no benefit to most asylum seekers.

2. Refugee leave and humanitarian protection

If you are an asylum seeker who is recognised by UK Visas and Immigration (UKVI) as a refugee or as being in need of humanitarian protection, you are granted refugee leave or humanitarian protection leave respectively.

Refugees and humanitarian protection

A **'refugee'** is someone who, owing to a well-founded fear of being persecuted because of race, religion, nationality, membership of a particular social group or political opinion, is outside the country of her/his nationality, and is unable to or, owing to such fear, is unwilling to avail her/himself of the protection of that country.

A person in need of **'humanitarian protection'** is someone who does not qualify as a refugee, but there are substantial grounds for believing that if s/he were returned to her/his country of origin, s/he would face a real risk of suffering serious harm. A person could, for example, face a risk of serious harm for reasons other than race, religion, nationality, membership of a particular social group or political opinion. It is arguable that this could include someone who faces a risk of serious harm on medical grounds.

An initial five years' leave to remain is usually granted, with the option of applying for indefinite leave shortly before this leave expires.

During the limited five-year period, your leave can be reviewed and revoked. A review may be triggered if:

- you are a refugee, but your actions bring you within the scope of the 1951 Refugee Convention 'cessation clauses' – eg, if you travel back to your country of origin without a reasonable explanation;[3] *or*
- there is a 'significant or non-temporary' change in the conditions in your country of origin (or part of the country) that means your continuing need for protection is now placed in doubt.

If you have been given refugee or humanitarian protection leave, your spouse and dependent children who formed part of your family unit prior to your departure from your country can apply to be reunited with you in the UK. This is commonly called 'family reunion'. There are no maintenance and accommodation requirements that must be met, and your spouse and children should be given leave in line with your own.

You can be excluded from refugee status or humanitarian protection status if:

- you have committed a crime against peace, a war crime, a crime against humanity or a serious non-political crime outside the UK before being admitted as a refugee; *or*
- you have been guilty of acts that are contrary to the purposes and principles of the United Nations. This could include being involved in terrorism or encouraging others to be involved.

If you are excluded from refugee or humanitarian protection status for these reasons, but you cannot be removed to your home country for human rights reasons (eg, because you face a risk of torture), you may be granted restricted leave (see p36).

3. Stateless people

A stateless person is defined by international law as someone who is 'not considered a national by any state under the operation of its law'.[4] On 6 April 2013, the UK introduced a provision in the Immigration Rules to recognise and grant leave to remain to certain stateless people.[5] Before this date, stateless people could obtain travel documents, but could not obtain leave. If you are recognised as being stateless in the UK, you can still obtain a stateless person's travel document.

4. Leave for human rights and compassionate reasons

Leave granted for Article 8 of the Human Rights Convention reasons

Article 8 of the European Convention on Human Rights guarantees enjoyment of private and family life without unnecessary or disproportionate interference. You may be able to rely on this Article if you have family in the UK and/or have lived in the UK for some time and developed ties here. If UK Visas and Immigration (UKVI) is considering removing you from the UK and this would disrupt (interfere with) these aspects of your life (eg, it would separate you from a loved one), under Article 8 you should only be removed if it is necessary and reasonable in the particular circumstances of your case. Since 9 July 2012, the Immigration Rules have set out the circumstances in which UKVI allows you to stay in the UK for private and family life reasons.

From 9 July 2012, leave is given for periods of no longer than 30 months, potentially leading to indefinite leave after 10 continuous years. UKVI policy is to grant you leave subject to a condition that you do not have recourse to public funds, unless there are exceptional circumstances that you have raised. These are explained in the application for leave. It is possible to apply for this condition to be lifted if there has been a change in your circumstances or if the circumstances were not known to UKVI at the time the leave was granted.[6] UKVI policy is that 'exceptional circumstances' only exist if you are destitute or if you are a parent on a low income and there are particularly compelling reasons relating to the welfare of your child.[7]

If you are a parent of a child who is a British citizen, you might have immigration rights under Article 8 of the European Convention on Human Rights, which may be recognised by UKVI as a derivative right to reside in UK under regulation 15A(4A) of the Immigration (European Economic Area) Regulations 2006. This is a right to reside in the UK on the basis that you are a non-European Union (EU) national and a primary carer of a British citizen and that requiring you to leave the UK would have the effect of forcing the child to leave the EU.[8] If you have been recognised as having a right of residence under regulation 15A(4A), you are not given leave to remain under the Immigration Rules and are not therefore prohibited from having recourse to public funds.

However, you are restricted by social security regulations from accessing benefits which require a right to reside (see p167). This is not stated on your residence card.

There are other potential advantages and disadvantages of being granted leave to remain as a parent of a British child, or having a derivative right to reside as such, for your being able to obtain permanent settlement in the UK in the longer term.

Note: before 9 July 2012, leave to remain given for Article 8 reasons was granted outside the Immigration Rules and was called **'discretionary leave'**. If you were granted limited discretionary leave before this date for Article 8 reasons, you should be able to apply to extend your leave under the old policy. This has the advantage of potentially leading to settlement after six years, as opposed to 10 years. Leave is usually granted for three years at a time and without a restriction on receiving public funds.

Domestic violence

If you are granted leave to enter or remain in the UK as a spouse, unmarried partner (including a same-sex partner) or civil partner of a British citizen, or of a person with indefinite leave to enter or remain in the UK or a member of HM Forces who has served for at least four years, you must usually complete a probationary period of limited leave in the UK with your partner before you can apply for indefinite leave to remain, to settle in the UK permanently with your partner. The probationary period is currently five years (two years if you were granted leave on this basis before 9 July 2012). However, you may be able to apply for indefinite leave to remain if your relationship has broken down as a result of domestic violence during the probationary period, under what is commonly known as the 'domestic violence rule'.[9]

If you are a victim of domestic violence in this situation, your limited leave will have been granted with a condition that you do not have recourse to public funds. However, if you are destitute, you can apply for public funds under the 'destitute domestic violence' concession.[10] If successful, you are granted limited leave to remain for three months with access to public funds, during which time you can apply for indefinite leave to remain under the domestic violence rule. If you do so, your 'destitute domestic violence' leave is extended, with no condition prohibiting you from claiming public funds, until your application (and any appeal or administrative review) has been decided (see p46).

Discretionary leave

Discretionary leave is granted:
- in medical cases. The threshold for leave on this basis is high: your illness must have: 'reached such a critical stage (ie, he is dying) that it would be inhuman treatment to deprive him of the care which he is currently receiving and send him home to an early death unless there is care available there to enable him to meet that fate with dignity.'[11] It is arguable that if you are granted leave for medical reasons, you should be granted humanitarian protection leave;
- if returning you would breach the European Convention on Human Rights – eg, if the government of the country to which you would need to go if you were not granted leave in the UK would flagrantly deny your rights to a fair trial under Article 6 of the Convention, or your rights to enjoy family and private life. This is different to cases where the UK government would breach your rights by removing you or refusing to grant you leave to enter or remain in the UK;
- to unaccompanied asylum-seeking children who do not qualify for refugee or humanitarian protection leave, but who cannot be removed because there are inadequate reception arrangements available in their own country to enable them to be removed there safely;
- in other exceptional circumstances specified in UKVI enforcement policies;
- if you have been identified as a victim of trafficking within the meaning of Article 4 of the Council of Europe Convention on Action Against Trafficking in Human Beings and your personal circumstances are so compelling that it is considered appropriate to grant some form of leave;
- if you are an unsuccessful asylum seeker, but it is considered appropriate to grant leave to you (the scope of this is unclear).

Note: from 9 July 2012, discretionary leave is no longer granted for reasons relating to Article 8 of the European Convention on Human Rights (see p33).

If you have been granted discretionary leave, you can have access to public funds (see p25) and are entitled to work.

Discretionary leave is normally granted for a period of 30 months, with the possibility of a further 30-month extension period. After you have had 10 continuous years of this type of leave, you can apply for indefinite leave to remain. The previous policy was normally to grant discretionary leave for three years, with the possibility of being able to apply to extend this, and of indefinite leave to remain after six continuous years. If you were granted leave before 9 July

2012, the previous policy continues to apply to you, with the benefit of a shorter required period before you can apply for indefinite leave to remain. The exception to this is if you were granted discretionary leave before 9 July 2012 because you were excluded from refugee or humanitarian protection leave but could not be removed from the UK for human rights reasons. In this case, the restricted leave policy now applies to you (see below).

If you apply to have your discretionary leave extended, or for indefinite leave to remain after completing the required period of time, your case is 'actively reviewed'. This means your circumstances are reviewed and leave is only granted if it continues to be justified for reasons such as those listed in the bullet points on p35.

In the case of an unaccompanied child, discretionary leave may be granted for up to 30 months or until the child is 17 and a half, whichever is the shorter period. At 17 and a half years, if s/he is not eligible for settlement, the child's case is actively reviewed. However, this does not automatically result in an extension of leave or settlement.

Restricted leave

If you are excluded from refugee or humanitarian protection leave (see above) for the reasons outlined on p32, but you cannot be removed from the UK for human rights reasons (eg, because you face a risk of torture if you were to be removed), you may be granted restricted leave. The previous policy was to grant discretionary leave for short periods.

Restricted leave is usually only granted for a maximum of six months at a time, with restrictions:

- on your employment or occupation in the UK;
- on where you can reside;
- requiring you to report to an immigration officer or UKVI at regular intervals;
- prohibiting your studying at an educational institution; *and*
- prohibiting your doing voluntary work with children and/or vulnerable adults.

If you knowingly fail to comply with any restrictions imposed, you may commit a criminal offence.

Exceptional leave

Exceptional leave was replaced by humanitarian protection and discretionary leave in 2003, but was granted for similar reasons. There were also blanket policies to grant exceptional leave to applicants from several countries experiencing civil or military upheaval.

Leave outside the Immigration Rules

It is possible to be given leave outside the Immigration Rules in special or unusual situations that would not otherwise be covered. UKVI policy is that this is mainly for non-asylum and non-protection cases and is only granted on a temporary basis – ie, such leave does not normally lead to settlement.[12] The potential reasons stated are:

- if you qualify under an immigration policy concession; *or*
- in particularly compelling circumstances.

If you are given leave to enter or remain outside the Immigration Rules for compassionate reasons, UKVI policy is to grant the leave subject to a condition of no public funds, unless there are exceptional circumstances. The policy is as for leave granted for human rights reasons described on p33.

If you or a member of you family applied for asylum before July 2006, instead of refugee or humanitarian protection leave, you may have been granted indefinite leave to remain or discretionary leave under the asylum 'legacy' case resolution exercise. This was intended to deal with a backlog of unresolved cases that were identified at the time by the Home Secretary.

5. **Fresh applications**

If you have made an asylum and/or human rights application that was unsuccessful and a decision was made to remove you from the UK, including if you appealed against such a decision and were unsuccessful, you must to make further submissions to UK Visas and Immigration (UKVI) if you want to avoid being removed. The submissions must usually be made in person. The location for doing so depends on when you made your first (refused) application, and on whether that was an asylum application and whether you have left the UK in the meantime.

UKVI considers whether the further submissions amount to a 'fresh application' – ie, an application that is significantly different to the failed application and which has a realistic prospect of resulting in your being allowed to stay in the UK. It might take many months or years before a decision is reached and you might only be notified of the decision when you are detained for removal.

If you are a failed asylum seeker, UKVI must usually provide you with accommodation if you have made further submissions that have yet to be considered and you would otherwise be destitute (see p329). The definition of a failed asylum seeker for these purposes includes someone who has made a refugee application and/or an application under Article 3 of the Human Rights Convention, which protects against torture and inhuman or degrading treatment.[13] It is likely that the definition also includes someone who has made a failed application for humanitarian protection. You may also be eligible to receive accommodation if you have been given temporary admission, temporary release or if you are seeking bail (see p344).

Notes

1. **Asylum seekers**
   1 s94(1) IAA 1999
   2 Art 11 EU Dir 2003/9; paras 360-61 IR

2. **Refugee leave and humanitarian protection**
   3 Art 1C(1)-(6) Convention Relating to the Status of Refugees 1951

3. **Stateless people**
   4 Convention Relating to the Status of Stateless Persons 1954
   5 Part 14 IR

4. **Leave for human rights and compassionate reasons**
   6 See www.gov.uk/government/uploads/ system/uploads/attachment_data/file/ 286132/change-condition.pdf
   7 The policy is contained in the IDI, 'Family Life (as a Partner or Parent)' FM 1.0a, and 'Partner and ECHR Article 8 Guidance', FM 8.0, which has been amended on several occasions.
   8 *Zambrano v ONEm*, C-34/09 [2011] ECR I-01177
   9 paras 289A-C IR
   10 www.gov.uk/government/publications/ application-for-benefits-for-visa-holder- domestic-violence
   11 *N (FC) v SSHD* [2005] UKHL 31
   12 Ch1, s14 IDI

5. **Fresh applications**
   13 s94(1) IAA 1999

Chapter 5

· ·

European Economic Area nationals and their families

This chapter covers:
1. The European Economic Area states (below)
2. Right of admission (below)
3. Documentation (p40)
4. Exclusion and removal (p40)

1. The European Economic Area states

· ·

The European Economic Area

The '**European Economic Area**' comprises the member states of the European Union (EU) plus the European Free Trade Association (EFTA) countries Norway, Liechtenstein and Iceland.

The current member states of the EU are: Austria, Belgium, Bulgaria, Croatia, Cyprus, Czech Republic, Denmark, Estonia, Finland, France, Germany, Greece, Hungary, Ireland, Italy, Latvia, Lithuania, Luxembourg, Malta, Netherlands, Poland, Portugal, Romania, Slovenia, Slovakia, Spain, Sweden and the UK.

Switzerland has a separate bilateral agreement with the EU.

· ·

2. Right of admission

If you are a European Economic Area (EEA) or Swiss national, you have an absolute right to be admitted to the UK (except for public policy, public security or public health reasons – see p40), provided you produce an identity card or passport, or you can otherwise prove your status – ie, you might not be required to obtain a visa (or equivalent) in order to enter the UK.

Certain family members of an EEA or Swiss national have similar rights to be admitted to the UK.

The rights of EEA and Swiss nationals and their family members to reside in the UK are covered in Chapter 12.

3. Documentation

If you are a European Economic Area (EEA) or Swiss national and have a right to reside in the UK, you have the right to be issued with a registration certificate by the Home Office. If you have acquired permanent residence, you have the right to be issued with a document certifying permanent residence. These documents are in the form of a vignette (sticker) fixed on a card booklet, separate from your passport.

If you are the family member of an EEA or a Swiss national and have a right to reside in the UK, you have the right to be issued with a residence card, or a permanent residence card if you have permanent residence. Alternatively, you may have been issued with a family permit entry visa before travelling to the UK. Each of these is usually a vignette (sticker) fixed in your passport.

If you have a right of residence derived from a relationship with an EEA or Swiss national, you have the right to be issued with a derivative residence card. Again, this is usually a vignette (sticker) fixed in your passport.

Note: the above documents are declaratory. It is not necessary to obtain such a document in order to have the rights recognised by it, and the period of validity should not to be regarded as a grant of permission to reside for that period. Similarly, the fact that you hold a valid residence card or registration certificate does not necessarily mean that you will continue to have the rights recognised by it in the future.

4. Exclusion and removal

If you are a European Economic Area (EEA) or Swiss national, the family member of an EEA or Swiss national, or a person with a right of residence derived from a relationship with an EEA or Swiss national, you can be refused admission to the UK, refused a right to reside, refused the documentation associated with such rights and removed from the UK for public policy, public security or public health reasons.[1]

A decision made on public policy, public security or public health grounds must:

- not be taken for the economic benefit of the UK;
- be 'proportionate';
- be based exclusively on the conduct of the individual concerned, which must represent a genuine, present and sufficiently serious threat, affecting one of the fundamental interests of society;

- be for reasons that relate to your case in particular, rather than being intended to deter others;
- not be justified by a person's previous criminal convictions alone;
- only be made after taking into account the person's age, state of health, family and economic situation, her/his length of residence in the UK, her/his social and cultural integration in the UK, and the extent of her/his links with her/his country of origin.

If you have permanent residence (acquired after five years' continuous lawful residence), the grounds for exclusion must be 'serious'.[2] An EEA or Swiss national aged under 18 cannot be excluded or removed unless it is in her/his best interests or her/his removal is imperative on grounds of public security.[3] Similarly, an EEA or Swiss national who has resided in the UK for 10 years cannot be excluded or removed except on imperative grounds of public security.[4] **Note:** a period of imprisonment does not, in itself, prevent you from accruing 10 years' residence for the purpose of enhanced protection against deportation, but might prevent you from accruing the five years' residence required for permanent residence.[5]

You may be prevented from re-entering the UK if you have been removed in the preceding 12 months on the grounds of not having a right to reside. The stated aim of this is to avoid someone repeatedly exiting and re-entering the UK, getting a new three-month period of residence each time.[6]

If UK Visas and Immigration thinks you are involved in a 'marriage of convenience' or other fraud, you may be refused entry, or have your right to reside taken away.[7]

Notes

4. **Exclusion and removal**
   1 Reg 19(5) I(EEA) Regs
   2 Reg 21(3) I(EEA) Regs
   3 Reg 21(4)(b) I(EEA) Regs
   4 Reg 21(4)(a) I(EEA) Regs
   5 *Secretary of State for the Home Department v FV (Italy)* [2012] EWCA Civ 1199
   6 Reg 21B I(EEA) Regs
   7 Reg 21B I(EEA) Regs

Chapter 6

. . . .

Checking your immigration status

This chapter covers:
1. British nationals and people with the right of abode (below)
2. People with leave to enter or remain (p43)
3. People without leave (p48)
4. Asylum seekers (p48)
5. European Economic Area and Swiss nationals (p49)
6. Passport issues (p49)

This chapter explains how to check your immigration status in order to establish your entitlement to social security benefits.

You can usually identify your immigration status in the UK from your passport and any endorsements in it by the UK immigration authorities (eg, stamps, stickers or vignettes) or, increasingly, from your biometric residence permit.

Note: some people's status (or nationality) may have changed since the passport, endorsement or card was issued. In addition, some people do not hold any of these.

If your immigration status is uncertain, you should contact a specialist adviser. A list of advisers and organisations is included in Appendix 2.

---

1. British nationals and people with the right of abode

If you are a British national, you can apply to HM Passport Office for a **UK passport** (see Appendix 6, Figure 1). However, not all British nationals have been issued with a passport and your British nationality does not depend on your being a passport holder.

UK passports are issued to all British nationals, not just British citizens, and it is important to distinguish between the different types of British nationality when checking your immigration status (see p15). Your passport specifies the type of British nationality you have. Holders of UK passports who have the right of abode in the UK are described as: 'British citizens or British subjects with the right of abode in the UK'.

Note: UK passports may also be issued to people whose right of abode is awaiting verification. The passport contains the endorsement: 'The holder's status under the Immigration Act 1971 has not yet been determined.'

If you have been granted British citizenship after applying to register or naturalise, you will have been issued with a certificate confirming this (see Appendix 6, Figure 2).

If you have the right of abode in the UK and are also a national of another Commonwealth country, you may have a **certificate of entitlement** endorsed in a passport issued by that country (see Appendix 6, Figure 3).

Although rare, a **certificate of patriality** issued under the Immigration Act 1971 and which was valid immediately before 1 January 1983 is regarded as a certificate of entitlement unless the holder no longer has the right of abode – eg, if you have renounced this, or if there has been independence legislation.[1]

Some people with the right of abode in the UK may hold a **confirmation of 'right of abode' document**. This was a non-statutory document issued for a brief period before the commencement of the Immigration Act 1988 to dual nationals with the right of abode who had opted to travel on non-British passports.

If you do not hold a passport or certificate confirming your British citizenship or right of abode, you may be able to prove that you have this status in some other manner – eg, by producing a birth certificate showing that you were born in the UK before 1983. If your claim to British citizenship or the right of abode is complicated, you may need to prove descent from your parents and/or grandparents, and/or marriage to a person and that person's place of birth, ancestry and/or nationality status at specific times. If this applies to you, it may be helpful to get specialist advice to check your citizenship and/or right of abode.

---

2. People with leave to enter or remain

Entry clearance confirming leave to enter

Entry clearance is endorsed by a sticker (known as a **'vignette'**) placed in a person's passport or travel document, or by data stored digitally in an identity card and government database (see p46).

The vignette endorsement may be designated as a visa (for visa nationals, stateless people and refugees), entry clearance (for non-visa nationals and British nationals other than British citizens) or a family permit (for dependants of European Economic Area nationals).

Two types of vignette are now issued. Which is used depends on the type of entry clearance given. Both include a photograph of the holder (see Appendix 6, Figure 9). Older versions look similar, but without a photograph (see Appendix

6, Figure 8). Even older ones were a smaller sticker, signed and date-stamped by an official (similar to the leave to remain endorsement vignette shown in Appendix 6, Figure 8).

Accompanying dependants whose details are included in the main applicant's passport receive their own vignettes, fixed in the main applicant's passport.

Entry clearance granting you leave to enter allows you to enter the UK at a port without having to demonstrate that you satisfy the requirements of the Immigration Rules (unless you commit an act of fraud or there is a material change in circumstances). The vignette endorsement is usually date-stamped on entry (see Appendix 6, Figure 10) and confirms that you have been granted leave to enter the UK, often for the remaining period of validity stated on the vignette.

In some circumstances, an immigration officer can vary or extend your leave on your arrival in the UK.

The date the entry clearance first becomes valid is usually the same as the date of authorisation. As the holder, you may present yourself for initial entry under the entry clearance at any time during its validity. However, entry clearance officers have the discretion to defer the date the entry clearance first becomes valid for up to three months after authorisation if, for example, you wish to delay travelling to the UK.

If you are granted entry clearance, you may travel to, and remain in, the UK for the purpose for which it was granted. You may be able to travel in and out of the UK repeatedly, provided your entry clearance remains valid. However, if entry clearance has been authorised for multiple journeys to the UK of a fixed duration (eg, under the visitor category of the Immigration Rules), the duration of each visit is limited to a maximum of six months. This limitation is stated on the vignette under the heading 'duration of stay'.

If you have been granted indefinite leave to enter the UK, your visa shows an 'expiry' or 'valid until' date. This is the date by when the entry clearance needs to be presented to enter the UK for the first time, after which you have indefinite leave and the date becomes irrelevant.[2]

If you have presented the entry clearance at a port, there should be an ink stamp showing where and on which date that occurred. The date when the entry clearance was presented is the date when the entry clearance took effect as indefinite leave.

If you are granted entry clearance with a vignette for leave to enter on certain conditions (eg, as a student on condition that you do not work except in authorised employment and do not have recourse to public funds), these should be stated on the endorsement (see Appendix 6, Figure 9). However, if you have been granted entry clearance for leave to enter on the basis of a sponsorship undertaking (see p28), this is not stated on the endorsement.

Leave to enter without entry clearance

Nationals of some countries cannot enter the UK for any purpose without first obtaining entry clearance (visa nationals). Others can apply at the port of entry for leave to enter for some of the purposes provided for under the Immigration Rules.

It is sometimes difficult to identify the purpose for which an endorsement of leave to enter has been given if you made an application at the port of entry. If limited leave has been granted, the endorsement may be an **ink stamp**, stating the duration of the leave period for which leave is granted and the conditions (if any) attached to the leave (see Appendix 6, Figure 8). Each stamped endorsement by an immigration officer granting leave to someone without entry clearance should be accompanied by a rectangular date stamp, showing when the leave was granted.

The example shown in Appendix 6, Figure 8 is the endorsement usually made in the passport of someone given leave to enter at a port of entry as a visitor or student on a short course (of six months or less). The endorsement shows that leave has been granted on condition that the holder does not engage in any employment or have recourse to public funds.

If you are returning to the UK and already have indefinite leave to enter or remain, you may simply be given a date stamp on being readmitted.

If you leave the UK and return during a period of leave that has been given for more than six months, an immigration officer may endorse a grant of leave to enter with the same conditions, using an ink stamp stating this.[3]

Some people, usually Commonwealth citizens, who entered the UK before the Immigration Act 1971 came into force may have received an ink stamp on entry with no conditions attached. These people are referred to as 'freely landed'. They may have been treated as having been given indefinite leave to enter or remain when the 1971 Act came into force and might have retained this status by remaining resident in the UK.

Leave to remain granted in the UK

The UK **residence permit** replaced all former stamp and ink endorsements for permission to stay in the UK for longer than six months. The permit is a vignette, similar in appearance to that used to endorse entry clearance (see p43), and includes a photograph of the holder (see Appendix 6, Figure 8).

Previously, leave may have been endorsed using a smaller vignette sticker or by a rectangular stamp accompanied by a pentagonal date stamp (see Appendix 6, Figure 8).

If you were granted leave to remain on certain conditions (eg, as a student on condition that you do not work except in authorised employment and do not have recourse to public funds), these should be stated on the permit (see Appendix

6, Figure 9). However, if you were granted leave to remain on the basis of a sponsorship undertaking (see p28), this is not stated on the permit.

Biometric residence permits

Biometric residence permit cards for foreign nationals have now replaced the vignette (sticker) endorsements and other UK immigration status documents (see Appendix 6, Figure 5). You are issued with one as an alternative to having a sticker or ink stamp endorsement placed in your passport, which is not endorsed with your immigration status at all.

A biometric residence permit is a plastic card, the same size as a debit or credit card, which bears the holder's photograph, name, date of birth, nationality and immigration status. An electronic chip attached to the card holds digitised biometric details, including fingerprints, a facial image and biographical information (including name, and date and place of birth).

The card also shows details of your immigration status and entitlements in the UK, including what kind of leave you have and whether you can work. A database holds a record of the biometrics of every person to whom a card has been issued, so these can be cross-checked.

If you have the new identity card, you may need to inform UK Visas and Immigration (UKVI) of specified changes in your circumstances. If you fail to do so, you may face prosecution or other sanctions (see p27).

Leave extended for an application or appeal

Limited leave is automatically extended beyond the date it is due to expire if you make a valid application to extend or vary your leave before this date.[4] Leave extended in this way continues until a decision is made by UKVI and, if you are then refused further leave, until any appeal rights are exhausted. The same conditions attached to your original leave continue to apply during the extension (apart from the time limit). This includes any restriction on having recourse to public funds (see p25). If you did not have a restriction on having recourse to public funds during the period of leave you had at the time of applying, you continue to have leave that is not subject to such a restriction while your application or any subsequent 'in-time' appeal remains pending.

Example
Valassene has discretionary leave to remain with no public funds restriction. He applies to extend this leave shortly before it expires. When he does so he is receiving income support (IS). Valassene's immigration status continues to allow him to claim IS while his application remains outstanding.

His application is then refused, but he has a right of appeal to the Immigration and Asylum Chamber of the First-tier Tribunal. Valassene's immigration status continues to allow him to claim IS during the period of time in which he can appeal – ie, before the time limit for doing so expires. If he appeals within this time, he can continue to claim IS while his appeal remains pending. If he subsequently wins his appeal (and there is no appeal by the losing party), he is treated as if the decision he appealed against was never made (ie, as a person whose leave is being extended while his application remains outstanding and until the decision maker makes a decision) and remains eligible for IS.

UKVI can take a long time to decide applications, and appeals against refusals to vary or to extend leave can take still longer, so you may have your leave extended in this way for many months, or even for years. Your passport or biometric residence permit, if you had one when you applied, may be retained all this time. For these reasons, it can be difficult to show that your leave is ongoing. UKVI may acknowledge a valid application for leave with a letter, but does not always do so, and offers to confirm specifically that you have ongoing leave if you request this. There is a special helpline for employers and prospective employers. The number for this service is available from the UKVI website.

Travel and status documents issued to non-UK nationals

Where necessary, leave to enter or leave to remain may have been endorsed on an **immigration status document** (which is simply an A4-sized piece of paper) – eg, because your passport was not available when your leave was granted. Refugee leave and humanitarian protection are never endorsed in a passport issued by the holder's government, because the use of such a passport is considered to be an indication that you are happy to be protected by the government that issued it, which would be incompatible with having asylum in the UK (see Appendix 6, Figure 4).

A dependant of a refugee or person with humanitarian protection may be granted entry clearance on the basis of refugee family reunion on a standard **European Union form**, if s/he has no passport or cannot obtain one. The previous version, **a GV3 document**, had an endorsement stating: 'visa family reunion – sponsor'. The sponsor referred to is the relative with refugee status who the dependant is joining in the UK. The endorsement does not indicate that a sponsorship undertaking has been given.

Refugees are entitled to a **Refugee Convention travel document** (coloured blue), which is similar in format to a passport (see Appendix 6, Figure 11).

People recognised as stateless under the terms of the 1954 United Nations Convention relating to the status of stateless people are entitled to a **stateless persons' document** (coloured red).

Someone granted indefinite leave but not recognised as a refugee, and someone granted exceptional leave, discretionary leave or humanitarian protection can apply for a **certificate of travel** (coloured black). However, to qualify for such a document, usually you must have applied to your national authorities for a passport or travel document and been formally and unreasonably refused one.

3. People without leave

If you have entered the UK without permission or remained in the UK after your limited leave to enter or remain has expired, you may have committed a criminal offence and could be arrested and detained for removal from the UK. This also applies if you have remained in the UK after you have been refused further leave or had your leave revoked or curtailed and any appeal rights have been exhausted. Any conditions attached to the limited leave that has expired or been revoked or curtailed ceases to apply.

If you are in the UK without leave and come to the attention of the authorities, you are likely to be served with a **notice** informing you that you are liable to be removed from the UK, and explaining why (see Appendix 6, Figure 12). You may also be detained or given temporary admission, temporary release or bail (see p14). If you have any of these types of status, you should have been issued with a notice informing you of this and of any conditions.

If further leave has been refused, a line may be drawn through the previous endorsement of leave in your passport. A decision refusing leave to enter at a port may be endorsed by a crossed-through ink date stamp.

You must be notified of any immigration decision in writing. Sending a notice to your last known address or the address of a representative (eg, a solicitor or other regulated person) might be sufficient, so you may not necessarily be aware of a decision concerning you. Get specialist advice if you are in any doubt.

4. Asylum seekers

People who have applied for refugee or humanitarian protection leave or other forms of international protection are commonly called 'asylum seekers' (see p30).

Until early 2002, asylum seekers were issued with a **standard acknowledgement letter** (SAL). A SAL1 was issued to those claiming asylum at the port of entry and a SAL2 was issued to those who applied for asylum once they were already in the UK. From 2002, UK Visas and Immigration (UKVI) has issued asylum seekers with an **application registration card** (ARC) (see Appendix 6, Figure 8). The ARC may state whether you have any dependants or permission to work.

Asylum seekers who apply at a port of entry and in-country applicants who do not have leave at the time of their application are usually given temporary admission to the UK until their application is decided. If they have been detained, they might have been granted temporary release or bail. If you have any of these types of status, you should have been issued with a notice informing you of this and of any conditions (see Appendix 6, Figure 13). See p14 for further information.

If you apply for asylum when you have leave to enter or remain for another purpose (although this is rare), your leave might be automatically extended on the same conditions beyond the date it is due to expire until a decision is made by UKVI and, if the application is refused, any appeal rights are exhausted.

5. European Economic Area and Swiss nationals

If you are a European Economic Area (EEA) or Swiss national and have a right to reside in the UK, you have the right to be issued with a **registration certificate** by the Home Office. If you have acquired permanent residence, you have the right to be issued with a **document certifying permanent residence** (see Appendix 6, Figure 6). These documents are in the form of a vignette (sticker) fixed on a card booklet, separate from your passport.

If you are the family member of an EEA or a Swiss national and have a right to reside in the UK, you have the right to be issued with a **residence card** (see Appendix 6, Figure 7), or a **permanent residence card** if you have permanent residence. Alternatively, you may have been issued with a **family permit entry visa** before travelling to the UK. Each of these is usually a vignette (sticker) fixed in your passport.

If you have a right of residence derived from a relationship with an EEA or Swiss national, you have the right to be issued with a **derivative residence card** (see Appendix 6, Figure 7). Again, this is usually a vignette (sticker) fixed in your passport.

Note: the above documents are declaratory. It is not necessary to obtain such a document in order to have the rights recognised by it, and the period of validity should not to be regarded as a grant of permission to reside for that period. Similarly, the fact that you hold a valid residence card or registration certificate does not necessarily mean that you will continue to have the rights recognised by it in the future.

6. Passport issues

Leaving the UK

Embarkation from (leaving) the UK used to be endorsed by a triangular ink stamp in the embarking person's passport (see Appendix 6, Figure 14). However, this practice was suspended in March 1998.

New or lost passports

If you have been granted leave to enter or remain that has been endorsed in a passport that has expired or been lost before your leave is due to expire, the expiry or loss of the passport does not affect your leave. This is most common for people granted indefinite leave – eg, if you had your leave endorsed in your passport, but this has now expired and your new passport is not endorsed.

In this situation, you can apply for confirmation of your status. This now takes the form of a biometric residence permit card (see p46).

Illegible passport stamps

Problems may arise if an endorsement on a passport is either unclear or illegible, or if the passport of someone requiring leave to enter was not endorsed on her/his last entry.

If your passport has been endorsed illegibly, you may be deemed to have been granted leave to enter for six months with a condition prohibiting employment,[5] or, if you arrived in the UK before 10 July 1998, to have been given indefinite leave to enter the UK.[6] If you required leave to enter the UK, but your passport was not endorsed on entry, you may be considered an illegal entrant.[7] Specialist advice should be sought.

Notes

1. **British nationals and people with the right of abode**
   1 s39(8) BNA 1981

2. **People with leave to enter or remain**
   2 See UKVI policy, 'Entry Clearance Guidance', ECB9.4, at www.gov.uk/government/publications/entry-clearance-vignettes-ecb09
   3 s3(3)(b) IA 1971
   4 s3C IA 1971

6. **Passport issues**
   5 Sch 2 para 6(1) IA 1971, as amended
   6 Sch 2 para 6(1) IA 1971, prior to amendment and as interpreted by the courts
   7 *Rehal v SSHD* [1989] Imm AR 576

Part 3

Benefits and immigration status

Chapter 7

. . . .

People subject to immigration control

This chapter covers:
1. Introduction (below)
2. The effect of immigration status on benefits and tax credits (p54)
3. Who is a 'person subject to immigration control' (p55)

You should check this chapter, together with Chapters 8 and 9, if you, your partner and children are not all European Economic Area (EEA) nationals (see p39). If you, your partner and children *are* all EEA nationals, the rules in these three chapters do not apply to you.

1. Introduction

Entitlement to many benefits and tax credits can depend on your immigration status. The immigration status of your partner can also affect how much you are paid. It is also important to know the immigration status of any child included in your claim. This chapter provides an overview of how immigration status affects your benefit and tax credit entitlement.

If you are defined as a 'person subject to immigration control', you are excluded from many benefits and tax credits. However, there are limited exceptions which mean that you can still be entitled, despite being a 'person subject to immigration control'. The relevant benefits and tax credits and the exempt groups are covered in Chapter 8 – this chapter also covers the rules on how your benefits or tax credits are affected if your partner or child is a 'person subject to immigration control'.

If you claimed asylum in the UK and have been granted refugee leave, humanitarian protection or discretionary leave to be in the UK, additional benefit rules apply (see Chapter 9).

In addition to immigration status restrictions, most benefits also have presence and residence conditions. If your immigration status does not exclude you from a benefit or tax credit, you must still satisfy these. See Part 4 for more details.

2. The effect of immigration status on benefits and tax credits

It is important to know your immigration status, and that of anyone included in your claim, before making a claim for a benefit or tax credit. This is because your immigration status affects your right to benefits and tax credits being paid. Also, an increased amount for someone included in your claim can affect her/his right to remain in the UK if her/his leave is subject to the condition that s/he has no recourse to public funds.

There are two ways in which your immigration status affects your entitlement to benefits and tax credits.

- Your immigration status may mean that you come within the definition of a 'person subject to immigration control'. In most cases, this means that you are excluded from many benefits and tax credits (although there are exceptions).
- Your immigration status can mean that you satisfy, or are exempt from, the residence requirements for the benefit or tax credit you want to claim.

In limited circumstances, receipt of benefits or tax credits can affect your immigration status.

As the rules are complicated, it is helpful to approach them systematically. If you are not a European Economic Area national, work through the following steps for you and anyone who you could include in your claim.

- **Step one:** be clear about your immigration status. See Chapter 6 for help in determining on what basis you are in the UK. If you are unsure about your immigration status, or that of anyone included in your claim, get specialist advice from your local law centre, Citizens Advice Bureau or other advice agency that gives immigration advice (see Appendix 2).
- **Step two:** check whether you are defined as a 'person subject to immigration control' (see p55). If you are not, you can claim the benefits you want, provided you meet the other conditions of entitlement, including any rules on residence and presence (see Part 4). Your partner's immigration status may still affect your entitlement (see Step five).
- **Step three:** check whether the particular benefit or tax credit is one that excludes 'people subject to immigration control' (see p63).
- **Step four:** if the benefit you want to claim is one from which 'people subject to immigration control' are generally excluded, check whether you fall into any of the limited exempt groups. These vary between the different benefits and tax credits (see p64). Even if you are in an exempt group, you must still satisfy all the other conditions of entitlement, including the residence and presence requirements (see Part 4).

- **Step five:** if you cannot claim the benefit you want, but you have a partner who can, or if you can but have a partner or child who is subject to immigration control, check the rules on partners and children (see p71).
- **Step six:** if you or a member of your family have leave to enter or remain in the UK on condition that you do not have 'recourse to public funds', check whether any claim for benefits or tax credits could affect your/their immigration status (see p57).

3. **Who is a 'person subject to immigration control'**

Most people, apart from British citizens, are subject to immigration control. However, for benefit and tax credit purposes, the term 'person subject to immigration control' has a specific meaning (see below). It is this meaning that is referred to when the phrase 'person subject to immigration control' is used in this *Handbook*.

In order to establish whether you are a 'person subject to immigration control', you must know:

- whether or not you require leave to enter or remain in the UK;
- if you require leave, whether or not you have it;
- if you have leave, what, if any, conditions are attached to it; *and*
- if you have leave, whether this was granted as a result of someone giving an undertaking to maintain and accommodate you.

For benefit and tax credit purposes, you are a **'person subject to immigration control'** if you are not a European Economic Area (EEA) national (see p39) and you:[1]

- require leave to enter or remain in the UK, but do not have it (see p56); *or*
- have leave to enter or remain in the UK which is subject to the condition that you do not have 'recourse to public funds' (see p57); *or*
- have leave to enter or remain in the UK, given as a result of a maintenance undertaking (see p59); *or*
- have leave to remain in the UK solely because you are appealing against a refusal to vary your previous leave (see p60).

Note: an EEA national (including a British national) can never be a 'person subject to immigration control' because the definition only applies to non-EEA nationals. If you are an EEA national, you cannot be refused benefit as a 'person subject to immigration control', and the rules in this part of this *Handbook* do not apply to you unless you are claiming for a partner or child who is a 'person subject to immigration control'. However, if you are an EEA national, you may still be refused benefit for other reasons, including if you do not satisfy the presence and residence conditions (see Part 4).

You require leave to enter or remain, but do not have it

If you are not an EEA national and require leave to enter or remain in the UK but do not have it, you are a person subject to immigration control.[2] If you are not an EEA national, you require leave to enter or remain in the UK unless you are:
- a person with the right of abode;
- a person with a right of residence in European Union (EU) law. This applies if, for example, you are:
  - a family member of an EEA national who has a right to reside in the UK (see p151);[3]
  - a Swiss national with a right to reside. As a result of an agreement between Switzerland and the EU, Swiss nationals, in general, have the same residence rights as EEA nationals and do not require leave to enter or, if they have a right to reside, leave to remain in the UK;[4]
  - a family member of a Swiss national with a right to reside;
  - the primary carer of a British citizen who is in the UK, and it is necessary for you to have a right to reside in the UK so that s/he can continue to reside within the EU. **Note:** although you do not require leave, you are still excluded from any benefits that require a right to reside (see p95). However, you are not excluded from other benefits that do not require a right to reside, such as personal independence payment (PIP) and carer's allowance (CA).[5] If the British citizen is a child, you may also be able to get support under the Children Act 1989 (or Children (Scotland) Act 1995) from your local authority (see p406).

All other non-EEA nationals require leave to enter or remain in the UK. If you are not an EEA national and not in any of the above groups, you are a person subject to immigration control if you do not have leave to enter or remain. For more information on when leave to enter or remain is granted see Chapter 3.

Examples of when you require leave to enter or remain but do not have it include if you:
- are an asylum seeker with temporary admission (see p14);
- have overstayed your limited leave to remain;
- have entered the UK illegally and since then have not obtained any leave to remain;
- are subject to a deportation order.

Note: there are close links between the benefit authorities and the Home Office UK Visas and Immigration (UKVI). Making a claim for benefit could alert the immigration authorities to your presence and status in the UK. If you are an illegal entrant or an overstayer, or you are unsure of your immigration status, you should get specialist immigration advice before making a claim for benefits (see Appendix 2).

Your leave has a public funds restriction

You are a 'person subject to immigration control' if you have leave to enter or remain in the UK which is subject to a condition that you do not have recourse to 'public funds'.[6]

Most people admitted to the UK with time-limited leave given for a particular purpose, such as spouses/civil partners, students or visitors, are given leave to stay subject to the condition that they do not have recourse to public funds. Increasingly, this condition is also being added to those given leave to remain for other reasons, such as family ties, so you should always check whether your leave is subject to the condition that you do not have recourse to public funds.

People granted refugee leave, humanitarian protection (see p32) or, in most cases, discretionary leave (see p35) do not have any condition restricting access to public funds.

Indefinite leave (see p23) is never given with this condition attached. However, if you have been granted indefinite leave as a result of someone else undertaking to maintain and accommodate you, you come into the definition of being a 'person subject to immigration control' (see p59).

What are public funds

'**Public funds**' are defined in the Immigration Rules as:[7]
- attendance allowance;
- CA;
- child benefit;
- child tax credit;
- council tax benefit (now abolished);
- council tax reduction;
- disability living allowance;
- income-related employment and support allowance (ESA);
- housing benefit (HB);
- income support (IS);
- income-based jobseeker's allowance (JSA);
- pension credit;
- PIP;
- severe disablement allowance;
- social fund payments;
- universal credit (UC);
- working tax credit.

Homelessness assistance and housing provided under specific provisions are also defined as public funds.

Only the benefits and tax credits listed in the Immigration Rules are public funds. Therefore, if you get any other benefit, you are not in breach of the 'no recourse to public funds' condition.

If you have recourse to public funds when your leave is subject to a 'no recourse to public funds' condition, you have breached a condition of your leave. This may affect your right to remain in the UK. You could be liable to be deported, have further leave refused and/or be prosecuted for committing a criminal offence.[8]

If you are subject to a no recourse to public funds condition, you are defined as a 'person subject to immigration control' and (unless you are exempt – see Chapter 8) you are not entitled to the benefits and tax credits defined as public funds.

If you come within one of the exceptions, however, you can claim and receive these benefits, as you are not regarded as having recourse to public funds under the Immigration Rules.[9]

Note: you are regarded as having recourse to public funds if someone else's benefit is increased because of your presence.[10] For example, if the amount of your partner's HB is greater because you are included in her/his claim, this counts as recourse to public funds. You have therefore breached a condition of your leave, which could jeopardise your immigration status (see p22). Seek specialist advice before making a claim (see Appendix 2).

Domestic violence

If you were granted leave to enter or remain in the UK as a spouse, unmarried partner (including a same-sex partner) or civil partner but that relationship has broken down because of domestic violence, you may be able to apply for leave to remain under the 'destitute domestic violence concession' (see p34). This leave lasts for three months and is not subject to a condition that you do not have recourse to public funds. During this period of leave you are not defined as a 'person subject to immigration control' and can, therefore, claim all benefits, subject to the normal conditions of entitlement.

If you apply for indefinite leave before this period of leave expires, your leave is extended while UKVI determines your application. You continue *not* to be defined as a 'person subject to immigration control and continue to be entitled to benefits.

If you do not apply for indefinite leave by the end of the three months, you once again become a 'person subject to immigration control'. If you are claiming any of the benefits listed on p63, your entitlement ceases unless you come into any of the exempt groups listed on p64.

Your leave is given as a result of a maintenance undertaking

If you are a non-EEA national who has leave to enter or remain in the UK given as a result of a maintenance undertaking, you are a 'person subject to immigration control'.[11]

Maintenance undertaking

A **'maintenance undertaking'** means a written undertaking given by another person under the Immigration Rules to be responsible for your maintenance and accommodation.[12]

There are specific Home Office forms on which an undertaking can be given. However, no official form need be used, provided the undertaking is sufficiently formal and definite.[13] The document must contain a promise or agreement that the other person will maintain and accommodate you in the future. If it merely contains a statement about her/his present abilities and intentions, it does not amount to an undertaking.[14]

Your leave is considered to be 'as a result of a maintenance undertaking' if this was a factor in granting it. It does not need to have been the only, or even a major, factor.[15] However, if the maintenance undertaking was not relevant to your being granted leave, its existence does not make you a 'person subject to immigration control'.

If it is unclear whether or not your leave was granted as a result of a maintenance undertaking, the onus is on the benefit authority to prove that it was.[16]

If you are in doubt about whether you have leave given as a result of an undertaking, get specialist advice (see Appendix 2).

Consequences for your sponsor if you claim benefits

If you have leave to enter or remain as a result of a maintenance undertaking and you claim benefits, it is possible that the person(s) who signed the undertaking to maintain and accommodate you could be asked to repay any IS, income-based JSA or income-related ESA paid to you. However, in practice, this provision is rarely used because the rules for these benefits exclude from entitlement people with this form of leave for the first five years (unless the person(s) who gave the undertaking has died – see p65).

In certain circumstances, the DWP can recover any IS or UC paid to you from the person who gave the undertaking.[17] Recovery is through the magistrates' court (in Scotland, the sheriff court).

The DWP also has a power to prosecute for failure to maintain if that failure results in the payment of IS, income-based JSA or UC.[18]

As the DWP has the power to recover benefit or to take court action, if the DWP approaches you about an undertaking you have made, you should obtain independent advice (see Appendix 2).

Sponsors

People who have been given leave to enter or remain as the result of a maintenance undertaking are often referred to as '**sponsored people**' and those giving the undertakings as '**sponsors**'. This terminology is used by the benefit authorities, including in their guidance to decision makers. However, the term 'sponsor' is also used in connection with other types of leave and this can lead to confusion and errors in decision making. For example, the word arises in the Immigration Rules in relation to those seeking leave to enter or remain on the basis of their relationship to their spouse/civil partner/fiancé(e),[19] and people commonly think of themselves as having been 'sponsored' by their partner when they are granted such leave. The Upper Tribunal has provided a helpful discussion of this confusion.[20]

Another common area of confusion is when a family member of someone with refugee leave or humanitarian protection is given leave to enter or remain under the family reunion provisions (see p77). Although the person with refugee leave or humanitarian protection is not required to provide a maintenance undertaking, the confusion arises because the Home Office policy on family reunion and the entry visa given to the family member uses the word 'sponsor'.

It is important to remember that it is only if you have been given leave to enter or remain as a result of an undertaking that you come within this group of people who are defined as 'people subject to immigration control'. However, if you have been given time-limited leave to enter or remain because, for example, you were 'sponsored' by your spouse/civil partner, your leave is not subject to a no recourse to public funds condition and you come within the second group within the definition of a 'person subject to immigration control' (see p57).

In order not to add to any existing confusion, this *Handbook* avoids using the word 'sponsor'.

If you have leave to remain only because you are appealing

If you are a non-EEA national who has leave to enter or remain, but only because your leave has been extended while you appeal against a decision to refuse or vary your leave (see p46), you may be a 'person subject to immigration control'.[21]

If you have time-limited leave (see p43), you can apply to extend your leave or for further leave to remain on a different basis. Provided you do this before your existing leave expires, this leave is extended until your application is decided by UKVI.[22] You therefore continue to have the same type of leave, subject to the same conditions, until your application is decided. If your application is refused, you continue to have the same type of leave during the short time period in which you can appeal (or seek an administrative review of that refusal).[23]

If you appeal (or seek an administrative review) within the time limit, your leave is extended until the appeal or review is dealt with.[24] You continue to have the same type of leave, subject to the same conditions, until your appeal or review is dealt with.

However, during the time when your leave is extended because your appeal is pending, you *may* count as a 'person subject to immigration control'.[25]

The reason why it is not completely clear is because this part of the definition of a 'person subject to immigration control' cross-refers to a provision that has now been revoked and the lack of clarity concerns whether the definition should be read as a reference to a different subsequent provision. It may be arguable, therefore, that no one is covered by this rule.

In practice, if the rule does apply, it only makes a difference to your benefit and tax credit entitlement if your original leave did not have a 'no recourse to public funds' condition. Otherwise, you were already a 'person subject to immigration control' and an extension of your leave simply means you carry on being a 'person subject to immigration control'.

Example

Banu is an Iranian national who, before 9 July 2012, was granted three years' discretionary leave in the UK. She is not a 'person subject to immigration control' and so has full access to benefits and tax credits during the period of her leave. Just before her discretionary leave expires she applies for a further period of discretionary leave. Her application is refused and she immediately appeals against this decision. Her discretionary leave is therefore extended while the appeal is pending. The benefit authorities may argue that she is now a 'person subject to immigration control' as she has leave only because she is appealing.

Notes

3. **Who is a 'person subject to immigration control'**
   1 s115(9) IAA 1999
   2 s115(9)(a) IAA 1999
   3 s7 IA 1988

4 *The Agreement Between the European Community and its Member States, of the one part, and the Swiss Confederation, of the other, on the Free Movement of Persons*, Luxembourg, 21 June 1999, Cmd 5639; reg 2 I(EEA) Regs defines Switzerland as an EEA state; reg 11 provides that no EEA national requires leave to enter the UK.

5 *Zambrano*, C-34/09 [2011] ECR, not yet
   reported; *Dereci and Others*, C-256/11
   [2011] ECR, not yet reported
6 s115(9)(b) IAA 1999
7 para 6 IR
8 s24(1)(b)(ii) IA 1971
9 para 6B IR
10 para 6A IR
11 s115(9)(c) IAA 1999
12 s115(10) IAA 1999
13 *R (Begum) v Social Security Commissioner*
   [2003] EWHC 3380 (Admin)); CIS/
   2474/1999; CIS/2816/2001 and CIS/
   47/2002
14 *Ahmed v SSWP* [2005] EWCA Civ 535;
   CIS/426/2003
15 CIS/3508/2001
16 R(PC) 1/09
17 s106 SSAA 1992
18 s105 SSAA 1992
19 para 6 IR
20 *OO v SSWP (SPC)* [2013] UKUT 0335
   (AAC)
21 s115(9)(d) IAA 1992
22 s3C(2)(a) IA 1971
23 s3C(2)(b) and (d) IA 1971
24 s3C(2)(c) and (d) IA 1971
25 s115(9)(d) IAA 1999 refers to leave
   continuing while you appeal because of
   the rule in Sch 4, para 17. Sch 4, para
   17 was repealed by NIAA 2002, which
   also inserted s3C into IA 1971. The
   reference to Sch 4, para 17 in
   s115(9)(d), therefore, now arguably has
   to be read as a reference to s3C IA 1971
   (see s17(2) IA 1978).

Chapter 8

People subject to immigration control and benefits

This chapter covers:
1. Benefits and tax credits affected by immigration status (below)
2. Who is not excluded (p64)
3. Partners and children who are subject to immigration control (p71)

Before using the information in this chapter, you should establish whether you, your partner or child are a 'person subject to immigration control'. This is explained in Chapter 7.

1. Benefits and tax credits affected by immigration status

The general rule is that if you are defined as a 'person subject to immigration control' (see p55), you are excluded from council tax reduction[1] (see p397) and the following benefits and tax credits:[2]

- attendance allowance;
- carer's allowance;
- child benefit;
- child tax credit;
- disability living allowance;
- contributory employment and support allowance (ESA) in youth;[3]
- income-related ESA;
- housing benefit;
- incapacity benefit in youth;[4]
- income support;
- income-based jobseeker's allowance (JSA);
- pension credit;
- personal independence payment;
- severe disablement allowance;

- social fund payments;
- universal credit;
- working tax credit.

However, there are limited exceptions when, despite being a 'person subject to immigration control', you can claim means-tested benefits (see below), non-means-tested benefits (see p66) and tax credits (see p68). Even if cannot claim yourself, a family member might be able to claim a benefit that includes an amount for you, or you might be able to make a joint claim (see p71).

A 'person subject to immigration control' is only excluded from the above benefits and tax credits, so you can claim any other benefit. For example, if you have paid sufficient national insurance contributions, you can claim any of the contributory benefits – eg, retirement pension, contribution-based JSA and contributory ESA. You can also claim benefits that depend on previous employment – eg, maternity allowance (MA) or industrial injuries benefits. **Note:** the government intends to make it a condition of entitlement to contribution-based JSA, contributory ESA, MA and statutory sick, maternity, paternity and adoption pay that you are entitled to work in the UK.[5] See CPAG's online service and *Welfare Rights Bulletin* for updates. You may also be able to get help from your local welfare assistance scheme (see p400).

2. **Who is not excluded**

Although the general rule is that you are excluded from the benefits and tax credits listed on p71 if you are defined as a 'person subject to immigration control', there are exceptions that mean you can still be entitled. The exceptions vary between the different categories of benefits and tax credits, so being in an exempt group for one category does not necessarily mean you can receive a benefit in a different category.

Note: if your leave prohibits you from having recourse to public funds (see p25), you can still claim any benefit to which you are entitled on the basis of being in an exempt group, even though these benefits (except employment and support allowance (ESA) in youth and incapacity benefit (IB) in youth) are defined as 'public funds'. This is because the Immigration Rules do not regard you as having recourse to public funds if you are entitled because you are in an exempt group (see p57).[6]

Means-tested benefits

If you are in any of the exempt groups below, being a 'person subject to immigration control' does not exclude you from getting:[7]

- income support (IS);
- income-based jobseeker's allowance (JSA);
- income-related ESA;
- pension credit;
- housing benefit;
- universal credit (UC).

Your leave is as a result of undertaking and you have been resident for five years

You are not excluded from the above means-tested benefits on the basis of being a 'person subject to immigration control' if you have:[8]

- leave to enter or remain given as a result of a maintenance undertaking (see p59); *and*
- been resident in the UK for at least five years since either the date the undertaking was given or the date when you came to the UK, whichever is later.

If you go abroad during the five years, you may still count as resident in the UK during your absence. This depends on the duration and circumstances of your absence (see p90).[9] If your absence abroad is such that you cease to be resident in the UK, you can add together periods of residency either side of the gaps in order to meet the five-year rule.[10]

Your leave is as result of undertaking and your sponsor has died

You are not excluded from the above means-tested benefits on the basis of being a 'person subject to immigration control' if:[11]

- you have leave to enter or remain given as a result of a maintenance undertaking (see p59); *and*
- the person who gave the undertaking (often referred to as your 'sponsor') has died. If the undertaking was given by more than one person, they must all have died.

Nationals of Turkey and Macedonia

You are not excluded from the above means-tested benefits on the basis of being a 'person subject to immigration control' if you are: [12]

- a national of a country that has ratified either the European Convention on Social and Medical Assistance or the European Social Charter (1961). The only non-European Economic Area (EEA) countries to which this applies are Turkey and Macedonia; *and*
- lawfully present in the UK. You satisfy this if you currently have leave to enter or remain in the UK.

Note: you must satisfy all the other conditions of entitlement, including the requirement to have a right to reside (see p107).[13] Therefore, if you are an asylum seeker with temporary admission in the UK, although you are 'lawfully present', you are likely to be excluded from benefit, as having temporary admission does not give you a right to reside.[14]

You applied for asylum before April 2000

You are not excluded from the above means-tested benefits (except UC) on the basis of being a 'person subject to immigration control' if:[15]

- you claimed asylum before 3 April 2000 and you have not had a decision on your asylum application (or appeal if it was against a decision made before 5 February 1996), or you were part of the benefit family of someone who applied for asylum and was receiving a means-tested benefit on 4 February 1996; *and*
- you are covered by the rules on transitional protection. See Chapter 58 of the 2011/12 edition of CPAG's *Welfare Benefits and Tax Credits Handbook* for these.

Non-means-tested benefits

If you are in any of the exempt groups below, being a 'person subject to immigration control' does not exclude you from getting any of the following non-means-tested benefits:[16]

- attendance allowance (AA);
- carer's allowance;
- child benefit;
- disability living allowance (DLA);
- ESA in youth;
- IB for incapacity in youth;
- personal independence payment (PIP);
- severe disablement allowance.

Your leave is as a result of an undertaking

You are not excluded from the above **non-means-tested** benefits on the basis of being a 'person subject to immigration control' if your leave to enter or remain was given as a result of a maintenance undertaking (see p59).[17]

Note: your entitlement to benefit still depends on your satisfying all the other conditions of entitlement, including those on presence and residence (see Part 4).

You are a family member of a European Economic Area national

You are not excluded from the above non-means-tested benefits on the basis of being a 'person subject to immigration control' if you are a 'family member' of an EEA national.[18]

'Family member' is not defined in the regulations and it is therefore arguable that it should be given its ordinary everyday meaning and include, for example, a sister or uncle, as well as a partner.

It is also arguable that no additional conditions should be placed on the EEA national, so, for example, British citizens who have never left the UK should be covered, as should other EEA nationals in the UK who do not have a right to reside.

In practice, decision makers often interpret who is covered in this way, and child benefit guidance states that you are covered if your family member is an EEA or Swiss national or 'UK national', including if s/he is the child for whom you are claiming child benefit or your partner or spouse.[19]

However, a much more restrictive view was taken by a commissioner in a case concerning DLA. This held that someone only comes into this exempt group if they are a 'family member' as narrowly defined in European law (see p152) and that EEA nationals are only covered if they are exercising certain EU rights – eg, as a 'worker'.[20]

If you are refused benefit because the decision maker has followed this decision and used a more restrictive interpretation of 'family member of an EEA national', you should challenge the decision on the basis that the case was wrongly decided. In support of your challenge, cite a more recent case in which a Northern Ireland commissioner did not follow this earlier decision.[21] Although Northern Irish decisions do not have to be followed in England, Scotland and Wales, they are still persuasive. This decision is also more fully reasoned than, and contains detailed consideration of, the earlier decision.

Note: 'family members' (as defined in European law) of EEA nationals who have residence rights (eg, as workers) are not excluded from non-means-tested benefits as they are not defined as 'people subject to immigration control'. This is because they do not require leave to be in the UK as they have rights under EU residence law (see p56).

If the First-tier Tribunal refuses your appeal, you can appeal to the Upper Tribunal, which can resolve the matter.

Nationals of Algeria, Morocco, San Marino, Tunisia and Turkey

You are not excluded from the non-means-tested benefits listed on p66 the basis of being a 'person subject to immigration control' if you:[22]

- are a national of Algeria, Morocco, San Marino, Tunisia or Turkey and you are either currently lawfully working (see below) in Great Britain, or you have ceased lawfully working for a reason such as pregnancy, childcare, illness or accident, or because you have reached retirement age;[23] *or*
- you are living with a member of your family (see p243) covered by the above bullet point.

Lawfully working

'**Lawfully working**' has been equated with being an 'insured person' under the European Union (EU) co-ordination rules (see p242).[24] In broad terms, this means that you must have worked in the UK and have (or should have) paid national insurance (NI) contributions. It is likely that you will only be accepted as 'lawfully working' if your work does not breach any work restrictions attached to your leave or, if you are an asylum seeker, you have permission to work from UK Visas and Immigration (UKVI).

For further details on the agreements with these countries, see p269.

You are covered by a reciprocal agreement

You are not excluded from claiming AA, DLA, PIP or child benefit (but not the other non-means-tested benefits listed above) on the basis of being a 'person subject to immigration control' if you are covered by a reciprocal agreement the UK has with another country.[25] In practice, this is most helpful for child benefit and, in particular, if you are covered by the agreement with former Yugoslavia which applies to Bosnia-Herzegovina, Kosovo, Macedonia, Montenegro, and Serbia.[26]

See p262 for more information about reciprocal agreements.

You have been in receipt of a benefit since 1996

You are not excluded from the above non-means-tested benefits on the basis of being a 'person subject to immigration control' if you have received that particular benefit continuously since 4 February 1996 (6 October 1996 for child benefit).[27]

This transitional protection only enables you to continue to receive that benefit. You cannot make a new claim. If you are receiving benefit on this basis, your transitional protection (and therefore your entitlement) ends if:

- your benefit award ends;
- you request a revision or supersession; *or*
- your asylum application (if any) is decided or abandoned.

If you think you may be getting benefit as a result of this transitional protection, it is therefore important that you do not request a revision or supersession, as this will bring your entitlement to an end. However, given that you must have been getting benefit continuously since 1996 and still be a 'person subject to immigration control', the number of claimants affected is extremely small.

Tax credits

If you are in any of the exempt groups below, being a 'person subject to immigration control' does not exclude you from getting child tax credit (CTC) or working tax credit (WTC).[28] Some of the exempt groups only apply to one of the tax credits, and some apply to both.

Note: if you are a 'person subject to immigration control', but your partner is not (or s/he is in one of the groups on pp69–70), you can make a joint claim for tax credits (see p73).

Your leave is as a result of undertaking and you have been resident for five years

You are not excluded from CTC or WTC on the basis of being a 'person subject to immigration control' if you have:[29]

• leave to enter or remain given as a result of a maintenance undertaking (see p59); *and*

• been resident in the UK for at least five years since either the date the undertaking was given or the date when you came to the UK, whichever is later.

If you go abroad during the five years, you may still count as resident in the UK during your absence. This depends on the duration and circumstances of your absence (see p90).[30] If your absence abroad is such that you cease to be resident in the UK, you can add together periods of residency either side of the gaps in order to meet the five-year rule.[31]

Your leave is as a result of undertaking and your sponsor has died

You are not excluded from CTC or WTC on the basis of being a 'person subject to immigration control' if:[32]

• you have leave to enter or remain given as a result of a maintenance undertaking (see p59); *and*

• the person who gave the undertaking (often referred to as your 'sponsor') has died. If the undertaking was given by more than one person, they must all have died.

Nationals of Turkey and Macedonia

You are not excluded from WTC on the basis of being a 'person subject to immigration control' if you are:[33]

• a national of a country that has ratified either the European Convention on Social and Medical Assistance or the European Social Charter (1961). The only non-EEA countries to which this applies are Turkey and Macedonia; *and*

• lawfully present. You satisfy this if you currently have leave to enter or remain in the UK.

Note: you must still satisfy all the other conditions of entitlement, including working a sufficient number of hours.

If you are an asylum seeker with temporary admission in the UK (see p14), you are accepted as 'lawfully present',[34] but you are only entitled to WTC if you satisfy the other conditions of entitlement. In practice, therefore, since you must work a sufficient number of hours and temporary admission usually prohibits you from working, you cannot benefit from this provision unless you have obtained permission to work from UKVI and you work in accordance with this (see p31).

Nationals of Algeria, Morocco, San Marino, Tunisia or Turkey

You are not excluded from CTC on the basis of being a 'person subject to immigration control' if you:[35]

- are a national of Algeria, Morocco, San Marino, Tunisia or Turkey and either you are currently lawfully working in the UK (see below), or you have ceased lawfully working for a reason such as pregnancy, childcare, illness or accident, or because you have reached retirement age;[36] *or*
- you are living with a member of your family (see p243) who is covered by the above bullet point.

Lawfully working

'Lawfully working' has been equated with being an 'insured person' under the EU co-ordination rules (see Chapter 16).[37] In broad terms, this means that you must have worked in the UK and have (or should have) paid NI contributions. It is likely that you will only be accepted as 'lawfully working' if your work does not breach any work restrictions attached to your leave or, if you are an asylum seeker, you have permission to work from UKVI.[38]

For further details on the agreements with these countries, see p269.

Your income support or income-based jobseeker's allowance claim has been transferred to child tax credit

You are not excluded from CTC on the basis of being a 'person subject to immigration control' if you:[39]

- claim CTC on or after 6 April 2004; *and*
- immediately before you claimed CTC, you were entitled to an increase in your IS or income-based JSA for a child because either:
  - you are Turkish and lawfully present (see p65); *or*
  - you applied for asylum before 3 April 2000 and are covered by the transitional protection rules (see p66).

This only applies if you are transferring to CTC from an IS or JSA claim that included amounts for a child. It does not apply if you have not been receiving IS or income-based JSA for a child.

Note: as Macedonia only ratified the European Social Charter on 31 March 2005, nationals of Macedonia cannot benefit from this provision (as they could not have established their entitlement to IS or income-based JSA for a child before 6 April 2004).

Social fund payments

You are not excluded from social fund payments on the basis of being a 'person subject to immigration control' if you are in one of the exempt groups for either means-tested benefits (see p64) or non-means-tested benefits (see p66).[40]

Chapter 8: People subject to immigration control and benefits
3. Partners and children who are subject to immigration control

8

However, you must meet the other conditions of entitlement, including (except for winter fuel payments) being in receipt of a qualifying benefit. What counts as a qualifying benefit varies for different social fund payments but is broadly the means-tested benefits and, in some circumstances, tax credits. See CPAG's *Welfare Benefits and Tax Credits Handbook* for details.

3. Partners and children who are subject to immigration control

Some benefits and tax credits have special rules that apply if your partner or child who lives with you is a 'person subject to immigration control'. These rules vary, so check the rules for the benefit or tax credit you want to claim.

Means-tested benefits

Income support, income-based jobseeker's allowance and income-related employment and support allowance

If your partner is a 'person subject to immigration control' (see p55), s/he is included in your claim for income support (IS), income-based jobseeker's allowance (JSA), including if you are a joint-claim couple, or income-related employment and support allowance (ESA). However, you are only paid a personal allowance at the single person's rate, unless s/he comes into one of the groups that can get the means-tested benefits on pp64–66. If s/he does fall into one of these groups, you are paid at the couple rate.[41]

In all cases, your partner is still treated as part of your household and part of your claim. Therefore, her/his work, income and capital can all affect your benefit entitlement. Her/his presence also means you cannot claim IS as a lone parent. Similarly, unless your partner receives a qualifying benefit or is registered blind, her/his presence might mean that you are not entitled to a severe disability premium.

Premiums are payable if either you or your partner satisfy the qualifying conditions and should be paid at the couple rate.

Note: if your partner's leave to enter or remain in the UK is subject to a condition that s/he does not have recourse to public funds, you should be aware that receiving the couple rate of a premium is a breach of the conditions of her/his leave and could affect her/his right to remain in the UK. Obtain specialist advice before making a claim that includes a higher level of premium on the basis of your partner (see Appendix 2).

Pension credit

If your partner is a 'person subject to immigration control' (irrespective of whether or not s/he is in one of the exempt groups listed on pp64–66), s/he is

8

Chapter 8: People subject to immigration control and benefits
3. Partners and children who are subject to immigration control

treated as not being part of your household.[42] This means that you are paid as a single person and your partner's income and capital do not affect your claim. If you would otherwise be entitled to the additional amount for severe disability, your partner's presence may mean that you are not entitled to it, as the DWP may count her/him as 'normally residing with' you for this purpose.[43] See CPAG's *Welfare Benefits and Tax Credits Handbook* for more details.

Housing benefit

If your partner and/or child for whom you are responsible is a 'person subject to immigration control', this does not affect the amount you are paid. Your partner is included in your claim and your applicable amount includes the couple rate of the personal allowance and any premiums to which either of you are entitled. Similarly, your child is included in your claim and your applicable amount includes a personal allowance for her/him, together with any premiums for which s/he qualifies.

Note: if your partner's and/or child's leave is subject to a condition that s/he does not have recourse to public funds, you should be aware that a claim for housing benefit could (depending on your circumstances) result in additional public funds being paid as a result of her/his presence. This could affect her/his right to remain in the UK (see p57). Obtain specialist advice before making a claim (see Appendix 2).

Council tax reduction (see p397) is also defined as a public fund, so if your council tax reduction is greater as a result of the presence of someone whose leave is subject to a 'no recourse to public funds' condition (eg, because you lose a single person's discount) that person's right to remain in the UK could be affected. Obtain specialist advice before making a claim (see Appendix 2).

Universal credit

If your partner is a 'person subject to immigration control' (see p55) and is not in one of the groups who can get universal credit (UC) listed on pp64–66, you must claim UC as a single person.[44] Your award is based on the maximum amount for a single person, but your partner's income and capital are taken into account.[45]

Non-means-tested benefits

Contributory non-means-tested benefits are not affected by your or your partner's or child's immigration status. **Note:** the government intends to make it a condition of entitlement to contribution-based JSA, contributory ESA, maternity allowance, and statutory sick, maternity, paternity and adoption pay that you are entitled to work in the UK.[46] See CPAG's online service and *Welfare Rights Bulletin* for updates.

Only the claimant's immigration status affects entitlement to non-contributory, non-means-tested benefits. Therefore, for **child benefit**, if you are

Chapter 8: People subject to immigration control and benefits
3. Partners and children who are subject to immigration control

8

not a 'person subject to immigration control' or you are but are in one of the exempt groups (see pp66–68), you can claim for any child for whom you are responsible, regardless of the child's immigration status. However, if your child has leave which is subject to a condition that s/he does not have recourse to public funds, you should be aware that a claim for child benefit will result in additional public funds being paid as a result of her/his presence. This could affect her/his right to remain in the UK (see p57). Obtain specialist advice before making a claim (see Appendix 2).

If your child is not a 'person subject to immigration control', or s/he is but s/he comes into one of the exempt groups on pp66–68, s/he can claim **disability living allowance**, even if you are a 'person subject to immigration control'.

Tax credits

If your partner is a 'person subject to immigration control' and you are not, or you are but are in one of the exempt groups on pp68–70, your joint claim for tax credits is treated as if your partner were not subject to immigration control. You are therefore entitled to working tax credit (WTC) and child tax credit (CTC).[47] However, unless you or your partner are responsible for a child, or your partner is a national of Macedonia or Turkey and is lawfully present in the UK, your WTC does not include the couple element.[48]

There are no immigration status conditions for children. Any child for whom you are responsible is included in your claim and your CTC and/or WTC includes amounts for her/him.

If your partner's leave is subject to a condition that s/he does not have recourse to public funds, s/he is not regarded as having such recourse by making a joint tax credits claim with you. This means that you and your partner can make the joint claim without it affecting her/his right to remain in the UK. If your joint claim includes a child whose leave is subject to a condition that s/he does not have recourse to public funds, any tax credits awarded in respect of that child are also not regarded as such recourse.[49]

If your claim for CTC or WTC is not a joint claim as described above (ie, it is a single claim or a joint claim but neither you nor your partner are a 'person subject to immigration control') and it includes an amount for a child whose leave is subject to a 'no recourse to public funds' condition, this breaches that condition and could affect her/his right to remain in the UK. Obtain specialist advice before making a claim (see Appendix 2).

Notes

1. Benefits and tax credits affected by immigration status

1 Sch para 22 CTRS(DS)E Regs; reg 13 CTRS(PR)E Regs; reg 19 CTR(SPC)S Regs; reg 19 CTR(S) Regs; reg 27 CTRSPR(W) Regs; Sch para 20 CTRS(DS)W Regs
2 s115(1) IAA 1999; reg 3(1) TC(Imm) Regs
3 Reg 11(1)(b) ESA Regs; reg 12(1)(b) ESA Regs 2013
4 Reg 16(1)(b) SS(IB) Regs
5 ss61-63 WRA 2012

2. Who is not excluded

6 para 6B IR
7 Reg 2(1) and Sch Part 1 SS(IA)CA Regs
8 Reg 2(1)-(1A) and Sch Part 1, para 3 SS(IA)CA Regs
9 CPC/1035/2005
10 R(IS) 2/02
11 Reg 2(1) and Sch Part 1, para 2 SS(IA)CA Regs
12 Reg 2(1)-(1A) and Sch Part 1, para 4 SS(IA)CA Regs
13 *Yesiloz v London Borough of Camden* [2009] EWCA Civ 415
14 *Szoma v SSWP* [2005] UKHL 64, reported as R(IS) 2/06 and see *Yesiloz v London Borough of Camden* [2009] EWCA Civ 415
15 Reg 12 SS(IA)CA Regs; reg 12 SS(PFA)MA Regs
16 Reg 2(2), (3) and (4)(b) and Sch Part 2 SS(IA)CA Regs; reg 2(1)(a)(ib) SS(AA) Regs; reg 9(1)(ia) SS(ICA) Regs; reg 16(d)(ii) SS(PIP) Regs; reg 2(1)(a)(ib) SS(DLA) Regs; reg 11(1)(b) and (3) ESA Regs; reg 12(1)(b) and (3) ESA 2013; reg 16(1)(b) and (5) SS(IB) Regs
17 Reg 2 and Sch Part 2, para 4 SS(IA)CA Regs
18 Reg 2 and Sch Part 2, para 1 SS(IA)CA Regs
19 para 10140 *Child Benefit Technical Manual*
20 CDLA/708/2007
21 *JFP v DSD (DLA)* [2012] NICom 267
22 Reg 2 and Part II SS(IA)CA Regs
23 *Zoulika Krid v Caisse Nationale d'Assurance Vieillesse des Travailleurs Salariés (CNAVTS)*, C-103/94 [1995] ECR I-00719, para 26
24 *Sema Sürül v Bundesanstalt für Arbeit*, C-262/96 [1999] ECR I-02685
25 Reg 2(3) SS(IA)CA Regs
26 The Family Allowances, National Insurance and Industrial Injuries (Yugoslavia) Order 1958, No.1263
27 Reg 12(10) SS(IA)CA Regs
28 Reg 3(1) TC(Imm) Regs
29 Reg 3(1) TC(Imm) Regs, case 1
30 CPC/1035/2005
31 R(IS) 2/02
32 Reg 3(1) TC(Imm) Regs, case 2
33 Reg 3(1) TC(Imm) Regs, case 4
34 *Szoma v SSWP* [2005] UKHL 64, reported as R(IS) 2/06 and see *Yesiloz v London Borough of Camden* [2009] EWCA Civ 415
35 Reg 3(1) TC(Imm) Regs, case 5
36 *Zoulika Krid v Caisse Nationale d'Assurance Vieillesse des Travailleurs Salariés (CNAVTS)*, C-103/94 [1995] ECR I-00719, para 26
37 *Sürül v Bundesanstalt für Arbeit*, C-262/96 [1999] ECR I-02685
38 para 02108 TCTM
39 Reg 5 TC(Imm) Regs
40 Reg 2 SS(IA)CA Regs

3. Partners and children who are subject to immigration control

41 **IS** Reg 21(3) and Sch 7 para 16A IS Regs
   JSA Reg 85(4) and Sch 5 para 13A JSA Regs
   ESA Reg 69 and Sch 5 para 10 ESA Regs
42 Reg 5(1)(h) SPC Regs
43 para 78946 DMG
44 Reg 3(3) UC Regs
45 Regs 18(2), 22(3) and 36(3) UC Regs
46 ss61-63 WRA 2012
47 Reg 3(2) TC(Imm) Regs
48 Reg 11(4) and (5) WTC(EMR) Regs
49 para 6B IR. The TC(Imm) Regs are made under s42 TCA 2002.

Chapter 9

•••

Asylum seekers and refugees

This chapter covers:
1. Asylum seekers (below)
2. Benefits and tax credits for refugees and others granted leave (p76)
3. Integration loans (p78)

This chapter explains some of the specific benefit and tax credit rules that apply to asylum seekers and to those who are granted refugee leave, humanitarian protection or discretionary leave following an asylum application. For more information about these categories of leave, see Chapter 4.

---

1. **Asylum seekers**

You are referred to as an **'asylum seeker'** while you are waiting for a Home Office decision on your application for refugee status (see p30). If you are a non-European Economic Area (EEA) national seeking asylum in the UK, unless you have leave on some other basis or you do not require it (eg, because you are joining your family member who is an EEA national with a right to reside in the UK), you come within the definition of a 'person subject to immigration control'. This is because you are someone who requires leave, but does not have it (see p56). You are therefore excluded from the social security benefits listed on p63, unless you are in one of the exempt groups (see p64).

Remember, even if you are in one of the exempt groups, you must still satisfy all the other conditions of entitlement for the particular benefit or tax credit, including the presence and residence conditions (see Part 4).

If benefit can be paid for you, either because you are not excluded from making a claim or because your partner can include you in her/his claim, this does not affect your asylum application. You can receive any benefit defined as a 'public fund' (see p57) because asylum seekers are not subject to a 'no recourse to public funds' condition. If you receive public funds, this does not affect the outcome of your asylum application.

If you are excluded from claiming social security benefits because you are a 'person subject to immigration control', you may be entitled to alternative forms of state support. If you are destitute, you may be eligible for asylum support from the Home Office (see Chapter 21).

Note: asylum support is taken into account as income when calculating any housing benefit your partner claims, but it is not taken into account as income for income support (IS), income-based jobseeker's allowance (JSA) or income-related employment and support allowance (ESA) and universal credit (UC).[1]

However, any IS, income-based JSA, income-related ESA or UC your partner receives is taken into account as income when calculating your asylum support.

If you are not eligible for asylum support or benefits, ask your local authority for help. If you have children, you may be eligible for support under the Children Act 1989 or Children (Scotland) Act 1995 (see p349). If you are sick or disabled, you may be eligible for help under the National Assistance Act 1948 (see p348). You may also be entitled to help from your local welfare assistance scheme (see p400). See Chapter 21 for more details.

2. Benefits and tax credits for refugees and others granted leave

If, following your asylum application, you are granted leave that is not subject to the condition that you do not have recourse to public funds, you are no longer a 'person subject to immigration control'. For example, if you are granted refugee leave, humanitarian protection, discretionary leave or indefinite leave under the 'case resolution exercise' (see p37), you are not a 'person subject to immigration control' during that period of leave. However, if you are granted leave that is subject to the condition that you do not have 'recourse to public funds', this brings you within the definition of a 'person subject to immigration control' (see p57) and you are excluded from the benefits and tax credits listed on p63, unless you are in an exempt group (see p64).

If the leave you have been granted following your asylum application means you are not a 'person subject to immigration control', you are no longer excluded from the benefits listed on p63 and can claim all benefits subject to the usual conditions of entitlement. The following rules may also affect you.

- If you are granted refugee leave, humanitarian protection or discretionary leave, you are exempt from the habitual residence test (see p99).
- If you are granted refugee leave or humanitarian protection, you can be joined by certain family members under family reunion provisions (see p32). The benefit authorities sometimes make mistakes about the benefit rights of these family members (see p77).
- If you are granted refugee leave, you may be able to claim backdated child benefit, child tax credit and working tax credit (WTC) (see p77).

- If you are granted refugee leave, you may be entitled to income support (IS) while you study English (see p78).
- If you are granted refugee leave or humanitarian protection, you may be eligible for an integration loan (see p78).

Family reunion

If you have been granted refugee leave or humanitarian protection, your spouse and dependent family members may join you under the family reunion rules (see p32).

A family member who comes to the UK and is given leave under these provisions is not a 'person subject to immigration control' and can claim all benefits, provided s/he meets the usual rules of entitlement.

However, sometimes the benefit authorities decide that your family member is a 'person subject to immigration control' on the basis that her/his Home Office documents describe you as her/his 'sponsor' and that your family member has been given leave as a result of a maintenance undertaking (see p59). This is incorrect. No such undertaking is required from a person with refugee leave or humanitarian protection and your family members who come to the UK under the family reunion provisions are not given leave a result of an undertaking.

If a family member has leave in the UK under the family reunion provisions and is refused benefits or tax credits because the decision maker decides s/he is a 'person subject to immigration control', s/he should challenge the decision.

Backdated child benefit and tax credits

If you have been granted refugee leave (not humanitarian protection or discretionary leave), you can claim child benefit, guardian's allowance and tax credits and have them backdated to the date of your asylum application (or 6 April 2003 for tax credits, if this is later).[2] Generally, you are required to reclaim tax credits each year. However, under the special backdating rules for refugees, the claim is treated as having been renewed each April.[3]

You must claim backdated tax credits within one month, and child benefit and guardian's allowance within three months, of receiving the Home Office letter granting you leave as a refugee.[4] If the Home Office letter is sent to a solicitor acting for you, the three- or one-month period starts from the date your solicitor receives it.[5]

The amount of tax credits paid is reduced by the amount of asylum support you received for your essential living needs over the period.[6]

In many cases, this is more than the amount of tax credits and, therefore, cancels out any entitlement over the backdated period. However, if you did not receive asylum support or your tax credit entitlement exceeds the amount of asylum support paid (eg, if you worked sufficient hours to qualify for WTC), you can be entitled to an amount of backdated tax credits.

The amount of child benefit and guardian's allowance paid is not reduced by any asylum support you may have received.

Income support for refugees studying English

Refugees who are studying English are one of the categories of people who are entitled to income support (IS).

If you have been granted refugee leave (not humanitarian protection or discretionary leave), you can claim IS for up to nine months while you are studying if you:[7]

- attend, for more than 15 hours a week, a course for the purpose of learning English so you may obtain employment; *and*
- have been in Great Britain for not more than 12 months on the date the course began.

---

3. **Integration loans**

Integration loans are interest-free loans, made to assist people who have recently been granted either refugee status or humanitarian protection integrate into UK society.

Note: you may also be entitled to help from local welfare assistance schemes (see p400). Depending on the nature of your local scheme, you may want to apply to this before applying for a repayable integration loan, but be aware that many local authorities do not give cash and some require the assistance to be repaid.

Who is eligible

An application for an integration loan is only considered if you are eligible to apply for one and you make a valid application (see p80). However, whether or not you are awarded a loan is at the discretion of the decision maker (see below).

You are eligible to apply for an integration loan if you:[8]

- have been granted, after 11 June 2007, refugee leave, humanitarian protection (see p32), or leave to enter or remain as a dependant of someone with either refugee leave or humanitarian protection;
- are aged 18 or over;
- have not previously had an integration loan; *and*
- are, in the view of the Home Secretary, capable of repaying the loan

In exercising her/his discretion and deciding whether to give you a loan, the decision maker must take into account:[9]

- the length of time since your leave was granted;
- your financial position – ie, your income, assets, liabilities and outgoings;
- your likely ability to repay the loan;

- what you intend to use the loan for; *and*
- the total available budget for loans.

Although the legislation does not specify which intended uses of a loan are more likely to be accepted, the application form provides the following headings for you to set amounts against, and guidance to decision makers confirms that these examples of 'integration needs' can be accepted (if they cannot be met through assistance available from Jobcentre Plus):[10]

- help with housing, including:
  - deposits for rented accommodation;
  - rent payments;
  - house-moving expenses;
  - essential items;
- help with finding work, including:
  - travel expenses to attend interviews;
  - work clothing/equipment;
  - initial childcare costs;
  - subsistence while training;
- help with education, including:
  - the cost of a training programme;
  - requalification/professional qualification.

There is also space on the form for other needs that would assist your integration. However, the guidance states that a loan should normally be refused for:

- non-essential items;
- domestic assistance and respite care;
- mobility items;
- general living expenses (including utility bills);
- council tax payments;
- medical items;
- cars, including a driving licence, unless it is connected to employment;
- repayment of debts;
- airfares for dependants to join you in the UK.

It is helpful to read the guidance before making your application, as it covers examples of factors that can be relevant. For example, in addition to how long you have been in the UK, your financial independence can also be relevant – your application may be considered weaker if you have been working and living independently in the UK for a long time before you apply than if you have been unable to work or live independently – eg, because you were receiving asylum support. The guidance also states that decision makers can take your 'character' into account – eg, a loan will usually be refused if you have been convicted of an offence.

Valid applications

It is advisable to apply for a loan by completing the form on the UK Visas and Immigration (UKVI) website, as this takes you through all the information required to make your application valid.[11]

To be valid, the application must contain your:[12]

- full name;
- other names you have used;
- date of birth;
- address;
- telephone number (if you have one);
- email address (if you have one);
- evidence about your leave to remain and your age;
- national insurance number;
- details of your (and any dependants') income, assets, liabilities and outgoings;
- confirmation as to whether any member of your household has applied for or received an integration loan; *and*
- the amount requested.

Decisions, payment and repayments

After you have applied for a loan, you should be sent a written decision stating:[13]

- whether the application was valid;
- if so, whether a loan will be made;
- if so, the amount, conditions and terms of repayment; *and*
- the deadline for responding to say whether you wish to take the loan.

If you are entitled to a loan, a loan agreement should be attached to the decision letter, which you can sign and return to the decision maker. Usually, you must do this within 14 days of being sent the decision. If you are unhappy with the decision, either because you were refused a loan or offered a smaller amount than you need, you can ask for a reconsideration, which is carried out by a different decision maker. Your request for a reconsideration must be received within 14 days of the date on the decision letter.[14] There is no right to an independent appeal.

If UKVI decides that you are entitled to an integration loan, it passes your details to the DWP, which then pays the loan and manages your repayments.

The DWP prefers to make the payment into a bank or building society account. If the loan is for more than £450, it can only be made into an account. Loans for less than £450 can be made by cheque, which can be redeemed at a post office specified on your application form.

Integration loans are recovered through direct deductions from benefits in the same way as for other third-party debts.[15] The rate of recovery and the start date of deductions should be notified to you. See CPAG's *Welfare Benefits and Tax Credits Handbook* for further details about deductions from benefit.

If direct deductions from your benefit are not possible (eg, because you do not receive a relevant benefit), you should be notified when repayments will begin and the method, amount and frequency of these.

If your circumstances change, you can ask the DWP to revise the terms of recovery. These should be notified to you in writing.[16]

Notes

1. **Asylum seekers**
   1 **IS** Sch 9 para 21 IS Regs
      JSA Sch 7 para 22 JSA Regs
      ESA Sch 8 para 22 ESA Regs
      HB Sch 5 para 23 HB Regs
      UC Reg 66 UC Regs

2. **Benefits and tax credits for refugees and others granted leave**
   2 **CB/GA** Reg 6(2)(d) CB&GA(Admin) Regs
      TC Regs 3(4)-(9) and 4 TC(Imm) Regs
   3 Reg 3(6)(b) TC(Imm) Regs
   4 **CB/GA** Reg 6(2)(d) CB&GA(Admin) Regs
      TC Reg 3(5) TC(Imm) Regs
   5 *Tkachuk v SSWP* [2007] EWCA Civ 515; CIS/3797/2003
   6 Reg 3(9) TC(Imm) Regs
   7 Reg 4ZA(3)(b) and Sch 1B para 18 IS Regs

3. **Integration loans**
   8 Reg 4 ILRFO Regs
   9 Reg 6 ILRFO Regs
   10 *Integration Loans Policy Guidance,* available at www.gov.uk/government/ uploads/system/uploads/ attachment_data/file/257390/ integration-loans-policyguidance.pdf
   11 www.gov.uk/refugee-integration-loan
   12 Reg 5 and Sch ILRFO Regs
   13 Reg 8(1) ILRFO Regs

   14 *Integration Loans Policy Guidance,* available at www.gov.uk/government/ uploads/system/uploads/ attachment_data/file/257390/ integration-loans-policyguidance.pdf, Part 12
   15 Reg 9(1) and (3) ILRFO Regs; Sch 9, para 1 SS(C&P) Regs; Sch 6 para 12 UC,PIP,JSA&ESA(C&P) Regs
   16 Reg 10 ILRFO Regs

Part 4

Benefits and residence rules

Chapter 10

. . . .

Residence and presence rules: overview

This chapter covers:

This chapter describes the different residence and presence conditions that apply when you make a claim for benefits and tax credits in the UK. The two most significant ones are the habitual residence test and the right to reside requirement, which are covered in Chapter 11. The groups of people who have a right to reside are covered in Chapter 12. The residence and presence requirements for individual benefits and tax credits are covered in Chapter 13.

If you are not a European Economic Area national (see p39), first check Part 3 to see if your immigration status means you are excluded from benefits as a 'person subject to immigration control'. If you are not excluded as a 'person subject to immigration control', you must still satisfy the residence and presence conditions described in this chapter.

If you, or a member of your family included in your claim, go abroad (either temporarily or to stay) see Part 5 for the way this affects your benefits and tax credits.

1. **Introduction**

There are residence and presence conditions for the following benefits and tax credits:
* attendance allowance;
* carer's allowance;
* child benefit;
* child tax credit;
* disability living allowance;
* contributory employment and support allowance (ESA) in youth;
* income-related ESA;
* guardian's allowance;
* housing benefit (residence conditions only);
* incapacity benefit (IB) for incapacity in youth;
* income support;
* income-based jobseeker's allowance (JSA);
* pension credit;
* personal independence payment;
* social fund payments;
* Category D retirement pension;
* severe disablement allowance;
* universal credit;
* working tax credit.

There are presence conditions for the following benefits:
* bereavement payment;
* contributory ESA;
* IB;
* industrial injuries benefit;
* contribution-based JSA;
* maternity allowance;
* retirement pensions;
* severe disablement allowance.

Council tax reduction also has residence conditions (see p397).

There are no residence or presence requirements for statutory sick pay, statutory maternity pay, statutory paternity pay or statutory adoption pay paid by your employer.

The residence and presence conditions vary between the different benefits and tax credits. If you satisfy the rules for one benefit or tax credit, it does not necessarily mean you will satisfy the rules for another.

The way in which the different residence and presence conditions affect your entitlement to benefit are set out in the UK benefits and tax credits legislation. Depending on the benefit or tax credit, you may be required to satisfy tests for:

- presence;
- past presence;
- living in for three months;
- residence;
- ordinary residence;
- habitual residence;
- the right to reside.

However, the way the requirements work can be modified by the following.

- The European Union (EU) rules on the co-ordination of social security. If these rules apply to you (see p242), they can help you to get benefits or tax credits in the UK – eg, by exempting you from certain past presence requirements or by enabling you to count periods of residence (or employment or national insurance contributions) in another European Economic Area (EEA) state to satisfy the conditions of entitlement (see p254). They can also allow you to 'export' certain benefits to other EEA states. **Note:** these rules are different from the residence rights provided under EU law, which can enable you to satisfy the right to reside requirement. In general, you do not need to know if you are covered by the co-ordination rules to know if you have a right to reside under EU law. The EU co-ordination rules are covered in Chapter 16, and the main ways they can assist with the residence and presence tests are highlighted for each benefit in Chapter 13.
- International agreements, including reciprocal agreements. Reciprocal agreements exist between the UK and some other EEA and non-EEA countries which can help you to qualify for benefits and tax credits if you have recently come to the UK or while you are abroad. They operate in similar ways to the EU co-ordination rules and, in general, apply only when the EU co-ordination rules cannot assist you. There are also some international agreements between EU and non-EU countries, which can also have similar effects (see Chapter 17).

Note: you must also check where you are required to satisfy a particular residence or presence test. This varies for different benefits and tax credits, and can be Great Britain, the UK or the common travel area – ie, the UK, Ireland, the Channel Islands and the Isle of Man.

2. **Presence**

Most benefits and tax credits have rules about presence and absence. You must usually be present in Great Britain at the time you make your benefit or tax credit claim and continue to be present. There are specific rules that allow you to be treated as present during some temporary absences (see p207) and the European Union co-ordination rules can also mean that the presence requirement does not apply if you are staying or living in another European Economic Area state (see p39). All these exceptions to the requirement to be present vary between the different benefits and tax credits and are covered in Chapters 14 and 15.

To satisfy the presence requirement, you must show that you are physically present in Great Britain. If a benefits authority wants to disqualify you from benefit because you were absent[1] from Great Britain, it must show you were absent throughout that day. This means that, on the day you leave Great Britain and the day you arrive in Great Britain, you count as present.

3. Past presence

The following benefits have a past presence requirement:
- attendance allowance;
- carer's allowance;
- disability living allowance;
- employment and support allowance in youth;
- incapacity benefit in youth;
- personal independence payment;
- severe disablement allowance.

In addition to being present at the time you make your claim for the above benefits, you must also have been present for a period of time before you become entitled. The requirement depends on the benefit you are claiming and, for some benefits, when you make your claim.

If you are covered by the European Union co-ordination rules (see p242), these can assist either by exempting you from the past presence requirement or by enabling you to count periods of time in another European Economic Area state.

For more details of the past presence test, including exemptions, for each benefit, see Chapter 13.

4. Living in for three months

There is a requirement to have been living, for the past three months, in:
- the common travel area (the UK, Ireland, Channel Islands and the Isle of Man) in order to satisfy the habitual residence test for income-based jobseeker's allowance (JSA) (see p89); or
- the UK for child benefit and child tax credit (CTC) (see p89).

The phrase 'living in' is not defined in the regulations and should therefore be given its ordinary, everyday meaning.

The three months do not have to be continuous, so you may satisfy this condition even if you have had one or more temporary absences during the three months. Factors such as the reasons for your absence, the intended and actual length of your absence and whether you maintained your accommodation in the common travel area/UK while you were gone are all relevant when deciding whether you ceased living in the common travel area/UK. See p208 for more information about temporary absences. Note also, for child benefit and child tax credit only, if you return to the UK after a specific temporary absence, you are exempt from the requirment to have been living in the UK for the past three months (see below).

If you are covered by the European Union (EU) co-ordination rules (see p242) and have moved to the UK from another European Economic Area (EEA) state, you may be able to use periods of residence there to satisfy this condition (see p254).

Income-based jobseeker's allowance

To satisfy the habitual residence test (see p98) for income-based JSA, you must have been living in the common travel area for the past three months (in addition to having a right to reside and being habitually resident 'in fact').[2] This requirement does not apply if:

- you are in one of the groups that are exempt from the habitual residence test (see p99); *or*
- your claim began before 1 January 2014.[3]

If you are covered by the EU co-ordination rules (see p242), it may be possible to argue that this requirement is unlawful. In the *Swaddling* case, the European Court of Justice held that someone covered by the co-ordination rules cannot be deemed not to be habitually resident in a state merely because the period of actual residence is too short.[4] See p105 for more details.

Child benefit and child tax credit

To be treated as present in Great Britain for child benefit and present in the UK for CTC, you must have been living in the UK for three months, ending on the first day of your entitlement.[5] This requirement does not apply if you:[6]

- most recently entered the UK before 1 July 2014;
- are an EEA national who is a 'worker' in the UK (see p129), including if you have retained that status (see p135);
- are an EEA national who is a self-employed person in the UK (see p141), including if you have retained that status (see p144);

- are a Croatian national working in accordance with your worker authorisation document (see p118);
- are a non-EEA national who would be classed as a worker or self-employed person if you were an EEA national;
- are a family member, other than an extended family member (see p152), of someone in any of the four groups immediately above;
- are a refugee;
- are a person with humanitarian protection;
- have been granted leave to enter or remain in the UK pending an application for indefinite leave to remain as a victim of domestic violence (see p34), leave granted outside the Immigration Rules with no restriction on accessing public funds, or leave under the displaced persons provisions;
- are returning to the UK, not as a worker or self-employed person, after a period working abroad and, except for last three months of your absence, you were paying UK Class 1 or Class 2 national insurance contributions;
- have been deported or otherwise legally removed from another country to the UK;[7]
- are returning to the UK after an absence of less than 52 weeks and either:
  - prior to departing the UK you were ordinarily resident for three months; *or*
  - you were covered by the rules that treat you as present during a temporary absence for eight or 12 weeks during payment of child benefit (see p222) or CTC (see p231).

5. **Residence**

The requirement to be simply 'resident', rather than 'ordinarily resident' or 'habitually resident', is only a condition for Category D retirement pension. However, it is a necessary part of being ordinarily resident (see p91) or habitually resident (see p94).

Residence is more than a physical presence in a country and you can be resident without being present – eg, if you are abroad for a short holiday. Similarly, you can be present without being resident.

To be resident in a country you must be seen to be making your home there for the time being; it need not be your only home, nor a permanent one.[8] You can remain resident during a temporary absence, depending on the duration and circumstances of your absence.[9] Your intentions to return, your accommodation, and where your family and your personal belongings are can all be relevant. It is possible to be resident in two countries at once.[10]

Children

The only benefits that can be claimed by a child under 16 that have residence requirements are disability living allowance (DLA), housing benefit (HB) and child benefit. For DLA and HB, the claimant must be habitually resident (unless, for DLA, s/he claimed before 8 April 2013, in which case s/he must be ordinarily resident until her/his award is terminated, revised or superseded, from which point s/he must be habitually resident). For child benefit, the claimant must have a right to reside.

Although children are covered by the same rules as for adults to decide whether or not they satisfy the residence requirement,[11] in practice, a child's habitual residence is usually decided by looking at the residence of her/his parent(s) or person(s) with parental responsibility (in Scotland, parental rights and responsibilities) for her/him. A child who lives with that person usually has the same habitual residence as her/him, so, a child who joins a parent (or person with parental responsibility) may become habitually resident almost immediately.[12] If there is only one person with parental responsibility, the child has the same habitual residence as her/him.[13]

Note: whether or not a child has a right to reside is determined in the same way as it is for an adult. So if a child under 16 is claiming child benefit, s/he (but not the child s/he is responsible for) must have a right to reside. If a child under 16 is claiming HB, s/he must have a right to reside in order to satisfy the habitual residence test.

---

6. **Ordinary residence**

The following benefits and tax credits have a requirement to be ordinarily resident:
- attendance allowance (if claimed before 8 April 2013 until the award is terminated, revised or superseded);
- carer's allowance (if claimed before 8 April 2013 until the award is terminated, revised or superseded);
- child benefit;
- child tax credit;
- disability living allowance (if claimed before 8 April 2013 until the award is terminated, revised or superseded);
- employment and support allowance in youth;
- incapacity benefit in youth;
- Category D retirement pension;
- severe disablement allowance;
- social fund funeral payments and winter fuel payments;
- working tax credit.

There are some limited exceptions to the requirement to be ordinarily resident, and if you are covered by the European Union (EU) co-ordination rules these may assist you in satisfying the requirement. The exceptions and assistance provided by the co-ordination rules vary between the different benefits and tax credits, and are covered in Chapter 13.

In practice, claims are rarely refused on the basis of ordinary residence.

You cannot be ordinarily resident without being resident (see p90).

The term 'ordinary residence' is not defined in the legislation, but caselaw has confirmed:

- the words should have their natural and ordinary meaning;[14]
- you are ordinarily resident in a country if you have a home there that you have adopted for a settled purpose and where you live for the time being (whether for a short or long duration);[15]
- ordinary residence can start on arrival (see below);
- a person in the UK for a temporary purpose can be ordinarily resident in the UK (see below);
- in general, your residence must be voluntary for you to be ordinarily resident (see p93);
- ordinary residence can continue during absences abroad, but leaving to settle abroad usually ends ordinary residence (see p93);
- although rare, it is possible for a person to be ordinarily resident in more than one place or country;[16]
- a person who lives in the UK but has no fixed abode can be ordinarily resident;[17]
- ordinary residence is different from the concept of 'domicile'.[18]

Ordinary residence on arrival

Ordinary residence can begin immediately on arrival in Great Britain.[19] In a family law case, a man who separated from his wife in one country (where he had lived and worked for three years) and went to live at his parent's house in another was found to become immediately ordinarily resident there. The Court of Appeal found that, where there is evidence that a person intends to make a place her/his home for an indefinite period, s/he is ordinarily resident when s/he arrives there.[20] In another case, a court decided that a woman returning from Australia after some months there had never lost her ordinary residence in England. However, if she had, she would have become ordinarily resident again when the boat embarked from Australia.[21] In a case involving students, they had to show that they were ordinarily resident within a few weeks of first arriving in the UK, and it was not argued that they could not be ordinarily resident because they had only just come to Great Britain.[22]

Ordinary residence while here for a temporary purpose

To be ordinarily resident in Great Britain, you do not have to intend, or be able, to live here permanently. The purpose can be for a limited period. In one case, Lord Scarman said that, 'Education, business or profession, employment, health, family, or merely love of the place spring to mind as common reasons for a choice of regular abode.'[23] If you are solely in the UK for business purposes, you can still be ordinarily resident here.[24] You may have several different reasons for a single stay – eg, to visit relatives, get medical advice, attend religious ceremonies and sort out personal affairs.[25]

The reason must be a settled one. This does not mean that the reason has to be long-standing,[26] but there must be evidence of it. Although in some cases concerning ordinary residence, the courts have looked back to see whether a person had been ordinarily resident months or years beforehand,[27] there is no minimum period of residence required before you are ordinarily resident. If, for example, you have arrived in the UK and started work, the benefit authorities should consider how long you are likely to reside in the UK. If you intend to live here for the time being, they should accept your intention as sufficient, unless it is clearly unlikely that you are going to be able to stay. The benefit authorities should not make a deep examination of your long-term intentions.[28] The type of accommodation you occupy may be relevant.[29] If you have made regular visits to the UK, this may be relevant.[30]

Involuntary residence

A person who is held in a place against her/his will is not usually ordinarily resident there. These cases are very rare.[31] However, it may be arguable that if you were taken out of the UK against your will (eg, as a child or for a forced marriage), you should still be ordinarily resident on your return. If you are in the UK because of circumstances that limit or remove your choice, this may not prevent you from being ordinarily resident here. For example, if you come to the UK for a visit and were held in hospital because of your mental health, you may be found to be ordinarily resident even though you have never decided to live here.[32]

Deportation to the UK does not prevent you from becoming ordinarily resident here.[33] The issue is whether your residence is part of your settled purpose. If you have decided to live in the UK, it does not matter if the reason for your decision is because you were deported here. For the purposes of tax credits and child benefit, you are treated as ordinarily resident if you are in the UK as a result of deportation or having been otherwise legally removed from another country.[34]

Absence from the UK

If you are ordinarily resident, you may lose this status if you go abroad, depending on:
- why you go abroad;
- how long you stay abroad;
- what connections you keep with the UK – eg, accommodation, furniture and other possessions.[35]

If you decide to move abroad for the foreseeable future, you normally stop being ordinarily resident in the UK on the day you leave.[36] There can be exceptions, which depend on your circumstances, including if your plans are clearly impractical and you return to the UK very quickly.

If your absence abroad is part of your normal pattern of life, your ordinary residence may not be affected.[37] This can apply if you are out of the UK for half, or even most, of the year – eg, if you spend each summer in the UK and the winter abroad, you may still be ordinarily resident in the UK.[38]

If your absence abroad is extraordinary or temporary and you intend to return to the UK, your ordinary residence may not be affected.[39]

In one case, a British woman who spent 15 months in Germany with her husband over a period of three years kept her ordinary residence in the UK. She had always intended to return here.[40]

However, if you are away from the UK for a long time and do not keep strong connections with Great Britain, you may lose your ordinary residence, even if you intend to return. In one case, a citizen of the UK and colonies lived in the UK for over four years and then returned to Kenya for two years and five months because her business here failed and there was a business opportunity in Kenya. She intended to make enough money to support herself on her return to the UK. Her parents and parents-in-law remained in the UK. She was found to have lost her ordinary residence during her absence.[41]

In deciding whether an absence affects your ordinary residence, the decision maker must consider all your circumstances. Every absence is unique and distinct, and you should provide full details of all your circumstances including:

- why you wish to go abroad;
- how long you intend to be abroad; *and*
- what you intend to do while you are abroad.

Each of these considerations needs to be taken into account, and it is your responsibility to demonstrate that your absence is to be a temporary one.[42]

Note: in addition to affecting your ordinary residence, an absence may also affect your benefit entitlement if it means you cease to satisfy the requirement to be present for the benefit or tax credit you are claiming (see p207) or if it means you cease to be treated as a couple (see p209).

7. **Habitual residence**

The following benefits and tax credits have a habitual residence requirement:

- attendance allowance (AA);
- carer's allowance (CA);
- disability living allowance (DLA);
- income-related employment and support allowance;
- housing benefit;
- income support;

- income-based jobseeker's allowance;
- pension credit;
- personal independence payment;
- universal credit.

You must satisfy (or be exempt from) the habitual residence test to get the above benefits (see p99). See Chapter 11 for details of the way the test works.
Note:
- You are also excluded from council tax reduction if you do not satisfy (and are not exempt from) the habitual residence test.[43]
- You may be entitled to a winter fuel payment from the social fund if, instead of being ordinarily resident in Great Britain, you are habitually resident in another European Economic Area country or Switzerland (see p197).
- If your claim for AA, DLA or CA began before 8 April 2013, you must be ordinarily, rather than habitually, resident until your award is revised or superseded.[44]

8. **The right to reside**

The following benefits and tax credits have a right to reside requirement:
- child benefit;
- child tax credit (CTC);
- income-related employment and support allowance;
- housing benefit;
- income support;
- income-based jobseeker's allowance;
- pension credit;
- universal credit.

The right to reside requirement for all the above benefits, other than child benefit and CTC, is part of the habitual residence test. For all the benefits and tax credits listed above, you must satisfy the right to reside requirement, unless, for the means-tested benefits only, you are in group that is exempt from the habitual residence test (see p99).

You are also excluded from council tax reduction if you do not satisfy the right to reside requirement.[45]

See Chapter 11 for details of the way the test works for each benefit and tax credit and Chapter 12 for who has a right to reside.

Notes

2. Presence
1 R(S) 1/66

4. Living in for three months
2 Reg 85A(2) JSA Regs
3 Reg 3 JSA(HR)A Regs
4 *Swaddling v Chief Adjudication Officer*, C-90/97 [1999] ECR I-01075
5 **CB** Reg 23(5) CB Regs
CTC Reg 3(6) TC(R) Regs
6 **CB** Reg 23(6) CB Regs
CTC Reg 3(7) TC(R) Regs
7 **CB** Reg 23(3) CB Regs
CTC Reg 3(3) TC(R) Regs

5. Residence
8 R(IS) 6/96, para 19; R(P) 2/67
9 CPC 1036/2005
10 R(IS)9/99, para 10
11 *Re A (A Minor) (Abduction: Child's Objections)* [1994] 2 FLR 126: on habitual residence, but also applies to ordinary residence
12 *Re M (Minors) (Residence Order: Jurisdiction)* [1993] 1 FLR 495
13 *Re J (A Minor) (Abduction: Custody Rights)* [1990] 2 AC 562 at p578

6. Ordinary residence
14 *Levene v Inland Revenue Commissioners* [1928] AC 217; R(M) 1/85
15 *R v Barnet London Borough Council ex parte Shah* [1983] 2 AC 309
16 *IRC v Lysaght* [1928] AC 234; R(P) 1/01; CIS/1691/2004
17 *Levene v Inland Revenue Commissioners* [1928] AC 217
18 *R v Barnet London Borough Council ex parte Shah* [1983] 2 AC 309, Lord Scarman at p345E-H
19 R(F) 1/62

20 *Macrae v Macrae* [1949] 2 All ER 34. The countries were Scotland and England which are separate for family law purposes. In R(IS) 6/96, para 27 the commissioner doubted the correctness of *Macrae* because he considered it used a test very close to the 'real home' test rejected in *Shah*. He does not seem to have heard any argument about this: *Macrae* was cited in *Shah* and was not one of the cases mentioned there as wrong: pp342-43.
21 *Lewis v Lewis* [1956] 1 All ER 375
22 *R v Barnet London Borough Council ex parte Shah* [1982] QB 688 at p717E
23 *R v Barnet London Borough Council ex parte Shah* [1983] 2 AC 309, Lord Scarman at p344C-D
24 *Inland Revenue Commissioners v Lysaght* [1928] AC 234; *AA v SSWP(IS)* [2013] UKUT 0406 (AAC)
25 *Levene v Inland Revenue Commissioners* [1928] AC 217, HL; *GC v HMRC (TC)* [2014] UKUT 0251 (AAC)
26 *Macrae v Macrae* [1949] 2 All ER 34
27 *R v Barnet London Borough Council ex parte Shah* [1983] 2 AC 309
28 *R v Barnet London Borough Council ex parte Shah* [1983] 2 AC 309, Lord Scarman at p344G
29 R(F) 1/82; R(F) 1/62; R(P) 1/62; R(P) 4/54
30 *GC v HMRC (TC)* [2004] UKUT 0251 (AAC)
31 *R v Barnet London Borough Council ex parte Shah* [1983] 2 AC 309
32 In *Re Mackenzie* [1941] 1 Chancery Reports 69
33 *Gout v Cimitian* [1922] 1 AC 105
34 **TC** Reg 3(3) TC(R) Regs
CB Reg 23(3) CB Regs
35 R(F) 1/62; R(M) 1/85
36 *Hopkins v Hopkins* [1951] P 116; *R v Hussain* [1971] 56 Crim App R 165; *R v IAT ex parte Ng* [1986] Imm AR 23 (QBD)
37 *R v Barnet London Borough Council ex parte Shah* [1983] 2 AC 309

38 *Levene v Inland Revenue Commissioners*
[1928] AC 217; *Inland Revenue
Commissioners v Lysaght* [1928] AC 234;
AA v SSWP(IS) [2013] UKUT 0406 (AAC)
39 *R v Barnet London Borough Council ex
parte Shah* [1983] 2 AC 309, Lord
Scarman at p342D
40 *Stransky v Stransky* [1954] 3 WLR 123,
[1954] 2 All ER 536
41 *Haria* [1986] Imm AR 165
42 *Chief Adjudication Officer v Ahmed and
others*, 16 March 1994

7. **Habitual residence**

43 Sch para 21 CTRS(DS)E Regs; reg 12
CTRS(PR)E Regs; reg 16 CTR(SPC)S
Regs; reg 16 CTR(S) Regs; reg 26
CTRSPR(W) Regs; Sch para 19
CTRS(DS)W Regs
44 Reg 1(2),(3) and (4) SS(DLA,AA&CA)(A)
Regs

8. **The right to reside**

45 Sch para 21 CTRS(DS)E Regs; reg 12
CTRS(PR)E Regs; reg 16 CTR(SPC)S
Regs; reg 16 CTR(S) Regs; reg 26
CTRSPR(W) Regs; Sch para 19
CTRS(DS)W Regs

Chapter 11

· ·

Habitual residence and the right to reside

This chapter covers:
1. The habitual residence test (below)
2. 'Habitual residence in fact' (p102)
3. The right to reside (p107)

This chapter explains the way in which the habitual residence test and the right to reside requirement apply to the various benefits and tax credits. For information on who has a right to reside, see Chapter 12.

---

1. **The habitual residence test**

The habitual residence test applies to the following benefits:
- attendance allowance (AA);
- carer's allowance (CA);
- disability living allowance (DLA);
- income-related employment and support allowance (ESA);
- housing benefit (HB);
- income support (IS);
- income-based jobseeker's allowance (JSA);
- pension credit (PC);
- personal independence payment (PIP);
- universal credit (UC).

To be entitled to one of the above benefits, you must be habitually resident in the 'common travel area' (ie, the UK, Ireland, the Channel Islands and the Isle of Man) or be exempt from the test (see p99).
    To satisfy the habitual residence test for **means-tested benefits**, you must:
- be 'habitually resident in fact' (see p102); *and*
- have a right to reside that is not excluded for the benefit you want to claim (see p107); *and*

- (for income-based JSA only) have been living in the common travel area for the past three months (see p88), unless your claim began before 1 January 2014.[1]

However, some groups of people are exempt from the habitual residence test for means-tested benefits (see below). If you are in one of these groups, you are treated as satisfying the test. Your residence is not examined further and, provided you meet the other conditions of entitlement, you are eligible for benefit.

In practice, the DWP or local authority first considers your right to reside. If you satisfy this requirement and you are claiming income-based JSA, it then considers whether you have been living here for the past three months and then (for all means-tested benefits) whether you are 'habitually resident in fact'. Whether or not you are exempt from the habitual residence test is not always considered. If you come into one of the exempt groups, make it clear to the DWP or local authority that you are exempt, particularly if you might not otherwise be accepted as habitually resident.

To satisfy the habitual residence test for **AA, DLA, PIP and CA**, you must be 'habitually resident in fact' (see p102).

Note: if your claim for AA, DLA or CA began before 8 April 2013, the previous requirement to be ordinarily, rather than habitually, resident continues to apply until your award is revised or superseded.[2]

Note also:

- You are also excluded from council tax reduction (see p397) if you do not satisfy (and are not exempt from) the habitual residence test.[3]
- You may be entitled to a winter fuel payment from the social fund if, instead of being ordinarily resident in Great Britain, you are habitually resident in another European Economic Area (EEA) country or Switzerland (see p197).

Who is exempt from the habitual residence test

You are exempt from the habitual residence test for **means-tested benefits** if you:[4]

- are an EEA national and are a 'worker' (see p129), including if you retain this status (see p135);
- are an EEA national and are a self-employed person (see p141), including if you retain this status (see p144);
- are the family member (see p151), other than an extended family member, of someone in either of the above two groups;
- are an EEA national with a permanent right of residence that you acquired in less than five years (the main groups cover certain former workers or self-employed people who have retired or are permanently incapacitated – see p174) or you are the family member of such a person;
- are a refugee;

- have humanitarian protection;
- have discretionary leave (see p35), leave granted under the 'destitute domestic violence concession' (see p34) or temporary protection granted under the displaced persons' provisions;
- have been deported, expelled or otherwise legally removed from another country to the UK and you are not a 'person subject to immigration control' (see p55);
- (for income-related ESA only) are being transferred from an award of IS which was transitionally protected from the requirement to have a right to reside (see p109);
- (for HB only) receive IS, income-related ESA or PC;
- (for HB only) receive income-based JSA and either:
  - you have a right to reside other than one that is excluded for HB (see p108); *or*
  - you have been receiving both HB and income-based JSA since 31 March 2014. Entitlement on this basis ends when either your entitlement to income-based JSA ceases or you make a new claim for HB.[5]

If you are not in one of the above groups, you must show that you have established 'habitual residence in fact' (see p102) in the common travel area and that you have a sufficient right to reside to claim the means-tested benefit you want (see p107). For income-based JSA only, you must also show that you have been living in the common travel area for the past three months (see p88).

The above exemptions do not apply to **AA, DLA, PIP and CA**. For these benefits, you must show that you have established 'habitual residence in fact' (see p102) in the common travel area unless you:

- are abroad in your capacity as a serving member of the forces; *or*
- are living with someone who is abroad as a serving member of the forces and s/he is your spouse, civil partner, son, stepson, daughter, stepdaughter, father, stepfather, father-in-law, mother, stepmother or mother-in-law.

If this applies to you, you are treated as being habitually resident (as well as treated as present).[6]

Who does the habitual residence test apply to

The habitual residence test applies to the benefit claimant.

For means-tested benefits, other than income-based JSA claimed as a joint-claim couple and UC, this means that it does not matter if your partner is not habitually resident or is not exempt. You are still paid as a couple. You and your partner should therefore consider who is most likely to satisfy, or be exempt from, the habitual residence test. For joint-claim JSA or UC couples, the rules are different (see p101).

Joint-claim jobseeker's allowance

If you are a member of a 'joint-claim couple' for income-based JSA (see CPAG's *Welfare Benefits and Tax Credits Handbook* for what this means) and either you or your partner do not satisfy, or you are not exempt from, the habitual residence test, a special rule applies. The partner who is habitually resident can claim income-based JSA for both of you without the other partner being required to be a claimant as part of the joint claim – ie, you do not need to make a joint claim.[7] You are paid as a couple.

Couples claiming universal credit

If you are a member of a couple and only one of you satisfies, or is exempt from, the habitual residence test, you cannot make a joint claim for UC. Instead the person who satisfies, or is exempt from, the habitual residence test can claim UC as a single person.[8]

However, if this applies to you, the following special rules apply to the calculation of your UC.
- The maximum amount of UC is that for a single person.[9]
- Your partner's capital is included in the amount of capital taken into account.[10]
- Your partner's income is included in the amount of income taken into account when calculating how much should be deducted from the maximum amount of UC. **Note:** the 'work allowance' (ie, the amount of earnings that can be ignored) is the same as for joint claimants – ie, the couple rate applies.[11]

If you fail the habitual residence test

The way in which your failure to satisfy, or be exempt from, the habitual residence test affects your benefit is slightly different for each benefit, but the outcome is the same: if you are not habitually resident in the common travel area, you are not entitled to IS, income-based JSA, income-related ESA, PC, HB, UC, AA, DLA, PIP and CA. The precise way in which that result is achieved for each benefit is as follows.
- For IS, income-based JSA, income-related ESA and HB, you are classed as a 'person from abroad'. This means for IS, income-based JSA and income-related ESA, you have an applicable amount of nil,[12] and for HB you are treated as not liable for rent.[13]
- For PC and UC, you are treated as not present in Great Britain.[14]
- For AA, DLA, PIP and CA, you have failed to meet the prescribed residence requirements.[15]

2. 'Habitual residence in fact'

There is no definition of habitual residence in the regulations. However, there is a considerable amount of caselaw on the meaning of 'habitual residence' and from this certain principles have emerged. To count as 'habitually resident in fact':

- you must be resident in the common travel area (see below);
- your residence must be voluntary (see below);
- you must have a settled intention to make the common travel area your home for the time being (see below);
- in most cases, you must have resided in the common travel area for an 'appreciable period of time' (see p104). **Note:** this is not a fixed period and there are some exceptions.

Of these four factors, most of the disputes about whether a person who has claimed a relevant benefit is habitually resident in fact concern the latter two.

The decision about whether or not you are habitually resident is a factual question and must be made on the 'balance of probabilities'. If the probabilities in favour of each answer are exactly equal, the decision should be that you *are* habitually resident. This is because the benefits authority must show that you are *not* habitually resident. However, it is preferable to examine the facts further rather than rely on the 'balance of probabilities'.[16]

You should therefore always provide as much evidence as you can about all your circumstances that are relevant to your habitual residence. See Chapter 20 for more information about providing evidence.

Residence

You cannot be habitually resident in the common travel area unless you are resident in the common travel area. It is not enough merely to intend to reside here in the future.[17] For information on residence, see p90.

Voluntary residence

You cannot be habitually resident in fact in the common travel area unless your residence is voluntary.[18] This factor, in practice, is rarely a barrier to your being found habitually resident in the common travel area. However, it can also be relevant if you are returning to live in the common travel area after having been taken or kept away against your will (see p104).

Settled intention

For your residence to become habitual, you must have a settled intention to reside in the common travel area. This is not determined just by your declaring your intention, but is a question of evidence about all the factors that are relevant to your intention.[19]

Your settled intention to reside in the common travel area does not need to be permanent; it is enough that you intend to make the common travel area your home for the time being.

Do you have a settled intention?

The following factors are relevant when determining whether or not you have a settled intention.

1. Your reasons for coming to the common travel area. If there is one or more clear reason why you have moved here (such as a family breakdown, a desire to study here or an offer of employment), this helps to show your settled intention.

2. The steps you took to prepare for coming to the common travel area – eg, the plans you made beforehand about where you would live, enquiries about work, making arrangements for your children to attend school, contacting people you know and settling your affairs in the country you were leaving, such as closing bank accounts, disposing of property and ending a tenancy.

3. The strength of your ties to the common travel area compared with your ties to other places (this is sometimes called your 'centre of interests') – eg, whether you have family or friends living in the common travel area, whether you have registered with a doctor or joined any clubs or associations here, whether your children are in school here, whether you have begun a course of study, or whether have spent money here (such as a deposit on a rented property). Similarly, if you have these sort of ties abroad, this may indicate a less strong settled intention.

4. The viability of your residence in the common travel area (see below).

As with the requirement to be resident (see p90), you must be seen to be making a home here, but it need not be your only home or a permanent one.[20] Therefore, a long-standing intention to move abroad (eg, when debts are paid) does not prevent someone from being habitually resident.[21]

Events after you claim benefit or receive a decision may confirm that your intention was always to reside in the UK – eg, if you are refused benefit because the DWP does not accept that you have a settled intention to stay in the UK, the fact that you are still here by the time of the appeal hearing may help show that you always intended to reside here. [22]

There is a close connection between 'settled intention' and 'appreciable period' (see p104): the stronger your settled intention, the shorter the period you need to reside in order to count as 'habitually resident in fact'.[23]

Viability of your residence

The viability of your continued residence, although a relevant factor, is not an additional requirement. This means that the question of whether you could survive in the common travel area without claiming the benefits to which the habitual residence test applies is not a separate question that must be answered positively in order for you to count as habitually resident in fact.[24] The viability of your residence is simply one factor that can be taken into account when considering your settled intention to reside in the common travel area.[25]

This means that you can be accepted as habitually resident in fact even though you have very few or no resources.

Appreciable period

In most cases, you do not count as habitually resident in fact until you have resided in the common travel area for an 'an appreciable period of time'.[26]

However, your appreciable period is reduced or may not apply at all if you:
- are a returning resident in certain circumstances (see below); *and/or*
- are covered by the European Union (EU) co-ordination rules (see p105).

There is no fixed period of time that amounts to an appreciable period and it depends on your circumstances.[27] Benefit authorities must not set a standard period of time for which all claimants must be resident before they can become habitually resident and any such policy should be challenged by judicial review. There is an extensive body of caselaw on what constitutes an appreciable period of residence. Periods of between one and three months are frequently cited,[28] but too much weight should not be put on any one decision, nor should any general rule about a specific time period be derived from it.[29]

Your appreciable period can include visits to prepare for settled residence made before that residence is taken up.[30]

The stronger your settled intention to make your home in the common travel area for the time being, the shorter your period of actual residence need be before you can be accepted as habitually resident in fact (and vice versa).[31]

Returning residents

If you were living in the common travel area in the past and you return here, you may count as habitually resident in fact either immediately on your return or after a much shorter period of residence than would otherwise be the case.[32]

Are you a returning resident?

The following issues must be considered:[33]

1. Were you habitually resident when you were previously here?

2. If you were, did you cease to be habitually resident when you went abroad either immediately on departure or while you were abroad?

3. If you ceased to be habitually resident while you were abroad, when did you resume habitual residence in the common travel area? This may involve deciding when you resumed residence, and then when that residence became habitual.

If you never stopped being habitually resident in fact, you continue to be habitually resident on your return. This could apply if you only went abroad for a short period – eg, for a holiday. Similarly, it can apply if your absence abroad was only ever intended to be for a temporary period – eg, in one case, a man was held not to have ceased to be habitually resident on his return from a two-year Voluntary Service Overseas placement, during which time he had given up his tenancy in the UK and placed his possessions in storage.[34] It may also apply if your absence abroad was involuntary. Guidance to decision makers states that people who leave, or remain away from, the UK because of a forced marriage are not considered to have lost their habitual residence as they were abroad through no fault of their own. They are therefore considered habitually resident from the date of their claim.[35]

If you have ceased to count as habitually resident in fact while outside the common travel area, whether or not you need to complete a further period of residence here on your return before you can resume your habitual residence depends on:[36]

- the circumstances in which your earlier habitual residence was lost. If you went abroad for a temporary or conditional reason and/or you stayed away longer because of circumstances beyond your control, you may be more likely to be found habitually resident immediately on your return;
- the links between you and the UK while abroad. This could include retaining property, bank accounts and membership of organisations, maintaining contact with family and friends and making visits back to the common travel area (their frequency, length and purpose are all relevant);
- the circumstances of your return to the UK. Evidence of your settled intention is relevant (see p102).

Applying the above factors in two cases that were heard jointly, a commissioner found both claimants to be habitually resident on the day of their return.[37]

Even if you are not able to resume your previous habitual residence immediately on your return, you may still be able to argue that your previous habitual residence here is a factor that reduces the period of time that counts as an appreciable period of actual residence.

If you are covered by the European Union co-ordination rules

If you are covered by the EU co-ordination rules (see p242), the period of time you must be resident before you can be found to be habitually resident in fact can be shorter than otherwise might be required and can be outweighed by other factors that show you are habitually resident. The co-ordination rules can only assist you to be found habitually resident in fact if you are claiming a 'special non-contributory benefit' (see p247) – ie:

- income-based jobseeker's allowance (JSA);

- income-related employment and support allowance (ESA);
- pension credit (PC);
- disability living allowance (DLA) mobility component.

The co-ordination rules state that you are entitled to 'special non-contributory benefits' in the member state in which you are 'resident'[38] and define 'residence' as the place where you 'habitually reside'.[39] See p249 for the factors that should be considered when deciding where you habitually reside for the purpose of the co-ordination rules.

The European Court of Justice (ECJ) has held that when assessing where someone habitually resides, her/his length of residence in the member state cannot be regarded as an intrinsic element of the concept of residence. The case concerned a British national who lived in the UK until he was 23 and then moved to France, where he worked for 14 years until he was made redundant. He returned to the UK and was refused benefit on the basis of not having completed an appreciable period of actual residence. The ECJ found that the claimant, who was covered by the EU co-ordination rules and was claiming a special non-contributory benefit, could not be deemed not to habitually reside merely because the period of residence completed was too short.[40] Although the case concerned a returning resident, subsequent caselaw confirms that the principle applies to any claimant covered by the EU co-ordination rules.[41] Consequently, while 'duration and continuity of presence' is one of the factors that should be considered when determining where you habitually reside, it is only one factor and can be outweighed by others. Therefore, you cannot be denied income-based JSA, income-related ESA, PC and DLA mobility component solely because you have not completed an 'appreciable period' of actual residence in the common travel area.

If you are refused benefit

If you are refused benefit because the decision maker says that you are not habitually resident in fact, you should challenge the decision. While challenging, you should also make a new claim for the benefit. If that claim is refused, you should also challenge that decision and make another new claim, and so on. This is because when the decision refusing your initial claim is looked at again, the decision maker or First-tier Tribunal cannot take account of circumstances that did not exist at the time the original decision was made.[42] So, if the decision maker considers that you were not habitually resident at the time benefit was originally refused, but you are now (because your period of residence now amounts to an appreciable period), s/he cannot take this into account when looking again at the decision in your case. However, s/he can take it into account if you had completed an appreciable period of residence before the date of the decision on your second, or subsequent, claim.

Sometimes benefit authorities state that you are not allowed to make a fresh claim in this way. This is not the case.[43] In these situations, it may help to refer to the fact that when amending regulations were introduced, the Secretary of State said in his report that 'it needs to be emphasised that neither the fact that a person's claim for benefit has been disallowed on the grounds that the habitual residence test has not been satisfied, nor the fact that there is an outstanding appeal against that decision, prevents that individual from making a fresh claim for benefit.'[44]

3. **The right to reside**

The right to reside requirement applies to:

- child benefit;
- child tax credit (CTC);
- income-related employment and support allowance (ESA);
- housing benefit (HB);
- income support (IS);
- income-based jobseeker's allowance (JSA);
- pension credit (PC);
- universal credit (UC).

Note: you are also excluded from council tax reduction (see p397) if you do not have a right to reside.[45]

The way the test works varies between the different benefits.

For **means-tested benefits**, the right to reside requirement forms part of the habitual residence test (see p98). Therefore, if you are exempt from the habitual residence test, you do not need to demonstrate your right to reside (see p99). If you are not exempt from the habitual residence test, in addition to being 'habitually resident in fact' (see p102) and, for income-based JSA, having lived in the common travel area for the past three months (see p88), you must satisfy the right to reside requirement.

For **child benefit** and CTC, the right to reside requirement is part of the presence test for these benefits.

Note: if you have been claiming benefits in the UK since 30 April 2004, you may have transitional protection from the right to reside requirement and do not need a right to reside (see p109).

If you do not have transitional protection and, for means-tested benefits, you are not exempt from the habitual residence test, you must have a right to reside that is sufficient for the benefit or tax credit you wish to claim. The regulations for each benefit or tax credit specifically exclude certain types of right to reside (see p108). However, you are only excluded if this is your only right to reside. If you have any other non-excluded right to reside, you satisfy the requirement for that benefit.

Means-tested benefits

To satisfy the right to reside requirement within the habitual residence test for IS, income-based JSA, income-related ESA, PC, HB, and UC, you must have a right to reside in the common travel area, other than as:[46]

- a European Economic Area (EEA) national with an initial right of residence during your first three months in the UK (see p122);
- a family member of the above;
- the 'primary carer' of a British citizen who is dependent on you and would have to leave the European Union (EU) if you were required to leave (see p167). **Note:** this exclusion is arguably unlawful and although legal challenges have not yet been successful, future ones may be.[47] See CPAG's online service and *Welfare Rights Bulletin* for updates;
- (except for income-based JSA and UC) an EEA jobseeker (see p123);
- (except for income-based JSA and UC) a family member of an EEA jobseeker.

Note: although having a right to reside as an EEA jobseeker is not sufficient to enable you to receive HB, if you have been receiving both HB and income-based JSA since 31 March 2014, you are (until either that income-based JSA award ceases or you make a new claim for HB) exempt from the habitual residence test for HB (see p99) and, therefore, if you lack any other right to reside this does not prevent you from receiving HB.

Child benefit and child tax credit

For child benefit and CTC, if you do not have a right to reside you are treated as not present in the UK and therefore not entitled to the benefit or tax credit.[48]

Any right of residence in the UK enables you to satisfy the requirement for child benefit and CTC *except* a right to reside as the primary carer of a British citizen who is dependent on you and who would have to leave the EU if you were required to leave (see p167).[49] **Note:** this exclusion is arguably unlawful and although legal challenges have not yet been successful, future challenges may be.[50] See CPAG's online service and *Welfare Rights Bulletin* for updates.

If you do not have a right to reside but you are covered by the EU co-ordination rules (see p242), note that the European Commission has asked the Court of Justice of the European Union to declare the right to reside test for child benefit and CTC unlawful, either because it is directly discriminatory (see p253) or because it imposes a condition that cannot be imposed under the co-ordination rules.[51] However, note also that the Court of Appeal in Northern Ireland has held that the right to reside requirement for child benefit is not unlawful.[52] Get specialist advice if you want to rely on this argument and see CPAG's online service and *Welfare Rights Bulletin* for updates.

Who does the right to reside test apply to

The right to reside test only applies to the claimant.

For means-tested benefits, other than income-based JSA claimed as a joint-claim couple and UC, if your partner does not have a right to reside, you can still include her/him in your claim and you are still paid as a couple. For joint-claim JSA and UC couples, the rules are different (see p100).

If you make a joint claim for CTC, both you and your partner must have a right to reside (see p199). If your partner does not have a right to reside, you may be able to make a single claim.

The right to reside requirement does not apply to a child for whom you are claiming CTC, child benefit or UC.

Transitional protection

If you have been receiving benefit since before 1 May 2004, you should check whether you have transitional protection from the requirement to have a right to reside. The rules vary depending on the benefit you are claiming.

Means-tested benefits

The right to reside requirement was introduced as part of the habitual residence test for means-tested benefits on 1 May 2004. If you have been receiving a means-tested benefit since 30 April 2004, you do not need a right to reside in order to continue to receive that benefit. Furthermore, you do not need a right to reside for a new claim for a different means-tested benefit, provided the periods of entitlement are continuous since 30 April 2004. The relevant benefits are:[53]

- council tax benefit (until it was abolished from 1 April 2013);
- income-related ESA (only from 31 October 2011);
- HB;
- IS;
- income-based JSA;
- PC.

The rules on transitional protection did not apply to income-related ESA when that benefit was introduced and it was only added to the list from 31 October 2011. In addition, if you are in receipt of income-related ESA and you then have a break in your award of less than 12 weeks, you are still transitionally protected and do not need a right to reside when you reclaim income-related ESA.

Example
Astrid is Swedish and came to the UK in March 2004 with her baby. She claimed IS as a lone parent while living with friends. In 2006, she moved into a bedsit and claimed HB. In 2008 her partner, who was working part time, moved in, so Astrid stopped claiming IS, but she continued to get HB as they had a low income. In 2010 Astrid's partner moved

out, but as Astrid now had another baby she once again claimed IS. In 2012 Astrid became
very ill, moved in with some friends, stopped claiming HB and claimed income-related ESA
instead of IS.
Astrid did not need to satisfy the right to reside requirement for any of these benefit claims
because she had been in receipt of one or more of the relevant benefits for every day since
30 April 2004.

If you have been receiving transitionally protected IS (ie, you have continuously
received this and/or another means-tested benefit since 30 April 2004) and your
award of IS on the grounds of disability or incapacity for work is converted to
income-related ESA, you are exempt from the habitual residence test at the date
of transfer.[54] If the decision maker suggests you are not entitled to income-related
ESA because you do not have a right to reside and this exemption applies to you,
you may need to explain this to the decision maker.

For transitional protection to apply, you must have been the claimant
throughout the whole period of continuous entitlement, rather than a partner or
parent.[55]

The benefit authorities rarely check, or even ask, whether you are transitionally
protected from the need to have a right to reside, so if you have been receiving
one or more of the above benefits since 30 April 2004, you should always make
this clear when you make your claim and provide evidence.

Child benefit and child tax credit

The right to reside test only applies to child benefit and CTC if you make a new
claim for one of these benefits on or after 1 May 2004.[56]

If you are still receiving the same award of **child benefit** that began before 1
May 2004, you do not need a right to reside.

If you have been claiming **CTC** since before 1 May 2004, you also do not need
a right to reside to continue to receive it. Although the tax credit rules treat you as
making a new claim each year when you respond to your annual declaration (or
when you receive a notice saying you will be treated as having made a declaration),
this renewal claim does not require a right to reside.[57]

Notes

1. The habitual residence test
1 Reg 3 JSA(HR)A Regs
2 Reg 1(2), (3) and (4) SS(DLA,AA&CA)(A) Regs
3 Sch para 21 CTRS(DS)E Regs; reg 12 CTRS(PR)E Regs; reg 16 CTR(SPC)S Regs; reg 16 CTR(S) Regs; reg 26 CTRSPR(W) Regs; Sch para 19 CTRS(DS)W Regs
4 **IS** Reg 21AA(4) IS Regs
   JSA Reg 85A(4) JSA Regs
   ESA Reg 70(4) ESA Regs
   PC Reg 2(4) SPC Regs
   HB Reg 10(3B) HB Regs; reg 10(4A) HB(SPC) Regs
   UC Reg 9(4) UC Regs
5 Reg 3 HB(HR)A Regs
6 **AA** Reg 2(2)&(3A) SS(AA) Regs
   DLA Reg 2(2)&(3A) SS(DLA) Regs
   PIP Regs 19 and 20 SS(PIP) Regs
   CA Reg 9(3) SS(ICA) Regs
7 Reg 3E(1) and (2)(d) JSA Regs
8 Reg 3(3) UC Regs
9 Regs 3(3) and 36(3) UC Regs
10 Regs 3(3) and 18(2) UC Regs
11 Regs 3(3) and 22(3) UC Regs
12 **IS** Regs 21 and 21AA and Sch 7 para 17 IS Regs
   JSA Regs 85 and 85A and Sch 5 para 14 JSA Regs
   ESA Regs 69 and 70 and Sch 5 para 11 ESA Regs
13 Reg 10(1) HB Regs; reg 10(1) HB(SPC) Regs
14 **PC** Reg 2 SPC Regs
   UC Reg 9 UC Regs
15 **AA** s35(1) SSA 1975; reg 2(1) SS(AA) Regs
   DLA s71(6) SSCBA 1992; reg 2(1) SS(DLA) Regs
   PIP s77(3) WRA 2012; reg 16 SS(PIP) Regs

2. 'Habitual residence in fact'
16 R(IS) 6/96, para 15
17 CIS/15927/1996
18 *R v Barnet London Borough Council ex parte Shah* [1983] 2 AC 309 at 342; *Cameron v Cameron* [1996] SLT 306; R(IS) 9/99

19 *Nessa v Chief Adjudication Officer* [1999] UKHL 41
20 R(IS) 6/96, para 19
21 *M v M (Abduction: England and Scotland)* [1997] 2 FLR 263
22 R(IS) 2/00, para 30
23 CJSA/1223/2006; R(IS 7/06; CIS/1304/97 and CJSA/5394/98, paras 29-31
24 CIS/4474/2003, paras 15-16
25 R(IS) 2/00, para 28, followed in CIS/1459/1996 and CIS/16097/1996
26 *Nessa v Chief Adjudication Officer* [1999] UKHL 41 (R(IS) 2/00)
27 *Nessa v Chief Adjudication Officer* [1999] UKHL 41; *Cameron v Cameron* [1996] SLT 306
28 CIS/4474/2003; R(IS) 7/06
29 CIS/1972/2003; CIS/2559/2005
30 R(IS) 2/00, para 26
31 CJSA/1223/2006; R(IS) 7/06; CIS/1304/97 and CJSA/5394/98, paras 29-31
32 *Nessa v Chief Adjudication Officer* [1999] UKHL 41
33 CIS/1304/1997 and CJSA/5394/1998, para 11
34 *KS v SSWP (SPC)* [2010] UKUT 156 (AAC)
35 HB/CTB Circular A22/2010, paras 11-12
36 CIS/1304/97 and CJSA/5394/98, paras 34-38
37 CIS/1304/97 and CJSA/5394/98, paras 40-41
38 Art 70(4) EU Reg 883/04
39 Art 1(j) EU Reg 883/04
40 *Swaddling v Chief Adjudication Officer*, C-90/97 [1999] ECR I-01075
41 R(IS) 3/00
42 Reg 3(9) SS&CS(DA) Regs; s12(8)(b) SSA 1998
43 s8(2) SSA 1998
44 Statement by the Secretary of State for Work and Pensions given as part of Cmd 7073, para 20, available at www.gov.uk/government/uploads/system/uploads/attachment_data/file/243307/7073.pdf

3. The right to reside

45 Sch para 21 CTRS(DS)E Regs; reg 12
CTRS(PR)E Regs; reg 16 CTR(SPC)S
Regs; reg 16 CTR(S) Regs; reg 26
CTRSPR(W) Regs; Sch para 19
CTRS(DS)W Regs

46 **IS** Reg 21AA(3) IS Regs
JSA Reg 85A(3) JSA Regs
ESA Reg 70(3) ESA Regs
PC Reg 2(3) SPC Regs
HB Reg 10(3A) HB Regs; reg 10(4)
HB(SPC) Regs
UC Reg 9(3) UC Regs

47 *R (HC) v SSWP* [2013] EWHC 3874
(Admin), currently under appeal to the
Court of Appeal

48 **CB** s146 SSCBA 1992; reg 23(4) CB
Regs
TC s3(3) TCA 2002; reg 3(5) TC(R) Regs

49 **CB** Reg 23(4) CB Regs
TC Reg 3(5) TC(R) Regs

50 *R (HC) v SSWP* [2013] EWHC 3874
(Admin), currently under appeal to the
Court of Appeal

51 *European Commission v UK,* C-308/14

52 *Commissioners for HMRC v Aiga
Spiridonova,* 13/115948

53 Reg 6(1) SS(HR)A Regs, preserved by reg
11(2) SS(PA)A Regs

54 Reg 70(4)(l) ESA Regs; reg 10A
ESA(TP)(EA) Regs

55 CIS/1096/2007

56 **CB** Reg 23(4) CB Regs
CTC Reg 3(5)(a) TC(R) Regs

57 Reg 3(5)(a) TC(R) Regs

Chapter 12

· ·

Who has a right to reside

This chapter covers:

This chapter explains who has a right to reside. For information on the benefits and tax credits that require a right to reside, details of how the requirement operates for each and the types of residency rights that are specifically excluded, see p107.

The right to reside requirement is only one of the residence and presence conditions that must be satisfied for each individual benefit and tax credit. See Chapter 13 for more information.

1. Overview

Whether or not you have a right to reside depends on the nationality, immigration status and other particular circumstance of you, your family members and certain people for whom you care. You may have a right of residence under UK law or one that comes directly from European Union law, or both. You may have more than one right of residence, or you may not have any.

Any residence right is sufficient to satisfy the right to reside requirement, unless it is specifically excluded for the benefit or tax credit you want to claim.

The residence rights of some people are more complicated than others. In general, if you are a European Economic Area (EEA) national (see p115), or a family member or primary carer of an EEA national, your residence rights are more complex. Consequently, the majority of this chapter focuses on these groups.

Note: the phrases 'right to reside' and 'right of residence' have the same meaning and are used interchangeably in this *Handbook*.

2. Non-European Economic Area nationals

If you are a non-European Economic Area (EEA) national, you have a right to reside if:

- you have been granted leave to enter or remain under UK immigration law. You have a right to reside during your period of leave. Any form of leave gives you a right to reside – eg, indefinite leave, refugee leave, humanitarian protection, discretionary leave and limited leave granted under the Immigration Rules, such as as a spouse or visitor. However, if you have leave which is subject to a condition that you do not have recourse to public funds, or indefinite leave granted as the result of a maintenance undertaking, you are defined as a 'person subject to immigration control' (see p55) and, therefore, likely to be excluded from benefits on that basis (see Part 3); *or*
- you are someone who does not need leave to enter or remain under UK immigration law because you have a right to reside under European law. The most common examples are if you are the family member (see p151) or primary carer (see p162) of an EEA national who has a right to reside and who confers her/his residence rights on you.

3. British, Irish and Commonwealth citizens

British citizens have an automatic right of residence in the UK. However, this right is under UK law and British citizens do not usually have residence rights in the UK under European Union law if they have not lived with a right to reside in another European Economic Area (EEA) country before returning to the UK. Therefore, unless otherwise stated, all references in this chapter to EEA nationals should be read as *not* including British citizens.

British citizens do not automatically confer residence rights on their family members. If you are not a British citizen, but you are the family member of a British citizen, see p155.

If you are the primary carer of a British citizen, see p167.

Irish nationals and nationals of other countries in the common travel area (ie, Ireland, Channel Islands, Isle of Man and the UK) have a right of residence in the common travel area and, therefore, satisfy the right to reside requirement for means-tested benefits.

Commonwealth citizens with the right of abode also have a right of residence in the UK (see p15).

4. **European Economic Area nationals**

In practice, the right to reside requirement mainly affects nationals from the European Economic Area (EEA). The residence rights of EEA nationals, their family members and carers can be complex, as both European Union (EU) law and UK law must be considered, and both are subject to a considerable amount of interpretation through caselaw.

Legal sources of European Economic Area residence rights

The right of residence of EEA nationals and their family members derives from the EU treaties, in particular the **Treaty of the Functioning of the European Union** (TFEU), or the EEA Agreement which provides similar (although not always equivalent) rights for Norway, Iceland and Liechtenstein. The most relevant provisions of the TFEU include the following.

- Discrimination on nationality grounds is prohibited wherever the provisions of the Treaty apply.[1]
- Every person holding a nationality of an EU state is an EU citizen and has certain rights that stem from this.[2]
- EU nationals have the right to move and reside freely within the territory of the EU states.

However, the right to move and reside freely within the EU is subject to the limitations and conditions set out in the TFEU and in other legislation that gives effect to it.[3] This means that those covered by the TFEU must satisfy certain conditions to have a right of residence. The most important secondary legislation that sets out residence rights and the conditions that must be satisfied is **EU Directive 2004/38**. This brings together most rights of residence under EU law into one piece of legislation and replaces many earlier directives and regulations, which previously set out EU residence rights. Directive 2004/38 has been in force since 30 April 2006 and was extended from 1 March 2009 to cover nationals of Norway, Iceland and Liechtenstein.[4] **Note:** while the EU Directive is the most important source of residence rights for EEA nationals and their family members, it is not the only one – eg, some derivative rights of residence (see p162) stem from other EU legislation.

Swiss nationals and their family members are covered by a separate agreement, which provides similar rights.[5]

The Immigration (European Economic Area) Regulations 2006, referred to in this *Handbook* as the **'EEA Regulations'**, apply to all EEA nationals (except British citizens – see p114) and Swiss nationals.[6] These give similar rights of residence to those contained in the Directive. Where they conflict with, or do not completely incorporate, EU Directive 2004/38, you can rely on whichever is more favourable to you.

Who can have European Economic Area residence rights

You *may* have EEA residence rights if you are:
- an EEA national (other than a British citizen, except in limited circumstances – see below) or a Swiss national; *or*
- a family member of an EEA national (other than a British citizen, except in limited circumstances – see below) or Swiss national who has a right to reside. You can have these rights whether or not *you* are an EEA national;
- someone who was previously in the above group; *or*
- the primary carer of certain EEA nationals (including British citizens).

In all cases, whether or not you have EEA residence rights also depends on other factors.

For a list of **EEA member states**, see p39. However, note that, unless otherwise stated, references to EEA nationals in this chapter should be read as *not* including British citizens (see below).

In general, **Swiss nationals** have the same residence rights as EEA nationals, so unless otherwise stated, references to EEA nationals include Swiss nationals.

British citizens have different rights in the UK compared to other EEA nationals. If you are a British citizen, you always have a right to reside in the UK under UK law. However, most British citizens do not have residence rights in the UK under EU law.[7] Therefore, unless otherwise stated, references to EEA nationals in this chapter do not include British citizens.[8]

The fact that most British citizens do not have residence rights in the UK under EU law means that family members and primary carers of British citizens do not have the same rights as family members and primary carers of other EEA nationals. If you are the family member of a British citizen, see p155. If you are the primary carer of a British citizen, see p162.

Croatian, A2 and A8 nationals can have their residence rights affected by additional restrictions. These countries are listed on p118. The restrictions are summarised on p119 and noted in the sections of this chapter where they are relevant.

Checklist

As EEA residence rights can be complex and affected by many different factors, it can be helpful to work through the following checklist of the main residence rights.

- **Step one:** are you an EEA national with a right to reside based on your current or previous employment, self-employment, jobseeking or self-sufficiency (including being self-sufficient while a student)? You have a right to reside if you:
  - are a 'qualified person'. You are a 'qualified person' if you are a:[9]
    - jobseeker (see p123);
    - worker (see p129), including if you have retained this status (see p135);
    - self-employed person (see p141), including if you have retained this status (see p144);
    - self-sufficient person, including a self-sufficient student (see p146); *or*
  - have a permanent right of residence (see p170). This is usually after five years of 'legal residence' but, in limited circumstances, can be acquired before five years.
- **Step two:** are you a 'family member' (see p151) of someone covered in Step one? You have a right to reside, even if you are not an EEA national yourself. In limited circumstances, you may have a right to reside if you were the family member of someone in Step one but s/he has now died, left the UK or your marriage or civil partnership has been terminated (see p157).
- **Step three:** do you have a 'derivative right to reside' – ie, through someone else's right to reside, but not as her/his family member? Certain primary carers and children have a 'derivative right to reside'. See p162 for more details.

Note:
- The term 'qualified person' appears in the EEA Regulations, but is not used in the EU Directive although the same groups of people are covered.
- You can have more than one right to reside at a time – eg, you may be a self-employed person and also the family member of someone with a permanent right of residence.[10]
- If you are an EEA national or family member of an EEA national, you also have an initial right of residence for the first three months that you are in the UK. However, if this is your only right to reside, it does not entitle you to means-tested benefits (see p122).
- If you are an Croatian, A2 or A8 national, a 'family member' (see p152) of an Croatian, A2 or A8 national, or if you have a derivative right to reside (see p162) as the child or primary carer of a Croatian, A2 or A8 national, see p118 for the additional restrictions that can affect your right to reside.

5. **Croatian, A2 and A8 nationals**

A2 and A8 states and Croatia

The A2 states are: Bulgaria and Romania.

These states joined the European Union (EU) on 1 January 2007.

The restrictions applied until 31 December 2013.

The A8 states are: Czech Republic, Estonia, Hungary, Latvia, Lithuania, Poland, Slovakia and Slovenia.

These states joined the EU on 1 May 2004.

The restrictions applied until 30 April 2011.

Croatia joined the EU on 1 July 2013.

The restrictions are currently in force until 30 June 2018.

The treaties under which the above 'accession' states joined the EU allowed existing member states to limit access to their labour markets for nationals of these states. The UK government imposed restrictions on the residence rights of workers and jobseekers from these countries. All these restrictions can only be imposed for a maximum of seven years from the date the states joined the EU.

Most Croatian nationals have (and most A2 and A8 nationals had) certain restrictions on their residence rights as jobseekers, workers or people who retain worker status. These restrictions on Croatian nationals have applied since 1 July 2013 and apply until 30 June 2018, but may be extended for a further two years. The restrictions on A2 nationals applied between 1 January 2007 and 31 December 2013 and on A8 nationals between 1 May 2004 and 30 April 2011. **Note:** although the restrictions on A2 and A8 nationals have now ended, in certain circumstances you may still need to know what they were and how they operated. This is because the residence rights you or your family member had in the past can affect current or future residence rights.

While in force, the restrictions apply unless you are in one of the exempt groups. If you are a Croatian national and are not exempt, you must obtain an 'accession worker authorisation document' (in most cases, an accession worker registration certificate, specifying the employer you can work for) before taking up employment, and then work in accordance with it. If you are an A2 national who was subject to restrictions, you were required to obtain an accession worker authorisation document (in most cases, an accession worker card specifying the employer you could work for) before taking up employment, and then work in accordance with it. If you are an A8 national who was subject to restrictions, you had to work for an 'authorised employer'.

Broadly speaking, this meant you had to register each job you took with the Worker Registration Scheme (but see p119 for the precise meaning as it can affect your residence rights).

Restrictions on residence rights

If you are a Croatian national, you are subject to worker authorisation unless you are in one of the groups listed on p120.[11]

If you are a Croatian national subject to worker authorisation, your residence rights are restricted until 30 June 2018 as follows.

- You do not have a right to reside as a jobseeker.
- You are only defined as a 'worker' if you have an accession worker authorisation document and are working in accordance with it.
- You cannot retain your worker status when you stop work in the ways other workers can (see p135).

If you are an A2 national who was subject to restrictions (see p120 for exemptions), you were required to obtain an accession worker authorisation document and your residence rights were restricted between 1 January 2007 and 31 December 2013 in the same way as Croatian nationals.[12]

If you are an A8 national who was subject to restrictions (see p121 for exemptions), you had to work for an 'authorised employer' (see below),[13] and your residence rights were restricted between 1 May 2004 and 30 April 2011 as follows.[14]

- You did not have a right to reside as a jobseeker.
- You were only defined as a 'worker' if you were working for an 'authorised employer' (see below).
- You could not retain your worker status when you stopped work in the ways other workers can (see p135). However, if you lost your job within the first month of employment, you could retain your status in those ways, but only until the end of the month.

The restrictions do not affect other residence rights you may have as an European Economic Area (EEA) national – eg, as a self-employed or self-sufficient person.

Authorised employer

If you were an A8 national subject to restrictions, you were defined as working for an 'authorised employer' if you:[15]

– were within the first month of employment;

– applied for a worker's registration certificate within the first month of work, but did not yet have a certificate or refusal;

– had a valid worker's registration certificate for that employer;

– had been legally working (see p121) for that employer since 30 April 2004;

– began work at an agricultural camp between 1 May 2004 and 31 December 2004, and before 1 May 2004 you had been issued with leave under the Immigration Act 1971 as a seasonal worker at such a camp.

If you only applied for a registration certificate after the first month of work, you only count as working for an 'authorised employer' from the date it was issued. It does not apply retrospectively.[16]

Croatian and A2 nationals not subject to worker authorisation

If you are a Croatian national, you are 'subject to worker authorisation' and have additional restrictions on your residence rights (see p119) unless you are in one of the groups listed below.

If you are an A2 national, you were 'subject to worker authorisation' until 31 December 2013 and had additional restrictions on your residence rights (see p119), unless you were in one of the groups listed below. **Note:** these restrictions for A2 nationals ended on 31 December 2013.

You are not subject to worker authorisation, and your residence rights are not restricted, if you:[17]

- have (or had on 30 June 2013 (Croatian) or 31 December 2006 (A2)) leave to enter or remain with no restriction on employment;
- were legally working (see p121) in the UK for 12 months without breaks of more than 30 days (in total), up to and including 31 December 2006 (A2) or 30 June 2013 (Croatian);
- have legally worked for 12 months (beginning before or after 31 December 2006 (A2) or 30 June 2013 (Croatian)), disregarding any breaks of less than 30 days (in total);
- are a posted worker – ie, you are working in the UK providing services on behalf of an employer who is not established in the UK;
- are a member of a diplomatic mission (or the family member of such a person) or a person otherwise entitled to diplomatic immunity;
- have dual nationality with the UK or another (non-A2/Croatian) EEA state;
- are the spouse/civil partner (or, Croatian only, unmarried or same-sex partner) of a UK national or of a person settled in the UK;
- are the spouse/civil partner (or, Croatian only, unmarried or same-sex partner) or child under 18 of a person with leave to enter or remain in the UK that allows employment;
- have a permanent right of residence (see p170);
- are a student with a registration certificate that states that you cannot work more than 20 hours a week (unless it is part of vocational training or during vacations) and you comply with this. If the certificate confirms you can work during the four months after the course ends, the exemption continues for this period;
- are a family member of an EEA national who has a right to reside, unless the EEA national is an A2 (or, if you are Croatian, a Croatian) national subject to worker authorisation (or, A2 only, the only reason s/he is not an A2 national subject to worker authorisation is because s/he is covered by the group below);
- are a family member of an A2 (or, if you are Croatian, a Croatian) national subject to worker authorisation who has a right to reside (for an A2 national only, as a worker, student, self-employed or self-sufficient person). If you are a

Croatian national (or an A2 national relying on an A2 worker), you are a 'family member' if you are the descendant and either under 21 or dependent, the spouse/civil partner, or (Croatians only) the unmarried or same-sex partner;
- are a 'highly skilled person' – ie, you:[18]
  - met the points-based criteria in the Immigration Rules for entering the UK on this basis; *or*
  - have a qualification at degree level or higher in the UK, or Higher National Diploma in Scotland and, within 12 months of this award, you apply for a registration certificate confirming your unconditional access to the labour market.

A8 nationals who were not required to register

If you are an A8 national, you were defined as 'requiring registration', any work you did had to be for an 'an authorised employer' (see p119) and your residence rights were restricted (see p119), unless you:[19]
- had leave to enter or remain on 30 April 2004 which had no restriction on employment;
- were legally working (see below) in the UK for 12 months, without breaks of more than 30 days (in total), up to and including 30 April 2004;
- had legally worked for 12 months (beginning before or after 30 April 2004), disregarding any breaks of less than 30 days (in total);
- were the spouse/civil partner or child under 18 of a person with leave to enter or remain in the UK that allowed employment;
- had dual nationality with the UK and another (non-A2/A8) EEA state or Switzerland;
- were a family member of another EEA or Swiss national who had a right to reside under the EEA Regulations (other than an A2/A8 national subject to registration/authorisation if her/his only right to reside was for the first three months in the UK);
- were the member of a diplomatic mission (or the family member of such a person) or a person otherwise entitled to diplomatic immunity;
- were a posted worker – ie, you were working in the UK providing services on behalf of an employer who was not established in the UK.

Legally working

The phrase 'legally working', referred to above, has a specific meaning and only refers to employment, not self-employment. Although there are no additional restrictions placed on self-employment, periods of self-employment do not bring you into a group that is exempt from authorisation (registration for A8 nationals).

If you are a Croatian national (or an A2 national before 1 January 2014), you are/were 'legally working' if:[20]

- you are/were working in accordance with your worker authorisation document; *or*
- you are/were working during a period when you are/were in one of the exempt groups on pp120–21 (other than posted workers); *or*
- the work was done before 1 July 2013 (for Croatian nationals) or before 1 January 2007 (for A2 nationals), either in accordance with any leave you had under the Immigration Act 1971 or when you did not require leave. The Court of Appeal has held that this does not apply to work done with permission from the Home Office while you were an asylum seeker.[21]

If you are an A8 national, you were 'legally working' before 1 May 2011 if:[22]
- you were working for an authorised employer (see p119); *or*
- you were working during a period when you were in one of the exempt groups on p121 (other than if you were the spouse/civil partner or child of a person whose leave to enter or remain in the UK allowed employment); *or*
- the work was done before 1 May 2004 either in accordance with any leave you had under the Immigration Act 1971 or when you did not require leave. The Court of Appeal has held that this does not apply to work done with permission from the Home Office while you were an asylum seeker.[23]

If you are a Croatian national and your employment ends, you stop legally working, stop being a 'worker' and, unless you are in an exempt group, you cannot retain your worker status. However, if you are still under a contract of employment, you continue to be legally working and a worker – eg, if you are on maternity leave, holiday leave, sick leave or compassionate leave (including if the leave is unpaid).[24]

The same applied to A2 nationals between 1 January 2007 and 31 December 2013 and A8 nationals between 1 May 2004 and 30 April 2011. If you stop working after these end dates, your rights are the same as for other non-accession state EEA nationals and the relevant question is whether you are still a 'worker' or can retain 'worker' status (see p135). However, it may still be relevant to know whether you were legally working before these dates in order to establish whether you had completed your 12 months of legal work or whether you were a 'worker' at a particular time, as it can affect your current residence rights and those of your family members.

6. **Initial right of residence**

All European Economic Area (EEA) nationals have a right to enter any member state. EEA nationals also have an initial right of residence in any member state for the first three months of their stay.[25] This is given whether or not you are working or seeking work, but is subject to your not becoming an unreasonable burden on the social assistance system of the UK.[26]

You also have a right of residence if you are not an EEA national, but are the family member of an EEA national who has an initial right of residence for three months.[27] For details of who counts as your family member, see p151.

Note: you can have one or more right of residence (eg, as the family member of a worker and/or as a jobseeker) in addition to your initial right of residence – ie, you do not have to wait for the three months to end before you have another right of residence.

If your *only* right of residence is on the basis of your (or your family member's) initial three-month right of residence, the benefit rules exclude you from entitlement to **income support, income-based jobseeker's allowance (JSA), income-related employment and support allowance, pension credit, housing benefit and universal credit**. However, if you have a right of residence on another basis during your initial three months in the UK, you can satisfy the right to reside requirement, provided it is not a residence right that is excluded for the means-tested benefit you want to claim (see p108).

Note: the requirement for you to have been living in the common travel area for the past three months for income-based JSA is a separate part of the habitual residence test (see p88) and unrelated to this initial right of residence.

If your *only* right of residence is on the basis of your (or your family member's) initial three-month right of residence, the **child benefit and child tax credit** (CTC) rules do not exclude you from entitlement. Therefore, you satisfy the right to reside requirement for child benefit and CTC, but only for the first three months of your residence in the UK, unless you have some other right of residence.

Note: the requirement for you to have been living in the UK for the past three months is a separate requirement (see p88) and unrelated to this initial right of residence.

7. **Jobseekers**

If you are a European Economic Area (EEA) national looking for work in the UK, you may have a right to reside as a 'jobseeker' (see p124). You may also have a right to reside if you are the family member (see p151) of a jobseeker. However, either of these residence rights only entitles you to certain benefits (see p127), so you should check whether you have a right of residence on some other basis. **Note:** if you have previously been a worker (see p129) and are now looking for work, in addition to having a right to reside as a jobseeker, you may also have a right of residence as someone who retains her/his status as a worker (see p135), which satisfies the right to reside requirement for all benefits.

Who has a right to reside as a jobseeker

If you are an EEA national, you have a right to reside as a jobseeker if:[28]
- you are in the UK and you can provide evidence that you are seeking employment and have a 'genuine chance of being engaged';
- you entered the UK in order to seek employment, or (EEA Regulations only – see below) you are present in the UK seeking employment immediately after having a right to reside as a worker (except if you retained worker status while involuntarily unemployed – see p135), a student, a self-employed or self-sufficient person; *and*
- (EEA Regulations only[29]) either you have not already had a right to reside as a jobseeker for 182 days or, if you have, the evidence you must provide to show that you are seeking employment and have a genuine chance of being engaged is 'compelling' (see p126).[30]

If you previously had a right to reside as a jobseeker for 182 days since 31 December 2013 (but not if since that time you have been absent from the UK continuously for at least 12 months), or you retained worker status while involuntarily unemployed (see p135) for at least six months, you must have since had an absence from the UK and the evidence you must provide must be 'compelling' from the start of your current period of residence as a jobseeker. Only periods since 31 December 2013 count towards any of the periods in this bullet point.

Note: if you are refused benefit because of a requirement that is in the EEA Regulations only, you should challenge the decision on the basis that the EEA Regulations interpret the category of jobseeker more narrowly than the European Court of Justice.[31]

Croatian, A2 and A8 nationals

If you are a Croatian national subject to worker authorisation (see p119), you do *not* have a right to reside as a jobseeker.[32] Similarly, before 1 January 2014, if you were an A2 national who was subject to worker authorisation, or before 1 May 2011 if you were an A8 national who was required to register your work (see p119), you did not have a right to reside as a jobseeker (see p119).[33]

Employment you must seek and have a genuine chance of obtaining

In order to have a right of residence as a jobseeker, you must be looking for, and have a genuine chance of obtaining, employment that would be sufficient for you to be a 'worker' (see p129) if you obtained it.[34]

If you are only looking for work as a self-employed person, this does not give you a right to reside as a jobseeker. However, if you are taking steps to establish self-employed activity, you may count as a self-employed person and have a right of residence on that basis (see p141).

In most cases, you should be accepted as seeking employment and having a genuine chance of being engaged if you are 'signing on' and are awarded either jobseeker's allowance (JSA) or national insurance (NI) credits, since both show that you have been accepted as being available for work and actively seeking work. Similarly, if you come under the universal credit (UC) system, you should be accepted as being a jobseeker if you meet all the work-related requirements. For an explanation of these requirements for JSA and UC, see CPAG's *Welfare Benefits and Tax Credits Handbook*. However, it has been held that, in rare circumstances, it is possible for someone to satisfy these conditions and not be accepted as having a genuine chance of being engaged.[35]

Have you not been accepted as having a genuine chance of finding work?

If the decision maker decides that, despite satisfying the benefit requirements regarding your work seeking and availability, you do not have a genuine chance of being engaged, you can try to argue that your case is not one of the rare cases where this applies.[36] It may help to look in detail at the provisions you have been held to satisfy. For example, to be accepted as actively seeking work for JSA, you must, in any week, take such steps as you can reasonably be expected to take in order to have the best prospects of securing employment.[37] Except in limited situations, if you put any restrictions on your availability for work, you must be able to show that you still have 'reasonable prospects of securing employment'.[38] If you have placed restrictions on your availability and these have been accepted as satisfying this requirement for JSA, it may be arguable that is then irrational to decide that you do not have a 'genuine chance of being engaged'.

After you have been looking for work for 182 days, the DWP may require you to provide 'compelling' evidence that you are continuing to seek work and have a genuine chance of being engaged (see p126). **Note:** there is no change to the type of work you must be seeking and have a genuine chance of obtaining.

Note: if your only right to reside is as a jobseeker and you are claiming UC, the UC regulations require you to be subject to all work-related requirements if you are someone who would otherwise be subject to only some or no work-related requirements (see p128).[39]

If you do not claim jobseeker's allowance or universal credit

There is no requirement that you must have claimed or be in receipt of JSA or UC in order to have a right to reside as a jobseeker. The requirements are simply that you are an EEA national who can provide evidence that you are seeking employment and have a genuine chance of being engaged.

The most straightforward way to be accepted as meeting these requirements is if you claim, and are entitled to, contribution-based or income-based JSA, UC and you satisfy the work search and work availability requirements, or NI credits on the basis of being available for and actively seeking work (or, if you come under the UC system, on the basis that you satisfy the work search and work availability requirements).

However, if you are not eligible for JSA, UC or NI credits, or you are still waiting for a decision on your claim, you can argue (eg, to HM Revenue and Customs in respect of a claim for child benefit or child tax credit (CTC)) that you still meet the essential requirements of being a jobseeker.[40]

For how long do you have a right to reside as a jobseeker

There is no time limit on how long you can have a right to reside as a jobseeker. It continues for as long as you can provide evidence that you are continuing to seek work and have a genuine chance of being engaged.[41]

However, the EEA Regulations require that to continue to have a right to reside as a jobseeker for longer than 182 days you must provide 'compelling' evidence that you are continuing to seek work and have a genuine chance of being engaged. The 182 days comprises any periods when you have had a right to reside as a jobseeker since 31 December 2013. This could be one continuous period or a cumulative total of shorter periods.[42]

If you are absent from the UK for a continuous period of at least 12 months, your 182-day period begins afresh on your return.[43]

The requirement for your evidence to be 'compelling' applies from the start of your period of residence as a jobseeker if you:[44]

- have been absent from the UK for a period of less than 12 months; *and*
- previously had a right to reside as a jobseeker for 182 days since 31 December 2013,[45] or you retained worker status while involuntarily unemployed (see p135) for at least six months.

Note:
- Under European Union (EU) law, although you must continue to provide evidence that you are continuing to seek work and have a genuine chance of being engaged in order to continue to have a right to reside as a jobseeker, there is no requirement for any change in this evidence after any period of time. Although you can argue that you continue to have a right to reside under EU law, the decision maker is likely to apply the EEA Regulations and refuse you benefit after 182 days if your evidence is not considered compelling. You may want to argue that not only is your evidence compelling, but also that, in any case, it does not need to be.
- The term 'compelling' is not defined and so should have its ordinary, everyday meaning.

- The DWP has produced guidance for JSA decision makers which, depending on your circumstances, may be helpful to refer to.[46] However, as guidance, it is not legally binding.
- If you have had a job that gives you 'worker' status since you previously had a right to reside as a jobseeker for 182 days or since you retained worker status while involuntarily unemployed for at least six months, you can retain your worker status while involuntarily unemployed if you satisfy the conditions on p135.[47]

The longer you have been a jobseeker without obtaining work, the more likely it is that the decision maker will argue that this shows you do not have a genuine chance of getting work. To avoid this, or to challenge a decision that you are not entitled to benefit because you do not currently have a right of residence as a jobseeker, you need evidence to demonstrate that you do have a genuine chance of being engaged, despite the long period of unemployment. See p321 for some types of evidence that may be helpful.

Benefit entitlement

If you have a right to reside as a jobseeker, this satisfies the right to reside requirement for:
- income-based JSA;
- UC (but see below);
- child benefit (but see below); and
- CTC (but see below).

Note:
- To satisfy the habitual residence test for income-based JSA, you must still be accepted as 'habitually resident in fact' (see p102) and have been living in the common travel area for the three months prior to your claim (see p88).
- To satisfy the habitual residence test for UC, you must still be accepted as 'habitually resident in fact' (see p102).
- You must have been living in the UK for the three months prior to your claim for child benefit and CTC, unless you are exempt from this requirement (see p89).

If you have a right to reside as a jobseeker, this does *not* satisfy the right to reside requirement for:
- income support (IS);
- income-related employment and support allowance (ESA) (but see p128);
- pension credit (PC); and
- housing benefit (HB) (but see p128).

You must therefore have another right to reside to get one of the above benefits.

Jobseekers have more limited benefit entitlement than most other groups with residence rights under EU law. EU Directive 2004/38 states that the host member state is not obliged to provide entitlement to social assistance to those with a right to reside as a jobseeker.[48] However, the UK government has chosen to provide the limited benefit entitlement, as set out on p127.

Note: periods when you have a right to reside as a jobseeker count towards the five years required to acquire permanent residence (see p170), which then satisfies the right to reside requirement for all benefits.

Income-related employment and support allowance

If your only right to reside is as a jobseeker, the UK rules state that this is not sufficient to obtain income-related ESA.[49] Therefore, if you can claim income-based JSA, this is generally easier than attempting to claim income-related ESA.

However, the UK is required to give EEA jobseekers who have established real links with the UK labour market equal access to benefits of a financial nature that are intended to facilitate access to the UK labour market as British citizens.[50] It is arguable that income-related ESA is such a benefit. This is because most claimants (other than those in the support group) are required to engage in work-related activity, which is intended to assist them to obtain a job.[51] If this is right, the decision maker may not legally be able to deny income-related ESA to an EEA national with a right to reside as a jobseeker.

If you try to argue this, it is likely that the decision maker will say that, regardless of whether ESA is a benefit of a financial nature intended to facilitate access to the labour market, you are not really a jobseeker because your health prohibits you from working – ie, you have limited capability for work. If this happens, you can point out that a person has limited capability for work if s/he has an illness or disability which makes it unreasonable to expect her/him to work, and that this is not the same as saying you are unable to work or you cannot choose to look for work. However, you must be able to demonstrate that you are looking for work and have a genuine chance of obtaining work.

Housing benefit

If you have a right to reside as a jobseeker, this does not satisfy the right to reside requirement for HB. However, if you have been in receipt of both income-based JSA and HB continuously since 31 March 2014, you are exempt from the habitual residence test for HB (see p99). You can therefore continue to receive HB until either:

- you cease to be entitled to income-based JSA; *or*
- you make a new claim for HB.

Universal credit

If your only right to reside is as a jobseeker, or a family member (other than an extended family member) of a jobseeker, you are not exempt from any of the UC work-related requirements, even if you would otherwise come into one of the exempt groups.[52] See CPAG's *Welfare Benefits and Tax Credits Handbook* for details of these.

It is arguable that this rule is unlawful. The UK is required to give EEA jobseekers who have established real links with the UK labour market equal access to benefits of a financial nature that are intended to facilitate access to the UK labour market as British citizens.[53] The UK benefit authorities (and, if necessary, the courts) must determine whether someone has established a genuine link to the labour market and assess whether a benefit is intended to facilitate access to the labour market.[54] Assessments therefore vary, depending on all the facts, including the exempt group that you would otherwise come into – eg, if you are responsible for a child under three or you have limited capability for work.

8. **Workers**

If you are a European Economic Area (EEA) national working in the UK, you may have a right to reside as a 'worker' (see below). You may also have a right to reside if you are the family member (see p151) of a worker. Once you have established worker status, it is important to be clear when you cease to be a worker (see p134). In limited circumstances, you can retain your worker status after you stop being a worker (see p135).

If you have a right to reside as a worker, as someone who has retained worker status, or as the family member of a worker, your right to reside satisfies the right to reside requirement for all benefits.

Who has a right to reside as a worker

If you are an EEA national and a worker, you have a right to reside.[55]

The term 'worker' is not defined in European Union (EU) legislation and the EEA Regulations simply cross-refer to EU law.[56] It should therefore be interpreted in accordance with EU law and the principles established through EU caselaw.

You count as a 'worker' if:

- you are in an employment relationship (see p131); *and*
- the work you do entails activities that are 'genuine and effective' rather than 'marginal and ancillary' (see p132).

The reason why you moved to the UK is irrelevant, provided you meet the above conditions.[57] For example, if your principle intention in coming to the UK was to pursue a course of study, this is not relevant when determining whether you are a worker.[58]

Your motives for seeking employment can be taken into account when determining whether you are pursuing activity as an employed person. However, once it is established that you are, your motives are irrelevant.[59]

Note: if you have been a worker, you do not necessarily lose this status just because you stop working. For more information on when you cease to be a worker, see p134, and for the circumstances in which you can retain your worker status, see p135.

Croatian, A2 and A8 workers

If you are a Croatian national subject to worker authorisation (see p119), you do *not* have a right to reside as a worker unless you hold a accession worker authorisation document and you are working in accordance with it (see p119).[60] Similarly, before 1 January 2014 if you were an A2 national who was subject to worker authorisation (see p119), you did not have a right to reside as a worker unless you held an accession worker authorisation document and worked in accordance with it (see p119).[61] Before 1 May 2011, if you were an A8 national who was required to register your work, you did not have a right to reside as a worker unless you were working for an 'authorised employer' (see p119).[62]

Guidance to decision makers

From March 2014, decision makers are advised to follow a two-tier process when determining whether or not someone is a worker (or self-employed).[63] Although this guidance is not legally binding, it is helpful to know its content either to offset potential problems before your claim is decided or to challenge an incorrect decision more effectively.

The first tier in deciding whether you are a worker (or self-employed) is to establish whether your average gross earnings reach a 'minimum earnings threshold' of 35 times the primary earnings threshold – ie, the level at which you start to pay national insurance contributions – £153 per week in 2014/15. If your gross earnings were at or above this amount for a continuous period of three months immediately before you claim benefit, you are automatically accepted as a worker (or self-employed).

The second tier applies if you do not satisfy the minimum earnings threshold for the relevant three-month period. If this is the case, the decision maker should, *in all cases,* assess your case and take into account all your circumstances to determine whether your activity was genuine and effective and not marginal and ancillary, and whether you are a worker (or self-employed).[64]

This guidance is clear that if you are not automatically accepted as a worker (or self-employed) under the first tier, the decision maker should go on to assess all your circumstances in relation to the criteria set out on pp131–34. You should not be told that you are not a worker (or self-employed) just because you have not met the minimum earnings threshold for three months.

Employment relationship

You count as being in an 'employment relationship' if you:[65]
- provide services;
- receive remuneration in return for those services (see below);
- perform your work under the direction of another person (see below).

The services you provide must entail activities that are 'genuine and effective' as opposed to 'marginal and ancillary' (see p132).

Although, in general, your employment must have begun for you to be a worker, in exceptional circumstances you may be a worker if you have moved to the UK to take up a job offer and it is not possible for you to begin work immediately but the offer is being held open for you.[66]

What counts as remuneration

In order to be a worker, you must receive 'remuneration' in return for the services you provide.

If you do voluntary work and receive payments for expenses, you are not a worker.[67] This is because the payments you receive are not provided in return for the services you perform, but rather to compensate you for the expenses you have incurred in providing them.

You can still count as a worker if the remuneration you receive is in the form of payment in kind rather than, or in addition to, in money.[68]

Working under the direction of another person

To count as a worker, you must perform the services for, and under the direction of, someone else – ie, there must be someone who can tell you how to do the work. If you provide services in return for remuneration and you are not under the direction of another person, you count as a person who is self-employed (see p141) rather than a worker.[69]

If you are taxed as a self-employed person, this fact by itself does not prevent you from being in an employment relationship, although it is a relevant factor in determining the question. For example, many people who work in the construction industry and pay tax as sub-contractors under the Construction Industry Scheme clearly provide services in return for payment and while at work are under the direction of another person. They are therefore workers and not self-employed.

It does not matter whether the person or organisation that provides the remuneration is the same as the person or organisation to whom you provide services.[70]

'Cash in hand' and agency work

You count as being in an 'employment relationship' if you provide services in return for renumeration under the direction of another person. This is not affected by the fact that:

- you are paid 'cash in hand'. The concept of 'worker' is an economic status, rather than a legal one.[71] However, you are still required to provide evidence of your employment and this may be harder to do if your work is paid cash in hand. See p319 for more information on providing evidence of your work;
- you did not declare the work to the DWP at the time.[72] This is likely to be most relevant when you are relying on past periods of employment;
- the person or organisation to whom you provide the services is different from the person or organisation that pays you for these – eg, if you are 'employed' by an employment agency.[73] However, the activities entailed in your provision of services must still be accepted as genuine and effective rather than marginal and ancillary (see below and in particular p133 regarding the regularity of the work). There is nothing inherent in working for an agency that would exclude this and it depends on the facts of each case.[74]

Example
Nora is a Hungarian national working as a nurse 'employed' by an employment agency. The payment she receives is via the agency, but the services are provided to a private care home. The care home has a contractual relationship with the agency, rather than with Nora, and pays the agency. Nora still counts as a worker in EU law because she is providing services and doing so in return for remuneration, even though there is a separation between the care home where she provides the services and the agency that pays her.

'Genuine and effective', not 'marginal and ancillary'

Even if you are in an employment relationship, you only have a right to reside as a worker if the services you provide entail activities that are 'genuine and effective' as opposed to those that are on such a small scale as to be regarded as 'marginal and ancillary'.[75]

The assessment of whether or not your employment is 'genuine and effective' must assess, as a whole, all the circumstances of your case.[76] See p130 for details of the guidance issued to decision makers. Relevant factors that must be considered include:

- the number of hours you work;
- the duration of your employment;
- the level of earnings;
- whether the work is regular or erratic;
- other employment rights;
- whether the work is not for the economic benefit of the employer or is just a small part of a larger relationship between the parties.

Number of hours worked

The number of hours you work in a given period is a relevant factor in determining whether your work is genuine and effective. There is no minimum number of hours you must work. Provided the other factors indicate that the work is genuine and effective, even work for a very small number of hours is capable of counting as genuine and effective.

In one case, the European Court of Justice held that, following an overall assessment of the employment relationship in question, the possibility could not be ruled out that someone who worked 5.5 hours a week could be a worker.[77] However, in most circumstances, you must work for more than 5.5 hours a week for your activity to be accepted as genuine and effective. Working as an au pair for 13 hours a week for £35 per week plus board and lodging for a period of 5.5 weeks was held in one case to result in worker status.[78]

The duration of employment

The duration of the employment is a relevant factor to consider when deciding whether or not your work is genuine and effective. However, it is not a conclusive factor, so if your work only lasts a short time, this fact by itself cannot exclude you from being a worker.[79]

Provided the other factors indicate that the work you do is genuine and effective, even very short periods of work can still be sufficient to mean that you have the status of being a worker while doing this work. In one case, the Court of Appeal found that someone was a worker during work which was, and was always known to be, of two weeks' duration.[80] Although a short duration of employment may still not be a barrier to being a worker, even if it was known to be such from the outset,[81] work that is curtailed prematurely may be more likely to be held to be genuine and effective.[82]

Level of earnings

If the level of earnings from your employment is very low, this may be a factor that indicates that your work is not genuine and effective. However, low earnings cannot, by themselves, prevent you from being found to be a worker. Even if the level of your earnings is so low that they do not meet your needs and you supplement them by claiming means-tested benefits, this does not prevent you from being a worker.[83]

Note: your earnings can include non-monetary payments in kind (see p131).

Irregular or erratic work

If you are in an employment relationship in which you are only occasionally called upon to work, this may indicate that the work is not genuine and effective. However, the decision maker must always look at all your circumstances. There is nothing inherent in an 'on-call' or 'zero-hours' contract that prevents you from being a worker; it depends on the work that you do.[84] Similarly, there is nothing inherent in doing temporary work for an agency that prevents you from being a worker. If the work is regular, rather than intermittent, and for a prolonged period or with a high likelihood of further work being obtained, you may be a worker.[85]

Other employment rights
Other contractual issues, such as the fact that you have a right to paid holidays or payment in the event of sickness, or that you are a member of a trade union recognised by your employer, are factors that may indicate that the employment is genuine and effective.[86]

Work not for an economic purpose or part of a wider relationship
Work may count as 'marginal' or 'ancillary' if it is done as part of some other relationship which is more significant, such as if a lodger performs a small task for her/his landlord as part of the terms of her/his tenancy.[87]

Work does not count as 'genuine and effective' if its main purpose is not for the economic benefit of the employer – eg, if the work is a means of rehabilitation to enable people with health problems to reintegrate into the labour market. Similarly, fostering children or caring for a person with disabilities have been held not to be economic activities and receipt of a fostering allowance or carer's allowance does not amount to remuneration in a commercial sense.[88]

Ceasing to be a worker

You only cease to be a worker when the employment relationship (see p131) ends. While you are still under a contract of employment, you continue to be a worker. Consequently, you are still a worker if you are a woman on maternity leave (including unpaid maternity leave), or if you are on holiday leave or sick leave (including if it is unpaid).[89]

If you have ceased to be a worker, you may retain your worker status in certain circumstances (see p135).

Benefit entitlement

If you are a worker, you have a right to reside for as long as you continue to be a worker. See p135 for the circumstances in which you can retain your worker status after you have ceased to be a worker.

If you have a right to reside as a worker, or as the family member (see p151) of a worker, this satisfies the right to reside requirement for all benefits that have such a requirement (see p107). You also come within one of the groups exempt from the habitual residence test for means-tested benefits (see p99). You therefore do not need to be 'habitually resident in fact' nor to have lived in the common travel area for the three months prior to your claim for income-based jobseeker's allowance.

Note: to claim benefit on the basis of being a worker, or the family member of a worker, you must provide evidence of this (see p319).

9. Retaining worker status

You can retain the status of 'worker', even though you are no longer working if:[90]
- you are involuntarily unemployed and registered as a jobseeker (see below);
- you are undertaking vocational training (see p137);
- you are temporarily unable to work because of an illness or accident (see p138);
- you are unable to work because you are in the late stages of pregnancy or have just given birth (see p138).[91]

Before arguing that you have retained your worker status, check whether you have ceased to be a worker (see p134). For example, if you are off work on unpaid sick leave but you can return to your job when you are better, you are still a worker, and so you do not need to argue that you have retained your worker status.

In addition to the four groups listed above, it may also be possible to argue that you can retain your worker status in other circumstances. The Court of Justice of the European Union has held that European Union (EU) Directive 2004/38 does not list exhaustively the circumstances in which a worker who is not longer in an employment relationship can continue to have the rights of a worker.[92]

Croatian, A2 and A8 nationals

If you are a Croatian national subject to worker authorisation (see p119), you cannot retain your worker status in the ways described in this section. Similarly if before 1 January 2014 you were an A2 national subject to worker authorisation (see p119), or before 1 May 2011 you were an A8 national who was required to register (see p119), you could not retain your worker status in the ways described in this section. However, if you were an A8 national required to register and you stopped working during the first month of employment, you could retain your worker status in the ways described in this section for the remainder of that month.[93]

Involuntarily unemployed and registered as a jobseeker

Note: the European Economic Area (EEA) Regulations impose additional requirements for you to be able to retain your worker status beyond those required under EU Directive 2004/38. Therefore, if you are refused benefit on the basis that you do not satisfy the additional requirements of the EEA Regulations, you should challenge the decision on the basis that these are not requirements under EU law.

Under **EU Directive 2004/38**, you retain your status as a worker if you:[94]
- are recorded as involuntarily unemployed (see p136); *and*
- have registered yourself as a jobseeker with the relevant employment office (see p136).

In addition to the above, under the **EEA Regulations** you must also:[95]
- provide evidence that you are seeking employment and have a genuine chance of being engaged; *and*
- either:
  - have entered the UK in order to seek employment; *or*
  - be present in the UK seeking employment immediately after having a right to reside as a worker (except if you retained your worker status on this basis), a student, or a self-employed or self-sufficient person.

Note: if your only right to reside is on the basis that you have retained your worker status while involuntarily unemployed and registered as a jobseeker, you are not exempt from the work-related requirements for universal credit, even if you would otherwise come within one of the exempt groups.[96] See CPAG's *Welfare Benefits and Tax Credits Handbook* for details of these. Arguably, this exclusion (and the similar one that applies to jobseekers) is unlawful and may be subject to legal challenge. See CPAG's online service and *Welfare Rights Bulletin* for updates.

Involuntary unemployment

You are 'involuntarily unemployed' if you are seeking and are available to take up a job. This depends on your remaining in the labour market. The circumstances in which you left your last job, including whether you left voluntarily, are relevant in determining whether you remained in the labour market. However, they are just one factor and your actions and circumstances, both at the time of leaving work and since then, should also be taken into account.[97]

Example
Karl is German. He was working at food processing factory for seven months. The shift times have changed recently, which means that when he is on late shifts he now has to catch three buses to get home from work. He finds this commute exhausting and asks his employer if he can just do the early shift when the bus connections are better. His employer says that all employees must work both early and late shifts, so Karl hands in his notice. Even while working his notice, Karl looks for other alternative work closer to home. He does not find any, but once his job ends he spends some time contacting potential employers. Karl counts as involuntarily unemployed, despite the fact that he left his previous employment voluntarily.

Registering as a jobseeker

You must register as a jobseeker with the 'relevant employment office'. In the UK, this is Jobcentre Plus.

The best way to register as a jobseeker is to claim jobseeker's allowance (JSA) and keep signing on, or, if you come under the universal credit (UC) system, to claim UC and accept the work search and work availability requirements, or if you are not entitled to benefit, claim national insurance credits under either system. You do not need to receive JSA or UC.

You may also satisfy the requirement to register as a jobseeker if you claim a different benefit, such as income support (IS) and you declare to the jobcentre in the course of making your claim that you are looking for work – eg, by stating this on your claim form or on your habitual residence questionnaire.[98] You should provide evidence of your work search. **Note:** this way of registering as a jobseeker is only relevant to retaining your worker status and claiming benefit on the basis of having a right to reside as a worker. It does not enable you to claim benefits, such as IS, if your only right to reside is as a jobseeker.

For how long can you retain worker status

The length of time you can retain your worker status while involuntarily unemployed depends on whether or not you have already been employed in the UK for more than a year.

Under EU Directive 2004/38, if you were employed for more than a year, you can retain your worker status on this basis indefinitely.[99]

In order to retain your worker status while involuntarily unemployed under the EEA Regulations, you must have been employed for at least a year and provide evidence that you are seeking employment and have a genuine chance of being engaged. In addition, once you have retained worker status on this basis for a continuous period of six months, this evidence must be 'compelling'.[100]

If you were employed for less than a year, the EEA Regulations limit the period during which you can retain your worker status while involuntarily unemployed to a maximum of six months.[101] The EU Directive allows you to retain worker status for no less than six months.[102]

Vocational training

You retain your worker status if you have either:
- started vocational training related to your previous employment; *or*
- started vocational training and you are 'involuntarily unemployed' (see p136). This applies if you have to retrain in order to find work that is reasonably equivalent to your former employment.[103]

In general, you should be able to argue that any training or study that can assist you in obtaining employment counts as vocational training. This can include a course leading to a qualification for a particular profession, trade or employment or a course that provides the necessary training or skills.[104] A course can be vocational for you even if it is not vocational for someone else – eg, a photography course if you want to work as a photographer.

Training related to previous employment

If you are not involuntarily unemployed, your vocational training must be related to your previous employment for you to retain your worker status. For this to apply, there must be a relationship between the purpose of the studies and your previous occupational activity.[105] The decision maker must take account of all your previous occupational activity in the UK, not just your most recent employment.[106] If you consider that the course you are pursuing is related to any of your previous employment in the UK, explain this relationship in detail to the decision maker and provide evidence.

Temporarily unable to work because of an illness or accident

You can retain your worker status if you are temporarily unable to work as a result of an illness or accident.[107]

As a result of an illness or accident

To retain your worker status on this basis, your inability to work must be as a result of an illness or accident. The test of your inability to work is unrelated to any test in the benefits system – eg, you do not need to show you have 'limited capability for work' or that you are 'incapable of work'. Instead, the test is whether you can be fairly described as unable to do the work you were doing or, if it follows a period in which you were seeking work, the sort of work you were seeking.[108] You do not need to have claimed a benefit payable on grounds of illness or disability, such as employment and support allowance (ESA), or any benefit at all to retain your right to reside as a worker on this basis. However, you must provide evidence of your inability to work, such as a medical certificate from your GP.

Your inability to work must be caused by an illness or accident which *you* have. You cannot retain your worker status if, for example, you are unable to work because you are looking after a child who is ill.[109]

Temporary inability to work

Your inability to work must be temporary. This simply means not permanent.[110] It is your inability to work that must be temporary not your health condition, so you can retain your worker status on the basis of a permanent illness or effect of an accident if this fluctuates and causes temporary periods when you are unable to work.[111]

You are considered temporarily unable to work if, taking into account all the available evidence, there is a realistic prospect of your being able to work again and re-enter the labour market.[112]

Pregnancy and childbirth

If you have established worker status and you are now not working because you are pregnant or have recently given birth, you may still count as a worker or you may be able to retain your worker status.

You do not cease to be a worker while you are still under a contract of employment (see p134). You are therefore still a worker while on maternity leave, whether or not it is paid. **Note:** this also applies to Croatian nationals from 1 July 2013, A2 nationals (including before 1 January 2014) and A8 nationals (including before 1 May 2011) who have established worker status.[113]

If you have ceased to be a worker, you may retain your worker status if you have a pregnancy-related illness that prevents you from working on the basis that you are 'temporarily unable to work due to illness or accident' (see p138).[114] You can also retain your worker status on this basis if you have another illness, unrelated to your pregnancy, that results in your being temporarily unable to work. **Note:** pregnancy itself does not mean you are 'temporarily unable to work due to illness or accident'.[115]

You also retain your worker status if you stop work because of the physical constraints of the late stages of pregnancy and the aftermath of childbirth, provided you start work again within a reasonable period after the birth of your child. In determining what is a 'reasonable period', the decision maker must take into account all your circumstances and UK law on the duration of maternity leave.[116]

If the basis on which you retain your worker status changes

You can retain your worker status if you are in one of the groups on p135 and continue to do so if you move into another category.[117]

Example
Nikolas is Greek. He worked for 13 months in a hotel. The hotel was losing money and Nikolas was made redundant. He claimed income-based JSA. Five months later, Nikolas became depressed and was unable to carry on looking for work, so he claimed income-related ESA. Nikolas was entitled to ESA because he had retained his right to reside as a worker – initially, as someone who was involuntarily unemployed and had registered as a jobseeker, and then because of his temporary inability to work as a result of his illness.

There is no limit to the number of times you can change the basis on which you retain worker status. However, if you lose worker status, you cannot regain it.

Gaps

If you cease to be a worker and do not retain your worker status, you cannot regain your worker status again. To be a worker in the future, you must acquire that status afresh. However, if there is just a gap between your having worker status and your being covered by one of the groups that can retain worker status on p135, you may not have lost the status of worker. Whether a gap prevents you from retaining worker status depends on all your circumstances, including the length of the gap.

A gap between your employment ending and your registering as a jobseeker is not necessarily 'fatal' and its significance depends on whether the length of the gap and the reasons for it indicate that you have left the labour market.[118] If the delay is for more than a few days, all your circumstances (including the reasons for the gap and what you did during that time) should be considered to establish whether there are reasonable grounds for the delay, so that it is not considered an 'undue delay'. The longer the gap, the more compelling the reasons must be.[119]

Arguably, you should be able to retain your worker status if there is a gap between your ceasing work and your being temporarily unable to work because of illness or an accident, since there is no requirement for the illness or accident to be the reason for your ceasing work. You do not need to have been receiving any benefit while you were temporarily unable to work, so if there was a delay before you claimed benefit, this does not necessarily mean there was a gap between your being a worker and retaining your worker status on the basis of your temporary inability to work.

***

Example

Rita is a Portuguese national who came to the UK a year ago and began full-time work in a restaurant. After eight months she was injured in a cycling accident and so left her job. She did not claim any benefits as she lived with her partner who supported her. She has just separated from her partner and has made a claim for income-based ESA, as she is still unable to work due to her injuries. Rita provides the DWP with a medical certificate that confirms her inability to work since the date of her accident. She satisfies the right to reside requirement for income-related ESA as she retains her worker status because she is temporarily unable to work as a result of her accident. There is no gap between her retaining her worker status on this basis and her last day of employment.

***

You can also retain your worker status during a short gap between two different bases on which you can retain worker status. Whether the gap is relevant also depends on your circumstances, the bases you are switching between, the length of the gap and your actions during it.

Benefit entitlement

If you retain your worker status, this satisfies the right to reside requirement for all benefits that have such a requirement (see p107).

If you are the family member (see p151) of someone who retains her/his worker status, your residence rights are the same as if you were the family member of someone who is a worker, and therefore you satisfy the right to reside requirement for all the benefits that have it.

If you retain worker status (or you are the family member of someone who does), you also come within one of the groups that are exempt from the habitual residence test for means-tested benefits (see p99). You therefore do not need to be 'habitually resident in fact' nor to have lived in the common travel area for the three months prior to your claim for income-based JSA.

Universal credit

If your only right to reside is as someone who has retained worker status, you are not exempt from any of the work-related requirements for UC, even if you would otherwise come within one of the exempt groups. See CPAG's *Welfare Benefits and Tax Credits Handbook* for details of these.[120]

It is arguable that this rule is unlawful. The UK is required to treat EEA workers the same as British workers and ensure that they have the same social and tax advantages.[121] This different treatment of EEA nationals who retain worker status as compared to British citizens appears to be a clear breach of these equal treatment obligations.

10. Self-employed people

If you are a European Economic Area (EEA) national undertaking self-employed activity in the UK, you may have a right to reside as a 'self-employed person' (see below). You may also have a right to reside if you are the family member (see p151) of a self-employed person. Once you have established your status as a self-employed person, it is important to be clear when you cease to self-employed (see p142). In limited circumstances, you can retain your status as a self-employed person even after you cease self-employed activity (see p144).

If you have a right to reside as a self-employed person, as someone who has retained status as a self-employed person, or as the family member of a self-employed person, your right to reside satisfies the right to reside requirement for all benefits.

Who has a right to reside as a self-employed person

If you are an EEA national and a 'self-employed person', you have a right to reside.[122]

The term 'self-employed person' is not defined in European Union (EU) legislation and the EEA Regulations simply cross-refer to EU law.[123] It should therefore be interpreted in accordance with EU law and the principles established through EU caselaw.

You count as a self-employed person if you:[124]

- provide services;
- receive remuneration in return for those services (see p131);

- do not perform your work under the direction of another person (see p131); *and*
- the work you do entails activities that are 'genuine and effective', rather than 'marginal and ancillary' (see p132).

The meanings of the above conditions are the same as they are for workers. The main difference between the definition of a self-employed person and a worker is that the work a self-employed person does is not done under the direction of another person.

Whether or not you satisfy these requirements always depends on all your circumstances. For example, in one case, the Upper Tribunal held that someone selling the *Big Issue* was self-employed, as the activities involved were 'genuine and effective'. Fostering children has been held not to be self-employment because it is not an economic activity and the fostering allowance received does not amount to remuneration in a commercial sense.[125]

From March 2014, decision makers are advised to follow a two-tier process when determining whether or not you are self-employed (or a worker).[126] Although this guidance is not legally binding, it is helpful to know its content either to offset potential problems before your claim is decided or to challenge an incorrect decision more effectively (see p130).

Croatian, A2 and A8 nationals

If you are a Croatian national, there are no additional restrictions that apply to you if you are a self-employed person. Your residence rights as a self-employed person are exactly the same as for nationals of any other EEA country.

Similarly, if you are an A2 or an A8 national, even during the seven years (up to 1 January 2014 for A2 and up to 1 May 2011 for A8) when other restrictions applied to you, no additional restrictions applied if you were a self-employed person. Your residence rights as a self-employed person were exactly the same as for nationals of any other EEA country.

For further details of the other restrictions that apply to Croatian nationals and that previously applied to A2 and A8 nationals, see p118.

What is self-employment

Whether you have become self-employed or you have ceased to be self-employed can be harder to determine than whether you have become a worker or you have ceased to be a worker. Unlike a person who is working, a person who is self-employed does not have a contract of employment that can be regarded as starting and ending on a particular date. It is possible that you may count as self-employed when you are setting yourself up to work as a self-employed person. Similarly, you may continue to count as self-employed, despite the fact that you have no work coming in for the time being.

Becoming self-employed

You count as self-employed when you establish yourself in order to pursue activity as a self-employed person.[127] You must have more than merely an intention to pursue self-employed activity and you must provide evidence of the steps you have taken or the ways in which you have set yourself up as self-employed.[128] Exactly what steps you must take depend on the nature of your self-employed activity and on your particular circumstances. It helps if you have registered with HM Revenue and Customs (HMRC) as self-employed. However, if you have not registered, this does not necessarily mean you are not self-employed.[129]

Relevant steps include:
- advertising your services;
- researching opportunities to find work;
- setting up your accounts;
- registering with HMRC as self-employed for purposes of national insurance contributions and taxes;
- obtaining equipment required for the work you intend to do;
- setting up a website for your business.

The above steps are only examples of the sort of steps that can contribute to your having established yourself in order to pursue self-employed activity. You do not have to take any of these particular steps, but the more you have done, the more likely it is that you will be accepted as having a right to reside as a self-employed person.

Ceasing to be self-employed

If you have stopped all self-employed activity and do not intend to resume that activity, it is clear that you have ceased to be a self-employed person. However, not all situations are as clear as this, and if you stop working, you do not necessarily cease to be self-employed. If you are in a temporary lull, you can continue to be self-employed. Whether you continue to be a self-employed person during a period when you have little or no work depends on your particular circumstances and the evidence you provide.[130]

Factors that are relevant in determining whether or not you have ceased self-employment include:[131]
- the amount of work you have coming in;
- steps you are taking to find new work;
- whether you are continuing to market your services;
- whether you are developing your business in new directions;
- whether you are maintaining your accounts;
- your motives and intentions.

Which factors are relevant depend on the nature of your self-employment and all your circumstances. However, the more factors that show you are still undertaking self-employed activity, the stronger your argument that you have not ceased to be a self-employed person. See below for the benefit implications of arguing that you have not ceased to be self-employed.

If you have ceased to be self-employed, you may be able to retain your self-employed status in certain circumstances (see below).

Pregnancy

If you are working on a self-employed basis and you become pregnant, you continue to count as self-employed during your maternity period when you do no self-employed work.[132]

Benefit entitlement

If you are a self-employed person, you have a right to reside for as long as you continue to be a self-employed person. See below for when you can retain your status as a self-employed person after you have ceased to be self-employed.

If you have a right to reside as a self-employed person, or as the family member (see p151) of a self-employed person, this satisfies the right to reside requirement for all benefits that have such a requirement (see p107). You also come within one of the groups exempt from the habitual residence test for means-tested benefits (see p99). You therefore do not need to be 'habitually resident in fact' nor to have lived in the common travel area for the three months prior to your claim for income-based jobseeker's allowance (JSA).

If you are not currently working, but you have not ceased to be self-employed (see p143), you may be entitled to income-based JSA based on your right to reside as a self-employed person, if you are seeking employment and satisfy the other conditions for JSA.[133] This is particularly significant if you are a Croatian national subject to restrictions and therefore with no right to reside as a jobseeker (see p119). It is also relevant if you want to claim housing benefit, as you will then have a non-excluded right to reside, as well as be in receipt of income-based JSA, and so will be in an exempt group (see p99).

See p319 for information on providing evidence of self-employment.

11. **Retaining self-employed status**

You can retain the status of a self-employed person, even though you are no longer working, if you are temporarily unable to work because of an illness or accident (see p145).[134] However, before arguing that you have retained your status as a self-employed person, check whether you have ceased to be a self-employed person, as you may still count as self-employed if you are just in a temporary period with little or no work (see p142).

If you have ceased your self-employment because of pregnancy or childbirth, see below.

You do not retain your self-employed status if you are involuntarily unemployed and registered as a jobseeker, and it is probable that you do not retain self-employed status if you are doing vocational training.[135]

Croatian, A2 and A8 nationals

If you are a Croatian national, you can retain your status as a self-employed person in exactly the same circumstances as nationals of any other European Economic Area (EEA) country. There are no additional restrictions that apply.

Similarly, if you are an A2 or an A8 national, even during the seven years (up to 1 January 2014 for A2 nationals and up to 1 May 2011 for A8 nationals) when other restrictions applied to you, no additional restrictions applied if you were retaining your status as a self-employed person. The circumstances in which you could retain your status as a self-employed person were exactly the same as for nationals of any other EEA country.

For further details of the other restrictions that apply to Croatian nationals, and that previously applied to A2 and A8 nationals, see p118.

Temporarily unable to work because of an illness or accident

If you have established self-employed status, you can retain this status if you have ceased to be self-employed and are temporarily unable to work because of an illness or accident.[136] The circumstances in which this applies are the same as those for retaining 'worker' status on this basis (see p138).

Pregnancy and childbirth

If you have established your status as a 'self-employed person' and you are now not working because of pregnancy or childbirth, you may still count as a 'self-employed person', or you may be able to retain your status as a 'self-employed person'.

You remain a self-employed person if you intend to resume your self-employment after your maternity period.[137]

If you have ceased to be a 'self-employed person' (see p143), you may retain this status if you have a pregnancy-related illness that means you are 'temporarily unable to work due to illness or accident' (see p145). You can also retain your worker status on this basis if you have another illness, unrelated to your pregnancy, that results in your being temporarily unable to work. **Note:** pregnancy in itself does not mean you are 'temporarily unable to work due to illness or accident.'[138]

You may also retain your status as a self-employed person if you cease self-employed activity because of the physical constraints of the late stages of pregnancy and the aftermath of childbirth, provided you start self-employed activity again within a reasonable period after the birth of your child. This argument depends on applying a judgment of the Court of Justice of the European Union, which concerned retaining worker status in these circumstances (see p138). You should argue that the same reasoning applies if you cease self-employment.[139] However, always check first whether you can argue that you have not ceased to be self-employed because you intend to resume self-employment after your maternity period.

Benefit entitlement

If you retain your status as a self-employed person, this satisfies the right to reside requirement for all benefits that have such a requirement.

If you are the family member (see p152) of someone who retains her/his status as a self-employed person, your residence rights are the same as if you were the family member of someone who is a self-employed person and, therefore, you satisfy the right to reside requirement for all benefits to which this applies.

If you retain your status as a self-employed person (or you are the family member of someone who does), you also come into one of the groups exempt from the habitual residence test for means-tested benefits (see p99). You therefore do not need to be 'habitually resident in fact' or have lived in the common travel area for the three months prior to your claim for income-based jobseeker's allowance.

12. **Self-sufficient people and students**

You have a right of residence as a self-sufficient person if you are a European Economic Area (EEA) national and you have:[140]
- sufficient resources (see p148) for yourself, and any family members who do not have an independent right to reside, not to become a burden on the social assistance system of the UK during your period of residence (see p148); *and*
- comprehensive sickness insurance cover in the UK (see p149).

You have a right to reside as a student if you are an EEA national and you:[141]
- are enrolled as a student in a government-accredited college;
- provide an assurance that you have sufficient resources (see p148) for yourself and your family members not to become a burden on the UK social assistance system during your period of residence (see p148);
- have comprehensive sickness insurance cover in the UK (see p149).

The requirements to have a right to reside as a student are very similar to the requirements to have a right to reside as a self-sufficient person. For this reason, those who have a right to reside as a student are referred to as 'self-sufficient students' in this section. The specific differences that apply to students are set out on p150.

You can also have a right to reside if you are the family member of a self-sufficient person, but note that the definition of 'family member' of a student is narrower than that which applies to family members of other EEA nationals (see p150).

Periods when you have a right to reside as a self-sufficient person or student, or family member of either, count as periods of 'residing legally' for the purposes of acquiring permanent residence after five years (see p170). This is the most common way in which periods of residence as a self-sufficient person or student can enable you to access benefits and tax credits, because during your period of self-sufficiency, your resources can exclude your from means-tested benefits. However, this is not always the case.

Croatian, A2 and A8 nationals

If you are a Croatian national, there are no additional restrictions that apply to you if you are a self-sufficient person or a self-sufficient student. Your residence rights as a self-sufficient person are the same as for nationals of any other EEA country.

Similarly, if you are an A2 or an A8 national, even during the seven years (up to 1 January 2014 for A2 nationals and up to 1 May 2011 for A8 nationals) when other restrictions applied to you, no additional restrictions applied if you were a self-sufficient person or a self-sufficient student. Your residence rights as a self-sufficient person or self-sufficient student were and are the same as for nationals of any other EEA country.

Note: certain students are exempt from the additional restrictions that apply to Croatian nationals and that applied to A2 nationals for the seven years up to 1 January 2014. You are/were not 'subject to worker authorisation' if you are a student with a registration certificate which states that you cannot work more than 20 hours a week (unless it is part of vocational training or during vacations) and you comply with this. If the certificate confirms that you can work during the four months after the course ends, the exemption continues for this period (see p120).

If this applies to you and you work no more than 20 hours a week, you may have a right to reside as a 'worker' (see p129). In addition, working while in the group counts as 'legally working' and, therefore, after a year of 'legally working' (see p121), you permanently cease to be 'subject to worker authorisation'.

If you are a Croatian national (or an A2 or an A8 national during the relevant periods of restrictions) employed in the UK but without a right to reside as a worker because your work is not in accordance with your worker authorisation document (or for an 'authorised employer' if you are an A8 national), you do not have a right to reside as a self-sufficient person on the basis of these earnings.[142]

For further details of other restrictions that apply to Croatian nationals and that previously applied to A2 and A8 nationals, see p118.

Sufficient resources

To know whether your resources are 'sufficient', it is necessary to appreciate what they must be sufficient for. The test is whether you have sufficient resources to avoid you, and any family members who do not have an independent right to reside, becoming a burden on the social assistance system of the UK (see below). The UK government cannot set a fixed amount to be regarded as 'sufficient resources' and must take account of your personal situation.[143]

You have 'sufficient resources' for the purpose of being either a self-sufficient person or a self-sufficient student if they:[144]

- exceed the maximum level you (and your family) can have to be eligible for 'social assistance' (see below); *or*
- do not exceed that level, but the decision maker considers that you still have sufficient resources, taking into account your (and your family's) personal situation.[145]

The 'maximum level' is the equivalent of your means-tested benefit applicable amount, including any premiums. Your resources also include your accommodation, so if your resources are more than your applicable amount plus your rent, they should be considered to be sufficient. You may also be self-sufficient if your resources are more than your applicable amount and you are provided with free and stable accommodation by friends or family.[146]

You do not need to own the resources that make you self-sufficient. It is enough if you have access to them – eg, if you are supported by someone else.[147]

The source of the resources does not matter.[148] However, you cannot rely on your earnings from employment carried out in the UK to give you self-sufficient status.[149] In most circumstances, this does not matter as your employment means you are a 'worker', but it is relevant if, for example, you do not (or did not) have worker status because you do not satisfy the additional conditions imposed on you as a Croatian, A2 or A8 national (see p147).

Not a burden on the social assistance system

You count as self-sufficient if you have sufficient resources 'not to become a burden on the social assistance system of the UK during your period of residence'.

'Burden' has been held to be an 'unreasonable burden'.[150]

The 'social assistance system of the UK' includes all means-tested benefits.[151] In its guidance, the DWP does not include child tax credit, but does list all the means-tested benefits.[152]

You cannot automatically be regarded as not self-sufficient just because you make a claim for a means-tested benefit. While such a claim could indicate that you do not have sufficient resources to avoid becoming an unreasonable burden on the social assistance system of the UK, the decision maker must carry out an assessment of the specific burden that granting a benefit would make on the system as a whole. This assessment must take all your circumstances into account, including the likely duration of your claim.[153] The assessment is done at the point you make your claim for benefit on the basis of your right to reside as a self-sufficient person so, for example, you do not need to have had sufficient resources at the start of your period of residence. However, from the point the assessment is carried out, you must show sufficient resources for your intended period of residence, including for five years if permanent residence is sought.[154]

Comprehensive sickness insurance

To have a right of residence as a self-sufficient person, in addition to having sufficient resources (see p148), you must also have comprehensive sickness insurance cover in the UK.

This requirement is satisfied if you have private health insurance.[155]

It is also satisfied if the UK can be reimbursed by another EEA state for any NHS costs you incur while in the UK.[156] This usually applies if you are covered by the European Union co-ordination rules (see p242) and another state continues to be your 'competent state' (see p248) – eg, if you are:

- resident in the UK but you are working or self-employed in another EEA member state;
- resident in the UK, you receive a pension from another EEA member state, you do not also receive a pension from the UK, and you are not working or self-employed in the UK (see p250);
- living temporarily in the UK (eg, you are a student on a course in the UK) and are entitled to health treatment in another EEA state because you are insured there. In this situation, you can get a European Health Insurance card.

If none of the above apply, seek specialist up-to-date advice, as this is an area in which other arguments are currently being considered by the courts. Existing caselaw has held that access to free NHS treatment where the UK bears this cost does not satisfy the requirement to have comprehensive sickness insurance cover in the UK.[157] However, there are likely to be other cases that consider this argument. Depending on your circumstances, you may also be able to argue that it is disproportionate to insist on this requirement being met if it is the only barrier to your having a right to reside as a self-sufficient person.[158]

Self-sufficient students

You have a right to reside as a student if you are an EEA national and you:[159]

- are enrolled as a student in a government-accredited establishment for the principal purpose of following a course of study (including vocational training); *and*
- provide an assurance that you have sufficient resources for yourself, and your family members (see below) who do not have an independent right of residence, not to become a burden on the UK social assistance system during your period of residence (see below); *and*
- have comprehensive sickness insurance (see p149).

The conditions for having a right of residence as a student are therefore very similar to the conditions for having a right of residence as a self-sufficient person. The only differences are as follows.

- To have the right to reside as a student, you must be enrolled on a course of study.
- The requirement to have sufficient resources is met by providing an assurance, either by means of a declaration or some other equivalent means that you choose, that you have 'sufficient resources'.
- The definition of family member is different (see below).

The assessment of what counts as 'sufficient resources' is the same as for a self-sufficient person (see p148). This requirement is satisfied by providing an assurance of these resources, but it is not clear what practical difference this makes. Although you may be more easily accepted as having a right to reside if you provide an assurance of your resources at the start of your studies, this does not prevent you from losing your right of residence if your circumstances change. However, such a loss is never automatic and always depends on your circumstances.[160] Furthermore, if the need for you to claim benefits is only likely to be temporary, depending on the length of your course, it may be easier to argue that any benefit claim does not amount to an unreasonable burden on the social assistance system of the UK (see p148).

Family members

Family member of a student

You are the **'family member'** of a student (once s/he has been in the UK for three months) if you are:[161]

– her/his spouse or civil partner; *or*

– her/his dependent child (regardless of your age); *or*

– the dependent child (regardless of your age) of the student's spouse or civil partner.

The definition of family member is narrower than that which generally applies (see p152) and only applies if the student does not have another right to reside that can confer a right of residence on you.

If you are the parent of a student who has been in the UK for at least three months, or a parent of her/his spouse or civil partner, you may be able to be treated as a family member on the basis of being an extended family member if you have the relevant documentation (see p154).[162]

This means that when assessing whether you have sufficient resources, you do not need to take account of anyone who does not come within this narrower definition of family member after you have lived in the UK for three months – eg, your resources do not need to be sufficient for your non-dependent children under 21 or dependent parent living in the UK.

Benefit entitlement

If you have a right to reside as a self-sufficient person, the family member (see below) of a self-sufficient person, or as a student or family member of a student (see p150), this satisfies the right to reside requirement for all benefits that have such a requirement (see p107).

Note: it cannot automatically be decided that you are not self-sufficient just because you have claimed a means-tested benefit (see p148).

However, the most common way in which periods of residence as a self-sufficient person or student (or family member of a self-sufficient person or student) can assist you to access benefits and tax credits that require a right to reside is when such periods are used towards the five years of residence required for permanent residency (see p170). This is because during your period of self-sufficiency, your resources can exclude you from means-tested benefits.

13. **Family members of European Economic Area nationals**

You have a right to reside if you are a 'family member' (see p152) of a European Economic Area (EEA) national who has:[163]
- a right to reside as a 'qualified person' – ie, a:[164]
  - jobseeker (see p123);
  - worker (see p129), including if s/he has retained this status (see p135);
  - self-employed person (see p141), including if s/he has retained this status (see p144);
  - self-sufficient person, including a self-sufficient student (see p146); *or*
- a permanent right of residence (see p170); *or*
- an initial right to reside (see p122).

You have this right to reside as a family member, whether or not you are an EEA national yourself.

You have a right to reside for as long as the EEA national has one of the residence rights listed above, and for as long as you remain her/his family member. In general, if s/he ceases to have a relevant right to reside or if you cease to be her/his family member, your right to reside ends. However, there are some limited circumstances in which you can continue to have residence rights as a former family member of an EEA national with a right to reside (see p157).

British citizens only give residence rights to their family members in limited circumstances (see p155).

The type of right to reside you have depends on the type of right to reside your family member has. For more information and the consequences of this for entitlement to benefits and tax credits with a right to reside requirement, see p160.

Croatian, A2 and A8 nationals

If you are a Croatian national and a family member of an EEA national with one of the residence rights listed on p151, you have a right to reside in the same way as any other national. In addition, this may mean that you come into one of the groups not subject to worker authorisation and that you do not have additional restrictions on your residence rights (see p120).

Similarly, if you are an A2 or an A8 national, during the seven years (up to 1 January 2014 for A2 nationals and up to 1 May 2011 for A8 nationals) no additional restrictions applied to you if you were the family member of an EEA national with a relevant right to reside. Being such a family member could have brought you into a group that was exempt from the additional restrictions. See p120 for A2 nationals and p121 for A8 nationals.

For further details of the other restrictions that apply to Croatian nationals and that previously applied to A2 and A8 nationals, see p118.

Who is a family member

To have a right to reside as a family member of an EEA national who has a relevant right to reside (see p151), you must come within the definition of 'family member'.

• •

Family member
You are a 'family member' of the EEA national if you are her/his:[165]
– spouse or civil partner;
– child, grandchild or great-grandchild or her/his spouse/civil partner and you are under 21;

– child, grandchild or great-grandchild or her/his spouse/civil partner, and you are dependent on her/him;
– parent, grandparent or great-grandparent or her/his spouse/civil partner, and you are dependent on her/him.

If you are not covered by the above definition of 'family member, you can be treated as a family member and have residence rights on that basis if:

- you are an 'extended family member' (see p154); *and*
- you have been issued with an EEA family permit, a registration certificate or a residence card (see p314). If you do not have this documentation, or it is no longer valid, you are not treated as a family member.[166]

Note: a narrower definition applies to family members of students who have been in the UK for at least three months (see p150).

Spouses and civil partners

Only spouses and civil partners are family members. If you are not married to, or in a civil partnership with, your partner, see p154.

You remain a spouse or civil partner if you have separated, including while you are in the process of getting divorced or dissolving a civil partnership. It is only once you are legally divorced (in the UK when the *decree nisi* is given) or the civil partnership has been legally terminated that you cease to count as the spouse or civil partner of the other person.[167]

Even when your marriage or civil partnership has been terminated (or if your spouse/civil partner dies or leaves the UK), you may still continue to have a right to reside (see p157).

Aged under 21

You count as a family member of a person if you are her/his child (or grandchild or great-grandchild), or a child of her/his spouse/civil partner, and you are aged under 21.

You do not need to show that you are dependent on the person in order to count as her/his family member. Therefore, you do not need to live with her/him or show you are receiving support from her/him, and it is irrelevant whether you do or not.[168]

Example
Greta is a Lithuanian national aged 18. She is eight months pregnant and lives in rented accommodation. She has claimed income support (IS) and housing benefit (HB). Her father is also Lithuanian and is working full time in the UK. Greta is estranged from her

father since she got pregnant. Despite this, she is still defined as his family member as she is his daughter and is under 21. Greta therefore has a right to reside as the family member of a worker and this enables her to be entitled to IS and HB.

For more information on providing evidence of your age, see p318.

Dependent

To count as a family member of someone, you may need to be dependent on that person – eg, if you are her/his parent or grandparent.

'Dependence' is not defined in the legislation, but caselaw has established a number of principles.[169]

There are only three things you must show in order to establish that you are dependent on a person.

- You receive support from her/him.
- The support you receive is 'material'. If the person is providing you with financial help, paying your bills, buying you food or providing your meals, providing you with accommodation or is providing you with care because you are ill or disabled, this should all count as material support.
- The support contributes to the 'basic necessities of life'.

It is irrelevant if there are alternative sources of support, including potential employment, available to you, either in your country of origin or in the UK.[170]

If you only became dependent on the EEA national in the UK, this does not prevent you from being classed as a family member. It is sufficient that you are dependent at the point when your claim for benefit is decided.[171] **Note:** this does not apply if you are an extended family member on the basis of dependency (see below). In this case, you must already have been dependent in the country from which you have come.[172]

If the decision maker decides that you cannot pass the right to reside test on the basis that you are the dependant of an EEA national because the benefit award would mean that you were no longer dependent on her/him, this is legally wrong. Your dependency should be considered independently of any benefit you claim.[173]

Extended family members

If you do not come within the definition of 'family member' on p152, but you have a relative in the UK who is an EEA national with a relevant right to reside (see p151), you can be treated as a family member, and therefore have residence rights on that basis, if you:

- are an 'extended family member' (see p155); *and*

- have been issued with an EEA family permit, a registration certificate or a residence card (see p314).[174] If you do not have this documentation, or it is no longer valid, you are not treated as a family member.[175]

Extended family member

You are an **'extended family member'** of an EEA national if you are her/his:[176]

– partner and you are in a durable relationship with her/him; *or*

– relative and would satisfy the requirements of the Immigration Rules for indefinite leave as her/his dependent relative if s/he were present and settled in the UK; *or*

– relative or her/his spouse/civil partner and:

  – you have serious health problems that require her/his care; *or*

  – you previously lived with, or were dependent on, the EEA national in a country other than the UK and either you are accompanying her/him to the UK, wish to join her/him in the UK, or you have joined her/him in the UK, and you continue to be dependent on her/him or to be a member of her/his household.

The term 'dependent' is not defined in legislation and its meaning is the same as that for a family member (see p154). However, if you are relying on being dependent on your relative to come within the definition of an 'extended family member', you must have previously been dependent on her/him in the country from which you have come.[177]

If you are the extended family member of a self-sufficient student (see p150), there are further limitations on when you can be treated as a family member depending on the basis on which the EEA family permit, a registration certificate or a residence card was issued to you.[178] **Note:** European Union (EU) Directive 2004/38 treats a student's parent (or her/his spouse or civil partner) who has been in the UK for at least three months as an 'extended family member'.[179]

Family members of a British citizen

British citizens do not automatically give residence rights to their family members. This is because most British citizens living in Britain do not generally have a right of residence under EU law, so they cannot confer an EU right of residence on their family members. EU Directive 2004/38 applies to people who 'move to or reside in' an EEA country 'other than that of which they are a national'.[180] The UK rules achieve a similar effect by setting out the residence rights of EEA nationals and their family members, but defining an EEA national 'as a national of an EEA state who is not also a British citizen'.[181]

However, there are circumstances in which a British citizen can have a right of residence under EU law. If you are that person's family member, s/he can then confer a right of residence on you.

The main ways in which s/he can do this are if:

- the British citizen has lived with a right to reside (eg, as a worker) in another EEA state. On her/his return to the UK, s/he has the same rights as other EEA nationals and can confer rights on you (see below);
- the British citizen is self-employed and carries out some of her/his business activities in another EEA state (see p157);
- s/he is a dual British national in limited circumstances (see p157).

In addition, you may have a right to reside in the following circumstances.
- If you are the primary carer of a British citizen who would not be able to continue live anywhere in the EEA if you were required to leave the UK, you may have a 'derivative right to reside' on this basis (see p167). **Note:** having a 'derivative right to reside' is different from having a right to reside as a family member (see p162).
- If you are a non-EEA national joining your family member who is British, and you have been given leave by UK Visas and Immigration (eg, as a spouse or civil partner), you have a right to reside during that period of leave. However, this is under domestic immigration law and not under EU law. See Part 2 for more information on immigration law. If your leave is subject to a condition that you do not have recourse to public funds, you are defined as a 'person subject to immigration control' (see p57) and excluded from all the benefits listed on p63, unless you come within an exempt group (see p64).

The British citizen has lived in another state

If you are a family member (see p152) of a British citizen, you have a right to reside on the basis of EU law as her/his family member if s/he has lived with a right to reside (eg, as a worker) in another EEA state and has now returned to the UK.[182]

The EEA Regulations contain these rights, but interpret them more restrictively than the European Court of Justice (ECJ) has done.[183] If your benefit is refused because the decision maker follows the more restrictive interpretation of the EEA Regulations, you should challenge the decision if the more generous interpretation by the ECJ would give you a right to reside.
- If you are the spouse or civil partner of a British citizen, the EEA Regulations state that you must have lived together in the other EEA state. This conflicts with an ECJ decision, which held that you can have residence rights as a family member if you became a family member either before or after entering the member state.[184]
- The EEA Regulations only treat a British national as an EEA national if s/he was a worker or self-employed person in the other EEA state.[185] Arguably, a British citizen should also be treated as an EEA national if s/he has been in another EEA state with another right to reside – eg, as a self-sufficient person.
- The EEA Regulations require the British citizen to have transferred her/his 'centre of life' to the other EEA state. The factors relevant to whether her/his

centre of life has been transferred include the period of residence in the other EEA state as a worker or self-employed person, the location of her/his principle residence and degree of integration in that country.[186] The condition to have transferred your centre of life is not required under the EEA Regulations if, on 1 January 2014, you had (and continue to have) a permanent right to reside or a residence document confirming your right to reside (or an outstanding application for such a document, or you were appealing against its refusal).[187] This requirement for the British citizen to have transferred her/his centre of life is not a condition under EU law.

- The EEA Regulations only give you a right to reside as a family member of a British citizen who has returned to the UK if s/he currently has a right to reside under these regulations. However, the ECJ has decided that it was not necessary for someone who had been a worker in another EEA state and then returned to her/his own state to carry out an economic activity in order for her/his family member to have a right of residence.[188]

The British citizen lives in UK and carries out activities in another state

If you are the family member (see p152) of a British citizen who is self-employed in the UK and whose business involves some activities in another EEA state, you may have a right of residence, depending on your circumstances. This right is not covered in the EEA Regulations, but is confirmed by the ECJ in a case concerning the spouse, who was a non-EEA national, of a British citizen who provided services to recipients in other member states from a business established in the UK.[189]

The British citizen also has citizenship of another state

A dual British/other EEA national does not have rights under EU law if s/he has lived all her/his life in the UK. She cannot therefore confer any rights on you as her/his family member.[190] However, if s/he has lived with a right of residence (eg, as a 'worker') in another member state (other than the one of which s/he is a national), when s/he returns to the UK s/he may have residence rights and be able to confer these on you in the same way as described on p156.

Until 16 October 2012, if you were the family member of someone who had both British and another EEA nationality, you had the same rights as family members of other EEA nationals.[191] If you had already acquired such a right before this date, it continues in limited circumstances.[192] See p1604 of the 2013/14 edition of the *Welfare Benefits and Tax Credits Handbook* for details.

Former family members

In general, if you are the family member of an EEA national who confers a right to reside on you, your right to reside ceases if s/he:

- stops being your 'family member' (see p152); *or*
- ceases to have a relevant right to reside.

However, there are some exceptions which mean that you can retain your right to reside in certain circumstances. Whether or not these apply to you depends on what right to reside your family member has. **Note:** several of these circumstances may mean that you have other residence rights that could be easier to prove or may apply instead (see p160).

When you may retain your right to reside

You may retain your right to reside if the EEA national who confers this right on you dies or leaves the UK, or if your marriage or civil partnership to her/him is terminated. These rights are in EU Directive 2004/38, but they are not exactly reproduced in the EEA Regulations (see below). The decision maker is more likely to accept that you retain your right to reside if you satisfy the requirements of the EEA Regulations, so you should check these first. If you cannot satisfy these, check whether you satisfy the requirements of the EU Directive (see p159). If you only have a right to reside under the Directive and are refused benefit, you should challenge this decision and seek specialist advice.

There are several differences in the specific wording of the provisions in the EEA Regulations and the EU Directive that could affect you. The two most significant differences are the following.

- Under the EEA Regulations, you can count periods of residence spent as a former family member who retains her/his right of residence towards the five years of residence required to aquire permanent residence (see p170).
- Under the EU Directive, if you are an EEA national, you retain your right to reside if your relevant family member dies or leaves the UK, or if your marriage or civil partnership to her/him is terminated, *without* needing to satisfy any other conditions. These rights are not reproduced in the EEA Regulations.

European Economic Area Regulations

You retain your right to reside under the EEA Regulations if you are a family member of a 'qualified person' (see p117) or a person with a permanent right to reside (see p170) and:[193]

- that person dies and you are:
  - not an EEA national, but if you were, you would be a worker, or a self-employed or self-sufficient person (or you are the family member of such a non-EEA national) and you resided in the UK with a right to reside under the EEA Regulations for at least a year immediately before s/he died; *or*
  - the child or grandchild of the qualified person (or her/his spouse or civil partner) and you were in education immediately before the death and you remain in education; *or*
  - a parent with custody of a child in the previous bullet point; *or*
- that person leaves the UK and you are:

- the child or grandchild of the qualified person (or her/his spouse or civil partner) and you were in education immediately before s/he left the UK and you remain in education; *or*
- a parent with custody of a child in the previous bullet point; *or*
- your marriage or civil partnership to that person is terminated, and you are not an EEA national, but if you were, you would be a worker or a self-employed or self-sufficient person (or you are the family member of such a non-EEA national), and you were residing in the UK with a right to reside under the EEA Regulations at the date of the termination and:
  - the marriage/civil partnership had, prior to the termination, lasted for at least three years with you both residing in the UK for at least one of those years; *or*
  - you have custody of the qualified person's child; *or*
  - you have a right of access to the qualified person's child which a court has said must take place in the UK; *or*
  - your continued right of residence in the UK is warranted by particularly difficult circumstances, such as your (or another family member's) being subject to domestic violence during the period of the marriage/civil partnership.

You have a right to reside on this basis for as long as the conditions apply to you,[194] until you can acquire a permanent right of residence (see p170).[195]

European Union Directive 2004/38

The rules under the EU Directive treat you differently depending on whether you are an EEA national (see p116) or not.

It is arguable that you retain your right to reside under EU Directive 2004/38 if you are a family member of an EEA national who has a right to reside as a worker, self-employed or self-sufficient person, or as a self-sufficient student and:

- the EEA national dies and you:[196]
  - are an EEA national; *or*
  - have lived in the UK as her/his family member for at least a year before her/his death and you are a non-EU national; *or*
- the EEA national leaves the UK and you are:[197]
  - an EEA national; *or*
  - the child, grandchild of great-grandchild of the EEA national and in education; *or*
  - the parent with custody of a child in education; *or*
- your marriage or civil partnership to the EEA national is terminated and:[198]
  - you are an EEA national; *or*
  - the marriage/civil partnership had, prior to the termination, lasted for at least three years with you both residing in the UK for at least one of those years; *or*

- you have custody of the EEA national's child; *or*
- you have a right of access to the EEA national's child, which a court has said must take place in the UK; *or*
- your continued right of residence in the UK is warranted by particularly difficult circumstances, such as your being subject to domestic violence during the period of the marriage/civil partnership.

You can only count periods when you have retained your right to reside as a former family member towards the five years required to acquire permanent residence if you are a non-EEA national and either:

- the EEA national who you were the family member of dies and you had lived in the UK as her/his family member for at least a year before the death; *or*
- your marriage or civil partnership is terminated and any of the circumstances listed under that heading on p159 apply.

In all other cases, periods when you have retained your right to reside as a former family member are not generally sufficient to enable you to acquire a permanent right of residence after five years, because you are also required to show that you are a worker, or a self-employed or a self-sufficient person, or you are the family member of such a person.[199]

Other residence rights

If you are covered by any of the circumstances that enable you to retain your right to reside as a family member, under either the EEA Regulations or the EU Directive, or if your circumstances are similar but you do not fit within these rules, check whether similar rights could apply to you. The main ones that might apply are the following.

- If you have had a right to reside in the UK as the family member of an EEA national who has conferred a right to reside on you for five years, you may have a permanent right to reside (see p170).
- If you were the family member of an EEA national who has died and s/he was a worker or a self-employed person, you may have a permanent right to reside (see p174).
- If you are the child of a worker and you are in education, or you are the primary carer of such a child, you may have a 'derivative right to reside' (see p162). **Note:** whereas periods during which you had a derivative right to reside do *not* count towards the five years needed to acquire permanent residence, time spent as a former family member who has retained her/his right to reside under the EEA Regulations *do* count towards the five years (see p170).

Benefit entitlement

Whether your right to reside as the family member of an EEA national satisfies the right to reside requirement depends on:

- the type of right to reside the EEA national has; *and*
- the benefit you want to claim.

Your right to reside is the equivalent of the EEA national's right to reside if s/he has:
- a right to reside as a 'qualified person' – ie, a:[200]
  - jobseeker (see p123);
  - worker (see p129), including if s/he has retained this status (see p135);
  - self-employed person (see p141), including if s/he has retained this status (see p144);
  - self-sufficient person, including a self-sufficient student (see p146);
- an initial right to reside (see p122).

This means the following.
- If you are the family member of a worker or self-employed person, you have the same residence rights as if you were a worker or a self-employed person yourself. Not only does this satisfy the right to reside requirement for all benefits that have such a requirement (see p107), but you also come within one of the groups exempt from the habitual residence test for means-tested benefits (see p99). You therefore do not need to be 'habitually resident in fact' nor have lived in the common travel area for the three months prior to your claim for income-based jobseeker's allowance (JSA).
- If you are the family member of a self-sufficient person or self-sufficient student, you have the same residence rights as if you were a self-sufficient person or student. This satisfies the right to reside requirement for all benefits that have such a requirement (see p107).
- If your only right to reside is as the family member of an EEA national who has a right to reside as a jobseeker, you have an equivalent right to reside. If this is your only right to reside, this does not enable you to satisfy the right to reside requirement for IS, income-related employment and support allowance (ESA), pension credit (PC) and HB (see p183).
- If you are the family member of an EEA national who has an initial right of residence for three months, you have an equivalent right to reside. If this is your only right to reside, this does not enable you to satisfy the right to reside requirement for IS, income-based JSA, income-related ESA, PC, HB and universal credit (see p183).

If you are the family member of an EEA national who has a permanent right of residence, your right to reside satisfies the right to reside requirement for all benefits that have such a requirement (see p107). However, you only have a permanent right to reside yourself, and are exempt from the habitual residence test (see p99), if you are the family member of an EEA national who acquired this permanent residency in less than five years (see p174).

If you have a right to reside as a former family member (see p157), your right to reside satisfies the right to reside requirement for all benefits that have such a requirement (see p107).

Note: to claim benefit on the basis of being a family member, you must provide evidence of this (see p315).

14. **Derivative residence rights**

You may be able to derive a right to reside from someone with a right to reside without being her/his family member. These rights are not listed in the European Union (EU) Directive 2004/38, but are based on other provisions of EU law as interpreted by caselaw. The European Economic Area (EEA) Regulations list these rights as 'derivative rights of residence'. However, the EEA Regulations interpret these rights more narrowly in some respects and impose some additional conditions. If these mean you do not have a right to reside, you can rely on the rights confirmed by the caselaw.

Note:
- You cannot count periods when you have a derivative right to reside towards the five years of residence required for permanent residency (see p170).
- Some of the circumstances below are similar to those that enable you to retain a right to reside if you are a former family member of an EEA national who conferred a right to reside on you and who has now died or left the UK, or your marriage or civil partnership to her/him has been terminated (see p157). Check whether these circumstances apply because, in some cases, you can count periods with a right to reside as a former family member towards the five years required for permanent residence.
- If you do not fit into any of the groups below, but your circumstances are similar, it may be arguable that you have a right to reside (see p168).

Who has a derivative right to reside

You have a derivative right to reside if you are not an 'exempt person' (see below) and you are:[201]
- the child of an EEA national who was a 'worker' in the UK (see p129) while you were living in the UK, and you are currently in education (see p164);[202] or
- the primary carer of a child in the above bullet point and the child would be unable to continue her/his education if you were required to leave (see p165);[203] or
- the primary carer of a self-sufficient child who is an EEA national, who would be unable to remain here if you were required to leave (see p166);[204] or
- a dependent child of a primary carer in either the second or third bullet points above, and s/he would be prevented from residing in the UK if you were

required to leave and you do not have leave to enter or remain in the UK (see p167); *or*

- the primary carer of a British citizen residing in the UK who would be unable to reside in the UK or another EEA state if you were required to leave (see p167).[205] **Note:** this right to reside does not satisfy the right to reside requirement for any of the benefits.

Who is exempt

The EEA Regulations exclude you from having a derivative right to reside if you are an 'exempt person'.[206] You are an 'exempt person' if you have a right to reside:[207]

- under any other provision of the EEA Regulations;
- as a British citizen or as a Commonwealth citizen with a right of abode;
- as a person with indefinite leave; *or*
- under provisions that exempt certain people from the requirement to have leave – eg, specified aircrew and diplomats.

If you are refused benefit on the basis that you do not have a derivative right to reside because you are an exempt person, but your other right to reside (eg, as a jobseeker) does not enable you to claim benefit, you should challenge the decision on the basis that you are not excluded under EU law, and refer to the EU caselaw in which your right to reside is confirmed.

Croatian, A2 and A8 nationals

The rules about derivative residence rights apply to Croatian nationals in exactly the same way as for other EEA nationals, and applied in exactly the same way to A2 or A8 nationals during the seven years (up to 1 January 2014 for A2 nationals and up to 1 May 2011 for A8 nationals) when other restrictions applied. However, if you are deriving your right to reside from being a worker's child in education, the primary carer of such as child, or a child of such a primary carer, the restrictions that do (or did) apply to workers could affect you, because they affect who can have 'worker' status.

If a Croatian national is subject to restrictions (see p119), the work s/he does only gives her/him worker status if it is done in accordance with her/his worker authorisation document. Similarly, if an A2 national subject to restrictions worked between 1 January 2007 and 31 December 2013, that work only gave her/him worker status if it was done in accordance with her/his 'worker authorisation document'. If you are the child of a Croatian or A2 national and you are in education, or you are the primary carer of such a child, check that the work done by the parent gave her/him worker status to establish whether you may have a derivative right to reside.

The situation for A8 nationals is slightly different. If an A8 national was subject to restrictions (see p119), the work that s/he did between 1 May 2004 and 30 April

2011 only gave her/him worker status if it was done for an 'authorised employer' (see p119). The first month of any employment counted as working for an authorised employer and, therefore, the A8 national would (provided s/he satisfied the requirements of being a worker, including that the work was accepted as 'genuine and effective' – see p129) have had worker status during that first month, even if s/he never registered her/his work. Consequently, if a child was in the UK while her/his parent did her/his first month of work between 1 May 2004 and 30 April 2011, s/he is a child of a worker based on that first month of work. If s/he is now in education in the UK, s/he has a derivative right to reside. If you are that child's primary carer, you also have a derivative right to reside.[208]

For further details of other restrictions that apply to Croatian nationals and that previously applied to A2 and A8 nationals, see p118.

Worker's child in education

A child (see below) has a right to reside if:
- s/he was living in the UK at a time when one of her/his parents had a right to reside in the UK as a worker (see p165); *and*
- s/he is now in education (see below).

The purpose of this right of residence is to enable a child to take up her/his right to be educated in the member state where her/his parent is employed if s/he is also living in that state.[209] For this right to education to be effective, the child must have a right of residence.[210] The right continues for as long as s/he is a child in education.

The nationality of the child does not affect this right of residence. However, the child's parent who had the right to reside as a worker must be an EEA national.

Who is a 'child in education'

To have a derivative right to reside as the 'child' of a worker in education, the child must generally need to be aged from around five and be under 18.

The lower age is determined by the need to be 'in education'. This excludes nursery education.[211] A child's rights begin when s/he enters compulsory education around the age of five and excludes preschool.[212] They may begin if s/he has started school in reception class but has not yet turned five.[213] Although there is no reception class in Scotland, it may be arguable that a child can be 'in education' when s/he is approaching age five.

Residence rights may apply beyond the age of 18 if someone is still in education, as the principle of equal treatment requires someone to be able to continue her/his studies in order to complete her/his education successfully.[214]

The child must have been in the UK while one of her/his parents was employed as a worker in the UK. The parent does not need to have been a worker when s/he entered education or at any time since then.[215]

Under the EEA Regulations, the child must have been in education at a time when her/his parent was in the UK.[216] It is arguable that this requirement is not consistent with EU law, as the European Court of Justice (ECJ) has consistently held that all that is required when a child starts education is for her/him to have lived in the member state during a period when one of her/his parents was exercising rights as migrant worker in that member state.[217]

Who is a 'worker'

The EEA Regulations state that, for this purpose, 'worker' does not include a jobseeker or someone who retains her/his worker status (see p135). It may be arguable that the latter exclusion is wrong. Caselaw consistently confirms that a child has a right to reside if s/he is now in education and was in the member state during a time when one of her/his parents was exercising rights of residence in that state as a 'worker' or a 'migrant worker'.[218] It appears from the wording of EU Directive 2004/38 that a person who retains her/his status as a worker does reside in a country as a 'migrant worker', as s/he has equivalent rights to 'workers', provided s/he continues to satisfy the conditions of retaining worker status. Furthermore, the family members of someone who has retained her/his status as a worker have equivalent rights of residence to family members of workers.

Absence of the child from the UK

A child may lose her/his right to reside as a worker's child in education if s/he leaves the UK but then returns. However, this depends on all the circumstances. The DWP takes the view that if a child leaves the UK, other than for a temporary reason, s/he may lose her/his right to education (and her/his associated right to reside) when s/he returns. DWP guidance suggests that, while a substantial period of habitual residence in another EEA state means that the right to education, and hence to reside, is lost, 'an absence that can properly be regarded as temporary will not have that effect'.[219] However, it may be arguable that what matters is whether the child's studies undertaken on her/his return are a continuation of her/his earlier education. The ECJ held that a worker's child in education continued to have his rights, despite an absence in which the child went back to his state of origin, because he returned to continue his studies, which he could not pursue in his own state.[220]

Primary carer of a worker's child in education

You have a derivative right to reside under the EEA Regulations if you:[221]
- are the 'primary carer' (see p166) of a child of a worker who is in education; *and*
- the child would be unable to continue to be educated in the UK if you were required to leave.

The basis of this right of residence builds on the residence rights of the child, which are necessary in order to be educated in the state where her/his parent is employed (see p164).[222] It is assumed that the child needs an adult to look after her/him and, consequently, her/his primary carer must also have a right of residence.[223]

You can have a right to reside as the primary carer of a worker's child in education if you were that worker or if the worker was someone else.

There is no need for the child or you, as her/his primary carer, to be self-sufficient in order to have residence rights.[224]

The nationality of you or the child does not affect this right of residence. However, the child's parent who had the right to reside as a worker must be an EEA national.

Who is a primary carer

Primary carer
The EEA Regulations define you as a **'primary carer'** of another person if you are her/his direct relative or legal guardian and either you:[225]
– have primary responsibility for that person's care; *or*
– share equally the responsibility for that person's care with one other person who is not an 'exempt person' (see p163).

Note: if you share care equally, whether or not the child would be unable to continue her/his education or remain in the UK, or the British citizen would be unable to reside in the EEA, is considered on the basis of both carers being required to leave the UK, unless the person with whom care is shared had already acquired a derivative right to reside before assuming equal care responsibility.

You are not regarded as someone's primary carer solely on the basis of a financial contribution you make towards her/his care.[226]

If you do not come within the above definition of 'primary carer', you may be able to argue that you have rights based on EU caselaw (see p162) – eg, if you are the primary carer of someone who is dependent on you, but you are not her/his direct relative or legal guardian.

Primary carer of a child who is self-sufficient

You have a derivative right to reside under the EEA Regulations if:[227]
* you are the 'primary carer' (see above) of a child under 18 who is residing in the UK as a self-sufficient person (see p146); *and*
* the child would be unable to remain in the UK if you were required to leave.

The basis of this right of residence is to make effective the rights of the child, as it is assumed that s/he needs an adult to look after her/him and, consequently, her/his primary carer must also have a right of residence.[228]

Your nationality does not affect this right of residence. However, the child must be an EEA national to have a right to reside as a self-sufficient person.

Child of a primary carer

You have a derivative right to reside under the EEA Regulations if:[229]
- you are the child under 18 of a 'primary carer' of either:
  - a worker's child in education (see p164); *or*
  - a child under 18 who is residing in the UK as a self-sufficient person (see p166); *and*
- you do not have leave to enter; *and*
- you were required to leave, it would prevent the primary carer from residing in the UK.

The basis of this right of residence is to make effective the rights of the primary carer and the other child for whom s/he is caring. Your nationality does not affect this right of residence.

Example
Veronika is Czech. She is aged 16, has learning difficulties and is eight months pregnant. She has stopped attending school. Veronika's mother last worked in the UK in 2012. She has a right to reside in order to look after Patrik, Veronika's younger brother, who is aged eight and is in school. Veronika has a derivative right to reside because her mother has to look after her, and if Veronika had to leave the UK so too would her mother. Therefore, Veronika can claim income support (IS) on the basis of her pregnancy and satisfies the right to reside requirement. When Veronika's baby is born, she will be able to claim child benefit and child tax credit, and continue to get IS as a lone parent.

Primary carer of a British citizen

You have a derivative right to reside under the EEA Regulations if you:[230]
- are the 'primary carer' (see p166) of a British citizen who is residing in the UK; *and*
- the British citizen would be unable to reside in the UK or another EEA state if you were required to leave.

This right of residence is based on the rights provided by Article 20 of the Treaty on the Functioning of the European Union (TFEU) for every person holding the nationality of an EU member state to be a citizen of the EU, and for every EU citizen to have the right to move and reside freely within the EU. If an EU citizen is dependent on another, to make her/his right effective, her/his primary carer must be given a right of residence.[231]

The British citizen, therefore, must be dependent on the primary carer – eg, because s/he is a child or has health problems that require another person's care.

The key question for this right of residence is whether the British citizen would be required to leave the territory of the EU (or, under the EEA Regulations, the EEA) if you were required to leave the UK. This is a question of fact to be determined by taking into account all the circumstances.[232] However, this is difficult to satisfy if you are an EEA national and, therefore, in most cases, this residence right only applies to non-EEA nationals.

Having a right to reside on the basis of being the primary carer of a British citizen does not enable you to be entitled to any benefit that requires you to have a right to reside. Since 8 November 2012, it is listed as an excluded right of residence in each of the benefit and tax credit regulations. This exclusion applies whether you have a derivative right to reside under the EEA Regulations or on the basis of Article 20 of the TFEU. **Note:** this exclusion is arguably unlawful and although legal challenges have not yet been successful, future challenges may be.[233] See CPAG's online service and *Welfare Rights Bulletin* for updates.

However, although this right of residence excludes you from benefits, it can mean that you are not defined as a 'person subject to immigration control' (see p56). This residence right therefore enables you to claim attendance allowance, disability living allowance, personal independence payment and carer's allowance, provided you meet all the other presence and residence requirements (see p190). You may also be entitled to working tax credit since you have a right to work in addition to your right to reside.

Other derivative rights

It is arguable that you may have a right to reside if your circumstances do not exactly fit the criteria for the derivative rights on p162, but they are similar and the legal principles underlying derivative residence rights could be applied. For example, you may be able to argue that you have a right to reside in the following situations.

- You are the child of a self-employed person in education or the primary carer of such a child. The question of whether a primary carer had a right of residence was referred to the Court of Justice of the European Union (CJEU) in two joined cases.[234] Although the CJEU stated that the provision that gives a right of education in the state where the child's parent has been a worker[235] cannot apply to the child of a self-employed person,[236] it did not consider other possible bases for such a right. It did not need to do so because the UK government conceded at the hearing that in each case the person had a right of residence on another basis. Consequently, further challenges are possible. The question of whether the primary carer of a (former) self-employed person's child in education remains to be determined in a future case.[237]

- You are the primary carer of a worker's child who is under school age. Such a child has a clear right to reside as the family member of a worker and, depending on the facts, it may be arguable that you need a right to reside to make the child's right effective.
- You are the primary carer of a child who has a permanent right to reside. The same principles that apply to give other primary carers residence rights arguably apply if the child has permanent residence – ie, to make effective the rights of the child.

There may be other circumstances in which you need a right to reside to make someone else's residence rights effective. The strength of your argument always depends on your circumstances and those of the other relevant people, but you may be able to apply some of the principles on which derivative rights are based.

Benefit entitlement

If you have a derivative right to reside (other than on the basis of being the primary carer of a British citizen), this satisfies the right to reside requirement for any of the benefits or tax credits to which that requirement applies (see p107).

If your right to reside is as a result of your being the primary carer of a British citizen, this is specifically excluded for each of the benefits and tax credits that have a right to reside requirement. This exclusion applies whether you have a derivative right to reside under the EEA Regulations or on the basis of Article 20 of the TFEU. **Note:** this exclusion is arguably unlawful and although legal challenges have not yet been successful, future challenges may be.[238] See CPAG's online service and *Welfare Rights Bulletin* for updates.

Note: the period of time when you have a derivative right to reside does not count towards the five years of residence required for acquiring permanent residence (see p170). This means that, unless you have another right to reside, when you cease to satisfy the conditions for your derivative right to reside, your residence rights end together with your entitlement to any benefits that have a right to reside requirement.

Example

Rosa is an Italian national who came to the UK in 2008 with her son Roberto. She worked for five months, but left her job because Roberto began to have night-time seizures and was awarded disability living allowance. Rosa then claimed IS as Roberto's carer for a couple of years. Her health deteriorated and so she switched to claiming income-related employment and support allowance (ESA). Roberto is just completing his A levels at school. When he leaves school, Rosa will cease to have a right to reside as it was based on being the primary carer of a worker's child in education, and her entitlement to income-related ESA and housing benefit will end (even though she has had a derivative right to reside for over five years).

15. **Permanent right to reside**

You can acquire a permanent right of residence after periods of residing with a right to reside in the UK. In most cases, you must have resided with a right to reside for a continuous period of five years, disregarding certain gaps (see below). However, in limited circumstances you can acquire a permanent right of residence after having resided for a shorter period of time (see p174).

Once you have a permanent right of residence, you do not need to satisfy any other conditions[239] (eg, you do not need to be a worker) and this right of residence satisfies the right to reside requirement for all the benefits that have such a requirement.

Once acquired, you only lose your permanent right of residence if you are absent from the UK for more than two consecutive years.[240]

Acquiring permanent residence after five years

You acquire a permanent right to reside if you have 'resided legally' (see below) for a continuous period of five years (see p173).[241]

You can acquire a permanent right of residence whether you are a European Economic Area (EEA) national or non-EEA national, provided you satisfy the criteria. However, if you are a non-EEA national, there are fewer ways in which you count as having resided legally (see p172). If you are a Croatian, A2 or A8 national, you can only count periods of residence in the UK before you became an EEA national in limited circumstances (see p173).

Note: in limited circumstances, you can acquire a right of residence in less than five years (see p174).

Legally resided

The European Union (EU) Directive requires you to have 'resided legally', and the EEA Regulations require you to have resided 'in accordance with these regulations', for a continuous period of five years in the UK.[242] In most cases, this makes no difference, and so the phrase 'resided legally' is used in this section and any difference between the EEA Regulations and EU Directive are noted where they are significant.

You always count as residing legally during periods when you have a right to reside as a:[243]

- worker (see p129), including if you have retained this status (see p135);
- self-employed person (see p141), including if you have retained this status (see p144);
- self-sufficient person, including a self-sufficient student (see p146); *or*
- family member (see p152) of any of the above.

Periods when you resided with another residence right can be more complicated.

The right of permanent residence was only introduced on 30 April 2006 when both the EU Directive 2004/38 and the EEA Regulations came into force. However, you can still count periods when you had a right of residence before 30 April 2006 towards the required five years if the residence was on the basis of one or more of those listed above. (These periods must be taken into account because each of the residence rights was provided under earlier EU[244] and UK[245] legislation.)

If you completed five years' legal residence before 30 April 2006 and then had a gap of less than two years when you were either out of the UK or residing in the UK but not counted as 'residing legally', this does not affect your acquisition of permanent residency.[246]

Jobseekers

You can count periods when you had a right to reside as a jobseeker (see p123) or a family member of a jobseeker from 30 April 2006 towards your five years of residing in accordance with the EEA Regulations.[247] You cannot count periods before this date, as jobseekers were not given a right to reside under earlier regulations. Therefore, if you need to rely on periods when you were seeking work before 30 April 2006, always check whether you had another residence right at that time – eg, if you retained worker status.

You cannot count periods when your only right of residence was as a jobseeker, or family member of a jobseeker, towards the five years required to give you permanent residence under the EU Directive, as it does not count as residing legally.[248]

Initial right of residence

You can count periods after 30 April 2006 when you had an initial right of residence for the first three months after your arrival in the UK (see p122), or as the family member of someone with an initial right of residence, towards your five years of residing in accordance with the EEA Regulations.[249] You can also count such periods towards the five years required to give you permanent residence under the EU Directive.[250]

There was no initial right of residence under earlier regulations or earlier EU law instruments, so it is not relevant to periods before 30 April 2006.

Family members

If you are the family member (see p152) of a person who has acquired permanent-residency after residing legally in the UK for five years, you have a right to reside for as long as you remain her/his family member.[251] Under the EEA Regulations, you can also use periods as a family member of a person with a permanent right of residence to count towards your five years of residing in accordance with those regulations, and so acquire a permanent right of residence yourself.[252]

Note: if you are the family member of a person who has acquired permanent residency in less than five years, you may have permanent residency yourself (see p174).

Former family members

You can count periods since 30 April 2006 when you had a right to reside as a former family member under the EEA Regulations (see p158) towards your five years of residing in accordance with the EEA Regulations. This only applies to periods since 30 April 2006, as this right of residence was not provided under earlier regulations. If you are a non-EEA national, you must have a right to reside as a former family member at the end of your five-year period to acquire a permanent right to reside under the EEA Regulations. [253]

If you have been a former family member under the EU Directive (see p159) for five years, this is not sufficient to enable you to acquire permanent residency under that Directive because, in most cases, you are also required to show that you are a worker, or a self-employed or self-sufficient person, or that you are the family member of such a person. [254] However, the exception is if you are a non-EEA national and you have retained your right to reside as a former family member on the basis of either the death of your spouse or civil partner, or the termination of your marriage/civil partnership (see p159). [255]

Non-European Economic Area nationals

Periods when you are in the UK with leave to enter or remain do not count as periods of 'residing legally'. They do not count under the EEA Regulations as they are not periods in which you resided in accordance with those regulations and the European Court of Justice has held that they do not count towards the five years required to acquire permanent residency under the EU Directive. [256]

If you are a non-EEA national, you cannot have a right of residence as a worker, self-employed person, person who retains either of these statuses, a self-sufficient person or as a self-sufficient student. However, you can have a right of residence as the family member of an EEA national who is in one of these groups.

In practice, therefore, the only ways for you to acquire a permanent right of residence after five years of residing legally is by either:

- residing for a five-year period as the family member of an EEA national who is legally residing; *or*
- retaining the right as a former family member on the basis of either the death of your spouse or civil partner or the termination of your marriage or civil partnership (see p159). [257]

Note: in limited circumstances, you can also acquire a right of permanent residence in less than five years if you are the family member of an EEA national who has acquired a permanent right of residence in less than five years (see p174).

Croatian, A2 and A8 nationals

If you are a Croatian, A2 or A8 national, you can acquire permanent residency after five years of residing legally in the same way as any other EEA national. However, if:

- you are relying on periods when you were subject to additional restrictions on your residence rights, these restrictions may affect whether you had a right to reside as a jobseeker or a worker, or retained worker status (see p118);
- you are relying on periods when you were living in the UK before your country joined the EU, you do not count as residing legally just on the basis that you had leave to enter or remain in the UK (see p172). However, you count as residing legally if:[258]
  - you had leave to enter or remain in the UK; *and*
  - you would have had a right of residence as a worker, self-employed person, person who retains one of those statuses, a self-sufficient person or self-sufficient student except for the fact that you were not an EU national at the time.

Derivative right to reside

Periods when you have resided with a derivative right to reside (see p162) do not count as periods of residing legally, and so you cannot count them towards your five years for the purposes of acquiring permanent residency under either the EEA Regulations or the EU Directive.[259]

Continuity of residence

You acquire permanent residency when you have been 'residing legally' (see above) for a continuous period of five years.[260] However, the continuity of your residence is not affected by certain absences (see below). It is also arguable that the continuity of your residence is not affected by certain gaps during the five years when you were in the UK, but did not count as 'residing legally' (see p174).

Absence from the UK

When calculating whether you have five years' continuous residence, temporary absences from the UK do not affect the continuity of your residence if:[261]

- they are not more than a total of six months a year;
- they comprise one absence of up to 12 consecutive months for important reasons, such as pregnancy and childbirth, serious illness, study or vocational training, or a posting abroad. These are just examples. If you have one absence of up to 12 months for a similar important reason, it should also not affect the continuity of your residence;[262] *or*
- they are for compulsory military service.

If you have one or more of the above temporary absences from the UK, you can count the time spent abroad as part of your five continuous years.[263]

Example

Botond is a Hungarian national. In August 2009 he came to the UK and began working as a self-employed carpenter. He had a successful business but ceased self-employment in November 2013, as he returned to Hungary because his father was terminally ill. Botond's father died in January and so he returned back to the UK in March 2014 and claimed jobseeker's allowance (JSA). Last month, Botond was involved in a serious car accident that has left him unable to work and so he claimed income-related employment and support allowance. Botond satisfies the right to reside right requirement for this benefit as he has legally resided in the UK for a continuous period of five years (including the five months he was in Hungary).

Your continuity of residence is broken if you are removed from the UK under the EEA Regulations.[264]

Gaps

Between periods when you are residing legally you may have one or more temporary periods when you remain in the UK, but you are not counted as 'residing legally'. You may be able to argue that the continuity of your residence is not affected by such a gap on the grounds that if the continuity of your residence is not affected by your being abroad for certain specified periods, it should also not be affected for equivalent periods when you remain in the UK, but do not count as residing legally.[265]

If the gap was spent in prison, however, this interrupts the continuity of your residence and you cannot count the time spent in prison towards your five years.[266] The Court of Justice of the Euroepan Union found that taking time spent in prison into account when calculating the five years would be contrary to the EU Directive's aim of strengthening social cohesion. This aim was a key element behind establishing the right of permanent residency. It was also the reason why permanenet residency was made dependent, not just on the duration, but also on the qualitative elements of residence relating to the level of integration in the member state. Receiving a prison sentence shows the person's non-compliance with the values of that state.[267]

This reasoning suggests that other gaps in your five-year period should be treated differently, particularly if they do not call into question your level of integration in the UK – eg, periods when you temporarily ceased to be a worker or self-employed because you were caring for someone.

Acquiring permanent residence in less than five years

You can acquire a permanent right of residence in less than five years in certain circumstances. You have a permanent right to reside if you: [268]
- are a worker (see p129) or self-employed person (see p141) and you:

> – have reached retirement age or taken early retirement and you either:
>   – have a spouse or civil partner who is a UK national (or who lost that nationality by marrying you); *or*
>   – have worked in the UK for the preceding year and resided in the UK continuously for more than three years; *or*
> – stopped working in the UK because of a permanent incapacity (see below) and:
>   – you have a spouse or civil partner who is a UK national (or who lost that nationality by marrying you); *or*
>   – you have resided in the UK continuously for more than two years; *or*
>   – the incapacity was as a result of an accident at work or occupational disease that resulted in benefit entitlement – eg, industrial injuries disablement benefit; *or*
> – have worked and resided in the UK continuously for three years and you then work in another member state and return to the UK at least once a week; *or*

- are the family member (see p176) of a worker or self-employed person in any of the above groups and you reside with her/him;[269] *or*
- are the family member of a worker or self-employed person who died while still working and who did not acquire a permanent right of residence under one of the above groups and:
  - s/he had lived in the UK for two years; *or*
  - the death resulted from an accident at work or an occupational disease; *or*
  - you lost your UK nationality as a result of marrying her/him.

Permanent incapacity

'Permanent incapacity' is the opposite of temporary incapacity.[270]

If your incapacity is not permanent, you may be able to retain your worker or self-employed status on the basis that you are temporarily unable to work due to illness or accident (see p138).

Calculating periods of work

When calculating whether you have worked for long enough to acquire a permanent right to reside in less than five years, you can count the following as periods of activity as a worker or self-employed person:[271]

- periods when you were not working for reasons not of your making;
- periods when you were not working due to an illness or accident;
- (workers only) periods of involuntary unemployment (see p136) recorded by the relevant employment office – ie, Jobcentre Plus.

If you are a Croatian, A2 or A8 national, there may be additional restrictions on your residence rights that apply, or that applied, to you (see p118).[272]

Residing in the UK

Some of the ways in which you can acquire permanent residence in less than five years require you to have resided in the UK for specified periods. Whether or not you satisfy this may be affected by the way this requirement is interpreted. The fact that acquiring permanent residency in less than five years is the exception to the general rule may have consequences for:

- calculating the period of residence. It is arguable that certain absences should not affect your continuity of residence in the same way as for acquiring permanent residence after five years (see p173); *and*
- the quality of the residence. The term 'reside' has been interpreted to mean 'legally reside'.[273] It may be possible to argue that this interpretation is wrong since it would mean that the provision under the EU Directive 2004/38 is more restrictive than under its predecessor[274] and the preamble to the Directive expressly states these rights will be maintained.[275]

Family members

You acquire permanent residence in less than five years if you are living in the UK and are the family member (see p152) of someone who has acquired a permanent right to reside under the first bullet point on pp174–75. You do not have to live with the person; it is sufficient that you are living in the UK now.[276] You do not have to have lived in the UK for the same period as the person of whom you are a family member, and you do not need to have been her/his family member throughout this time.[277]

Loss of permanent right to reside

Once you have acquired a permanent right to reside, whether because of residing legally in the UK for at least five years or under the rules that enable you to acquire permanent residence in less than five years, you can only lose this right if you are absent from the UK for more than two consecutive years.[278]

Benefit entitlement

If you have a permanent right to reside, this satisfies the right to reside requirement for all the benefits that have this requirement (see p107).

If you acquired a permanent right to reside under the rules that enable you to do so in less than five years, you are exempt from the habitual residence test for means-tested benefits (see p99). You therefore do not need to be 'habitually resident in fact' nor have lived in the common travel area for the three months prior to your claim for income-based JSA.

Notes

4. European Economic Area nationals
1 Art 18 TFEU
2 Art 20 TFEU
3 Arts 20 and 21 TFEU
4 EEA Joint Committee Decision No.158/2007
5 *Agreement between the European Community and its Member States, of the one part, and the Swiss Confederation, of the other on the free movement of persons,* Cmd 5639, 21 June 1999 (in force on 1 June 2002)
6 Reg 2(1) I(EEA) Regs
7 Art 3(1) EU Dir 2004/38
8 This approach is taken in the I(EEA) Regs – see reg 2(1) I(EEA) Regs, definition of 'EEA national'
9 Regs 6 and 14(1) I(EEA) Regs. The same groups are covered in Arts 7 and 14 EU Dir 2004/38, although the term 'qualified person' is not used.
10 *SSWP v JB (JSA)* [2011] UKUT 96 (AAC)

5. Croatian, A2 and A8 nationals
11 Regs 4 and 5 AC(IWA) Regs
12 Reg 6 A(IWA) Regs; reg 7B EEA Regs
13 Reg 7 A(IWR) Regs
14 Reg 5 A(IWR) Regs; reg 7A I(EEA) Regs
15 Reg 7 A(IWR) Regs
16 *SSWP v ZA* [2009] UKUT 294 (AAC); *Szpak v SSWP* [2013] EWCA Civ 46
17 Reg 2 AC(IWA) Regs; reg 2 A(IWA) Regs
18 Reg 3 AC(IWA) Regs; reg 4 A(IWA) Regs
19 Reg 2 A(IWR) Regs
20 Reg 2(5) AC(IWA) Regs; reg 2(12) A(IWA) Regs
21 *Miskovic and Another v SSWP* [2011] EWCA Civ 16
22 Reg 2(7) A(IWR) Regs
23 *Miskovic and Another v SSWP* [2011] EWCA Civ 16
24 *BS v SSWP* [2009] UKUT 16 (AAC)

6. Initial right of residence
25 Reg 13(1) I(EEA) Regs; Art 6(1) EU Dir 2004/38
26 Reg 13(3) I(EEA) Regs; Art 14(1) EU Dir 2004/38
27 Reg 13(2) I(EEA) Regs; Art 6(2) EU Dir 2004/38

7. Jobseekers
28 Art 45 TFEU; Art 14 EU Dir 2004/38; reg 6 I(EEA) Regs
29 Reg 4 I(EEA)A Regs 2014
30 Sch 3 para 1 I(EEA)A Regs 2013; reg 4 I(EEA)A Regs 2014
31 Art 45 TFEU; *The Queen v Immigration Appeal Tribunal, ex parte Gustaff Desiderius Antonissen,* C-292/89 [1991] ECR I-00745
32 Reg 5 AC(IWA) Regs
33 **A2** Reg 6 A(IWA) Regs
   A8 Regs 4(2) and (4) and 5(2) A(IWR) Regs
34 CH/3314/2005
35 R(IS) 8/08; CIS 1951/2008, para 21
36 R(IS) 8/08, para 6; CIS 1951/2008, para 21
37 s7 JSA 1995
38 Reg 8 JSA Regs
39 Reg 92 UC Regs
40 *The Queen v Immigration Appeal Tribunal, ex parte Gustaff Desiderius Antonissen,* C-292/89 [1991] ECR I-00745, para 21; R(IS) 8/08, para 5
41 *The Queen v Immigration Appeal Tribunal, ex parte Gustaff Desiderius Antonissen,* C-292/89 [1991] ECR I-00745, para 21
42 Reg 6(7) and (8) I(EEA) Regs; Sch 3 para 1 I(EEA)A 2013 Regs; reg 4 I(EEA)A Regs 2014
43 Reg 6(8)(b) and (9) I(EEA) Regs
44 Reg 6(4) and (8)-(11) I(EEA) Regs
45 Reg 4 I(EEA)A Regs 2014
46 Memo DMG 15/14
47 Confirmed in Memo DMG 15/14, paras 17 and 21
48 Art 24(2) EU Dir 2004/38
49 Reg 70(3)(b) and (d) ESA Regs
50 *Athanasios Vatsouras and Josif Koupatantze v Arbeitsgemeinschaft Nürnberg,* C-23/08) [2009] ECR I-04585, para 40
51 s13 WRA 2007
52 Reg 92 UC Regs
53 *Athanasios Vatsouras and Josif Koupatantze v Arbeitsgemeinschaft Nürnberg,* C-23/08 [2009] ECR I-04585, para 40

54 *Athanasios Vatsouras and Josif Koupatantze v Arbeitsgemeinschaft Nürnberg,* C-23/08 [2009] ECR I-04585, para 41

8. Workers

55 Reg 6(1)(b) I(EEA) Regs; Art 7(1)(a) EU Dir 2004/38
56 Reg 4(1)(a) I(EEA) Regs
57 *Levin v Staatssecretaris van Justitie,* C-53/81 [1982] ECR I-1035
58 *LN v Styrelsen for Videregående Uddannelser og Uddannelsesstøtte,* C-46/12 [2013] ECR, not yet reported
59 *MDB (Italy) v SSHD* [2012] EWCA Civ 1015, paras 61-65
60 Reg 5 AC(IWA) Regs
61 Reg 6 A(IWA) Regs
62 Reg 5(2) A(IWR) Regs
63 DMG Memo 1/14; HB A3/2014; 'Child Benefit and Child Tax Credit: right to reside establishing whether an EEA national is/was a worker or a self-employed person under EU law', February 2014
64 DMG Memo 1/14 para 7; HB A3/2014 para 15; 'Child Benefit and Child Tax Credit: right to reside establishing whether an EEA national is/was a worker or a self-employed person under EU law', February 2014, para 7
65 *Raulin v Minister van Onderwijs en Wetenschappen,* C-357/89 [1992] ECR I-1027, para 10
66 *SSWP v RR (IS)* [2013] UKUT 21 (AAC)
67 CIS/868/2008; CIS/1837/2006
68 *Steymann v Staatssecretaris van Justitie,* C-196/87 [1988] ECR 06159; R(IS) 12/98
69 *Jany v Staatssecretaris van Justitie,* C-268/99 [2001] ECR I-08615, para 34
70 *SSWP v KP (JSA)* [2011] UKUT 241 (AAC)
71 *Bettray v Staatssecretaris van Justitie,* C-344/87 [1989] ECR 1621, para 16; *JA v SSWP(ESA)* [2012] UKUT 122 (AAC)
72 *Barry v London Borough of Southwark* [2008] EWCA Civ 1440, para 45; *NE v SSWP* [2009] UKUT 38 (AAC), para 4
73 *Bettray v Staatssecretaris van Justitie,* C-344/87 [1989] ECR 1621; *SSWP v KP(JSA)* [2011] UKUT 241 (AAC)
74 *NE v SSWP* [2009] UKUT 38 (AAC), para 9
75 *Levin v Staatssecretaris van Justitie,* C-53/81 [1982] ECR 1035, para 17
76 *Ninni-Orasche v Bundesminister für Wissenschaft, Verkehr und Kunst,* C-413/01 [2003] ECR I-13187, para 27

77 *Genc v Land Berlin,* C-14/09 [2010] ECR I-00931
78 R(IS) 12/98
79 *Ninni-Orasche v Bundesminister für Wissenschaft, Verkehr und Kunst,* C-413/01 [2003] ECR I-13187, para 25
80 *Barry v London Borough of Southwark* [2008] EWCA Civ 1440
81 *Ninni-Orasche v Bundesminister für Wissenschaft, Verkehr und Kunst,* C-413/01 [2003] ECR I-13187, para 19
82 In *NE v SSWP* [2009] UKUT 38 (AAC), para 9; R(IS) 12/98
83 *Vatsouras and Koupantze v Arbeitsgemeinschaft (ARGE) Nürnberg 900* [2009] C-22/08 and C-23/08 [2009] ECR I-04585, paras 27 and 28
84 *Raulin v Minister van Onderwijs en Wetenschappen,* C-357/89 [1992] ECR I-1027
85 *NE v SSWP* [2009] UKUT 38 (AAC); CIS/1793/2007
86 *Genc v Land Berlin,* C-14/09 [2010] ECR I-00931
87 *Barry v London Borough of Southwark* [2008] EWCA Civ 1440, para 20
88 *SSWP v SY (IS)* [2012] UKUT 233 (AAC); *JR v SSWP (IS)* [2014] UKUT 0154 (AAC); *JR v Leeds City Council (HB)* [2014] UKUT 0154 (AAC)
89 *BS v SSWP* [2009] UKUT 16 (AAC); CIS/4237/2007

9. Retaining worker status

90 Art 7(3) EU Dir 2004/38; reg 6(2), (2A) and (5)-(8) I(EEA) Regs
91 *Jessy Saint Prix v SSWP,* C-507/12 [2014] ECR, not yet reported
92 *Jessy Saint Prix v SSWP,* C-507/12 [2014] ECR, not yet reported, para 38
93 Reg 5(4) A(IWR) Regs; reg 7A(4) I(EEA) Regs
94 Art 7(3)(b) and (c) EU Dir 2004/38; reg 6(2)(b) I(EEA) Regs
95 Reg 6(2)(b) and (ba),(5) and (6) I(EEA) Regs
96 Reg 92 UC Regs
97 CH/3314/2005, para 11; confirmed in *SSWP v EM (IS)* [2009] UKUT 146 (AAC), para 10; *SSWP v MK* [2013] UKUT 0163 (AAC), paras 44-47
98 *SSWP v Elmi* [2011] EWCA Civ 1403; paras 071183-84 DMG
99 Art 7(3)(b) EU Dir 2004/38
100 Reg 6(2)(b) and (5)-(8) I(EEA) Regs
101 Reg 6(2)(ba), (2A), (5) and (6) I(EEA) Regs
102 Art 7(3)(c) EU Dir 2004/38

103 *SSWP v EM (IS)* [2009] UKUT 146 (AAC), para 10
104 *Steven Malcolm Brown v Secretary of State for Scotland,* C-197/86 [1988] ECR I-03205
105 *Lair v Universität Hannover,* C-39/86 [1988] ECR I-03161, para 37
106 *Raulin v Minister van Onderwijs en Wetenschappen,* C-357/89 [1992] ECR I-01027, paras 18 and 19
107 Art 7(3)(a) EU Dir 2004/38; reg 6(2)(a) I(EEA) Regs
108 CIS/4304/2007, para 35
109 CIS/3182/2005
110 *SSHD v FB* [2010] UKUT 447 (IAC), para 23
111 CIS/3890/2005
112 *De Brito v SSHD* [2012] EWCA Civ 709; *Konodyba v Royal Borough of Kensington and Chelsea* [2012] EWCA Civ 982; *Samin v SSHD* [2012] EWCA Civ 1468
113 CIS/4237/2007
114 CIS/731/2007
115 CIS/4010/2006
116 *Jessy Saint Prix v SSWP,* C-507/12 [2014] ECR, not yet reported
117 CIS/4304/2007, para 34; *SSWP v IR* [2009] UKUT 11 (AAC)
118 CIS/1934/2006; *SSWP v IR(IS)* [2009] UKUT 11 (AAC)
119 *SSWP v MK* [2013] UKUT 0163 (AAC); *VP v SSWP (JSA)* [2014] UKUT 0032 (AAC), paras 56-61
120 Reg 92 UC Regs
121 Art 7 EU Reg 492/2011

10. Self-employed people
122 Reg 6(1)(c) I(EEA) Regs; Art 7(1)(a) EU Dir 2004/38
123 Reg 4(1)(b) I(EEA) Regs
124 *Aldona Malgorzata Jany and Others v Staatssecretaris van Justitie,* C-268/99 [2001] ECR I-08615
125 *SSWP v SY (IS)* [2012] UKUT 233 (AAC)
126 DMG Memo 1/14; HB A3/2014; *Child Benefit and Child Tax Credit: right to reside establishing whether an EEA national is/ was a worker or a self-employed person under EU law,* February 2014
127 Reg 4(1)(b) I(EEA) Regs; R(IS) 6/00
128 R(IS) 6/00, para 31
129 *TG v SSWP* [2009] UKUT 58 (AAC), para 5
130 *SSWP v JS (IS)* [2010] UKUT 240 (AAC), paras 5 and 8; *RJ v SSWP (JSA)* [2011] UKUT 477 (AAC), paras 9 and 17
131 *SSWP v JS (IS)* [2010] UKUT 240 (AAC), para 5

132 CIS/1042/2008
133 *SSWP v JB (JSA)* [2011] UKUT 96 (AAC)

11. Retaining self-employed status
134 Art 7(3)(a) EU Dir 2004/38; reg 6(3) I(EEA) Regs
135 *R (Tilianu) v SSWP* [2010] EWCA Civ 1397

0. Croatian, A2 and A8 nationals
136 Art 7(3)(a) EU Dir 2004/38; reg 6(3) I(EEA) Regs
137 CIS/1042/2008
138 CIS/4010/2006
139 *Jessy Saint Prix v SSWP,* C-507/12 [2014] ECR, not yet reported

12. Self-sufficient people and students
140 Art 7(1) EU Dir 2004/38; regs 4(1)(c), 6(1) and 14(1) I(EEA) Regs
141 Art 7(1) EU Dir 2004/38; regs 4(1)(d), 6(1) and 14(1) I(EEA) Regs
142 *VP v SSWP (JSA)* [2014] UKUT 0032 (AAC), paras 88-97
143 Art 8(4) EU Dir 2004/38
144 Reg 4(4) I(EEA) Regs
145 With effect from 2 June 2011
146 *SG v Tameside MBC (HB)* [2010] UKUT 243 (AAC)
147 *Zhu and Chen v SSHD,* C-200/02 [2004] ECR I-09925
148 *Commission of the European Communities v Kingdom Belgium,* C-408/03 [2006] ECR I-02647; *Zhu and Chen v SSHD,* C-200/02 [2004] ECR I-09925
149 *VP v SSWP (JSA)* [2014] UKUT 0032 (AAC), paras 88-97
150 *Pensionsversicherungsanstalt v Brey,* C-140/12 [2013] ECR, not yet reported, paras 54-57
151 CH/1400/2006; *SG v Tameside MBC (HB)* [2010] UKUT 243 (AAC); *Pensionsversicherungsanstalt v Brey,* C-140/12 [2013] ECR, not yet reported
152 para 071243 DMG
153 *Pensionsversicherungsanstalt v Brey,* C-140/12 [2013] ECR, not yet reported, paras 64 and 75-78
154 *VP v SSWP (JSA)* [2014] UKUT 0032 (AAC), paras 77, 84 and 94
155 *W (China) and Another v SSHD* [2006] EWCA Civ 1494
156 *SG v Tameside MBC (HB)* [2010] UKUT 243 (AAC); *VP v SSWP (JSA)* [2014] UKUT 0032 (AAC); para 07145 DMG
157 *FK (Kenya) v SSHD* [2010] EWCA Civ 1302; *VP v SSWP (JSA)* [2014] UKUT 0032 (AAC); *Ahmad v SSHD* [2014] EWCA Civ 988

158 *Baumbast and R v SSHD,* C-413/99
[2002] ECR I-07091
159 Art 7(1) EU Dir 2004/38; regs 4(1)(d),
6(1) and 14(1) I(EEA) Regs
160 *Rudy Grzelczyk v Centre Public d'aide
Sociale d'Ottignies-Louvain-la-Neuve,* C-
184/09 [2001] ECR I-06193
161 Art 7(4) EU Dir 2004/38; reg 7(2) I(EEA)
Regs
162 Art 7(4) EU Dir 2004/38

13. **Family members of European
Economic Area nationals**
163 Art 7(2) EU Dir 2004/38; *Clauder,* C-E-4/
11 [2011] EFTACR 216, para 43; reg
14(2) I(EEA) Regs
164 Regs 6 and 14(1) I(EEA) Regs. The same
groups are covered in Arts 7 and 14 EU
Dir 2004/38, although the term
'qualified person' is not used.
165 Art 2(2) EU Dir 2004/38; reg 7(1) I(EEA)
Regs
166 Reg 7(3) I(EEA) Regs; CPC/3588/2006;
SS v SSWP (ESA) [2011] UKUT 8 (AAC)
167 *Aissatou Diatta v Land Berlin,* C-267/83
[1985] ECR I-00567
168 CF/1863/2007
169 CIS/2100/2007, which considers the
findings of *Centre Public d'Aide Sociale de
Courcelles v Lebon,* 316/85 [1987] ECR I-
02811, *Zhu and Chen v SSHD,* C-200/02
[2004] ECR I-09925 and *Jia v
Migrationsverket,* C-1/05 [2007] ECR I-
00001
170 *Flora May Reyes v Migrationsverket* C-
423/12 [2014] ECR, not yet reported;
*Centre Publique d'Aide Social de Courcelles
vLebon* C-316/85 [1987] ECR 02811;
ECO v Lim (EEA dependency) [2013]
UKUT 437 (IAC)
171 *Pedro v SSWP* [2009] EWCA Civ 1358.
Arguably, this remains good law despite
the assumptions made in *Flora May
Reyes v Migrationsverket,* C-423/12
[2014] ECR, not yet reported
172 *SSHD v Rahman and Others,* C-83/11
[2012] ECR, not yet reported; *Oboh and
Others v SSHD* [2013] EWCA Civ 1525
173 *Centre Publique d'Aide Social de Courcelles
v Lebon,* C-316/85 [1987] ECR I-02811,
para 20
174 Reg 7(3) I(EEA) Regs
175 CPC/3588/2006; *SS v SSWP(ESA)* [2011]
UKUT 8 (AAC); *SSWP v LZ (SPC)* [2014]
UKUT 0147 (AAC)
176 Reg 7(3) and 8 I(EEA) Regs; the same
groups are covered in Art 3 EU Dir 2004/
38, but the term is not used.

177 *SSHD v Rahman and Others,* C-83/11
[2012] ECR, not yet reported; *Oboh and
Others v SSHD* [2013] EWCA Civ 1525
178 Reg 7(4) I(EEA) Regs
179 Art 7(4) EU Dir 2004/38
180 Art 3(1) EU Dir 2004/38
181 Reg 2(1) I(EEA) Regs
182 Art 7(2) EU Dir 2004/38
183 Reg 9 I(EEA) Regs
184 *Blaise Baheten Metock and Others v
Minister for Justice, Equality and Law
Reform,* C-127/08 [2008] ECR I-06241
185 Reg 9(2) I(EEA) Regs
186 Reg 9(2) and (3) I(EEA) Regs
187 Sch 3 para 2 I(EEA)A 2013 Regs
188 *Minister voor Vreemdelingenzaken en
Integratie v Eind,* C-291/05 [2007] ECR I-
10719, para 45. The case relates to an
earlier EU Regulation, but the same
reasoning applies to Art 7(2) EU Dir
2004/38.
189 *Mary Carpenter v SSHD,* C-60/00 [2002]
ECR I-06279, para 46
190 *McCarthy v SSHD,* C-434-09 [2011] ECR
I-03375
191 *AA v SSWP* [2009] UKUT 249 (AAC); *HG
v SSWP (SPC)* [2011] UKUT 382 (AAC)
192 Sch 3 I(EEA)A Regs 2012
193 Regs 10 and 14(3) I(EEA) Regs
194 Reg 14(3) I(EEA) Regs
195 Reg 10(8) I(EEA) Regs
196 Art 12 EU Dir 2004/38
197 Art 12 EU Dir 2004/38
198 Art 13 EU Dir 2004/38
199 Art 12(2) and 13(1) EU Dir 2004/38
200 Regs 6 and 14(1) I(EEA) Regs. The same
groups are covered in Arts 7 and 14 EU
Dir 2004/38, although the term
'qualified person' is not used.

14. **Derivative residence rights**
201 Reg 15A I(EEA) Regs
202 See also *London Borough of Harrow v
Nimco Hassan Ibrahim and SSHD,* C-310/
08 [2010] ECR I-01065; *Maria Teixeira v
London Borough of Lambeth and SSHD,*
C-480/08 [2010] ECR I-01107; *GBC
Echternach and A Moritz v Minister van
Onderwijs en Wetenschappen,* joined
cases 389/87 and 390/87 [1989] ECR
00723; *Baumbast and R v SSHD,* C-413/
99 [2002] ECR I-07091

203 See also *London Borough of Harrow v
Nimco Hassan Ibrahim and SSHD*, C-310/
08 [2010] ECR I-01065; *Maria Teixeira v
London Borough of Lambeth and SSHD*,
C-480/08 [2010] ECR I-01107; *GBC
Echternach and A Moritz v Minister van
Onderwijs en Wetenschappen*, joined
cases 389/87 and 390/87 [1989] ECR
00723; *Baumbast and R v SSHD*, C-413/
99 [2002] ECR I-07091

204 See also *Zhu and Chen v SSHD*, C-200/02
[2004] ECR I-09925

205 See also *Zambrano v ONEm*, C-34/09
[2011] ECR I-01177; *Dereci and Others v
Bundesministerium für Inneres*, C-256/11
[2011] ECR I-11315

206 Reg 15A(1) I(EEA) Regs

207 Reg 15A(6)(c) I(EEA) Regs

208 *DJ v SSWP* [2013] UKUT 0113 (AAC)

209 Art 10 EU Reg 492/2011 (before 1 June
2012, Art 12 EC Reg 1612/68 was in
identical terms)

210 *Baumbast and R v SSHD*, C-413/99
[2002] ECR I-07091

211 Reg 15A(6)(a) I(EEA) Regs; CIS/3960/
2007

212 *SSWP v IM (IS)* [2011] UKUT 231 (AAC),
paras 17 and 28

213 *Shabani v SSHD* [2013] UKUT 00315
(IAC)

214 *Landesamt für Ausbildungsförderung
Nordrhein-Westfalen v Lubor Gaal*, C-7/
94 [1995] ECR I-1031, paras 24 and 25

215 *Maria Teixeira v London Borough
of Lambeth and SSHD*, C-480/08 [2010]
ECR I-01107, para 74

216 Reg 15A(3)(c) I(EEA) Regs

217 *Maria Teixeira v London Borough
of Lambeth and SSHD*, C-480/08 [2010]
ECR I-01107, para 74; *Baumbast and R v
SSHD*, C-413/99 [2002] ECR I-07091,
para 63

218 *London Borough of Harrow v Nimco
Hassan Ibrahim and SSHD*, C-310/08
[2010] ECR I-01065; *Maria Teixeira v
London Borough of Lambeth and SSHD*,
C-480/08 [2010] ECR I-
01107; *Baumbast and R v SSHD*, C-413/
99 [2002] ECR I-07091; *SSWP v Czop
and SSWP v Punakova* joined cases, C-
147/11 and C-148/11 [2012] ECR, not
yet reported; *Landesamt für
Ausbildungsförderung Nordrhein-
Westfalen v Lubor Gaal*, C-7/94 [1995]
ECR I-1031

219 para 071276 DMG

220 *Echternach and Moritz v Netherlands
Minister for Education and Science*, joined
cases 389/87 and 390/87 [1989] ECR
00723, paras 18-23

221 Reg 15A(1) and (4) I(EEA) Regs

222 Art 10 EU Reg 492/2011 (before 1 June
2012 Art 12 EC Reg 1612/68 was in
identical terms)

223 *Baumbast and R v SSHD*, C-413/99
[2002] ECR I-07091

224 *Maria Teixeira v London Borough of
Lambeth and SSHD*, C-480/08 [2010]
ECR I-01107, para 3

225 Reg 15A(7) I(EEA) Regs

226 Reg 15A(8) I(EEA) Regs

227 Reg 15A(1) and (2) I(EEA) Regs

228 *Zhu and Chen v SSHD*, C-200/02 [2004]
ECR I-09925

229 Reg 15A(1) and (2) I(EEA) Regs

230 Reg 15A(1) and (4A) I(EEA) Regs

231 *Zambrano v ONEm*, C-34/09 [2011] ECR
I-01177; *Dereci and Others v
Bundesministerium für Inneres*, C-256/11
[2011] ECR I-11315

232 *Harrison and AB v SSHD* [2012] EWCA
Civ 1736; *O and S v
Maahanmuuttovirasto and
Maahanmuuttovirasto v L*, joined cases
C-356/11 and C-357/11 [2012] ECR,
not yet reported.

233 *R (HC) v SSWP* [2013] EWHC 3874
(Admin), currently under appeal to the
Court of Appeal

234 *SSWP v Lucja Czop and Margita
Punakova*, joined cases C-147/11 and C-
148/11 [2012] ECR, not yet reported

235 Art 12 EC Reg 1612/68 replaced, in
identical terms, by Art 10 EU Reg 492/
2011 since 1 June 2012

236 *SSWP v Lucja Czop and Margita
Punakova*, joined cases C-147/11 and C-
148/11 [2012] ECR, not yet reported,
para 33

237 Confirmed by the judge when the
joined cases were referred back to the
Upper Tribunal: *SSWP v Punakova*
[2012] UKUT 352 (AAC) and *SSWP v
Czop* [2012] UKUT 351 (AAC)

238 *R (HC) v SSWP* [2013] EWHC 3874
(Admin), currently under appeal to the
Court of Appeal

15. Permanent right to reside

239 Art 16(1) EU Dir 2004/38

240 Art 16(4) EU Dir 2004/38; reg 15(2)
I(EEA) Regs

241 Art 16(1) EU Dir 2004/38; reg 15(1)
I(EEA) Regs

242 Art 16(1) EU Dir 2004/38; reg 15(1)(a)
I(EEA) Regs

243 Art 7 EU Dir 2004/38; regs 6, 14 and 15
EEA Regs; *Tomasz Ziolkowski and
Barbara Szeja v Land Berlin*, joined cases
C-424/10 and C-425/10 [2011] ECR I-
14035

244 *SSWP v Lassal*, C-162/09 [2010] ECR I-
09217; *Alarape and Tijani v SSHD*, C-
529/11 [2013] ECR, not yet reported

245 Sch 4 para 6 I(EEA) Regs

246 *SSWP v Lassal*, C-162/09 [2010] ECR I-
09217; *SSWP v Dias*, C-325/09 [2011]
ECR I-06387; Sch 4 para 6(4) I(EEA) Regs

247 Regs 6(1)(a), 7, 14(1) and (2) and 15(1)
I(EEA) Regs

248 *Ziolkowski and Szeja,* joined cases C424/
10 and C425/10 [2011] ECR, not yet
reported

249 Regs 13 and 15(1) I(EEA) Regs 2006

250 *Ziolkowski and Szeja,* joined cases C424/
10 and C425/10 [2011] ECR I-14035,
para 46

251 Reg 14(2) I(EEA) Regs; *Clauder*, E-4/11
[2011] EFTACR 216, para 43

252 Regs 14(2) and 15(1)(a) and (b) I(EEA)
Regs

253 Reg 15(1)(f) I(EEA) Regs

254 Arts 12(2) and 13(1) EU Dir 2004/38;
Ziolkowski and Szeja, joined cases C424/
10 and C425/10 [2011] ECR I-14035

255 Art 18 EU Dir 2004/38

256 *Ziolkowski and Szeja,* joined cases C424/
10 and C425/10 [2011] ECR I-14035

257 Art 18 EU Dir 2004/38

258 *Ziolkowski and Szeja,* joined cases C424/
10 and C425/10 [2011] ECR I-14035;
Sch 4, para 6(1) and (3) I(EEA) Regs;
SSWP v LS (IS) [2012] UKUT 207 (AAC)

259 *Oakfor and Others v SSHD* [2011] EWCA
Civ 499; *Alarape and Tijani v SSHD*, C-
529/11 [2013] ECR, not yet reported;
Bee and Another v SSHD [2013] UKUT
00083 (IAC); reg 15(1A) I(EEA) Regs

260 Art 16(1) EU Dir 2004/38; reg 15(1)
I(EEA) Regs

261 Art 16(3) EU Dir 2004/38; reg 3 I(EEA)
Regs

262 *Babajanov v SSHD* [2013] UKUT 00513
(IAC)

263 *Idezuna v SSHD* [2011] UKUT 474 (IAC);
Babajanov v SSHD [2013] UKUT 00513
(IAC)

264 Reg 3(3) I(EEA) Regs

265 Following *SSWP v Dias*, C-325/09 [2011]
ECR I-06387; see also *Jessy Saint Prix v
SSWP*, C-507/12 [2014] ECR, not yet
reported, paras 45 and 46

266 *Nnamdi Onuekwere v SSHD*, C-378/12
[2014] ECR, not yet reported

267 *Nnamdi Onuekwere v SSHD*, C-378/12
[2014] ECR, not yet reported, paras 24-
26

268 Regs 5 and 15 I(EEA) Regs; Art 17 EU Dir
2004/38

269 *PM (EEA – spouse -'residing with') Turkey*
[2011] UKUT 89 (IAC)

270 *SSHD v FB* [2010] UKUT 447 (IAC) para
23

271 Reg 5(7) I(EEA) Regs; Art 17(1) EU Dir
2004/38

272 Reg 5(7) I(EEA) Regs

273 *ID v SSWP (IS)* [2011] UKUT 401 (AAC),
paras 17 and 18

274 EC Reg 1251/70

275 Recital 19 preamble to EU Dir 2004/38

276 *PM (EEA – spouse – 'residing with') Turkey*
[2011] UKUT 89 (IAC)

277 Reg 15(1)(d) and (e) I(EEA) Regs and Art
17(3) EU Dir 2004/38; see also paras 62-
64 of the Advocate General's opinion in
Givane, C-257/00 [2003] ECR I-00345,
although the ECJ did not address the
issue itself.

278 Reg 15(2) I(EEA) Regs; Art 16(4) EU Dir
2004/38

Chapter 13

•••

Residence and presence: rules for individual benefits

This chapter covers:
1. Means-tested benefits (below)
2. Bereavement benefits (p187)
3. Child benefit and guardian's allowance (p190)
4. Disability and carers' benefits (p190)
5. Industrial injuries benefits (p192)
6. Contribution-based jobseeker's allowance and contributory employment and support allowance (p194)
7. Maternity allowance (p195)
8. Retirement pensions (p195)
9. Social fund funeral and winter fuel payments (p196)
10. Tax credits (p198)

This chapter explains the residence and presence rules for each benefit. It also covers how you may be assisted by the European Union co-ordination rules. Further information on the different residence and presence tests is in Chapter 10, and further information on the habitual residence and right to reside tests is in Chapter 11. This chapter does not explain the rules on being paid while you are abroad. These are covered in Part 5.

1. Means-tested benefits

To be entitled to **income support (IS)**, **income-based jobseeker's allowance (JSA)**, **income-related employment and support allowance (ESA)**, **pension credit (PC)** and **universal credit (UC)**, you (and your partner for UC) must:
- be present in Great Britain (see p87);[1] *and*
- satisfy the habitual residence test (see p98) or be in a group that is exempt (see p99).[2]

To satisfy the habitual residence test for these benefits, in addition to being 'habitually resident in fact' (see p102), you must have a right to reside (see p107) in the common travel area – ie, the UK, Ireland, Channel Islands and the Isle of Man. For income-based JSA only, you must also have been living in the common travel area for the past three months (see p88).

In certain circumstances, the rules treat you as present in Great Britain during a temporary absence, so you can continue to receive these benefits while you are abroad for limited periods (see Chapter 15).

For all means-tested benefits other than UC, the habitual residence test only applies to the claimant. For UC, if you live with your partner, you make a joint claim and you must both satisfy the habitual residence test. If your partner fails the habitual residence test, you must claim UC as a single person. Your award is based on the maximum amount for a single person, but your partner's income and capital are taken into account.[3]

Note: if you come under the UC system as part of the pathfinder (see CPAG's *Welfare Benefits and Tax Credits Handbook* for more details on this), you must satisfy additional residence and presence rules for UC. You must:[4]

- be a British citizen; *and*
- have resided in the UK throughout the two years before the date of your claim; *and*
- not have left the UK for a continuous period of more than four weeks during the above period.

If you do not satisfy the requirements for UC, you may be able to claim existing means-tested benefits. For further details, see CPAG's *Welfare Benefits and Tax Credits Handbook*.

To be entitled to **housing benefit (HB)**, you must be habitually resident (see p98), including having a right to reside, (see p107) in the common travel area, unless you are in a group that is exempt from the habitual residence test (see p99).[5]

There is no requirement to be present in Great Britain for HB. However, you must be liable to make payments in respect of a dwelling in Great Britain, which you occupy as your home.[6] There are rules that treat you as occupying your home, including during a temporary absence from it.[7] Although these rules are not specific to absences abroad, they determine whether you can be entitled to HB while you are abroad (see p209).

If your partner is abroad

If you have a partner who is abroad, the effect this has on your benefit depends on whether the separation is permanent or, if temporary, whether you still count as members of the same household.

If you are still regarded as a couple, your partner's absence abroad can affect your benefit in two ways.

- At some point, you will cease to be paid an amount of benefit for your partner.
- Your partner's capital and income can continue to affect your entitlement.

If you separate permanently (ie, you do not intend to resume living with your partner), you no longer count as a couple.[8]

If you and your partner are living apart temporarily, you continue to count as a couple because you are still treated as members of the same household, unless:[9]

- for **IS, income-based JSA, income-related ESA, PC and HB**, you are likely to be separated for more than 52 weeks. However, you still count as a couple if you are unlikely to be separated for 'substantially' longer than 52 weeks and there are exceptional circumstances, such as a stay in hospital, or if you have no control over the length of the absence;
- for **IS, income-based JSA, income-related ESA** and **PC**, you or your partner are detained in custody or in a high-security psychiatric hospital, or are on temporary release, or are living permanently in a care home;
- for **UC**, you have been separated (or expect to be separated) for more than six months.

Your partner's absence is from *you*, not from the family home, so these rules can apply even if your partner has never lived in your current home and your former household need not have been in this country.[10] The length of the absence is calculated from when it started to when it is likely to finish.

Where questions of 'intention' are involved (eg, when deciding whether you or your partner intend to resume living with your family), the intention must be 'unqualified'. This means that it must not depend on a factor over which you have no control – eg, the right of entry to the UK being granted by the Home Office[11] or the offer of a suitable job.[12]

If you still count as a couple, there are rules that allow you to continue to receive an amount of benefit for your partner while s/he is abroad for a limited period depending on the circumstances. These rules vary between the different means-tested benefits (see Chapter 15).

If these rules do not apply, or at the end of the limited period:

- for **IS, income-based JSA, income-related ESA and HB**, your applicable amount no longer includes an amount for your partner. However, your partner's capital, income and work are still taken into account as s/he is still treated as part of your household;[13]
- for **PC**, you are paid as a single person. Your partner's income and capital are ignored because s/he is no longer treated as part of your household;[14]
- for **UC**, you cease to be entitled as joint claimants and must claim as a single person. Your award is based on the maximum amount for a single person, but your partner's income and capital are taken into account until you have been, or you expect to be, apart for six months (as then you cease to be treated as a

couple).[15] **Note:** if your partner's absence abroad means s/he ceases to be habitually resident (including if s/he ceases to have a right to reside) in the common travel area, s/he is treated as no longer present. You can claim as a single person, but your partner's income and capital are taken into account.[16]

If your child is abroad

If you have a child who is abroad, the effect this has on your benefit depends on whether s/he is still treated as being part of your household, despite temporarily living away from you.

S/he ceases to be treated as part of your household if:[17]

- for **IS, JSA, ESA** and **HB**, s/he is not living with you and:
  - has no intention of resuming living with you; or
  - is likely to be absent for more than 52 weeks, unless there are exceptional circumstances, such as being in hospital, or if you have no control over the length of absence and the absence is unlikely to be substantially longer than 52 weeks;
- for **IS, JSA** and **ESA**, s/he is not living with you and has been abroad for more than:
  - four weeks; or
  - eight weeks (26 weeks for ESA) to get medical treatment;
- there are other reasons that are not related to residence or presence, such as being fostered. See CPAG's *Welfare Benefits and Tax Credits Handbook* for more information.

For **IS** or **income-based JSA**, once the child ceases to be treated as part of your household, s/he permanently ceases to be included in your applicable amount. If s/he returns to your household, you must claim child tax credit for her/him instead. See p214 for IS and p217 for income-based JSA.

The rules for **UC** are different. You cease to be responsible for a child if s/he is absent from your household and the absence exceeds, or is expected to exceed, one month, or up to six months in limited circumstances (see p221).[18]

European Union co-ordination rules

If you are covered by the European Union (EU) co-ordination rules, these can assist you to satisfy the habitual residence test for some of the means-tested benefits sooner than might otherwise be the case.

If you are covered by the EU co-ordination rules (see p242) and you are claiming:

- **income-based JSA, income-related ESA** or **PC**, you cannot be denied benefit on the basis that you have not been actually resident for an 'appreciable period' of time, because your length of actual residence is only one relevant factor in

determining whether you are 'habitually residence in fact' and can be outweighed by others (see p105);
- **income-based JSA,** you may be able to argue that it is unlawful to exclude you from benefit until you have been living in the common travel area for three months if you are 'habitually resident in fact' and have a right to reside (see p88).

2. **Bereavement benefits**

You do not need to satisfy any residence or presence rules to be entitled to bereavement benefits. There is one exception, which only applies to bereavement payment.

If you are absent from Great Britain when you claim bereavement payment, you can only be entitled if:[19]
- your late spouse or civil partner was in Great Britain when s/he died; *or*
- you were in Great Britain on the date of the death of your spouse or civil partner; *or*
- neither of the above two bullets apply, but you returned to Great Britain within four weeks of the death of your late spouse or civil partner; *or*
- your late spouse's/civil partner's national insurance (NI) contribution record is sufficient for you to satisfy the contribution conditions for widowed parent's allowance and bereavement allowance; *or*
- your spouse or civil partner died while abroad in another European Economic Area (EEA) state and the European Union (EU) co-ordination rules apply to you (see p242); *or*
- your spouse or civil partner died while abroad in a state which has a reciprocal agreement with the UK that covers your entitlement to bereavement payment.

According to official guidance, the DWP takes the view that if you and your late spouse or civil partner were outside Great Britain when s/he died and you do not return to Great Britain within four weeks of the death (and none of the last three bullets above apply), you are disqualified from bereavement payment, even if you claim within the necessary time limit when you are back in Great Britain.[20] It is arguable that this approach is incorrect and you should only be disqualified if you are absent from Great Britain when you make your claim (and none of the above bullets apply).

European Union co-ordination rules

If you are covered by the EU co-ordination rules (see p242) and the UK is your 'competent state' (see p248):

- you can, if necessary, rely on NI contributions paid by your late spouse or civil partner in other EEA states to calculate your entitlement to bereavement benefits under the aggregation principle (see p254);
- if your late spouse/civil partner died in another EEA state, s/he can be treated as having died in the UK for the purposes of entitlement to a bereavement payment.[21]

Reciprocal and other international agreements

If you have lived and worked in a country with which the UK has a reciprocal agreement (see p262), you may be able to count periods of insurance paid in that country towards your bereavement benefit entitlement. Similarly, if you are covered by an international agreement between the EU and another state, you may be able to do the same (see p269).

3. **Child benefit and guardian's allowance**

Child benefit

To be entitled to child benefit, you and your child(ren) must be present in Great Britain (see p87).[22]

You are treated as not present and, therefore, not eligible for child benefit if:[23]

- you are not ordinarily resident in the UK (see p91); *or*
- you do not have a right to reside in the UK (see p107); *or*
- you have not been living in the UK for the three months prior to your claim, unless you are exempt from this requirement (see p88).

Note: you do not need to have a right to reside if you claimed child benefit before 1 May 2004 and you have been receiving it since that date.

You are treated as present if you are:[24]

- a Crown servant posted overseas and:
  - you are, or immediately before your posting abroad you were, ordinarily resident in the UK; *or*
  - immediately before your posting you were in the UK in connection with that posting; *or*
- the partner of a Crown servant posted overseas and in the same country as her/ him, or temporarily absent from that country under the same exceptions that enable child benefit to continue during a temporary absence from Great Britain (see p222); *or*
- a person who is in the UK as a result of your being deported or legally removed from another country.

You and/or your child can be treated as present for limited periods during a temporary absence (see p222).

While you are treated as present, you continue to satisfy that condition of entitlement. This means that you can continue to receive child benefit if it is already being paid and you can also make a fresh claim during your, or your child's, absence. If you, or your child, spend longer abroad than the permitted periods (see p222), you (or s/he) cease to satisfy the presence condition and your entitlement to child benefit ends.

Guardian's allowance

Entitlement to guardian's allowance depends on entitlement to child benefit, so you must meet the conditions for child benefit set out above. In addition, at least one of the child's parents must:[25]

- have been born in the UK; *or*
- have spent a total of 52 weeks in any two-year period in Great Britain at some time after reaching the age of 16.

In order to satisfy the second condition above, you are treated as being present in Great Britain during any absence abroad which is due to your employment as a serving member of the forces, an airman or airwoman, mariner or continental shelf worker.

European Union co-ordination rules

If you are covered by the European Union (EU) co-ordination rules (see p242), you may be able to:

- use periods of residence in another European Economic Area (EEA) country to satisfy the child benefit requirement to have been 'living in' the UK for the past three months (see p254);
- use time spent in another EEA state to satisfy the guardian's allowance requirement to have spent 52 weeks in any two-year period in Great Britain (see above). It may also be arguable that this condition should not apply to you if you are covered by the co-ordination rules and have a 'genuine and sufficient link to the UK social security system' (see p192);[26]
- be paid child benefit, and, if applicable, guardian's allowance, for a child resident in another EEA country without her/him needing to satisfy the UK rules on temporary absences. Child benefit and guardian's allowance are classified as 'family benefits' under the EU co-ordination rules. For more details on the payment of these, see p257;
- argue that the right to reside requirement for child benefit is unlawful (see p108).

4. **Disability and carers' benefits**

For **attendance allowance (AA), disability living allowance (DLA), personal independence payment (PIP) and carer's allowance (CA),** you must satisfy the presence, past presence and habitual residence tests. This means you must:[27]
- be present in Great Britain at the time of your claim;
- have been present in Great Britain for at least 104 weeks in the last 156 weeks (the 'past presence test'). See p88, but see also below;
- be habitually resident in the common travel area (see p98).

However, if you were entitled to AA, DLA or CA on 7 April 2013, the rules that applied when you claimed (which are the same as those described below for employment and support allowance (ESA) in youth) continue to apply until your benefit award is terminated unless:[28]
- your benefit award is revised or superseded. You must then be habitually resident rather than ordinarily resident in Great Britain; *or*
- your benefit award continues until 7 April 2015. In this case, you must have been present for at least 104 weeks in the last 156 weeks, rather than 26 weeks in the last 52.

If the DLA claimant is a child under 16, her/his residence is generally determined by the residence of the person responsible for her/him (see p90). For AA, DLA, PIP and CA, you are treated as habitually resident (as well as treated as present) if you:[29]
- are abroad in your capacity as a serving member of the armed forces; *or*
- are living with someone who is abroad as a serving member of the armed forces and s/he is your spouse, civil partner, son, stepson, daughter, stepdaughter, father, stepfather, father-in-law, mother, stepmother or mother-in-law.

For **ESA in youth, incapacity benefit (IB) in youth and severe disablement allowance (SDA),** you must satisfy the presence, past presence and ordinary residence tests. This means to be entitled to each of these benefits you must:[30]
- be present in Great Britain at the time of claim (see p87);
- have been present in Great Britain for not less than 26 weeks in the last 52 weeks (the 'past presence' test – see p88);
- be ordinarily resident in Great Britain (see p91).

For ESA in youth, IB in youth and SDA, once you pass the residence and presence tests, you do not need to satisfy them again while you are in the same period of limited capability for work or incapacity for work.[31]

When you can be treated as present

You are treated as being present during certain absences (see p223). Any period when you are treated as present can be counted to satisfy both the presence and the past presence tests.

Exceptions to the past presence test

If you are claiming the DLA care component for a baby under six months old, there is a shorter 13-week past presence test. If covered by this, it continues to apply until your child's first birthday. If your child becomes entitled to DLA aged between six months and 36 months, the past presence test is 26 weeks in the last 156 weeks.

For AA, DLA and PIP, the 104-week (or 26-week or 13-week) past presence test does not apply if you are terminally ill.[32]

The definition of 'terminal illness' is the same as applies for other purposes for these benefits – ie, that you have a progressive disease and your death in consequence of that disease can reasonably be expected within six months.[33]

European Union co-ordination rules

The European Union (EU) co-ordination rules can make it easier to claim AA, DLA, PIP and CA in the UK and can also enable you to make a new claim if you live in another European Economic Area (EEA) state.

The past presence test does not apply to AA, DLA, PIP and CA if:[34]

- you are habitually resident in Great Britain; *and*
- you are covered by the co-ordination rules (see p242); *and*
- you can demonstrate 'a genuine and sufficient link to the UK social security system' (see p192).

If you are covered by the co-ordination rules (see p242), but are not exempt from the past presence test because you are not accepted as having 'a genuine and sufficient link to the UK social security system', you may be able to count periods of residence in another EEA member state to satisfy the past presence test for these benefits (and also for ESA in youth). This is achieved under the aggregation principle of the co-ordination rules (see p254).

If you are living in another EEA member state, you can make a new claim for AA, DLA care component, the daily living component of PIP or CA without needing to satisfy the habitual residence in Great Britain and the presence and past presence requirements if the UK is your 'competent state' (see p248)[35] if:[36]

- you are habitually resident in another EEA state or Switzerland; *and*
- you are covered by the co-ordination rules (see p242); *and*
- you can demonstrate a genuine and sufficient link to the UK social security system (see p192).

Whether you are in the UK or another EEA state, if you are covered by the co-ordination rules (see p242), you can only be entitled to AA, DLA care component, the daily living component of PIP or CA if the UK is your 'competent state' (see p248).[37] This might not be the case if you (or your family member who brings you within the co-ordination rules) receive a pension from another member state (see p250).

DLA mobility component is listed as, and PIP mobility component is treated by the DWP as, a special non-contributory benefit and is therefore not 'exportable'.[38] You can only be paid these in the state where you are resident.[39] Under the EU co-ordination rules, this means where you 'habitually reside'.[40] The EU co-ordination rules can still assist you to be entitled to the DLA or PIP mobility component sooner than you would otherwise be because, if you are covered by these rules (see p242), you cannot be denied benefit on the basis that you have not been actually resident for an 'appreciable period' of time and your length of actual residence is only one relevant factor in determining whether you are 'habitually residence in fact' and can be outweighed by other factors (see p105).

Genuine and sufficient link to the UK social security system

The phrase **'genuine and sufficient link to the UK social security system'** is not defined in regulations, but comes from a case decided by the Court of Justice of the European Union (CJEU).[41] The circumstances which applied in that case and which were held to have amounted to a 'genuine and sufficient link to the UK social security system' are therefore relevant, but they do not form an exhaustive list and other factors may be equally or more relevant in your case. Relevant factors accepted by the CJEU include:

– whether you have worked in the UK;
– whether you have spent a significant part of your life in the UK;
– whether you are receiving a UK contributory benefit or you are dependent on a family member who has worked in the UK and/or receives a UK contributory benefit.[42]

You must show that you have a genuine and sufficient link to the UK social security system for the purpose of the benefit you are claiming, taking all your circumstances into account.[43]

---

5. **Industrial injuries benefits**

Industrial injuries benefits are:
- industrial injuries disablement benefit;
- reduced earnings allowance;
- retirement allowance;
- constant attendance allowance;
- exceptionally severe disablement allowance.

To be entitled to any of these benefits, you must have been:
- in Great Britain when the accident at work happened;[44] *or*
- engaged in Great Britain in the employment that caused the disease (even if you have also been engaged outside Great Britain in that employment);[45] *or*
- paying UK national insurance (NI) contributions, either at Class 1 rate or at Class 2 rate as a volunteer development worker when the accident at work happened or you contracted the disease. Benefit is not payable until you return to Great Britain.[46]

There are exceptions to these rules which mean you can qualify for benefit in respect of an accident which happens, or a disease which is contracted, outside Great Britain while you are:[47]
- employed as a mariner or airman or airwoman;
- employed as an apprentice pilot on board a ship or vessel;
- on board an aircraft on a test flight starting in Great Britain in the course of your employment.

In these cases, there are also more generous rules for defining when accidents arise 'out of and in the course of' your employment, and for complying with time limits under benefit rules.[48]

European Union co-ordination rules

If you are covered by the European Union (EU) co-ordination rules (see p242), you can, if necessary, rely on periods of employment and NI paid in other European Economic Area (EEA) states in order to qualify for industrial injuries benefits in the UK. This is achieved under the aggregation principle (see p254).

Industrial injuries benefits, except retirement allowance, are classed as 'benefits for accidents at work and occupational diseases' under the EU co-ordination rules (see p245).

If you have an accident while travelling abroad in another member state, this can be deemed to have occurred in the state liable to pay benefits for accidents at work and occupational diseases. If one state determines that you have had an accident or contracted a disease, this should be accepted by the state liable to pay benefit in respect of that accident or disease. These outcomes are achieved under the principle of equal treatment of facts of events (see p254).[49]

If you have worked in two or more EEA states in a job that gave you a prescribed industrial disease, you only get benefit from the member state in which you last worked in that job.[50]

13

Chapter 13: Residence and presence: rules for individual benefits
6. Contribution-based JSA and contributory ESA

6. Contribution-based jobseeker's allowance and contributory employment and support allowance

To be entitled to contribution-based jobseeker's allowance (JSA) or contributory employment and support allowance (ESA), you must be in Great Britain.[51] The rules about when you can be paid during a temporary absence abroad are covered on p215 and p217. There are no residence conditions, unless you are claiming contributory ESA in youth (see p190).

See p183 for the residence and presence conditions for income-based JSA and income-related ESA.

European Union co-ordination rules

Contribution-based jobseeker's allowance

If you are covered by the co-ordination rules (see p242) you can, if necessary, rely on national insurance (NI) contributions paid in another European Economic Area (EEA) state to entitle you to contribution-based JSA in the UK. This is achieved under the principle of aggregation. However, an additional condition applies for unemployment benefits that means that, in most cases, you can only aggregate your contributions if your most recent period of paying or being credited with those contributions was in the UK.[52] See p254 for more details.

If you are coming to, or returning to, the UK to look for work and have been insured in another EEA member state, you may be able to get the other member state's unemployment benefit for up to three months if:[53]

- you were getting that unemployment benefit immediately before coming to the UK;
- you have been registered as available for work for four weeks (or less if the member state's rules allow) in the other member state;
- you claim JSA within seven days after you were last registered in the other member state; *and*
- you meet whichever of the jobseeking requirements apply for the type of contribution-based JSA you are claiming – eg, if you do not come under the universal credit (UC) system, you satisfy the JSA jobseeking conditions or, if you come under the UC system, you accept a claimant commitment and you meet any work-related requirements that have been imposed on you.

The three months can be extended to a maximum of six months if the state from which you are claiming the unemployment benefit agrees.[54]

Contributory employment and support allowance

If you are covered by the EU co-ordination rules (see p242) you can, if necessary, rely on NI contributions paid in another EEA state to entitle you to contributory ESA in the UK. This is achieved under the principle of aggregation (see p254).

If you are covered by the EU co-ordination rules (see p242) and have moved to the UK from another EEA state, you maybe able to continue to receive a sickness or invalidity benefit from that other EEA state if it continues to be your competent state for the payment of that benefit (see p248).

Reciprocal and other international agreements

If you have lived and worked in a country with which the UK has a reciprocal agreement (see p262), you may be able to count periods of insurance paid in that country towards your entitlement to contribution-based JSA or contributory ESA in the UK. Similarly, if you are covered by another type of international agreement between the EU and another state, you may be able to do the same (see p269).

7. **Maternity allowance**

Entitlement to maternity allowance (MA) is based on past employment. There are no residence requirements, but you are disqualified if you are absent from Great Britain.[55] See p227 for the rules allowing you to be paid during a temporary absence.

European Union co-ordination rules

If you are covered by the co-ordination rules (see p242) you can, if necessary, rely on periods of employment in other European Economic Area states in order to qualify for MA in the UK. This is under the principle of aggregation (see p254).

8. **Retirement pensions**

Retirement pensions, other than a Category D retirement pension, do not have any residence or presence conditions.[56] They can be paid without time limit, whether or not you are present in Great Britain. The exception to this is the annual uprating, which is only paid while you are abroad in certain circumstances (see p230).

To be entitled to a Category D retirement pension, you must have been:
- resident in Great Britain for at least 10 years in any continuous period of 20 years ending on or after your 80th birthday; *and*
- ordinarily resident (see p91) in Great Britain on either:

13

Chapter 13: Residence and presence: rules for individual benefits
9. Social fund funeral and winter fuel payments

– your 80th birthday; *or*
– the date on which you claimed the Category D pension, if later.

European Union co-ordination rules

If you are covered by the European Union (EU) co-ordination rules (see p242), you can, if necessary, rely on national insurance contributions paid in other European Economic Area (EEA) states to calculate your entitlement to retirement pensions in the UK. Similarly, for a Category D retirement pension, you can count periods of residence in other EEA states to meet the residence requirement. Both of these possibilities are achieved under the aggregation principle (see p254).

Note: your award may be reduced to reflect the proportion of years of contributions paid, or periods of residence completed, in the UK out of the total years of contributions paid or periods of residence completed in all states.[57]

The requirement to be ordinarily resident for a Category D retirement pension may not apply to you if you are covered by the EU co-ordination rules and you can show that you have a 'genuine and sufficient link to the UK social security system' (see p192).[58]

Reciprocal and other international agreements

If you have lived and worked in a country with which the UK has a reciprocal agreement (see p262), you may be able to count periods of residence or insurance paid in that country towards your UK retirement pension entitlement. Similarly, if you are covered by another international agreement between the EU and another state, you may be able to do the same (see p269).

9. Social fund funeral and winter fuel payments

The only two social fund payments that have residence conditions are funeral expenses payments and winter fuel payments.

Funeral expenses payment

To qualify for a funeral expenses payment:
- the deceased must have been ordinarily resident (see p91) in the UK;[59]
- the funeral must take place in the UK. However, it can take place in any European Economic Area (EEA) country if you or your partner are:[60]
  - an EEA national and a 'worker' (see p129), including if you have retained this status (see p135);
  - an EEA national and a self-employed person (see p141), including if you have retained this status (see p144);

Chapter 13: Residence and presence: rules for individual benefits
9. Social fund funeral and winter fuel payments

13

– a family member of one of the above (see p151);
– an EEA national with a permanent right of residence acquired in less than five years, or you are the family member of such a person (see p174);
– arguably a person with any other right of residence in the UK under European Union (EU) law (see below).

It is arguable that you can also qualify for a funeral expenses payment if the funeral takes place in an EEA state other than the UK if you have *any* right to reside in the UK under EU law. This is because the EU law on residence rights has developed since the above provisions were introduced and now covers additional groups of EEA nationals and their family members. The above provisions were introduced following a case in which the European Court of Justice held that the rule which required the funeral to be in the UK was unlawfully discriminatory against EU migrant workers.[61] Arguably, the same applies to other groups who now have residence rights under EU law, but who are not listed in the funeral payment regulations – eg, people who have a permanent right of residence following five years of legal residence in the UK. Furthermore, EU Directive 2004/38 contains a general rule that (subject to certain limitations) prohibits discrimination against anyone with a right of residence.[62]

Winter fuel payment

To qualify for a winter fuel payment, you must be ordinarily resident (see p91) in Great Britain on any day in the qualifying week.[63]

The qualifying week
The '**qualifying week**' is the week beginning on the third Monday in September before the winter you want to be paid for.

European Union co-ordination rules

You are not required to be ordinarily resident in Great Britain in order to be entitled to a winter fuel payment if, on any day in the qualifying week, you are:[64]

- covered by the EU co-ordination rules (see p242);
- habitually resident in an EEA country (other than the UK) or Switzerland; *and*
- can demonstrate a 'genuine and sufficient link to the UK social security system' (see p192).

Was your application for a winter fuel payment refused before September 2013?
The EU rules were only included within the UK regulations from 16 September 2013. However, they are based on a judgment of the Court of Justice of the European Union, dated 21 July 2011.[65] If you had your winter fuel payment refused because, at the relevant time, you were not ordinarily resident in Great Britain, but you did satisfy the

above rules, you can request that the decision be revised. The DWP will revise its decision on the grounds of official error if it was made on or after 21 July 2011.[66] If the decision was made before this date, the DWP's position is that it can only be revised if another ground for revision is available.[67] For a discussion of similar issues in relation to previous refusals of disability benefits, see p224.

10. **Tax credits**

To be entitled to **child tax credit** (CTC), you (and your partner if you are making a joint claim) must:[68]
- be present in the UK (see p87); *and*
- be ordinarily resident in the UK (see p91); *and*
- have a right to reside in the UK (see p95); *and*
- unless you are also claiming working tax credit (WTC), have been living in the UK for the three months prior to your claim (see p88).

To be entitled to **WTC**, you (and your partner if you are making a joint claim) must be:[69]
- present in the UK (see p87); *and*
- ordinarily resident in the UK (see p91).

There are, however, some exceptions.[70]
- You do not need to have a right to reside for CTC if you claimed CTC before 1 May 2004 and you have been receiving it since that date.
- You are treated as ordinarily resident in the UK for CTC and WTC and, if you are claiming CTC only, you are not required to have been living in the UK for the past three months, if you have been deported or otherwise legally removed from another country to the UK.
- You are treated as ordinarily resident in the UK for WTC if you have a right to reside under European Union (EU) Directive 2004/38 (see p115). However, in practice, being accepted as ordinarily resident is rarely a problem.
- There are several groups of people who are exempt from the requirement to have been living in the UK for three months prior to the claim (see p89).
- You can be treated as present for either eight or 12 weeks during a temporary absence, or while you or your partner are a Crown servant posted overseas (see p231). While you are treated as present, you continue to satisfy the conditions of entitlement to tax credits. This means that you can continue to receive tax credits that are already in payment and can make a fresh or renewal claim during your absence. If you spend longer abroad than the permitted periods, you cease to satisfy the presence condition and your tax credit entitlement ends.

Being absent (other than while you are treated as present), ceasing to be ordinarily resident or losing your right to reside are all changes that you must notify to HM Revenue and Customs (HMRC) within one month. Failure to notify may result in your being overpaid and/or being subject to a penalty.

Couples and children

If you are a member of a **couple** and make a joint tax credit claim, you must both satisfy the residence requirements. Your entitlement to tax credits as a couple ends if either you or your partner:

- are abroad for longer than a permitted temporary absence of eight or 12 weeks (see p231);
- (for CTC only) lose the right to reside;
- cease to be ordinarily resident.

The person who continues to satisfy the residence rules can make a fresh claim for CTC and/or WTC as a single person if s/he is entitled on that basis.

If your partner returns to the UK, or becomes ordinarily resident or acquires a right to reside, you must terminate your single person claim and claim again as a couple.

If you or your partner are abroad (even for a permitted temporary absence of less than eight or 12 weeks) and you (or s/he) were the only partner in full-time work, you may lose entitlement to WTC if the requirement to be in full-time work is no longer satisfied.

If at any point HMRC considers that you and your partner have separated and this is likely to be permanent, you cease to be entitled to make a joint claim as a couple and each of you may be entitled to make single claims.[71]

You have a duty to notify HMRC of any of the above changes within one month of their taking place. Failure to notify may result in your being overpaid or being subject to a penalty, as well as missing out on any potential alternative entitlement that you may have as a single person or as a couple.

There are no presence or residence requirements for any **child** in your claim, but you must be responsible for the child. You count as responsible if the child normally lives with you or, if there are competing claims, you have main responsibility for her/him.[72]

European Union co-ordination rules

If you are covered by the EU co-ordination rules (see p242), you may be able to be paid CTC for a partner or child resident in another European Economic Area (EEA) country. CTC is classed as a 'family benefit' under the EU co-ordination rules. For more details on the payment of family benefits, see p257.

WTC is not covered by the EU co-ordination rules. Therefore, if your partner is in another EEA country, although you may be able to make a joint claim for CTC as a couple, your WTC claim is treated as a single claim.[73] If you or your partner are working in another EEA country but live in the UK, and therefore remain present and ordinarily resident in the UK, this work can count for the purposes of your WTC claim.[74]

Note: the European Commission has asked the Court of Justice of the European Union to declare the right to reside test for CTC unlawful (see p108).[75]

Notes

1. **Means-tested benefits**
1   **IS** s124(1) SSCBA 1992
    JSA s1(2)(i) JSA 1995
    ESA s1(3)(d) WRA 2007
    PC s1(2)(a) SPCA 2002
    UC s4(1)(c) WRA 2012
2   **IS** Regs 21-21AA IS Regs
    JSA Regs 85-85A JSA Regs
    ESA Regs 69-70 ESA Regs
    PC Reg 2 SPC Regs
    UC Reg 9 UC Regs
3   Regs 3(3), 18(2), 22(3) and 36(3) UC Regs
4   Reg 5 UC(TP) Regs
5   Reg 10 HB Regs; reg 10 HB(SPC) Regs
6   s130(1)(a) SSCBA 1992
7   Reg 7 HB Regs; reg 7 HB(SPC) Regs
8   **IS** Reg 16(2)(a) IS Regs
    JSA Reg 78(2)(a) JSA Regs
    ESA Reg 156(3)(a) ESA Regs
    PC Reg 5(1)(a)(i) SPC Regs
    HB Reg 21(2)(a) HB Regs; reg 21(2)(a) HB(SPC) Regs
    UC Reg 3(6) UC Regs
9   **IS** Reg 16(1)-(3) IS Regs
    JSA Reg 78(1)-(3) JSA Regs
    ESA Reg 156(1)-(4) ESA Regs
    PC Reg 5 SPC Regs
    HB Reg 21(1)and(2) HB Regs; reg 21(1) and(2) HB(SPC) Regs
    UC Reg 3(6) UC Regs
10 CIS/508/1992
11 CIS/508/1992; CIS/13805/1996
12 CIS/484/1993
13 **IS** Regs 4, 16 and 21 and Sch 7 paras 11 and 11A IS Regs
    JSA Regs 78 and 85 and Sch 5 paras 10 and 11 JSA Regs
    ESA Reg 156 and Sch 5 paras 6 and 7 ESA Regs
    HB Reg 21 HB Regs; reg 21 HB(SPC) Regs
14 Regs 3-5 SPC Regs
15 Regs 3(3) and (6), 18(2), 22(3) and 36(3) UC Regs
16 Regs 3(3), 9, 18(2), 22(3) and 36(3) UC Regs
17 **IS** Reg 16 IS Regs
    JSA Reg 78 JSA regs
    ESA Reg 156 ESA Regs
    HB Reg 21 HB Regs; reg 21 HB(SPC) Regs
18 Reg 4(7) UC Regs

2. **Bereavement benefits**
19 s113 SSCBA 1992; reg 4(1) and (2B) SSB(PA) Regs
20 para 073081 DMG, Example 2
21 Arts 5 and 42 EU Reg 883/04

3. **Child benefit and guardian's allowance**
22 s146 SSCBA 1992
23 Reg 23 CB Regs
24 Regs 23, 30 and 31 CB Regs
25 Reg 9 GA(Gen) Regs
26 *Stewart v SSWP*, C-503/09 [2011] ECR I-06497; *SSWP v JG (IS)* [2013] UKUT 0298 (AAC); *SSWP v JG (RP)* [2013] UKUT 0300 (AAC), currently under appeal to the Court of Appeal

4. Disability and carers' benefits
27 **AA** Reg 2 SS(AA) Regs
DLA Reg 2 SS(DLA) Regs
PIP Reg 16 SS(PIP) Regs
CA Reg 9 SS(ICA) Regs
28 Reg 1 SS(DLA,AA&CA)(A) Regs
29 **AA** Reg 2(2) and (3A) SS(AA) Regs
DLA Reg 2(2) and (3A) SS(DLA) Regs
PIP Regs 19 and 20 SS(PIP) Regs
CA Reg 9(3) SS(ICA) Regs
30 **ESA** Reg 11 ESA Regs; reg 12 ESA Regs
2013
AA Reg 2 SS(AA) Regs
DLA Reg 2 SS(DLA) Regs
CA Reg 9 SS(ICA) Regs
IB Reg 16 SS(IB) Regs
SDA Reg 3 SS(SDA) Regs
31 **ESA** Reg 11(4) ESA Regs; reg 12(4) ESA
Regs 2013
IB Reg 16(6) SS(IB) Regs
SDA Reg 3(3) SS(SDA) Regs
32 **AA** Reg 2(3) SS(AA) Regs
DLA Reg 2(4) SS(DLA) Regs
PIP Reg 21 SS(PIP) Regs
33 **AA** s35(2C) SSA 1975
DLA s66(2) SSCBA 1992
PIP s82(4) WRA 2012
34 **AA** Reg 2A SS(AA) Regs
DLA Reg 2A SS(DLA) Regs
PIP Reg 22 SS(PIP) Regs
CA Reg 9A SS(ICA) Regs
35 ss65(7), 70(4A) and 72(7B) SSCBA
1992; s84 WRA 2012
36 **AA** Reg 2B SS(AA) Regs
DLA Reg 2B SS(DLA) Regs
PIP Reg 23 SS(PIP) Regs
CA Reg 9B SS(ICA) Regs
37 ss65(7), 70(4A) and 72(7B) SSCBA; s84
WRA 2012
38 *Bartlett and Others v SSWP*, C-537/09
[2011] ECR I-03417
39 Art 70 EU Reg 883/04; *Robin Swaddling v
Adjudication Officer*, C-90/97 [1999] ECR
I-01075
40 Art 1(j) EU Reg 883/04
41 *Stewart v SSWP*, C-503/09 [2011] ECR I-
06497
42 *Stewart v SSWP*, C-503/09 [2011] ECR I-
06497
43 *SSWP v JG (IS)* [2013] UKUT 0298 (AAC);
SSWP v JG (RP) [2013] UKUT 0300
(AAC), currently under appeal to the
Court of Appeal

5. Industrial injuries benefits
44 s94(5) SSCBA 1992
45 Reg 14 SS(IIPD) Regs
46 Reg 10C(5) and (6) SSB(PA) Regs

47 Reg 2 SS(II)(AB) Regs 1975; SS(II)(MB)
Regs
48 Regs 3, 4, 6 and 8 SS(II)(MB) Regs; regs
3 and 6 SS(II)(AB) Regs
49 Art 5 EU Reg 883/04
50 Art 38 EU Reg 883/04

6. Contribution-based jobseeker's allowance and contributory employment and support allowance
51 **JSA** s1(2)(i) JSA 1995
ESA ss1(3)(d) and 18(4)(a) WRA 2007
52 Art 61(2) EU Reg 883/04
53 Art 64 EU Reg 883/04
54 Art 64(3) EU Reg 883/04

7. Maternity allowance
55 s113(1) SSCBA 1992

8. Retirement pensions
56 s113 SSCBA 1992; reg 4(1) SSB(PA)
Regs
57 Art 52 EU Reg 883/04
58 *Stewart v SSWP*, C-503/09 [2011] ECR, I-
06497; *SSWP v JG (RP)* [2013] UKUT 300
(AAC), currently under appeal to the
Court of Appeal

9. Social fund funeral and winter fuel payments
59 Reg 7(5) SFM&FE Regs
60 Reg 7(9) and (10) SFM&FE Regs
61 *John O'Flynn v Adjudication Officer*, C-
237/94 [1996] ECR I-02617; R(IS) 4/98
62 Art 24 EU Dir 2004/38
63 Reg 2 SFWFP Regs
64 Reg 2 SFWFP Regs
65 *Stewart v SSWP*, C-503/09 [2011] ECR I-
06497
66 Reg 3(5)(a) SS&CS(D&A) Regs; para
73245 and vol 2 Part 6 Appendix 1 para
10 DMG
67 vol 2 Part 6 Appendix 1 para 11 DMG

10. Tax credits
68 s3(3) TCA 2002; reg 3(1) and (5) TC(R)
Regs
69 s3(3) TCA 2002; reg 3(1) TC(R) Regs
70 Reg 3 TC(R) Regs
71 s3(5A) TCA 2002
72 s8(2) TCA; reg 3(1) CTC Regs
73 paras 20090, 20160 and 20170 TCCCM
74 para 0288580 TCM; see also *GC v
CHMRC (TC)* [2014] UKUT 0251 (AAC)
75 *European Commission v UK*, C-308/14

Part 5

Benefits while abroad

Chapter 14

Going abroad

This chapter covers:
1. Introduction (below)
2. How your benefits and tax credits are affected (p207)

This chapter provides an overview of the way your entitlement to benefits and tax credits is affected if you, or a member of your family for whom you claim, go abroad. The specific information about individual benefits and tax credits is in Chapter 15.

---

1. Introduction

Most benefits and tax credits are affected if you, or your partner or child, go abroad. The rules vary between different benefits and tax credits. Some can always be paid abroad, some can only be paid in certain circumstances and for limited periods, and some benefits have rules affecting the amount that can be paid if you are abroad.

Your entitlement while you, or your partner or child, are abroad depends on any or all of the following factors:
- the benefit or tax credit you are claiming (see Chapter 15);
- the reason for going abroad;
- whether the absence is temporary or permanent;
- the length of time the absence will last;
- the country to which you are, or s/he is, going;
- whether you are covered by the European Union (EU) co-ordination rules;
- whether you are covered by a reciprocal agreement the UK has with the country you, or your partner or child, are going to.

In addition to the above factors, other changes that occur indirectly as a consequence of your being abroad can also affect your entitlement – eg, if your income changes, or you cease to count as being in full-time work for the benefit or tax credit you are claiming. Further details on the way these other changes affect your entitlement are covered in CPAG's *Welfare Benefits and Tax Credits Handbook*.

Before you go abroad

If you are thinking about going abroad, check how your entitlement will be affected well in advance of your departure, as this could affect the decisions you make. It also ensures you have sufficient time to take any necessary action before you leave the UK. You should notify the Jobcentre Plus/local authority/HM Revenue and Customs office that pays your benefit before you leave, providing details of your destination, purpose and expected duration of your absence abroad. If it is possible for you get your UK benefit paid abroad, you should give the benefit authority as much notice as possible, as it can be very slow in making these arrangements.

To see how going abroad affects your entitlement, check which rules apply (see below) and then check the rules for the specific benefit or tax credit you are claiming (see Chapter 15).

If you might want to claim a benefit from the country you are going to, it is worth checking what the conditions of entitlement are as you might want to take relevant documents with you – eg, a statement of the national insurance contributions you have paid, which you can obtain from the DWP, or proof of your past employment. **Note:** check whether claiming a benefit in another country could affect your entitlement to benefits paid abroad by the UK – eg, if you claim benefits in another European Economic Area (EEA) state and this causes the UK to cease to be your 'competent state' for the purposes of the EU co-ordination rules (see p248).

Which rules apply

Your entitlement to UK benefits or tax credits while you, or a family member, are abroad can be affected by three different sets of rules.
- The **UK benefit and tax credit legislation** contains rules about how your absence, or the absence of a family member, affects your entitlement (see p207). You should check these rules first. If your circumstances mean that, under these rules, you can obtain the benefits you want when you or your family member is outside the UK, you do not need to check the other rules.
- If you or your family member are going to another EEA state (see p39 for a list of EEA states), even if you have no entitlement under UK legislation, you might be able to receive UK benefits because of the **EU co-ordination rules** (see p210). If these rules apply to you (see p242) and provide for receipt of benefit outside the UK, they override any specific UK rules that prevent you getting your benefit outside the UK.
- **Reciprocal agreements** exist between the UK and some other countries and can assist in similar ways to the EU co-ordination rules (see p210). In general, they will only apply if the EU co-ordination rules do not assist you.

2. **How your benefits and tax credits are affected**

UK law

There are different ways in which the UK benefits and tax credits rules can affect your entitlement when you (or your family member) go abroad.

The main ways in which they result in your not getting benefit (or not being paid for your family member) when you (or s/he) are abroad are as follows.

- During your (or her/his) absence, you do not (or s/he does not) meet the condition of entitlement to be ordinarily resident in the UK (see below).
- During your (or her/his) absence, you do not (or s/he does not) meet the condition of entitlement to be present in Great Britain (see p207).
- The fact that your partner is abroad can mean you no longer count as a couple (see p209).
- Your child's absence abroad can mean s/he is no longer included in your claim (see p209).
- You stop being covered by the rules that allow you to receive housing costs for a certain period while you are absent from your home (see p209).

All of these rules contain exceptions. In particular, there are rules that allow you to be treated as present in certain circumstances, provided that your absence is temporary.

An overview of the way these different rules affect your entitlement when you go abroad is provided below. For details on how to satisfy the presence and residence rules when you are in the UK, see Part 4.

Ordinary residence

In order to be entitled to some benefits and tax credits, you must be ordinarily resident in Great Britain. See p91 for an explanation of what 'ordinary residence' means. If, by going abroad, you cease to be ordinarily resident, your entitlement to any benefit or tax credit that requires you to be ordinarily resident (see p91) ends. However, if your absence abroad is temporary and you intend to return to the UK, your ordinary residence is not usually affected.[1] It is very rare that ceasing to be ordinarily resident is the reason why your entitlement ends when you go abroad. It is more likely that your entitlement ends simply because you are absent (see below). If you receive a decision that your entitlement to a benefit or tax credit has ended because you have ceased to be ordinarily resident, ask for the decision to be looked at again and obtain specialist advice.

Presence and absence

Most benefits require you to be present in Great Britain (or, for tax credits, the UK). There are rules that allow you to be treated as present and, therefore, continue to be entitled to the benefit or tax credit, during a temporary absence in specified circumstances (see below). Some benefits also have a rule that disqualifies you from entitlement if you are absent from Great Britain. There are specified exemptions to this rule for each benefit.

Presence and absence

'**Presence**' means being physically present in Great Britain and '**absence**' means 'not physically present' in Great Britain. If the DWP, HM Revenue and Customs (HMRC) or a local authority wants to disqualify you from benefit because you were absent from Great Britain, it must show that you were absent throughout that day. This means that, on the day you leave Great Britain and the day you arrive in Great Britain, you count as present.

Temporary absence

Many benefits or tax credits allow you to be treated as present, and therefore entitled to that benefit or tax credit, during a temporary absence in specified circumstances. Your entitlement depends on:

- whether your absence counts as 'temporary' for the benefit or tax credit you are claiming (see below); *and*
- how long (if at all) during your temporary absence do the rules for that benefit or tax credit allow you to be treated as present and, therefore, entitled to benefit (see Chapter 15).

Temporary absence

The attendance allowance, disability living allowance, personal independence payment (PIP), tax credits and (for the claimant's, but not the child's, absence) child benefit regulations specify that you are '**temporarily absent**' from the UK if, at the beginning of the period of absence, it is unlikely to exceed 52 weeks.[2]

For all other benefits, temporary absence is not defined. It is your responsibility to demonstrate that your absence will be temporary, and you should therefore provide full details of why you are going abroad, how long you intend to be abroad and what you intend to do while you are abroad.[3] However, although your intentions are relevant, they are not decisive.[4] The nature of an absence can also change over time. If your absence is found to be temporary at the beginning of the period, it does not mean that it will always remain temporary. If your circumstances change while you are abroad (eg, you go abroad for one reason and decide to stay abroad for a different purpose), your absence may no longer be regarded as temporary.[5] Although for benefits other than those listed above there is no set period that counts as a temporary absence, as a general rule, absences of more than 12 months are not temporary unless there are exceptional circumstances.[6] If the purpose of your trip abroad is obviously temporary (eg, for a holiday, to visit friends or relatives or for a particular course of medical treatment) and you buy a return ticket, your absence should be viewed as temporary.

If your absence counts as temporary for the benefit or tax credit you are claiming (see p208), you are entitled to receive the benefit or tax credit for a specified period. This period varies for each benefit or tax credit and according to your circumstances. Many of the rules that entitle you to benefit during a specified period only do so if certain circumstances apply, but some rules simply state a maximum period. See Chapter 15 for information on the specific benefit you are claiming.

Note: for many benefits and tax credits, your intended absence still counts as temporary even if it is longer than the maximum period for which the benefit or tax credit is payable.

Example
Mohsen receives PIP. He goes to visit family in Iran and buys a return ticket to come back after seven months. Mohsen is entitled to PIP for the first 13 weeks of his absence (the maximum period in these circumstances – see p223). Although his intended period of absence is longer than this maximum period, it is still a temporary absence.

Couples and children living apart

There are UK benefit and tax credit rules on when members of a couple who are living apart continue to count as a couple and when a child living elsewhere is still included in your claim. Although these rules are not only about situations where one member of a couple or a child is living abroad, when this is the case, these rules can affect your benefit.

If your partner goes abroad, this can affect your benefit or tax credit in one or more of the following ways:
- for tax credits and universal credit (UC), you may cease to be entitled to make a joint claim as a couple and may need to make a single claim;
- depending on the circumstances, including the permanence or duration of your partner's absence, at some point you will cease to be paid for your partner;
- even if you are not paid for your partner, in some circumstances her/his income and capital can still affect your claim.

If your child goes abroad, depending on the circumstances, including the duration, s/he can cease to be part of your claim. This can affect your entitlement, as either you cease to be paid for her/him or your entitlement ends altogether.

For further details of the rules about couples and children for means-tested benefits see p184, and for tax credits, see p199.

Absence from your home

If you are temporarily absent from the accommodation you normally occupy as your home, you can be treated as occupying it for a period. These rules apply to housing benefit (HB) and to housing costs within income support (IS), income-based jobseeker's allowance (JSA), income-related employment and support allowance (ESA), pension credit (PC) and UC. They mean you can continue to receive payments during your temporary absence.

These rules are not specific to your being abroad, but they still affect you if you are absent from your home because you are abroad. As such, they are only briefly summarised in this *Handbook*. For further details, see CPAG's *Welfare Benefits and Tax Credits Handbook*.

If you are temporarily absent from home, have not rented out your home and intend to return to it, you can continue to be paid **HB**, or **housing costs within your IS, income-based JSA, income-related ESA or PC** (provided you remain entitled to these benefits). You can be paid for up to:

- **13 weeks** while you are absent, whatever the reason. You must be unlikely to be away for longer than this;[7]
- **52 weeks** if you come into one of a list of specific groups.[8] See CPAG's *Welfare Benefits and Tax Credits Handbook* for more details.

A new period of absence starts if you return home, even for a short stay. A stay of at least 24 hours may be enough.[9]

If you are temporarily absent from your home, you can continue to be paid **UC housing costs** for up to six months while you are absent for any reason. You are no longer treated as occupying your home once your absence has lasted, or is expected to last, longer than six months.[10] The main exception to this is if you are absent because of a fear of domestic violence, in which case you can be treated as occupying your home for up to 12 months.[11]

European Union co-ordination rules

If you are a European Economic Area (EEA) national (including a UK national) or a family member of an EEA national, and you are going to another EEA state, you may be able to benefit from the European Union (EU) co-ordination rules. These can help you to be paid your benefits or tax credits when you go abroad for longer than would be the case under UK law. The EU co-ordination rules can also enable you to be paid benefit for a family member living in another EEA state. See Chapter 15 for information on the individual benefits and tax credits and Chapter 16 for further information on the co-ordination rules.

Reciprocal agreements

The UK has reciprocal agreements with several EEA and non-EEA countries. For a list of these and further information, see p262. In general, a reciprocal agreement only applies if the EU co-ordination rules do not assist you and so are of most relevance for the non-EEA countries. In addition, the EU and the Council of Europe have agreements with some countries that can also affect your entitlement (see Chapter 17).

Notes

2. **How your benefits and tax credits are affected**

1 *R v Barnet London Borough Council ex parte Shah* [1983] 2 AC 309, Lord Scarman at p342D

2 **AA** Reg 2(3C) SS(AA) Regs
DLA Reg 2(3C) SS(DLA) Regs
PIP Reg 17(2) SS(PIP) Regs
CB Reg 24(2) CB Regs
TC Reg 4(2) TC(R) Regs

3 *Chief Adjudication Officer v Ahmed and Others,* 16 March 1994, the *Guardian,* 15 April 1994, reported as R(S)1/96

4 *Chief Adjudication Officer v Ahmed and Others,* 16 March 1994, the *Guardian,* 15 April 1994, reported as R(S)1/96

5 R(S) 1/85

6 R(U) 16/62

7 **IS** Sch 3 para 3(10) IS Regs
JSA Sch 2 para 3(10) JSA Regs
ESA Sch 6 para 5(10) ESA Regs
PC Sch 2 para 4(10) SPC Regs
HB Reg 7(13) HB Regs; reg 7(13) HB(SPC) Regs

8 **IS** Sch 3 para 3(11)-(13) IS Regs
JSA Sch 2 para 3(11)-(13) JSA Regs
ESA Sch 6 para 5(11)-(13) ESA Regs
PC Sch 2 para 4(11)-(13) SPC Regs
HB Reg 7(16)-(18) HB Regs; reg 7(16)-(18) HB(SPC) Regs

9 *R v Penwith District Council ex parte Burt* [1988] 22 HLR 292 (QBD); para A3/3.460 GM

10 Sch 3 para 9(1) UC Regs

11 Sch 3 paras 6 and 9(3) UC Regs

Chapter 15

· ·

Going abroad: rules for individual benefits

This chapter covers:

This chapter explains the UK benefit and tax credit rules on being paid when either you or your family members are abroad. It also covers the ways in which the European Union (EU) co-ordination rules may affect whether you can be paid benefit. See Chapter 14 for an overview of how the UK benefit rules and the EU co-ordination rules operate and see Chapters 16 and 17 for more details on the EU co-ordination rules and international agreements.

1. Means-tested benefits

You cannot usually receive means-tested benefits when you are abroad, because the rules for each benefit (except for housing benefit – HB) require you to be present in Great Britain. However, you can be treated as present in certain circumstances. These rules differ between the different means-tested benefits and are set out on pp213–21.

Although you do not need to be present in Great Britain to get HB, rules about occupying your home determine whether or not you are entitled to HB while you are away.

Income support

You cannot usually get income support (IS) if you are not in Great Britain.[1] However, IS can be paid while you are temporarily absent from Great Britain in the circumstances listed below, provided you meet the other conditions of entitlement.

If you were entitled to IS immediately before leaving Great Britain and are temporarily absent, your entitlement can continue:[2]

- **indefinitely** if your absence is for NHS treatment at a hospital or other institution outside Great Britain;
- during the first **four weeks** of your absence, if it is unlikely to exceed 52 weeks and:
  – you are in Northern Ireland; *or*
  – you and your partner are both abroad and s/he satisfies the conditions for one of the pensioner premiums, a disability premium or a severe disability premium; *or*
  – you are claiming IS on the grounds of being incapable of work and are abroad for the sole purpose of receiving treatment for that incapacity. The treatment must be carried out by, or under the supervision of, a person qualified to provide medical treatment, physiotherapy or similar treatment; *or*
  – you are incapable of work and:
    – you have been continuously incapable of work for the previous 28 weeks and you are terminally ill or receiving the highest rate of disability living allowance care component, the enhanced rate of the daily living component of personal independence payment or armed forces idependence payment; *or*
    – you have been continuously incapable of work for 364 days; *or*
  – you come within one of the groups of people who can claim IS (see CPAG's *Welfare Benefits and Tax Credits Handbook* for these) other than if you are:
    – in 'relevant education'; *or*
    – involved in a trade dispute, or have returned to work for 15 days or less following the dispute; *or*
    – entitled to statutory sick pay; *or*
    – appealing a decision that you are not incapable of work; *or*
    – incapable of work and not covered by one of the groups of people incapable of work listed above;
- during the first **eight weeks** of your absence, if it is unlikely to exceed 52 weeks and is solely in connection with arrangements made for the treatment of a

disease or disablement of a child or qualifying young person. The treatment must be carried out by, or under the supervision of, a person qualified to provide medical treatment, physiotherapy or similar treatment, and the child or young person must be someone for whom you count as responsible under the IS rules. See CPAG's *Welfare Benefits and Tax Credits Handbook* for who counts as a child or young person and when you count as responsible for her/him.

If you are entitled to housing costs in your IS, your temporary absence from your home can mean that you cease to be entitled to receive these (see p209).

If your partner is abroad

If you are the IS claimant and you stay in Great Britain, your IS applicable amount includes an amount for your partner who is abroad for:[3]

- the first **four weeks**; *or*
- the first **eight weeks** if s/he meets the conditions of the eight-week rule above.

If you are the IS claimant and both you and your partner are abroad, your IS includes an amount for your partner for the first eight weeks if both of you meet the conditions of the eight-week rule above.[4]

After this four- or eight-week period, your benefit is reduced because your applicable amount is calculated as if you have no partner. However, your partner is still treated as being part of your household and, therefore, her/his work, income and capital affect your IS entitlement, unless you are no longer treated as a couple (see p209).[5]

If your child is abroad

If you were getting an amount in your IS for your child before s/he went abroad, you continue to be paid for her/him for:[6]

- the first **four weeks**; *or*
- the first **eight weeks** if your child meets the conditions of the eight-week rule above.

After this four- or eight-week period, you cease to be paid IS in respect of your child. When s/he returns to Great Britain, you must claim child tax credit (CTC) for her/him instead.[7]

European Union co-ordination rules

IS is not classified as a 'social security benefit' under the European Union (EU) co-ordination rules (see p246). This means that the co-ordination rules cannot assist you. If you go to another European Economic Area (EEA) state, you can only be paid under the UK rules above.

Income-based jobseeker's allowance

You cannot usually get jobseeker's allowance (JSA) if you are not in Great Britain.[8] However, both income-based JSA and contribution-based JSA can be paid when you are temporarily absent from Great Britain in the circumstances listed below, provided you meet the other conditions of entitlement.

You can be treated as available for work and actively seeking work during certain temporary absences abroad. These are similar to, but more limited than, those listed below.[9] Similarly, if you are getting contribution-based JSA and you come under the universal credit (UC) system, you are exempt from the work search requirement and are treated as 'able and willing immediately to take up work' during these absences.

If you are temporarily absent from Great Britain, you are treated as being in Great Britain and can therefore be paid JSA:[10]

- **indefinitely** if you are entitled to JSA immediately before leaving Great Britain and your absence is for NHS treatment at a hospital or other institution outside Great Britain;
- for up to **four weeks** if you are entitled to JSA immediately before leaving Great Britain and:
  - your absence is unlikely to exceed 52 weeks, you continue to satisfy the conditions of entitlement and you are in Northern Ireland; *or*
  - (except if you come under the UC system) your absence is unlikely to exceed 52 weeks, you continue to satisfy the conditions of entitlement and your partner satisfies the conditions for one of the pensioner premiums, a disability premium or a severe disability premium; *or*
  - (except if you come under the UC system) you are in receipt of a specified type of training allowance that means you do not have to satisfy the JSA jobseeking conditions;[11]
- for up to **eight weeks** if you are entitled to JSA immediately before leaving Great Britain and your absence is unlikely to exceed 52 weeks and is solely in connection with arrangements made for the treatment of a disease or disablement of a child or qualifying young person. The treatment must be carried out by, or under the supervision of, a person qualified to provide medical treatment, physiotherapy or similar treatment and you must count as responsible for the child or young person in the same way as for the similar rule on temporary absence for IS (see p213);
- for an absence of up to **seven days** if you are attending a job interview and you notified the employment officer before you left (in writing if required). On your return, you must satisfy the employment officer that you attended the interview as stated;
- for an absence of up to **15 days** for the purpose of training as a member of the territorial or reserve forces.

If you are entitled to housing costs in your income-based JSA, your temporary absence from your home can mean that you cease to be entitled to receive these (see p209).

Joint-claim jobseeker's allowance if your partner is abroad

If you are a member of a 'joint-claim couple' (see CPAG's *Welfare Benefits and Tax Credits Handbook* for what this means) and your partner is temporarily absent from Great Britain **on the date you make your claim**, you are paid as a couple for:[12]

- an absence of up to **seven days** if your partner is attending a job interview;
- up to **four weeks** if your partner is:
  - in Northern Ireland and her/his absence is unlikely to exceed 52 weeks; *or*
  - in receipt of a specified type of training allowance that means s/he does not have to satisfy the JSA jobseeking conditions.

After this seven-day/four-week period, your JSA is reduced because your applicable amount is calculated as if you have no partner.[13] However, your partner is still treated as part of your household and, therefore, her/his work, income and capital affects your joint-claim JSA entitlement, unless you are no longer treated as a couple (see p209).[14]

If you are a joint-claim couple and your partner goes abroad **after you claimed JSA**, you continue to be paid as a joint-claim couple:[15]

- for up to **four weeks** if you were entitled to joint-claim JSA immediately before s/he left Great Britain and:
  - her/his absence is unlikely to exceed 52 weeks, you continue to satisfy the conditions of entitlement and your partner satisfies the conditions for one of the pensioner premiums, a disability premium or a severe disability premium; *or*
  - her/his absence is unlikely to exceed 52 weeks, you both continue to satisfy the conditions of entitlement and your partner is in Northern Ireland; *or*
  - your partner is in receipt of a specified type of training allowance that means s/he does not have to satisfy the JSA jobseeking conditions.[16]
- for an absence of up to **seven days** if your partner is attending a job interview and has notified the employment officer before leaving (in writing if required). On her/his return, s/he must satisfy the employment officer at Jobcentre Plus that s/he attended the interview as stated.

Income-based jobseeker's allowance if your partner is abroad

If you are the income-based JSA claimant and you stay in Great Britain, your applicable amount includes an amount for your partner while s/he is abroad for:[17]

- the first **four weeks** of a temporary absence; *or*
- the first **eight weeks** if your partner meets the conditions of the eight-week rule on p215.

If you are the income-based JSA claimant and both you and your partner are abroad, your applicable amount includes an amount for your partner for the first eight weeks if both of you meet the conditions of the eight-week rule on p215.[18]

After this four- or eight-week period, your benefit is reduced because your applicable amount is calculated as if you have no partner. However, your partner is still treated as part of your household and, therefore, her/his work, income and capital affect your income-based JSA entitlement, unless you are no longer treated as a couple (see p209).[19]

Income-based jobseeker's allowance if your child is abroad

If you were getting JSA for your child before s/he went abroad, you can continue to be paid for her/him for:[20]
- the first **four weeks**; or
- the first **eight weeks** if your child meets the conditions of the eight-week rule on p215.

After this four- or eight-week period, you cease to be paid income-based JSA in respect of your child. When s/he returns to Great Britain, you must claim CTC for her/him instead.[21]

European Union co-ordination rules

Income-based JSA is classed as a 'special non-contributory benefit' under the EU co-ordination rules (see p247) and therefore cannot be exported. This means that if you go to another EEA country, the co-ordination rules cannot assist you and you can only be paid income-based JSA abroad under the UK rules explained above.

However, the co-ordination rules may enable you to be paid contribution-based JSA for up to three months if you go to another EEA country (see p229).

Income-related employment and support allowance

You cannot usually get employment and support allowance (ESA) if you are not in Great Britain.[22] However, both income-related ESA and contributory ESA can be paid when you are temporarily absent from Great Britain in the circumstances listed below, provided you meet the other conditions of entitlement.

If you were entitled to ESA immediately before leaving Great Britain and are temporarily absent, you can continue to be entitled:[23]
- **indefinitely** if:
  - your absence is for NHS treatment at a hospital or other institution outside Great Britain; or
  - you are living with your spouse, civil partner, son, daughter, stepson, stepdaughter, father, father-in-law, stepfather, mother, mother-in-law or stepmother who is a serving member of the armed forces;
- for the first **four weeks** if your absence is unlikely to exceed 52 weeks;

- for the first **26 weeks** if your absence is unlikely to exceed 52 weeks and is solely in connection with arrangements made for the treatment of:
  - your disease or disablement that is directly related to your limited capability for work which began before you left Great Britain; *or*
  - the disease or disablement of a dependent child who you are accompanying.

The treatment must be carried out by, or under the supervision of, a person qualified to provide medical treatment, physiotherapy or similar treatment.

If you are due to have a medical examination to assess your limited capability for work when you go abroad, you can ask for this to be carried out in the country you are going to, or to be postponed until you return. If your request is refused and you go abroad and miss your medical, your ESA will be stopped because you failed to attend your medical unless it is accepted that you had a good cause for not attending. In deciding whether you had good cause, the decision maker must take all your circumstances into account, including the fact that you were outside Great Britain.[24] See CPAG's *Welfare Benefits and Tax Credits Handbook* for further details.

If you are entitled to housing costs in your income-related ESA, your temporary absence from your home can mean that you cease to be entitled to receive these (see p209).

If you move from Great Britain to Northern Ireland or vice versa, the DWP should make an extra-statutory payment to make up any loss of income-related (or contributory) ESA that results from having to make a new claim (see p266).

If your partner is abroad

If you are the claimant and you stay in Great Britain, your income-related ESA includes an amount for your partner for:[25]

- the first **four weeks**; *or*
- the first **26 weeks** if s/he is accompanying a child abroad for treatment in line with the 26-week rule above.

If you are the claimant and both you and your partner are abroad, your income-related ESA includes an amount for your partner for the first 26 weeks if both of you are accompanying a child abroad for treatment in line with the 26-week rule above.[26]

After this four- or 26-week period, your benefit is reduced because your applicable amount is calculated as if you have no partner. However, your partner is still treated as part of your household and, therefore, her/his work, income and capital affect your income-related ESA entitlement, unless you are no longer treated as a couple (see p209).[27]

European Union co-ordination rules

Income-related ESA is listed under the co-ordination rules as a 'special non-contributory benefit' (see p247) and is therefore not exportable. This means that if you go to another EEA country, the EU co-ordination rules cannot assist you and you can only be paid income-related ESA abroad under the UK rules explained above.

However, the co-ordination rules may enable you to continue to be paid contributory ESA if you go to live in another EEA country (see p229).

Pension credit

You cannot usually get pension credit (PC) if you are not in Great Britain.[28] However, PC can be paid when you are temporarily absent from Great Britain in the circumstances listed below, provided you meet the other conditions of entitlement.

If you were entitled to PC immediately before leaving Great Britain and are temporarily absent, your entitlement can continue:[29]

- **indefinitely** if your absence is for NHS treatment at a hospital or other institution outside Great Britain; *or*
- for up to **13 weeks** if your absence is unlikely to exceed 52 weeks.

If you are entitled to housing costs in your PC, your temporary absence from your home can mean that you cease to be entitled to receive these (see p209).

If your partner is abroad

If your partner is abroad and you are entitled to PC, either while in Great Britain or abroad because you are covered by the rules above, your PC only includes an amount for her/him if s/he is also covered by the above rules. After this, s/he is not treated as part of your household, you are paid as a single person and her/his income and capital do not affect your claim.[30] For further information about your partner going abroad, see p209.

European Union co-ordination rules

PC is classed as a 'special non-contributory benefit' under the EU co-ordination rules (see p247) and therefore cannot be exported. This means that if you go abroad, the co-ordination rules cannot assist you. You can only be paid PC abroad under the UK rules above.

Housing benefit

There is no requirement to be present in Great Britain to be entitled to HB. However, you must be liable to make payments in respect of a dwelling in Great Britain, which you occupy as your home.[31] There are rules that treat you as occupying your home, including when you are temporarily absent from it.[32] If you are going abroad, these rules determine whether you can be entitled to HB while you are away (see p209).

If your partner or child is abroad

Whether or not you have amounts included in your HB for your partner or child who is abroad depends on whether s/he is treated as part of your household (see p184 and p186).

Universal credit

You cannot usually be paid universal credit (UC) if you (and your partner if it is a joint claim) are not in Great Britain.[33] However, UC can be paid while you are temporarily absent from Great Britain in the circumstances outlined below, provided you meet the other conditions of entitlement.

If you were entitled to UC immediately before leaving Great Britain and are temporarily absent, you can continue to be entitled for:[34]

- a **month** if your absence is not expected to exceed, and does not exceed, one month; *or*
- **two months** if your absence is in connection with the death of your partner or child, or a close relative of yours (or of your partner or child), and it would be unreasonable for you to return to Great Britain within the first month; *or*
- **six months** if your absence is not expected to exceed, and does not exceed, six months and you are a mariner or continental shelf worker; *or*
- **six months** if your absence is not expected to exceed, and does not exceed, six months and is solely in connection with the medically approved care, convalesence or treatment of you, your partner or child. You are automatically exempt from the work search requirement and are also treated as 'able and willing immediately to take up work' during this period.[35]

If you are entitled to housing costs in your UC, your temporary absence from your home can mean that you cease to be entitled to receive these (see p209).

If your partner is abroad

If you have a joint claim for UC and both you and your partner go abroad, this does not affect your entitlement during the period when one of the situations listed above applies to both of you. After this time, if you both remain abroad, your entitlement ends.

If you stay in Great Britain while your partner is abroad, her/his absence does not affect your entitlement during the one-, two- or six-month period if the circumstances listed above apply to her/him. After this time, you cease to be entitled as joint claimants. If you and your partner have been, and expect to be, apart for less than six months, you must claim as a single person. Your award is based on the maximum amount for a single person, but your partner's income and capital are taken into account.[36] However, once you have been, or expect to be, apart for six months, you cease to be treated as a couple.[37] Your entitlement is then unaffected by your absent partner.

In addition, if your partner's absence abroad means that s/he stops being habitually resident (including if s/he no longer has a right to reside) in the common travel area, s/he is treated as no longer present (see p87). You can claim as a single person, but your partner's income and capital are taken into account.[38]

If your child is abroad

If your child is abroad, you cease to be entitled for her/him if her/his absence abroad is, or is expected to be, longer than the one-, two- or six-month periods allowed in the circumstances set out above. The circumstances must apply to your child.[39]

European Union co-ordination rules

The DWP considers that UC is not a 'social security benefit' under the EU co-ordination rules (see p248). This means that the co-ordination rules cannot assist you and, if you go to another EEA state, you can only be paid under the UK rules above.

2. **Bereavement benefits**

In general, bereavement benefits are payable while you are abroad. However, your benefit is not uprated each year if, on the day before the annual uprating takes place, you have ceased to be 'ordinarily resident' (see p91) in Great Britain, unless you have gone to another European Economic Area (EEA) state and you are covered by the European Union (EU) co-ordination rules (see p242) or you can rely on a reciprocal agreement (see Chapter 17).[40]

If you are absent from Great Britain when you claim a bereavement payment, you are only entitled in limited circumstances. See p187 for further details.

European Union co-ordination rules

Bereavement benefits are classed as 'survivors' benefits' under the EU co-ordination rules (see p246) and are therefore fully exportable. If these rules apply to you (see p242) and you go to stay or live in another EEA state, you can be paid your bereavement benefits without a time limit and they are fully uprated each year.

If the co-ordination rules apply to you and your late spouse/civil partner died in another EEA state, s/he can be treated as having died in the UK for the purpose of your entitlement to a bereavement payment, provided the UK is your 'competent state' (see p248).[41]

3. **Child benefit and guardian's allowance**

Child benefit

You and your child can be treated as present in Great Britain and, therefore, you can continue to be entitled to child benefit for a limited period during a 'temporary absence' (see p208).

Provided you are ordinarily resident (see p91), you are treated as present during a temporary absence for:[42]
- the first **eight weeks**; *or*
- the first **12 weeks** of any period of absence, or any extension to that period, which is in connection with:
  - the treatment of an illness or disability of you, your partner, a child for whom you are responsible, or another relative of yours or your partner's; *or*
  - the death of your partner, a child or qualifying young person for whom you or your partner are responsible, or another relative of yours or your partner's.

'**Relative**' means brother, sister, parent, grandparent, great-grandparent or child, grandchild or great-grandchild.[43]

Your child is treated as present during a temporary absence for:[44]
- the first **12 weeks** of any period of absence; *or*
- **any period** during which s/he is absent for the specific purpose of being treated for an illness or disability which began before her/his absence began; *or*
- **any period** when s/he is in Northern Ireland; *or*
- **any period** during which s/he is absent only because s/he is:
  - receiving full-time education at a school or college in another European Economic Area (EEA) state or in Switzerland; *or*
  - engaged in an educational exchange or visit made with the written approval of the school or college s/he normally attends; *or*
  - a child who normally lives with a Crown servant posted overseas who is either in the same country as her/him or is absent from that country for one of the reasons in the two bullet points immediately above.[45]

If a child is born outside Great Britain during the eight- or 12-week period in which you were treated as present in Great Britain, s/he is treated as being in Great Britain for up to 12 weeks from the start of your absence.[46]

While you and your child are present, or treated as present, you satisfy that condition of entitlement. This means that you can continue to receive any child benefit already in payment and can also make a fresh claim during your, or her/his, absence.

Guardian's allowance

Entitlement to guardian's allowance depends on entitlement to child benefit, so you can be paid guardian's allowance abroad for the same period as child benefit (see p222).

However, your guardian's allowance is not uprated each year if you have ceased to be ordinarily resident (see p91) in Great Britain on the day before the annual uprating takes place, unless you have gone to another EEA state and you are covered by the European Union (EU) co-ordination rules (see below) or you can rely on a reciprocal agreement.[47]

European Union co-ordination rules

Child benefit and guardian's allowance are classed as 'family benefits' under the EU co-ordination rules (see p246). If these rules apply to you (see p242):
- you can be paid child benefit, and guardian's allowance for a child resident in another EEA country. The child does not have to be in education; *and/or*
- you can be paid child benefit and guardian's allowance if you are an EEA national and you go to stay or live in another EEA country, and your benefit is uprated in the normal way.

See p257 for more information on the payment of family benefits under the EU co-ordination rules.

---

4. Disability and carers' benefits

If you go abroad, you can be treated as present in Great Britain and therefore continue to be entitled to attendance allowance (AA), disability living allowance (DLA), personal independence payment (PIP) or carer's allowance (CA) for a limited period.

Provided you satisfy the residence condition (see below), you are treated as present and can continue to receive AA, DLA, PIP or CA during an absence from Great Britain:[48]
- (for AA, DLA and PIP only) for the first **13 weeks** of a 'temporary absence' (see p208);
- (for AA, DLA and PIP only) for the first **26 weeks** of a 'temporary absence' (see p208) if the absence is solely in connection with medical treatment for your illness or disability that began before you left Great Britain;
- (for CA only) for up to **four weeks** if your absence is, and was when it began, for a temporary purpose and does not exceed four weeks. You must be accompanied by the disabled person for whom you are caring (unless you qualify for CA during a break from caring (see CPAG's *Welfare Benefits and Tax Credits Handbook* for the rules on this);

- (for CA only) if your absence is temporary and for the specific purpose of caring for a disabled person who is also absent from Great Britain and who continues to receive AA, DLA care component paid at the highest or middle rate, the daily living component of PIP, armed forces independence payment or constant attendance allowance;
- while you are abroad as an airwoman/man or mariner or continental shelf worker;
- while you are a serving member of the armed forces, or you are living with your spouse, civil partner, son, daughter, stepson, stepdaughter, father, father-in-law, stepfather, mother, mother-in-law or stepmother who is a serving member of the armed forces.

The residence condition

You must be **habitually resident** (see p94), unless your current award of AA, DLA or CA began before 8 April 2013, in which case, you must be be **ordinarily resident** (see p91) until that award is terminated, revised or superseeded.[49] You are treated as habitually resident if you are covered by the last bullet point above.

The temporary absence rules were more generous before 8 April 2013. If you were already abroad on this date and continued to be entitled to AA or DLA because your absence is temporary and for the specific purpose of being treated for an illness or disability that began before you left Great Britain, and the DWP has agreed that you should be treated as present, you continue to be treated as present in Great Britain until either you return or your award is revised or superseded.[50]

If you lose your entitlement to CA, you should still be eligible for a carer premium paid with your income support, income-based jobseeker's allowance, income-related employment and support allowance or housing benefit for a further period of eight weeks, provided you remain entitled to these benefits while you are away.[51] If you lose your entitlement to CA while you are abroad and the disabled person for whom you care is staying in the UK, s/he may be able to claim a severe disability premium during your absence instead. For further information on premiums, see CPAG's *Welfare Benefits and Tax Credits Handbook*.

You can continue to be paid an increase in your CA for your spouse/civil partner or dependent adult while s/he is abroad if:[52]

- you are entitled to CA; *and*
- you are residing with her/him. **Note:** you can be treated as residing together during a temporary absence from each other.[53]

European Union co-ordination rules

If you move to another European Economic Area (EEA) state, you can continue to be paid (or make a new claim for) AA, DLA care component, PIP daily living component and CA without needing to satisfy the usual presence and residence requirements (see p190) if:[54]

- you are habitually resident in another EEA state or Switzerland; *and*
- you are covered by the European Union (EU) co-ordination rules (see p242); *and*
- you can demonstrate a 'genuine and sufficient link to the UK social security system'.

You can continue to be paid for as long as the UK is your 'competent state' (see p248).[55]

A genuine and sufficient link to the UK social security system

The following factors are relevant when demonstrating that you have a **'genuine and sufficient link to the UK social security system'**:

– whether you have worked in the UK;

– whether you have spent a significant part of your life in the UK;

– whether you are receiving a UK contributory benefit;

– whether you are dependent on a family member who has worked in the UK and/or who receives a UK contributory benefit.[56]

The test is whether you have a 'genuine and sufficient link to the UK social security system' for the purpose of the benefit you are claiming, taking all your circumstances into account.[57] **Note:** the interpretation of this phrase is still evolving and will be affected by developments in caselaw. See CPAG's online service and *Welfare Rights Bulletin* for updates.

The above provision has only been in force since April 2013. Whether or not you can be paid in another EEA state before this date depends on the date your entitlement began, as AA, DLA and CA have been categorised in different ways under the co-ordination rules at different times.

Before 1 June 1992, AA, DLA and CA were classed as 'invalidity benefits' (see p246). If your entitlement began before this date, you can export your benefit without any time limit to any EEA state.

From 1 June 1992, the UK government categorised AA, DLA and CA as 'special non-contributory benefits' (see p247). These are not exportable. However, the European Court of Justice (ECJ) declared that this was wrong and that these benefits (except DLA mobility component) were 'sickness benefits'.[58] This means they *are* exportable and you should continue to receive the benefit for as long as the UK remains your competent state (see p250).[59]

DLA mobility component is listed as (and PIP mobility component is treated by DWP as) as 'special non-contributory benefit' and is not exportable.[60] You can only be paid in the state where you are resident under the co-ordination rules.[61] See p249 for details on where you are considered 'resident'.

If you receive CA while in the UK and the EU co-ordination rules apply to you (see p242), you may be able to continue to be paid an addition for an adult or child if s/he goes to stay or live in another EEA state. These additions count as 'family benefits' under the co-ordination rules (see p257).

Was your benefit stopped because you moved to another European Economic Area state on or after 8 March 2001?

If your AA, DLA care component or CA was stopped solely because you moved to another EEA state on or after 8 March 2001, this decision was wrong.[62]

The DWP can restore your entitlement and pay arrears from 18 October 2007 (or the date your payment was stopped if this is later).[63] The DWP pays arrears from this date because it was when the ECJ decided these benefits had been wrongly categorised.

To get your entitlement restored and arrears paid for any period between 8 March 2001 and 18 October 2007, you should do the following.

1. If you appealed within the time limit against the decision that stopped your benefit, the First-tier Tribunal should be able to reinstate it from the date it was stopped. If your appeal is waiting to be determined, the DWP can revise the decision and pay your arrears of benefit in full.

2. If you did not appeal, the DWP can only correct its decision and pay arrears from the date your benefit was stopped if that decision was made because of an 'official error'. However, if a mistake in a decision was not known to be a mistake at the time, but is only shown to have been a mistake by a later court decision, the mistake does not count as an official error.[64] It has been decided that it only became clear that AA, DLA care component and CA were exportable benefits under the EU co-ordination rules when the ECJ decided that they had been wrongly categorised (on 18 October 2007).[65] Therefore, if the decision stopping your benefit (solely because it was mistakenly categorised as a special non-contributory benefit and therefore not exportable) was made before 18 October 2007, this decision does not count as an official error. If the decision is revised, your benefit can only be restored from the date of the revision (although the DWP pays arrears outside these rules back to 18 October 2007).

3. You may be able to get around the above difficulty if you can identify another error in the decision to stop your benefit when you moved to another EEA state which can count as an 'official error', thus enabling the decision to be revised and your entitlement reinstated from the date it was stopped.[66] One fairly common mistake that may count as another error if made before 10 April 2006, was a decision, made after you went abroad, to stop your AA or DLA care component from the date you went abroad rather than from the date of that decision.[67] Whether errors such as these can enable all aspects of the decision to be revised on grounds of 'official error' is due to be considered in a case currently before the Upper Tribunal.[68] See CPAG's online service and *Welfare Rights Bulletin* for updates.

Chapter 15: Going abroad: rules for individual benefits
5. Incapacity benefit, severe disablement allowance and maternity allowance

15

5. Incapacity benefit, severe disablement allowance and maternity allowance

If you are temporarily absent from Great Britain, you can continue to be paid incapacity benefit (IB), severe disablement allowance (SDA) and maternity allowance (MA) if:[69]

- you are receiving attendance allowance (AA), disability living allowance (DLA), personal independence payment (PIP) or armed forces independence payment. For when AA, DLA or PIP can be paid abroad, see p223; or
- the DWP certifies that you should continue to be paid. You can then receive the benefit for the first 26 weeks of your temporary absence; or
- you are the spouse, civil partner, son, stepson, daughter, stepdaughter, father, stepfather, father-in-law, mother, stepmother, or mother-in-law of a serving member of the armed forces and you are abroad only because you are living with her/him.

In addition:

- when you left Great Britain, you must have been continuously incapable of work for six months and have been continuously incapable since your departure; or
- your absence from Great Britain must be for the specific purpose of being treated for an incapacity which began before you left Great Britain; or
- for IB only, your incapacity for work is the result of a personal injury caused by an accident at work and your absence from Great Britain is for the specific purpose of receiving treatment for that injury. See CPAG's *Welfare Benefits and Tax Credits Handbook* for more information on industrial injuries.

If you are due to have a medical examination, this can be arranged abroad.

Note: IB and SDA are being replaced by employment and support allowance (ESA). If you do not lose your entitlement to IB or SDA by going abroad, at some future point you will be reassessed for ESA. When your award of IB or SDA is converted to an award of contributory ESA, you do not need to resatisfy the national insurance (NI) contribution conditions. However, if you are getting IB or SDA and lose entitlement because you go abroad for more than 26 weeks, you do not requalify for IB or SDA on your return to Great Britain, and you can only get contributory ESA if you satisfy all the conditions of entitlement, including the NI contribution conditions. Losing entitlement now could therefore result in a loss of potential future benefit.

You can continue to be paid an increase in your IB or SDA for your spouse/civil partner or dependent adult while s/he is abroad if you are residing with her/him.[70] **Note:** you can be treated as residing together during a temporary absence from each other.[71]

European Union co-ordination rules

Long-term IB and SDA are classed as 'invalidity benefits' under the European Union (EU) co-ordination rules (see p246). If these rules apply to you (see p242) and the UK is your 'competent state' (see p248), you can export your IB and SDA if you go to live in another European Economic Area (EEA) state. Provided you continue to satisfy the rules of entitlement, benefit is paid without any time limit and at the same rate as if you were still in the UK, including your annual uprating.

The state from which you claim benefit is the one that determines your degree of invalidity, but any checks and medicals take place in the state in which you live and the reports are then sent to the paying state.[72]

If the co-ordination rules apply to you and you remain in the UK, you may be able to continue to be paid an increase for an adult or child if s/he goes to stay or live in another EEA state. Such increases are classified as 'family benefits'. See p257 for details about when you can receive these for a family member living abroad.

MA is classed as a 'maternity benefit' under the EU co-ordination rules (see p246). If these rules apply to you (see p242) and the UK is your competent state (see p248), you can be paid MA if you go to live or stay in another EEA country.[73] See p255 for more details.

6. Industrial injuries benefits

Industrial injuries benefits are:
- disablement benefit;
- reduced earnings allowance (REA);
- retirement allowance;
- constant attendance allowance;
- exceptionally severe disablement allowance.

Disablement benefit and retirement allowance are not affected if you go abroad.[74]

Constant attendance allowance and exceptionally severe disablement allowance are payable for the first six months of a temporary absence, or a longer period that the DWP may allow.[75]

REA can be paid while you are temporarily absent abroad for the first three months (or longer if the DWP allows) if:[76]
- your absence from Great Britain is not in connection with employment, trade or business; *and*
- your claim was made before you left Great Britain; *and*
- you were entitled to REA before going abroad.

Note: REA has now been abolished. If you break your claim, you may no longer be eligible for benefit.

European Union co-ordination rules

Industrial injuries benefits, with the exception of retirement allowance, are classed as 'benefits for accidents at work and occupational diseases' under the European Union co-ordination rules (see p246) and are therefore fully exportable. If these rules apply to you (see p242) and you go to stay or live in another European Economic Area state, you can be paid without any time limit and they are fully uprated each year. See p255 for more details.

7. **Contribution-based jobseeker's allowance and contributory employment and support allowance**

You cannot usually get jobseeker's allowance (JSA) or employment and support allowance (ESA) if you are not in Great Britain.[77] However, contribution-based JSA can be paid when you are temporarily absent from Great Britain in the same circumstances as income-based JSA (see p215) and contributory ESA can be paid when you are temporarily absent from Great Britain in the same circumstances as income-related ESA (see p217).

European Union co-ordination rules

Contribution-based jobseeker's allowance

Contribution-based JSA is classed as an unemployment benefit under the European Union (EU) co-ordination rules (see p246). If these rules apply to you (see p242) and the UK is your 'competent state' (see p248), you can be paid contribution-based JSA for up to three months if:[78]

- you satisfied the conditions for contribution-based JSA before you left the UK for at least four weeks, unless authorised by the DWP to go abroad before you have claimed for four weeks; *and*
- you register as unemployed in the European Economic Area (EEA) state you go to within seven days and comply with its procedures.

Contributory employment and support allowance

If the EU co-ordination rules apply to you (see p242) and the UK is your competent state (see p248), you can generally continue to be paid contributory ESA if you go to live in another EEA state.

Contributory ESA is classed under the co-ordination rules as a 'sickness benefit' during the assessment phase and as an 'invalidity benefit' after the assessment phase. In cases of long-term or permanent disability, it is arguable that contributory ESA during the assessment phase should be regarded as an 'invalidity benefit' (see p246).[79] However, in most cases, this distinction does not matter as sickness benefits are exportable in similar circumstances to invalidity benefits (see p255).

If the UK continues to pay your contributory ESA while you are resident in another EEA state, the DWP continues to assess your limited capability for work and your limited capability for work-related activity. However, any checks and medicals take place in the state in which you are living, with reports then sent to the DWP.[80]

8. **Retirement pensions**

With the exception of Category D retirement pension, all retirement pensions are payable without time limit while you are abroad.[81] However, your benefit is not uprated each year if you have ceased to be 'ordinarily resident' (see p91) on the day before the annual uprating takes place, unless you have gone to another European Economic Area (EEA) state and you are covered by the European Union (EU) co-ordination rules (see below) or you can rely on a reciprocal agreement.[82]

For the residence requirements for Category D retirement pension, see p195.

Note: you cannot 'de-retire' if you are not ordinarily resident in Great Britain.[83]

If you live abroad, your retirement pension can be paid either into a bank in the country where you live or a bank or building society in the UK.

You can continue to be paid an increase in your Category A retirement pension for your spouse/civil partner or dependent adult while s/he is abroad if:[84]

- you are entitled to the pension; *and*
- you are residing with her/him. You can be treated as residing together during a temporary absence from each other.[85]

European Union co-ordination rules

Retirement pensions are classed as 'old age benefits' under the EU co-ordination rules (see p246). If these rules apply to you (see p242) and the UK is your 'competent state' (see p248), you can export your retirement pension if you go to live in another EEA state. It is paid without time limit and at the same rate as if you were still in the UK, including your annual uprating.

If the EU co-ordination rules apply and you remain in the UK, you may be able to continue to be paid an increase for an adult or child if s/he goes to stay or live in another EEA state. These increases count as 'family benefits' under the co-ordination rules. See p257 for more details.

9. **Statutory sick, maternity, paternity and adoption pay**

There are no presence or residence rules for statutory sick pay (SSP), statutory maternity pay (SMP), statutory paternity pay (SPP) and statutory adoption pay (SAP). You remain entitled to these benefits if you go abroad, provided you meet the usual rules of entitlement.[86]

Even while you are employed abroad, you count as an employee for the purpose of these benefits in certain circumstances, including if:[87]

- your employer is required to pay secondary Class 1 national insurance (NI) contributions for you; *or*
- you are a continental shelf worker or, in certain circumstances, an airwoman/ man or mariner; *or*
- you are employed in another European Economic Area (EEA) state and, had you been employed in Great Britain, you would have been considered an employee, and the UK is the competent state under the European Union (EU) co-ordination rules (see p248).

Your employer is not required to pay you SSP, SMP, SPP or SAP if:[88]

- your employer is not required by law to pay employer's Class 1 NI contributions (even if these contributions are, in fact, made) because, at the time they become payable, your employer:
  - is not resident or present in Great Britain; *or*
  - does not have (or is treated as not having) a place of business in Great Britain; *or*
- because of an international treaty or convention your employer is exempt from the Social Security Acts or those Acts are not enforceable against your employer.

European Union co-ordination rules

It is arguable that SSP is a 'sickness benefit' and SMP and SPP are 'maternity/ paternity benefits' under the EU co-ordination rules (see p246). However, given the generosity of the above UK rules, it is unlikely that you will need to rely on the EU co-ordination rules directly.

10. **Tax credits**

You can be treated as present and, therefore, entitled to child tax credit (CTC) and working tax credit (WTC) for limited periods during a 'temporary absence' (see p208).

You are treated as present for both CTC and WTC during a temporary absence, provided you are ordinarily resident (see p91), for:[89]
- the first **eight weeks**; *or*
- the first **12 weeks** of any period of absence, or any extension to that period, which is in connection with:
  - the treatment of an illness or disability of you, your partner, a child for whom you are responsible, or another relative (see below) of either you or your partner; *or*
  - the death of your partner, a child or qualifying young person for whom you or your partner are responsible, or another relative (see below) of you or your partner.

'**Relative**' means brother, sister, parent, grandparent, grandchild or great-grandparent or child.[90]

You are also treated as present if you are:[91]
- a Crown servant posted overseas and:
  - you are, or immediately before your posting abroad you were, ordinarily resident in the UK; *or*
  - immediately before your posting you were in the UK in connection with that posting; *or*
- the partner of a Crown servant posted overseas and in the same country as her/him or temporarily absent from that country under the same exceptions that enable tax credits to continue during a temporary absence from Great Britain.

While you are treated as present in any of the ways above, you continue to satisfy that condition of entitlement. This means that you can continue to receive any tax credits that are already in payment and can make a fresh or renewal claim during your absence.

Your tax credit entitlement ends if:
- you (or your partner if you are making a joint claim) spend longer abroad than the permitted temporary absence periods, as you cease to satisfy the presence condition; *or*
- you (or your partner if you are making a joint claim) cease to be ordinarily resident; *or*
- you are making a joint claim and separate from your partner in circumstances in which the separation is likely to be permanent, as you cease to count as a couple.[92]

If your entitlement to a joint claim as a couple ends, you may be able to make a single claim. See p199 for considerations if you are making a joint claim as a couple.

European Union co-ordination rules

CTC is classed as a 'family benefit' under the European Union (EU) co-ordination rules (see p246). If these rules apply to you (see p242), you can be paid CTC:
- for a child resident in another European Economic Area (EEA) state; *and/or*
- if you are an EEA national and you go to stay or live in another EEA state.

See p257 for more details on the payment of family benefits under the EU co-ordination rules.

WTC is not covered by the EU co-ordination rules. Therefore, if your partner is in another EEA country, although you may be able to make a joint claim for CTC as a couple, your WTC claim is treated as a single claim.[93]

If you or your partner are working in another EEA country but live in the UK and therefore remain present and ordinarily resident in the UK, this work can count for the purposes of your WTC claim.[94]

Notes

1. Means-tested benefits
1 s124(1) SSCBA 1992
2 Reg 4 IS Regs
3 Reg 21 and Sch 7 paras 11 and 11A IS Regs
4 Reg 21 and Sch 7 para 11A IS Regs
5 Reg 16 IS Regs
6 Reg 16(5) IS Regs
7 Reg 1(4B) SS(WTCCTC)(CA) Regs
8 s1(2)(i) JSA 1995
9 Regs 14 and 19 JSA Regs; reg 16 JSA Regs 2013
10 s21 and Sch 1 para 11 JSA 1995; reg 50 JSA Regs; reg 41 JSA Regs 2013
11 Regs 50(4) and 170 JSA Regs
12 Regs 50(6B), 86C and 170 and Sch 5A para 7 JSA Regs
13 Sch 5A para 7 JSA Regs
14 Reg 78 JSA Regs
15 Reg 50(3) and (6C) and Sch 5A para 7 JSA Regs
16 Regs 50(4) and 170 JSA Regs
17 Reg 85 and Sch 5 paras 10 and 11 JSA Regs
18 Reg 85 and Sch 5 para 11 JSA Regs
19 Reg 78 JSA Regs
20 Reg 78(5) JSA Regs

21 Reg 1(8B) SS(WTCCTC)(CA) Regs
22 ss1(3)(d) and 18(4)(a) WRA 2007
23 Regs 151-55 ESA Regs; regs 88-92 ESA Regs 2013
24 Reg 24 ESA Regs; reg 20 ESA Regs 2013
25 Reg 156 and Sch 5 paras 6 and 7 ESA Regs
26 Reg 156 and Sch 5 para 7 ESA Regs
27 Reg 156 ESA Regs
28 s1(2)(a) SPCA 2002
29 Regs 3 and 4 SPC Regs
30 Regs 4 and 5 SPC Regs
31 s130(1)(a) SSCBA 1992
32 Reg 7 HB Regs; reg 7 HB(SPC) Regs
33 ss3 and 4(1)(c) WRA 2012
34 Reg 11 UC Regs
35 Reg 99(1)-(3) UC Regs
36 Regs 3, 8, 22 and 36 UC Regs
37 Reg 3(6) UC Regs
38 Regs 3(3), 9, 18(2), 22(3) and 36(3) UC Regs
39 Reg 4(7) UC Regs

2. Bereavement benefits
40 Reg 5 SSB(PA) Regs
41 Arts 5, 42 and 43 EU Reg 883/04

3. Child benefit and guardian's allowance
42 Reg 24 CB Regs
43 Reg 24(1) CB Regs
44 Reg 21 CB Regs
45 Reg 32 CB Regs
46 Reg 21(2) CB Regs
47 Reg 5 SSB(PA) Regs

4. Disability and carers' benefits
48 **AA** Reg 2(2), (3B) and (3C) SS(AA) Regs
DLA Reg 2(2), (3B) and (3C) SS(DLA) Regs
PIP Regs 17-20 SS(PIP) Regs
CA Reg 9(2) and (3) SS(ICA) Regs
49 Reg 1(2), (3) and (4) SS(DLA,AA&CA)(A) Regs
50 Reg 5 SS(DLA,AA&CA)(A) Regs
51 **IS** Sch 2 para 14ZA IS Regs
JSA Sch 1 para 17 JSA Regs
ESA Sch 4 para 8 ESA Regs
HB Sch 3 para 17 HB Regs
52 Reg 13 SSB(PA) Regs; Sch 2 para 7 SSB(Dep) Regs
53 Reg 2(4) SSB(PRT) Regs
54 **AA** Reg 2B SS(AA) Regs
DLA Reg 2B SS(DLA) Regs
PIP Reg 23 SS(PIP) Regs
CA Reg 9B SS(ICA) Regs
55 **AA** s65(7) SSCBA 1992
DLA s72(7B) SSCBA 1992
PIP s84 WRA 2012
CA s70(4A) SSCBA 1992
56 *Stewart v SSWP*, C-503/09 [2011] ECR I-06497
57 *SSWP v JG* [2013] UKUT 0298 (AAC); *SSWP v JG* [2013] UKUT 0300 (AAC), currently under appeal to the Court of Appeal
58 *Commission of the European Communities v European Parliament and Council of the European Union*, C-299/05 [2007] ECR I-08695, 18 October 2007
59 ss65(7), 70(4A) and 72(7B) SSCBA 1992; s84 WRA 2012
60 *Bartlett and Others v SSWP*, C-537/09 [2011] ECR I-03417
61 Art 70 EU Reg 883/04; *Robin Swaddling v AO*, C-90/97 [1999] ECR I-01075
62 *Commission of the European Communities v European Parliament and Council of the European Union*, C-299/05 [2007] ECR I-08695, 18 October 2007
63 Reg 6(35)-(37) SS(C&P) Regs; reg 7(9A) SS&CS(DA) Regs
64 Reg 1(3) SS&CS(DA) Regs
65 *CK and JK v SSWP (CA, DLA)* [2013] UKUT 218 (AAC)
66 *BD v SSWP (DLA)* [2013] UKUT 216 (AAC), para 15, but note that this part of the decision is not binding.
67 CIB/736/2004; *BD v SSWP (DLA)* [2013] UKUT 216 (AAC), para 14, but note that this part of the decision is not binding.
68 CDLA/3276/2012

5. Incapacity benefit, severe disablement allowance and maternity allowance
69 Reg 2 SSB(PA) Regs
70 Reg 13 SSB(PA) Regs; reg 14 SS(IB-ID) Regs
71 Reg 2(4) SSB(PRT) Regs
72 Arts 5, 46 and 82 EU Reg 883/04; Arts 27, 46, 49 and 87 EU Reg 987/2009
73 Arts 7 and 21 EU Reg 883/04

6. Industrial injuries benefits
74 Reg 9(3) SSB(PA) Regs
75 Reg 9(4) SSB(PA) Regs
76 Reg 9(5) SSB(PA) Regs

7. Contribution-based jobseeker's allowance and contributory employment and support allowance
77 s1(2)(i) JSA 1995; ss1(3)(d) and 18(4)(a) WRA 2007
78 Art 64 EU Reg 883/04
79 *Stewart v SSWP*, C-503/09 [2011] ECR, not yet reported
80 Arts 5, 46 and 82 EU Reg 883/04; Arts 27, 46, 49 and 87 EU Reg 987/2009

8. Retirement pensions
81 s113 SSCBA 1992; reg 4(1) SSB(PA) Regs
82 Reg 4(3) SSB(PA) Regs
83 Reg 6 SSB(PA) Regs
84 Reg 13 SSB(PA) Regs
85 Reg 2(4) SSB(PRT) Regs

9. Statutory sick, maternity, paternity and adoption pay
86 **SSP** Reg 10 SSP(MAPA) Regs
SMP Reg 2A SMP(PAM) Regs
SAP/SPP Reg 4 SPPSAP(PAM) Regs
87 Art 6 EU Reg 883/04
SSP s163(1) SSCBA 1992; reg 16 SSP Regs; regs 5-10 SSP(MAPA) Regs
SMP s171(1) SSCBA 1992; regs 2, 2A, 7 and 8 SMP(PAM) Regs
SAP/SPP ss171ZJ(2)-(3) and 171ZS(2)-(3) SSCBA 1992; regs 3, 4, 8 and 9 SPPSAP(PAM) Regs

88 **SSP** Reg 16(2) SSP Regs
SMP Reg 3 SMP(PAM) Regs; reg 17(3)
SMP Regs
SAP/SPP Reg 2 SPPSAP(PAM) Regs; reg
32(3) SPPSAP(G) Regs; reg 24(4)
ASPP(G) Regs

10. **Tax credits**
89 Reg 4 TC(R) Regs
90 Reg 2(1) TC(R) Regs
91 Regs 3, 5 and 6 TC(R) Regs
92 s3(5A) TCA 2002
93 paras 20090, 20160 and 20170 TCCCM
94 para 0288580 TCM; see also *GC v
CHMRC (TC)* [2014] UKUT 0251 (AAC)

Part 6

European co-ordination rules and international agreements

Chapter 16

European Union co-ordination rules

This chapter covers:
1. Introduction (below)
2. Who is covered (p242)
3. Which benefits are covered (p245)
4. Principles of co-ordination (p248)

This chapter describes the way in which the European Union social security co-ordination rules can assist you to satisfy the entitlement conditions for UK benefits and tax credits if you have moved from another European Economic Area (EEA) state to the UK, and to be paid benefits and tax credits when you or a family member go to live in another EEA state.

The residence and presence conditions for the individual benefits that affect your entitlement while you are in Great Britain are covered in Part 4 and the rules that affect your entitlement to benefits and tax credits if you go abroad are covered in Part 5.

If you are not an EEA national, check Part 3 first as your immigration status may exclude you from the benefit or tax credit you want to claim.

---

1. Introduction

If you are a European Economic Area (EEA) national (see p39), a family member (see p243) of an EEA national or, in some cases, a non-EEA national (a 'third country national'), you may be able to benefit from the European Union (EU) social security co-ordination rules. These rules and the European caselaw about their application and meaning apply in the UK and throughout the EEA.

Note: there are two main parts of EU law affecting benefit and tax credit entitlement that are covered in this *Handbook*: the residence rights that enable you to satisfy the right to reside requirement, covered in Part 4, and the social security co-ordination rules, which are summarised in this chapter. In general, you do not need to know whether you have a right to reside in order to understand how the co-ordination rules affect you.

The co-ordination rules can help you qualify for benefits in the UK – eg, by enabling you to count periods of residence, insurance and employment in any EEA state to meet the conditions of entitlement. For the ways the co-ordination rules can help you qualify for individual benefits, see Chapter 13. They can also help you be paid a UK benefit in another EEA state for longer than you would be able to do under UK law alone. See Chapter 15 for the ways the co-ordination rules can help you claim or continue to receive individual UK benefits if you or your family member are in another EEA state.

The co-ordination rules

In order to secure and promote freedom of movement, EU law co-ordinates all the social security systems within the EEA. The intention is that people should not lose out on social security protection because they move to another member state. The rules do not seek to harmonise the social security systems of individual states; their sole objective is to co-ordinate the different schemes.

The co-ordination rules contain the following principles.

- **The single state principle.** You can generally only claim benefit from one member state (see p248).
- **Equal treatment of people.** Discrimination on the grounds of nationality in terms of access to, or the rate of payment of, the benefits that are covered is prohibited (see p253).
- **Equal treatment of benefits, income, facts and events.** If receipt of a benefit, or a fact or an event, has a legal consequence in one member state, this must be recognised in the same way by other member states (see p253).
- **Aggregation.** Periods of residence, insurance and employment in any EEA state can be used towards entitlement to benefit in another (see p254).
- **Exportability of certain benefits.** The co-ordination rules allow you to continue to be paid certain benefits abroad if you go to another member state. These rules generally mean that you can take benefit abroad for longer than under the UK rules (see p255).
- **Administrative co-operation.** Member states undertake to co-operate in the administration of the co-ordination rules.

The co-ordination rules set out the above general principles. There are exceptions to these principles for specific categories of benefits and, in some cases, there are more detailed provisions on how the principle should apply in certain circumstances. It is therefore helpful to understand the sources of the rules and the structure of the main regulation that sets these out.

The current co-ordination rules succeed and build on, but do not repeal, the previous set of rules. These are referred to in this *Handbook* as 'the old co-ordination rules' (see p242).

Sources of the co-ordination rules

Article 48 of the Treaty on the Functioning of the European Union (TFEU) requires the European Parliament and the Council of Ministers to make such rules in the field of social security:

'as are necessary to provide freedom of movement for workers; to this end, they shall make arrangements to secure for employed and self-employed migrant workers and their dependants:

(a) aggregation, for the purpose of acquiring and retaining the right to benefit and of calculating the amount of benefit, of all periods taken into account under the laws of the several countries;

(b) payment of benefits to persons resident in the territories of Member States.'

Under this Article, the following further legislation has been made.

- **EU Regulation 883/2004** sets out the rules for co-ordinating the different social security systems of the various EU states. The structure of this Regulation is as follows.
  - Preamble. This contains numbered 'recitals' that explain the purpose of the Regulation and the principles it contains. These recitals can be used as an aid to interpret the subsequent substantive Articles.
  - General Provisions. Article 1 contains important definitions. Article 2 explains the 'personal scope' of the Regulation (the people to whom it applies – see p242). Article 3 sets out the 'material scope' (the categories of benefits to which the Regulation applies – see p245). Articles 4 to 10 contain the general principles of the Regulation.
  - Determination of the Legislation Applicable. Articles 11 to 16 contain the general rules for working out which is the competent state (see p248).
  - Special Provisions Concerning the Various Categories of Benefits. Articles 17 to 70 contain more specific rules for different categories of benefits and are divided into chapters – one for each category of benefits.
  - Administrative Commission and Advisory Committee. Articles 71 to 75 establish organisations to oversee and implement the working of the Regulation.
  - Miscellaneous Provisions. Articles 76 to 86 contain various miscellaneous rules on practical issues of administration.
  - Transitional and Final Provisions. Articles 87 to 91 provide for the implementation of the Regulation and transitional measures.
  - Annexes. These contain further rules, most of which concern specific rules for individual member states.
- **EU Regulation 987/2009** contains procedures for implementing EU Regulation 883/2004.

Note: EU Regulation 883/2004 is the successor to Regulation 1408/71, which (together with its implementing regulation, EU Regulation 574/72) came into force on 1 April 1973 and is referred to in this chapter as the '**old co-ordination rules**'. The current co-ordination rules build on their predecessor, taking account of developments in European caselaw and national legislation to modernise and simplify the rules. However, the old co-ordination rules have not been repealed and continue to apply to limited groups (see p244). Since the majority of claims are now determined under the current co-ordination rules, this *Handbook* only covers these. For further information on the old co-ordination rules, see the 2012/13 edition of CPAG's *Welfare Benefits and Tax Credits Handbook*.

The other relevant law in the field of EU co-ordination comprises:
- the provisions in the TFEU on freedom of movement for workers, the self-employed and citizenship. Even if the EU co-ordination rules do not provide for entitlement to benefits, these provisions may;
- the Charter of Fundamental Rights of the European Union;
- judgments of the Court of Justice of the European Union.

Using the co-ordination rules

In order to establish whether you can rely on the co-ordination rules, you must do the following.
- **Step one:** check whether you are covered by the current or the old co-ordination rules (see p244).
- **Step two:** check whether you are within the 'personal scope' of the co-ordination rules (see below).
- **Step three:** check whether the particular benefit you want to claim is covered by the co-ordination rules and into which category it falls (see p245).
- **Step four:** check which state is the 'competent state' (see p248).
- **Step five:** check the principle you want to apply – eg, exporting benefit or aggregating periods of insurance (see pp253–55).
- **Step six:** check the individual benefit and tax credit rules in Chapter 13 if you want to check entitlement in the UK, and in Chapter 15 if you want to be paid when you or your family are in another EEA state.

2. **Who is covered**

In order to be covered by the co-ordination rules, you must come within the range of people to whom the rules apply. This is known as their '**personal scope**'.

You are within the personal scope of the co-ordination rules if:[1]
- you have been 'subject to the legislation of one or more member states' (see p243) and you are:
  – a European Economic Area (EEA) national; *or*

– a refugee; *or*
– a stateless person; *or*
• a family member (see below) or a survivor of one of the above. **Note:** the old co-ordination rules defined 'survivor' in terms of national legislation, so in the UK it meant a widow, widower or surviving civil partner.[2] However, there is no definition in the current rules, so it might be possible to argue a wider meaning could apply.

For the co-ordination rules to apply, your situation must involve more than one member state. This generally means that you must have moved between EEA states, or you live in one and work in another, or you live in one and are the national of another.[3]

Note: if you are covered by the co-ordination rules, check which state is the 'competent state' (see p248).

Subject to the legislation of a member state

You have been '**subject to the legislation of a member state**' if you have worked in, and paid (or should have paid) national insurance (NI) contributions to, or have received any social security (see p246) or special non-contributory benefit (see p247) from, that member state. You may also be subject to the legislation if you are potentially eligible for any social security benefit or special non-contributory benefit.

'**Legislation**' is defined as 'in respect of each member state, laws, regulations and other statutory provisions and all other implementing measures relating to the social security branches covered by Article 3(1) of the Regulation.'[4]

The '**social security branches**' referred to in this definition include UK benefits which are intended to assist you in the event of one of the risks covered by the co-ordination rules (see p246). Examples include attendance allowance, disability living allowance, personal independence payment, carer's allowance, child benefit and child tax credit. None of these depend on your being an employee or self-employed at any time. Potentially, therefore, even if you have never worked, you can be covered by the co-ordination rules.

Family members

A family member of someone covered by the co-ordination rules can also rely on the rules that cover that person (which can vary depending on the type of benefit claimed). The definition of member of the family under the co-ordination rules is different to the definition that applies in EU residence law (see p151). It is also affected by national social security legislation and can therefore vary between member states.

Note: as economically inactive people, including in some circumstances children, are now covered under the current co-ordination rules, you may not need to rely on being a family member. If you are both a family member of a person covered by the rules and also covered by the rules yourself, you can rely on either coverage.

Family member

You are a **'member of the family'** of a person covered by the co-ordination rules if you are:[5]

– a person defined or recognised as a member of the family, or designated as a member of the household, by the legislation under which benefits are provided; *or*

– if the legislation under which benefits are provided does not make a distinction between the members of the family and other people to whom the legislation is applicable, the covered person's spouse or child either under the age of majority (18 in England, Wales and Northern Ireland; 16 in Scotland) or older but dependent on the person covered.

If, under the legislation in either bullet above, you are only considered to be a member of the family or member of the household if you are living in the same household as the person, this condition is considered to be satisfied if you are mainly dependent on her/him.

The 'legislation under which benefits are provided' in the above definition should cover the legislation providing for the particular benefit you are claiming. However, it may be arguable that a broader category of social security legislation should apply. Get specialist advice if this affects you.

In a case concerning child benefit, the Upper Tribunal found that the relevant legislation was that of child benefit and held that the claimant's niece and nephew living in a different member state did not count as members of the claimant's family.[6] **Note:** this case concerned the old co-ordination rules and while the judge commented that the same would apply under the current co-ordination rules, it is arguable that insufficient consideration was given to the possibility of the children being designated as members of the household. Since they were not living in the same household as the claimant, this would have required a finding that they were mainly dependent on the claimant.

When the old co-ordination rules apply

The current co-ordination rules[7] apply to the vast majority of current benefit claims. However, the old co-ordination rules[8] (see p241) apply to you if:

• you are in receipt of a benefit because you qualified for it under the old co-ordination rules. A benefit claim is determined under the rules applicable at the time it is made. This depends on your nationality (see dates below). You remain subject to the legislation of a member state determined in accordance with the old co-ordination rules during a transitional period of up to 10 years, provided your circumstances do not change. This transitional period is intended to protect anyone who might otherwise have lost benefit under the new rules. However, you can ask to be transferred and considered under the new rules if this would be better for you. If so, the new rules take effect from the start of the following month;[9] *or*

- you are a 'third-country national' (other than a refugee) – ie, you are not an EEA national yourself, you are legally resident in the UK[10] and you have been employed or self-employed and subject to the legislation of a member state because you have paid (or should have paid) NI contributions or you have been a student and subject to the legislation of an EEA state. You continue to be covered by the old co-ordination rules if the UK is one of the member states where you have legally resided. This is because the UK obtained an opt-out, allowing it not to extend the current rules to third-country nationals.[11]

Relevant dates

The current co-ordination rules apply to nationals (and their family members) of:[12]

– the EU member states (and refugees and stateless people) from 1 May 2010;

– Switzerland from 1 April 2012;

– Iceland, Liechtenstein and Norway from 1 June 2012.

As most claims are now determined under the current co-ordination rules, this *Handbook* only covers these. For further information on the old co-ordination rules, see the 2012/13 edition of CPAG's *Welfare Benefits and Tax Credits Handbook*.

3. **Which benefits are covered**

The benefits to which the co-ordination rules apply are referred to as being within the '**material scope**' of the rules.

Individual social security benefits are not directly referred to. Instead, the rules have broad categories of benefits such as for 'old age' or 'maternity'. The rules refer to these categories as benefits designed to cover certain 'risks'. Any social security benefit in a member state designed to provide assistance in the event of a particular risk falls into that particular category of benefit. Each state must then list the benefits it considers are designed to assist with that risk. **Note:** the UK has no pre-retirement benefits.

Benefits are also divided into the following types, depending on the conditions of eligibility:

- social security benefits (see p246);
- special non-contributory benefits (see p247);
- social and medical assistance (see p248).

Those benefits deemed to be social security benefits have the most rights and special non-contributory benefits provide fewer rights. Social and medical assistance is not covered by the co-ordination rules.

Social security benefits

Social security benefits are categorised according to the risk against which they are designed to provide financial protection.[13]

Risk	UK benefit
Sickness	Attendance allowance (AA) (but see p247)
	Disability living allowance (DLA) care component (but see p247)
	Personal independence payment (PIP) daily living component
	Carer's allowance (CA) (but see p247)
	Statutory sick pay
	Contributory employment and support allowance (ESA) in the assessment phase (but see p247)
Maternity	Maternity allowance
	Statutory maternity pay
Paternity	Statutory paternity pay
Invalidity	AA, DLA care and mobility component and CA if you were in receipt of benefit before 1 June 1992. If you claimed after this date, see the note on p247
	Long-term incapacity benefit
	Severe disablement allowance
	Contributory ESA after the assessment phase
	Arguably, contributory ESA during the assessment phase (see p247)
	Additional pension
Old age	Graduated retirement benefit
	Winter fuel payments
	Increments – eg, to pensions
	Increases of retirement pension for an adult
	Age addition in pensions
Pre-retirement	None
Survivors	Bereavement benefits
Death grants	Bereavement payment
Accidents at work and occupational diseases	Industrial injuries disablement benefit
	Constant attendance allowance
	Exceptionally severe disablement allowance
	Reduced earnings allowance

Unemployment	Contribution-based jobseeker's allowance (JSA)
Family benefits (see p257)	Child benefit
	Guardian's allowance
	Child tax credit
	Increases in other benefits for an adult or a child

Note: AA, DLA care component and CA have been categorised as assisting with different risks at different times. Until 1 June 1992 they were categorised as invalidity benefits. They were then categorised as special non-contributory benefits until this was held to be wrong and they were then re-categorised as sickness benefits.[14] For the relevance of this if you want to export one of these benefits to another European Economic Area state, see p224.

The mobility component of DLA continues to be listed as a special non-contributory benefit and this has been held to be lawful.[15] The mobility component of PIP is treated by the DWP as a special non-contributory benefit. Therefore, you cannot export either mobility component (see p224).

Note:
- If you have a long-term or permanent disability, it is arguable that contributory ESA during the assessment phase, as well as after, should be regarded as an invalidity benefit.[16] However, in most cases it makes no difference to when it can be paid.
- For rules on exporting family benefits, see p257.
- The DWP considers that universal credit (UC) is neither a social security nor a special non-contributory benefit and so the co-ordination rules do not apply to it.[17] This view is likely to be subject to legal challenge. See CPAG's online service and *Welfare Rights Bulletin* for updates.

Special non-contributory benefits

Special non-contributory benefits are:[18]
- intended to provide supplementary or ancillary cover against the above risks or solely specific protection for disabled people closely linked to a person's social environment in the state concerned; *and*
- funded solely from general taxation and do not depend on having made contributions as a condition of entitlement; *and*
- listed as such in EU Regulation 833/2004 (see below).

The last criterion above requires each member state to list in an annex to EU Regulation 833/2004 the benefits it considers to be 'special non-contributory benefits'. The UK government has only listed the four benefits on p248.[19] However, it is expected that the mobility component of PIP will also be listed as a special non-contributory benefit and, until then, the DWP is treating it as such. Income-related ESA replaced income support (IS) in the list from 28 June 2012.

Special non-contributory benefits
DLA mobility component
Income-related ESA
Income-based JSA
Pension credit

Special non-contributory benefits can only be paid in the state in which you are 'resident'.[20] See p249 for details of when you count as resident.

Although you cannot 'export' special non-contributory benefits, all the other co-ordination principles apply.

Social and medical assistance

The UK does not specify which benefits it considers to be social assistance and consequently excluded from the co-ordination rules.

However, it has made it clear that it does not consider UC to be either a social security or a special non-contributory benefit.[21] This view is likely to be subject to legal challenge. See CPAG's online service and *Welfare Rights Bulletin* for updates.

It has also been decided that housing benefit[22] and working tax credit[23] are not social security or special non-contributory benefits. It is likely that the government would argue that IS is now also outside the scope of the EU co-ordination rules, since its removal from the list of special non-contributory benefits on 28 June 2012.

4. **Principles of co-ordination**

The co-ordination rules set out several general principles. There are exceptions to these principles for specific categories of benefits and, in some cases, there are more detailed provisions on how the principle should apply in certain circumstances. The following information provides an overview of the principles, as it is beyond the scope of this *Handbook* to cover all the exceptions and additional provisions in detail. You should therefore get specialist advice about the way the co-ordination rules apply to your particular circumstances.

The single competent state

Under the co-ordination rules you are generally only able to claim a particular type of benefit from one member state and only liable to pay national insurance (NI) contributions (or their equivalent) to one member state. This is expressed as the general principle that you can be subject to the legislation of a single member state only.[24]

The competent state and competent institution

The '**competent state**' is the state in which the 'competent institution' is situated.[25] It is the state that is responsible for paying your benefit and to which you are liable to pay NI contributions.

The '**competent institution**' is broadly the institution which is responsible for paying your benefit and to which you are liable to pay NI contributions.[26] The DWP is the UK's primary competent institution.

The general rule is that the competent state is the one in which you are:[27]

- employed or self-employed;
- resident and from which you receive an unemployment benefit;
- a conscripted member of the armed forces or someone doing compulsory civilian service;
- a civil servant.

However, there are exceptions for sickness benefits if you (or your family member who brings you within the co-ordination rules) receive a pension from a state other than the one in which you reside (see p250).

Note: you are treated as still employed or self-employed if, as a result of that activity, you are receiving cash benefits (other than for the risks of invalidity, sickness, old age, being a survivor or accidents at work).[28]

If you work simultaneously in two or more member states, you are subject to the legislation of the member state of residence if you pursue a substantial part (generally, at least 25 per cent) of your activities there.[29]

If your employer's business is normally in one member state but you are sent to another state to work and it is anticipated that the posting will last for no more than 24 months, you remain subject to the legislation of the first state. Similarly, if you are self-employed in one state and go to another state to provide similar services as a self-employed person, you remain subject to the legislation of the first member state, provided the anticipated duration of your time abroad does not exceed 24 months.[30]

If none of the above bullet points apply, the competent state is the state in which you are 'resident' (see below).[31]

How residence is determined

'**Residence**' is defined in the co-ordination rules as 'the place where a person habitually resides'.[32] The following information outlines the factors that should be considered when determining where you habitually reside. Although this list of factors is in a rule which explains what should be done if there is a difference of views between two states or institutions about where you are resident, it is clear that it should also be used where there is no such dispute. Firstly, it should be established by common agreement where your centre of interests lies. This is based on an overall assessment of the relevant facts, including:[33]

- the duration and continuity of presence in the state(s) concerned;
- your personal situation, including:
  - the nature and specific characteristics of any activity pursued, in particular the place where such activity is habitually pursued, the stability of the activity, and the duration of any work contract;
  - your family status and family ties;
  - any unpaid activity, such as voluntary work;
  - if you are a student, the source of your income;
  - your housing situation, in particular how permanent it is;
  - the member state in which you are deemed to reside for tax purposes.

If there is still a dispute about your place of residence, your intentions should be considered, especially the reasons why you moved. This is decisive in establishing your actual place of residence.

When the UK remains the competent state

If you are subject to the legislation of the UK, either because you last worked in the UK or you are resident in the UK, the UK remains your competent state until:[34]

- you start to work in another European Economic Area (EEA) member state;
- (unless you last worked in the UK) you receive a pension from another EEA member state and request that the UK ceases to be your competent state;[35]
- in some circumstances, you move to another EEA member state and become resident there (see below).

These general rules can be supplemented by other rules which are specific to the category of benefit being paid.[36]

The point at which the UK stops being responsible for paying your benefit if you move to another state is not always clear and most of the caselaw has considered the old co-ordination rules, which differ in some respects from the current ones (see p241). However, in general, if you continue to be entitled to a UK benefit when you move to another EEA state, the UK remains the competent state for paying that benefit until either you become employed/self-employed in the other EEA state or, in certain circumstances, you start to receive a benefit from that state.[37]

Sickness benefits

The general rule for determining the competent state for paying 'cash' sickness benefits (see p246) does not apply if you, or your family member (see p243) who brings you within the co-ordination rules, are a pensioner living in a state other than the one paying you a pension (even if this is your only pension).

Instead, the competent state for paying sickness benefits to a pensioner is the one responsible for meeting the cost of sickness benefits in kind – eg, in the UK, NHS treatment.[38] Although you receive sickness benefits in kind in the state in which you are resident, the cost of these can be borne by another state. This means that you need to establish which state must bear the cost of sickness benefits in kind to work out which is state is competent for payment of a cash sickness benefit.

There are several possible scenarios (although see p252 for some exceptions).

- If you live in the UK (or another state which also has a system of entitlement to sickness benefits in kind on the basis of residence, rather than insurance or employment) and you (or your family member who brings you within the co-ordination rules) receive a pension from one or more states but not from the UK (or the other state where you live), although you can receive sickness benefits in kind from the UK (or the other state), the cost of these is borne by one of the other states that pays a pension, to the extent that you would be entitled to receive sickness benefits in kind from that state if you lived there.[39]

Example
Emil is a Swedish national and receives a small Swedish old-age state pension. Emil moves to the UK and claims attendance allowance (AA). As he receives a pension from another state (Sweden), that state is responsible to the UK for reimbursing the cost of any NHS treatment he has. Consequently, provided Emil would be entitled to sickness benefits in kind (eg, healthcare) if he were resident in Sweden, he is not entitled to AA.

- If you receive a pension from two or more states and one of them is the state in which you reside, that state is responsible for the cost of your sickness benefits in kind (and is therefore the competent state for paying cash sickness benefits).[40]

Example
Emil becomes eligible for and claims a Category D retirement pension. He is now able to claim AA because he receives a pension from two or more states, including the one in which he resides. Therefore that state (the UK) is responsible for the cost of his NHS treatment.

- If you are the family member of a person receiving a pension and reside in a different state to her/him, whichever state must meet the cost of the sickness benefits in kind for that pensioner must also meet the cost of sickness benefits in kind for you (and is therefore the competent state for paying cash sickness benefits).[41]

The above rules do not apply if:

- you (or your family member who is a pensioner) are entitled to benefits under the legislation of a state because that state is the competent one on the basis of an activity as an employed or self-employed person;[42]

Example

Sophia is Portuguese and lives in the UK. She receives a small pension from Portugal. However, Sophia works part time as a self-employed cleaner and claims child benefit and child tax credit (CTC) for her disabled granddaughter who lives with her. Sophia can claim carer's allowance (CA), as the UK is the competent state for the payment of benefits to her on the basis of her self-employment here.

- you are the family member of a pensioner, but you have an independent right to benefits in kind, either under the legislation of a state or under the co-ordination rules, unless that independent right exists solely because of your residence in that state.[43]

UK legislation specifies that you are only entitled to AA, disability living allowance (DLA) care component, the daily living component of personal independence payment (PIP) and CA if the UK is the competent state under the co-ordination rules for cash sickness benefits.[44] Therefore, to see if you are entitled to one of these benefits if you are living in the UK and you (or your family member who brings you within the co-ordination rules) are receiving a pension from another member state, you should use the rules described above to determine whether the UK is competent for paying you such benefits.

Are you excluded by the rules for sickness benefits?

If you are residing in the UK and you receive a decision that the rules for sickness benefits exclude you from entitlement to AA, DLA care component, the daily living component of PIP or CA, or you think these rules might exclude you, check the following.

1. Are you (or your family member who brings you within the co-ordination rules) receiving a pension from another state? This must be a pension received under the legislation of a member state, so private and occupational pensions should not bring you within the above rules. **Note:** it is not always clear what counts as a pension and the term can apply to more than retirement pensions.[45] Most of the caselaw considering what counts as a pension does so in the context of the old co-ordination rules, which differ in some respects from the current co-ordination rules.[46]

2. Do, or could, you (or your family member who brings you within the co-ordination rules) receive a pension from the UK as well as from another state? If this applies, the UK is responsible for the cost of your NHS treatment, and so is also the competent state for paying sickness benefits (see the example of Emil on p251).

3. Although withdrawing your (or your family member's) claim for a pension from the other state could mean the above rules cease to apply you (or her/him), get advice before doing so as it could affect your (or her/his) future pension entitlement.

4. It may be possible to argue that the exclusion from AA, DLA care component or the daily living component of PIP on the basis that the UK is not your competent state does not apply. Depending on your circumstances, the basis of this argument could be that:

– if you are claiming AA, the exclusion does not apply to AA claims made on the grounds of terminal illness, since the location of the exclusion in the legislation[47] does not affect these awards as they are made under a separate provision;[48]

– if your health condition is permanent or long term, the exclusion should not apply because it only applies to cash sickness benefits and it was held by the Court of Justice of the European Union (CJEU) that a benefit claimed by someone whose disability is permanent or long term should be classed as an invalidity benefit rather than a sickness benefit;[49]

– if you are the dependent family member of an EEA worker, the exclusion is prohibited by the principle of equal treatment (see below) if the refusal of a disability benefit reduces or impedes her/his ability to work.

Equal treatment of people

If you are covered by the co-ordination rules, you are entitled to the same benefits under the legislation of the 'competent state' (see p248) as a national of that state. Equal treatment is one of the fundamental rights of European Union law, and the principle of non-discrimination prohibits discrimination based on your nationality. Both direct discrimination and, if it cannot be justified as proportionate and in pursuit of a legitimate aim, indirect discrimination are prohibited.

Direct discrimination arises when one person is treated less favourably than another. Indirect discrimination arises when rules which, although apparently neutral and non-discriminatory, have, in practice, a greater adverse impact on some people than others – eg, non-nationals of the competent state over nationals of the competent state. For example, the right to reside test in UK law would appear to apply equally to all EEA nationals. However, British and Irish citizens will always have a right to reside in the common travel area and therefore satisfy the test for means-tested benefits, whereas other EEA nationals will only satisfy it in certain circumstances. Therefore, the test is indirectly discriminatory. However, the Supreme Court decided in a case concerning pension credit that this discrimination is justified and, therefore, legal.[50] Although a different view was taken by the Northern Ireland Chief Commissioner who found that, for the purposes of child benefit, the right to reside test was either directly or indirectly discriminatory, this was overturned by the Court of Appeal in Northern Ireland.[51] However, note that one of the bases on which the European Commission has asked the Court of Justice of the European Union to declare the right to reside test for child benefit and CTC unlawful is because it is directly discriminatory.[52] See CPAG's online service and *Welfare Rights Bulletin* for updates.

Equal treatment of facts and events

The co-ordination rules provide for the 'equal treatment of benefits, income, facts or events'.[53] This is sometimes referred to as the 'principle of the assimilation of facts'. This principle is designed to ensure that if the competent state regards the receipt of a particular benefit or income, or the occurrence of certain facts or events, as producing certain legal effects, it should regard the receipt of an equivalent benefit or income from another state, or the occurrence of particular facts or events in another state, as producing the same effect. For example, a person receiving AA is entitled to a disability premium within her/his housing benefit (HB). Therefore, someone receiving a benefit equivalent to AA from another state who claims HB can argue that s/he should get the disability premium in her/his applicable amount. Similarly, if one member state has determined that a person has had an industrial accident, that fact must be accepted, for the purpose of awarding benefit, in another member state.

There are exceptions to the general principle of the assimilation of facts, some of which are set out in the co-ordination rules, and others arise as a result of a conflict between this principle and other principles of the co-ordination rules. An example of the latter is that the assimilation of facts cannot render another member state competent.[54] The competent state should first be determined (see p248) and then that state should assimilate facts for the purposes of its own legislation. Another example of the assimilation principle not being absolute is that it should not interfere with the principle of aggregation (see below).[55] Therefore, the competent state should count periods of insurance in another member state (under the aggregation principle) without needing to address the question of whether they count as periods of insurance for the assimilation principle to apply. If it counts as a period of insurance under the legislation of the state in which it took place, that period can be aggregated.

Aggregation

The principle of aggregation for the purpose of acquiring and calculating entitlement to benefits is a key co-ordinating principle.[56]

'**Aggregation**' means adding together periods of NI contributions, residence or employment/self-employment completed under the legislation of other member states to satisfy the conditions of entitlement for a benefit. This may be necessary if your entitlement to a benefit depends on your fulfilling a certain period of residence, employment or insurance. For example, if you want to claim a UK contribution-based benefit such as contributory employment and support allowance (ESA), but you have not paid sufficient NI contributions, you can rely on contributions you have paid in other EEA states in order to satisfy the UK contribution rules. What constitutes a period of residence, employment or insurance is determined by the legislation of the state in which it took place.[57]

The principle is that you should not lose out if you choose to exercise your rights to move within the EEA. If you were to be at a disadvantage should you need to claim benefit, this may deter you from moving.

Example
Sancha is a Portuguese national who has worked for many years in Portugal. She leaves her job in Portugal and moves to the UK. She works for three weeks before being made redundant. Sancha is expecting a baby in two months' time and claims maternity allowance (MA). She is entitled to MA because she can rely on her periods of employment in Portugal to satisfy the condition of having worked for 26 out of the last 66 weeks.

Unemployment benefits

When determining entitlement to unemployment benefits, the principle of aggregation has an additional condition. Your periods of insurance or employment/self-employment completed in all member states are only aggregated if you were last insured or last worked under the legislation of the state from which you are claiming benefit.[58]

Example
Tomasz is Polish and after working and being insured in Poland for four years became unemployed, and so moved to the UK to look for work. If he claims contribution-based jobseeker's allowance (JSA) he cannot use his periods of insurance from Poland to satisfy the NI contribution conditions. However, if he takes two weeks' full-time temporary work in the UK and then claims contribution-based JSA, he can then aggregate his periods of insurance in Poland and the NI contributions paid in the UK to be able to qualify for contribution-based JSA.

However, this additional condition does not apply if, during your last period of employment or self-employment, you resided in a state other than your competent state. In this case, if you claim an unemployment benefit in the state in which you reside you *can* aggregate periods of insurance or employment or self-employment in order to be entitled to that benefit.[59]

Exporting benefits

The co-ordination rules allow you to 'export' certain social security benefits to another state if you cease to be resident in the member state in which the entitlement arose.

This means that certain benefits may not be reduced, modified, suspended, withdrawn or confiscated just because you go to live in a different member state.[60] The rules for exporting vary according to the benefit concerned: some are fully exportable, some may be exportable on a temporary basis, and some are not exportable at all.

Check the individual benefit rules in Chapter 15 to see whether that benefit can be exported. If it can, you should contact the office that pays your benefit well in advance so that arrangements can be made to pay you in the other EEA state. The rules covering periodic reassessments still apply so, for example, if you export contributory ESA, the DWP continues to assess your limited capability for work and your limited capability for work-related activity. However, any checks and medicals take place in the state in which you are living, with reports then sent to the DWP.[61]

Under the co-ordination rules, all benefits categorised as social security benefits are exportable. See p246 for a list of the UK benefits covered.

The following benefits are fully exportable and can be exported indefinitely:
- invalidity benefits;
- old age benefits;
- survivors' benefits;
- pensions for accidents at work or occupational diseases;
- death grants.

The following benefits can be exported for a limited period or subject to certain restrictions:
- unemployment benefits;
- sickness, maternity and paternity benefits. However, in most cases these benefits are exportable in a similar way to the fully exportable benefits.[62]

Special non-contributory benefits (see p247) **cannot be exported**. They are paid only in the state in which you are 'resident'.[63] See p249 for details of when you count as resident.

Overlapping benefit rules

A general principle of the EU rules on co-ordination is that you should not use one period of compulsory insurance to obtain more than one benefit derived from that period of insurance.[64] In general, you are only insured in one EEA member state for any one period, so you cannot use insurance from that one period to obtain entitlement to benefits of the same kind from more than one member state. Usually, benefits are adjusted to ensure that either only one state (the 'competent state' – see p248) pays the benefit, taking into account periods of insurance in other EEA member states, or that the benefit is paid pro rata according to the lengths of the periods of insurance in different member states.

In certain cases, however, you may be paid both the full level of a UK benefit and a proportion of a benefit from another member state, accrued as a result of having paid national insurance contributions there. EEA states are not allowed to apply provisions preventing the overlapping of their own benefits with those of other member states if it would reduce what you would have received from your years of contributions in the first member state alone.[65]

There are particular overlapping rules on specific categories of benefits – eg, family benefits[66] (see p258), old age and survivors' benefits.[67]

Family benefits

Under the co-ordination rules, family benefits in the UK include child benefit, child tax credit (CTC), guardian's allowance and child dependants' additions in other benefits. For the definition of family member, see p243.

You can export family benefits without any time limit and they are uprated in the normal way. You can also be paid for family members living in another member state.[68]

Special rules apply if there is entitlement to family benefits from more than one member state in respect of the same person and for the same period. The rules determine which state has priority when these entitlements overlap (see p258).

Family members resident in another state

Generally, you are entitled to receive family benefits from your competent st-ate, determined in the usual way (see p248), even when the family member for whom you are claiming is resident in another state.[69] In this case, the family member is treated as if s/he were resident in the competent state.

Example

Carla is Italian. She is working in the UK. Carla's two children live with their grandmother in Italy. Carla is entitled to child benefit and CTC in respect of her children.

However, if you are receiving a pension, the member state that is competent for paying your pension is the one from which you claim family benefits.[70]

Example

Julien is a French national. He receives a small state pension from France and has moved to the UK. Julien's 15-year-old twin daughters remain living in France. Julien also runs a small business in the UK. Normally, because Julien is working in the UK, the UK would be the state competent for payment of family benefits. However, because Julien is in receipt of a pension from France, he is only entitled to claim French family benefits.

Priority when family benefits overlap

It is not uncommon for entitlement to family benefits to be provided for under the legislation of more than one member state in respect of the same family member and for the same period. This can arise when two people are entitled to benefit for the same child – eg, if a mother resides in one state and the father in another and both can claim family benefits for their child. It can also arise when the same person has an entitlement from more than one member state – eg, if a parent lives in one state with her children, but works in another.

The general principle in the EU co-ordination rules is that equivalent family benefits should not be payable by more than one state in respect of the same family member for the same period. To achieve this, there are rules which set out which member state has 'priority' – ie, must pay the family benefits.

The way these rules operate depends on:

- the basis on which each of the family benefits in question is paid. Different member states have different criteria for entitlement. In some states, family benefits may be payable on the condition that you live there (payable on the basis of 'residence'); in others, the criterion might be that you must work in that particular state (payable on the basis of 'employment or self-employment'); or family benefits may be paid on the basis that you receive a pension (payable on the basis of 'receipt of a pension'). Working out the basis on which a family benefit from another state is paid can be difficult, but the European Commission has online information on the conditions for each state.[71] In the majority of states, including the UK, family benefits are mostly payable on the basis of residence, rather than employment or receipt of a pension – eg, there are no employment conditions or a requirement to receive a pension in order to obtain child benefit or CTC;
- the member state in which the child lives.

If there is entitlement to a family benefit in respect of the same family member for the same period from more than one state, and the family benefits from each state are payable on a different basis, the member state which has priority (ie, must pay) is the one whose family benefits are payable under the first of the following bases:[72]

- employment or self-employment;
- receipt of a pension;
- residence.

If there is entitlement to a family benefit in respect of the same family member for the same period from more than one state, and the family benefits from each state are payable on the same basis, the member state which has priority (ie, must pay) is as follows.[73]

- If family benefits are based on employment/self-employment in both states, the state with priority is the one where the child resides, if you (or if there is another potential claimant, s/he) work there, otherwise it is the state that pays the highest amount.

- If family benefits are based on receipt of a pension in both states, the state with priority is the one where the child resides if that state also pays the pension, otherwise the state where you, or the other potential claimant, have been insured or resided for the longest period.
- If family benefits are based on residence, the state with priority is the one where the child resides.

If there is an entitlement to family benefits from the state that has priority, the entitlement to family benefits from the other state(s) with lower priority is suspended up to the amount provided under the legislation of the former state. If this suspension does not wipe out all entitlement, a differential supplement is paid to 'top up' the family benefits paid by the priority state. However, this top-up need not be paid for children residing in another state when entitlement to family benefits is based on residence only.[74]

Examples

Marie and her two children moved to the UK from Belgium four months ago when she separated from their father, Arnaud. Marie is looking for work but has not found a job yet. She claims child benefit and CTC. However, Arnaud, who is working in Belgium, is still receiving the Belgian family benefit and sending this money to Marie for the children. The Belgian family benefit is payable on the basis of employment and, therefore, has priority over the UK family benefits since the latter are based on residence. If the UK family benefits are more than the Belgian family benefits, Marie should be paid the difference to top up the Belgian family benefits.

Alica moved to the UK from Slovakia to take up a job, but was made redundant after four months. Her husband and their two children stayed in Slovakia. Alicia's husband receives Slovakian family benefits, which are payable on the basis of residence. Alicia claims child benefit and CTC. Since these are also payable on the basis of residence, Slovakia has priority since the children live there. The UK does not need to pay a top-up, even though its family benefits are more generous than the Slovakian benefits.

Note: if entitlement to a family benefit in one state depends on a claim having been made and no claim has been made, entitlement to the family benefit that has been claimed in another state cannot be suspended.[75] It is therefore not necessary to consider whether family benefits in another member state have priority or are payable at a higher rate if a claim is required for entitlement and no claim has been made.

If family benefits are paid to someone who is not using them to maintain the family member, the member state paying the benefit can make payments to the person who is, in fact, maintaining the family member. This is done at the request of, and through, the relevant institution in the state where the person who is maintaining the family member lives.[76]

There are rules that cover the administration of claims for family benefits, including procedures that should be followed if a claim for a family benefit is made to a member state that does not have priority.[77]

Notes

2. Who is covered
1 Art 2 EU Reg 883/04
2 Art 1(g) EU Reg 1408/71
3 *Petit v Office National de Pensions*, C-153/91 [1992] ECR I-04973
4 Art 1(l) EU Reg 883/04
5 Arts 1(i) and 2 EU Reg 883/04
6 *KT v HMRC (CB)* [2013] UKUT 151 (AAC)
7 EU Reg 883/04
8 EU Reg 10408/71
9 Art 87(8) EU Reg 883/04
10 Art 1 EU Reg 859/2003
11 Recital 18 EU Reg 1231/2010
12 The UK's attempt to challenge this extension of the current co-ordination rules failed in relation to:
Switzerland: *UK v Council of the European Union*, C-656/11 [2014] not yet reported;
Iceland, Liechtenstein and Norway: *UK v Council of the European Union*, C-431/11 [2013] not yet reported

3. Which benefits are covered
13 Art 3 EU Reg 883/04
14 *Commission of the European Communities v European Parliament and Council of the European Union*, C-299/05 [2007] ECR I-08695
15 *Bartlett and Others v SSWP*, C-537/09 [2011] ECR I-03417
16 *Stewart v SSWP*, C-503/09 [2011] ECR I-06497
17 SSAC, *Universal Credit and Related Regulations Report and Government Response,* December 2012
18 Art 70(1) and (2) and Annex X EU Reg 883/04

19 Annex X EU Reg 883/04
20 Art 70 EU Reg 883/04
21 SSAC, *Universal Credit and Related Regulations Report and Government Response,* December 2012
22 CH/1400/2006, paras 37-40
23 *MR v HMRC (TC)* [2011] UKUT 40 (AAC), para 17

4. Principles of co-ordination
24 Art 11 EU Reg 883/04
25 Art 1(s) EU Reg 883/04
26 Art 1(q) EU Reg 883/04
27 Art 11 EU Reg 883/04
28 Art 11(2) EU Reg 883/04
29 Art 13 EU Reg 883/04
30 Art 12 EU Reg 883/04
31 Art 11(3)(e) EU Reg 883/04
32 Art 1(j) EU Reg 883/04
33 Art 11 EU Reg 987/2009
34 Arts 11-16 EU Reg 883/04
35 Art 16(2) EU Reg 883/04
36 Title III EU Reg 883/04
37 See for example, *Kuusijärvi v Riksförsäkringsverket,* C-275/96 [1998] ECR I-03419; *SSWP v LT (DLA)* [2012] UKUT 282 (AAC) (granted leave to appeal to the Supreme Court as *SSWP v Tolley*); *SSWP v HR (AA)* [2013] UKUT 66 (AAC)
38 Art 29 EU Reg 883/04
39 Art 25 EU Reg 883/04
40 Art 23 EU Reg 883/04
41 Art 26 EU Reg 883/04
42 Art 31 EU Reg 883/04
43 Art 32(1) EU Reg 883/04

44 **AA** s65(7) SSCBA 1992
   DLA s72(7B) SSCBA 1992
   PIP s84 WRA 2012
   CA s70(4A) SSCBA 1992
45 Art 1(w) EU Reg 883/04
46 See for example, *JS v SSWP (DLA)* [2009] UKUT 81(AAC), para 14 and *KS v SSWP (DLA)* [2014] UKUT 19 (AAC), para 81. These cases accepted that invalidity benefits were pensions under EU Reg 1408/71.
47 s65(7) SSCBA 1992
48 s66 SSCBA 1992
49 *Stewart v SSWP*, C-503/09 [2011] ECR I-06497, especially paras 53-54
50 *Patmalniece v SSWP* [2011] UKSC 11
51 *Commissioners for HMRC v Aiga Spiridonova*, 13/115948
52 *European Commission v UK*, C-308/14
53 Art 5 EU Reg 883/04
54 Recital 11 EU Reg 883/04
55 Recital 10 EU Reg 883/04
56 Art 6 EU Reg 883/04; see also Art 48 TFEU
57 *Fonds National de Retraite des Ouvriers Mineurs v Giovanni Mura*, C-22/77 [1977] ECR 01699; but see also *Maria Frangiamore v Office National de l'Emploi*, C-126/77 [1978] 00725 and *Bestuur van de Nieuwe Algemene Bedrijfsvereniging v WFJM Warmerdam-Steggerda*, C-388/87 [1989] ECR 01203
58 Art 61 EU Reg 883/04
59 Arts 61(2) and 65(5)(a) EU Reg 883/04
60 Art 7 EU Reg 883/04
61 Arts 5, 46 and 82 EU Reg 883/04; Arts 27, 46, 49 and 87 EU Reg 987/2009
62 Art 7 EU Reg 883/04
63 Art 70 EU Reg 883/04
64 Art 10 EU Reg 883/04
65 *Teresa and Silvana Petroni v Office National des Pensions Pour Travailleurs Salariés (ONPTS), Bruxelles* 24-75 [1975] ECR 01149
66 Art 68 EU Reg 883/04
67 Arts 53-55 EU Reg 883/04
68 Art 67 EU Reg 883/04
69 Art 67 EU Reg 883/04
70 Art 67 EU Reg 883/04, second sentence
71 http://ec.europa.eu/social/main.jsp?catId=858&langId=en
72 Art 68(1)(a) EU Reg 883/04
73 Art 68(1)(b) EU Reg 883/04
74 Art 68(2) EU Reg 883/04
75 *Gudrun Schwemmer v Agentur für Arbeit Villingen-Schwenningen – Familienkasse*, C-16/09 [2010] ECR I-09717
76 Art 68a EU Reg 883/04
77 Arts 58-61 EU Reg 987/2009

Chapter 17

International agreements

This chapter covers:
1. Reciprocal agreements (below)
2. Council of Europe conventions and agreements (p268)
3. European Union co-operation and association agreements (p269)

The rules in this chapter may help you to obtain benefits in the UK, or to export benefits to certain countries. However, if you are moving within the European Economic Area, the European Union co-ordination rules may be more generous. See Chapter 16 for whether these apply to you.

1. Reciprocal agreements

A reciprocal agreement is a bilateral agreement made between the UK and another country. Reciprocal agreements are part of UK law and their purpose is to protect your entitlement to benefits if you move from one country that is a party to an agreement to the other.[1] A reciprocal agreement can help you qualify for certain benefits by allowing periods of residence and contributions paid in each of the two countries to be aggregated. It can also mean that you are paid more generously when you go abroad than you would be under the UK rules. Furthermore, they often specify that you must receive equal treatment with nationals of the country to which you have moved.

The scope of the reciprocal agreements differs greatly, not only in terms of the benefits covered and the provisions made, but also in respect of the people covered. It is therefore crucial to check the individual agreement. You can find the agreements in the *Law Related to Social Security* at www.lawvolumes.dwp.gov.uk.

This section provides an outline of the benefits covered and the general principles relating to the agreements. A list of all the countries and the benefits covered is in Appenidx 5.

Note: the following benefits are *not* covered by any of the agreements:
* income support;
* income-based jobseeker's allowance (JSA);

- employment and support allowance (ESA) – but see p266 for Northern Ireland;
- personal independence payment;
- social fund payments;
- child tax credit;
- working tax credit.

Agreements with non-European Economic Area countries

The UK has reciprocal agreements with some countries outside the European Economic Area (EEA). Each reciprocal agreement is different in terms of who is covered and which benefits are included. For a full list of the countries and the benefits covered, see Appendix 5.

Agreements with Northern Ireland, the Channel Islands and the Isle of Man

Technically, the rules relating to most social security and tax credits apply only to Great Britain – ie, England, Wales and Scotland. This does not include Northern Ireland, the Channel Islands or the Isle of Man, which have their own social security legislation. There are reciprocal agreements between all of these to ensure you do not lose out if you move between them. However, not all benefits are covered.

Agreements with European Economic Area states

The UK has reciprocal agreements with all the established EEA member states, except Greece and Liechenstein. Of the newer member states, only Croatia, Cyprus, Malta and Slovenia have agreements. Appendix 5 lists the countries with which the UK has social security agreements, and the benefits covered by each.

In general, reciprocal agreements can be relied on by EEA nationals if the European Union (EU) co-ordination rules (see Chapter 16) do not apply.[2] You cannot qualify for benefits using a reciprocal agreement if you:
- come within the 'personal scope' of the co-ordination rules (see p242);[3] *and*
- acquired your right to benefit on, or after, the date the EU provisions applied.[4]

If you are not covered by the co-ordination rules, you may be able to get benefits using a reciprocal agreement. Agreements between EEA states continue to apply if you do not come within the personal scope of the co-ordination rules, but you are within the scope of the reciprocal agreement.[5]

Agreements between EEA member states can also continue to apply if:
- the provisions of an agreement are more beneficial to you than the EU provisions; *and*

- your right to benefit from the reciprocal agreement was acquired before:
  - the EU provisions applied to the UK on 1 April 1973; *or*
  - the other member state joined the EU/EEA.[6]

Note: the UK's agreement with Denmark applies in both the Faroes and Greenland, as they are not part of the EU/EEA. Greenland left the EU on 1 February 1985.

People covered by the agreements

Some of the agreements cover nationals of the contracting countries, while others apply to 'people going from one member state to another'. This may be particularly significant if you are a non-EEA national who has worked in two or more EEA states but you cannot benefit under the co-ordination rules (see p242). Of the member states that now comprise the EEA (see p39), the agreements with Belgium, Denmark, France, Italy and Luxembourg are confined to nationals only.[7] The convention with the Netherlands extends to all people moving from one member state to the other who fall within its scope.

The reciprocal agreements define who is counted as a national for the purpose of the agreement where nationality is an issue. In all of these, a UK national is defined as a 'citizen of the United Kingdom and Colonies'.[8]

This category of people disappeared on 1 January 1983 when the British Nationality Act 1981 came into force. From this date, a person who had previously held citizenship of the UK and Colonies became:

- a British citizen;
- a British dependent territories citizen;
- a British overseas citizen; *or*
- a British subject.

For the purpose of the UK social security 'nationals only' conventions with Belgium, Denmark, France, Italy and Luxembourg, a UK national now includes anyone in one of the above four categories.

See p15 for further details of British nationality.

The definition of nationality contained in the agreements with Denmark, Italy and Luxembourg is simply that of a 'Danish' or 'Italian' or 'Luxemburger' national.[9] These agreements confer no rights if you are not a national of one of these states. The agreement with Belgium, however, covers a 'person having Belgian nationality or a native of the Belgian Congo or Ruanda-Urundi'. The agreement with France refers to 'a person having French nationality' and 'any French-protected person belonging to French Togoland or the French Cameroons'.

When these agreements came into force in 1958, the Belgian Congo and Ruanda-Urundi and French Togoland and the French Cameroons were Belgian and French territories respectively. Which Belgian and French nationals are covered by the agreements is a matter for the Belgian and French authorities. If you come from one of these countries (present-day Democratic Republic of Congo, Rwanda, Burundi, Togolese Republic and the Republic of Cameroon), enquire whether you are covered by these agreements with the Belgian or French authorities.

The agreements give equal treatment to nationals of the contracting countries, stating that a 'national of one contracting party shall be entitled to receive the benefits of the legislation of the other contracting party under the same conditions as if he were a national of the latter contracting party'.[10]

The agreements with Finland, Iceland, Ireland, Portugal, Spain and Sweden are not confined to nationals but give rights to:

- 'people who go from one country to another' (Ireland);
- 'a person subject to the legislation of one contracting party who becomes resident in the territory of the other party' (Portugal);
- 'a national of one contracting party, or a person subject to the legislation of that party, who becomes resident in the territory of the other contracting party' (Spain);
- 'a national of the state and person deriving their rights from such nationals and other people who are, or have been, covered by the legislation of either of the states and people deriving their rights from such a person' (Sweden).

The agreements with Austria and Norway have nationality restrictions that apply to the protocol on benefits in kind (eg, medical treatment), but not to social security contributions and benefits. A national of the UK is defined as anyone who is recognised by the UK government as a UK national, provided s/he is 'ordinarily resident' in the UK.

The agreement with Germany is not restricted to nationals of either agreement member state insofar as social security benefits are concerned. However, a nationality provision applies to the Articles relating to contribution liability.

Even if you are not a national of one of the contracting parties to these agreements, you may still be able to benefit from their provisions.

Benefits covered by the agreements

The following benefits are covered by some of the reciprocal agreements. See Appendix 5 for a full list of which benefits apply to which countries.

Unemployment benefits

The relevant benefit in the UK is contribution-based JSA.

None of the agreements allow you to receive unemployment benefits outside the country in which you have paid your national insurance (NI) contributions. However, some allow NI paid in one country to count towards satisfying the conditions of entitlement in another. This is the case with the UK agreements with Austria, Cyprus, Finland, Iceland, Malta, New Zealand and Norway.

Sickness benefits

In the UK, the relevant sickness benefit is short-term incapacity benefit (IB).

Note: from 27 October 2008, IB was abolished for new claims and replaced with ESA, but the reciprocal agreements in the UK were not amended to include ESA. Therefore, both contributory and income-related ESA are not covered by reciprocal agreements, but see below for Northern Ireland.

If you are entitled to sickness benefits, some of the agreements allow you to receive your benefit in another country. In other cases, contributions paid under one country's scheme may be taken into account to help you satisfy the conditions of entitlement in another.

Invalidity benefits

The relevant benefit in the UK is long-term IB and, for Northern Ireland only, ESA (see below).

Note: from 27 October 2008, IB was abolished for new claims and replaced by ESA. If you continue to be entitled to IB after the introduction of ESA, you are still covered by the reciprocal agreements. The reciprocal agreements that covered IB were not extended or amended to include ESA.[11] However, it is has since been decided to amend the reciprocal arrangements between Great Britain and Northern Ireland to cover both contributory and income-related ESA. Until this happens, the DWP makes extra-statutory payments to make up any loss of ESA that results from having to make a new claim when moving from Northern Ireland to Great Britain or vice versa.[12]

A number of agreements allow you to receive invalidity benefits in another country. The agreements with Austria, Cyprus, Iceland, Norway and Sweden allow you to continue to receive your long-term IB in these countries, subject to medical controls being undertaken in the agreement country. Similarly, you can receive the other country's invalidity benefits in the UK. The agreement with Barbados allows a certificate of permanent incapacity to be issued, permitting you to receive long-term IB without medical controls.

Maternity benefits

In the UK, the relevant maternity benefit is maternity allowance (MA).

If you are entitled to maternity benefits, some of the agreements allow you to receive your benefit in another country. You may be entitled to MA, or continue to be paid MA, when absent from the UK, under the reciprocal agreements with: Barbados, Cyprus, the Isle of Man, Jersey and Guernsey, Switzerland, Turkey and the countries of the former Republic of Yugoslavia (Bosnia-Hercegovina, Croatia, Kosovo, Macedonia, Montenegro, Serbia and Slovenia). The circumstances under which you may be able to claim or retain MA differ from agreement to agreement.

Benefits for industrial injuries

The relevant benefits in the UK are industrial injuries disablement benefit (including any constant attendance allowance or exceptionally severe disablement allowance), reduced earnings allowance and retirement allowance.

Most of the agreements include industrial injuries benefits. The arrangements determine which country's legislation applies to new accidents or diseases, depending on where you are insured at the time. Many of the agreements allow you to combine industrial injuries incurred in each country when assessing the degree of your latest injury. Furthermore, if you work in one country and remain insured under the other country's scheme and you have an industrial injury, you can be treated as though the injury arose in the country in which you are insured. Most agreements include arrangements to allow you to receive all three of the UK benefits for industrial injuries indefinitely in the other country.

Retirement pensions and bereavement benefits

All the agreements include retirement pensions and bereavement benefits. In the UK, the relevant benefits are retirement pensions, bereavement allowance and widowed parent's allowance. In most cases, you can receive a retirement pension or bereavement benefit in the agreement country at the same rate as you would be paid in the country where you are insured. This is the case under all the agreements except those with Canada and New Zealand, which do not permit the uprating of these benefits. If you go to live in either of these countries, your retirement pension (and any other long-term benefit) is 'frozen' at the rate payable either when you left the UK or when you became entitled to your pension abroad.

If you do not qualify for a retirement pension or bereavement benefit from either the UK or the other country, or you qualify for a pension or bereavement benefit from one country but not the other, the agreements with the following countries allow you to be paid basic old age and bereavement benefits on a pro rata basis, with your insurance under both schemes taken into account: Austria, Barbados, Bermuda, Cyprus, Finland, Iceland, Israel, Jamaica, Malta, Mauritius, Norway, the Philippines, Sweden, Switzerland, Turkey, the USA and the countries of the former Republic of Yugoslavia (Bosnia-Hercegovina, Croatia, Kosovo, Macedonia, Montenegro, Serbia and Slovenia).

Family benefits

In the UK, the relevant family benefits are child benefit and guardian's allowance. The provisions concerning these two benefits enable periods of residence and/or presence in the other country to be treated as residence and/or presence in Great Britain. The extent to which reciprocity exists varies, however, according to the particular agreement. For example, residence or contributions paid in the following countries count towards your satisfying UK residence conditions for guardian's allowance: Cyprus, Israel, Jamaica, Jersey/Guernsey, Mauritius and Turkey.

If you are a 'person subject to immigration control' (see p55) and you are covered by a reciprocal agreement for child benefit, you immigration status does not exclude you from entitlement to child benefit (see p66), provided you meet the other conditions of entitlement, including the residence and presence requirements (see p188).

Dependants' benefits

In the UK, a dependant's benefit is an increase to the benefit covered by the agreement. Dependants' increases can be paid if the dependant is in either country to the agreement.

2. Council of Europe conventions and agreements

There are numerous European conventions and agreements. These are prepared and negotiated within the Council of Europe. The most well known is perhaps the European Convention on Human Rights. The purpose of these conventions is to address issues of common concern in economic, social, cultural, scientific, legal and administrative matters and in human rights. However, such agreements and conventions are not legally binding in the UK unless or until they are incorporated into UK law, or legislation is enacted to give specific effect to the Treaty obligations in question – eg, the UK Human Rights Act in respect of the European Convention on Human Rights. They are statements of intent of the individual countries that are signatories. The UK is a signatory to a number of these agreements, including two that are significant for social security.

The European Convention on Social and Medical Assistance

The European Convention on Social and Medical Assistance has been in force since 1954. It requires that ratifying states provide assistance in cash and in kind to nationals of other ratifying states, who are lawfully present in their territories and who are without sufficient resources on the same conditions as their own nationals. It also prevents ratifying states repatriating a lawfully present national of other ratifying states simply because s/he is in need of assistance.

All the European Economic Area (EEA) countries (see p39) plus Turkey have signed and ratified this agreement. The rights given are recognised in UK law.

However, the European Union (EU) co-ordination rules are more generous than the Convention, so it would not normally need to be relied on by EEA nationals. They mainly assist you if you are a national of Turkey and are defined as a 'person subject to immigration control' (see p55), as the Convention exempts those covered from being excluded from means-tested benefits (see p64) and working tax credit (WTC) (see p68).

You can only benefit from the Convention if you are 'lawfully present' in the UK. If you are a national of Turkey, this means you must be within a period in which you have leave to enter or remain in the UK.

Note: you still must satisfy the other conditions of entitlement including, for means-tested benefits, having a right to reside (see p107).[13] Consequently, although the House of Lords held that an asylum seeker with temporary admission is 'lawfully present' and so potentially able to benefit from the Convention,[14] this will rarely assist you, as temporary admission does not give you a right to reside.[15]

The 1961 European Social Charter

This agreement is similar to the European Convention on Social and Medical Assistance. The ratifying states are all EEA countries (see p39), plus Macedonia and Turkey. The main relevance of this agreement for entitlement to benefits and tax credits is that if you are a national of Macedonia or Turkey and you are lawfully present, as with the Convention, you are not excluded from means-tested benefits or WTC if you are a 'person subject to immigration control' (see above).

It is only this 1961 Charter that gives access to UK social security benefits. If you are a national of a country that has signed a later charter only and are a 'person subject to immigration control', you are not exempt from being excluded from means-tested benefits and WTC.

3. **European Union co-operation and association agreements**

The Treaty on the Functioning of the European Union provides for agreements to be made with countries outside the European Union (EU).[16] These co-operation and association agreements are of greater significance than the other agreements outlined in this chapter as they are part of EU law and, therefore, have the potential to override UK rules.

The EU co-operation and association agreements can be divided into those that include a rule on equal treatment and have quite a wide scope and those that do not include an equal treatment rule and whose scope is much narrower (see p270).

Agreements with equal treatment provisions

The agreements that most directly affect benefits in the UK are those with Algeria, Morocco, San Marino, Tunisia and Turkey.

All of these agreements contain provisions specifying that there must be equal treatment for those covered by the agreement in matters of 'social security'.

UK regulations specify that if you are defined as a 'person subject to immigration control' (see p55), you are exempt from the exclusion from certain non-contributory benefits that would otherwise apply (see p66).

However, the EU agreements offer equal treatment to a wider range of benefits. The European Court of Justice (ECJ) found, in one case, the Turkish agreement and, in another, the Algerian agreement, to be inspired by the old EU co-ordination rules and that these rules should be looked to for guidance in interpreting the agreements. The ECJ held that the benefits covered by these agreements were the social security benefits covered by the co-ordination rules.[17] Under the co-ordination rules, 'social security' refers to certain benefits intended for the risks of unemployment, sickness, maternity, old age, bereavement, industrial injury and death. See p246 for a full list of these benefits.

Who is covered

To benefit from the agreements, you must be within their 'personal scope' – ie, you must be a national of Algeria, Israel, Morocco, Tunisia, San Marino or Turkey and you must be lawfully working in the UK. This has been equated with being an 'insured person' under the EU co-ordination rules.[18] In broad terms, this means that you must have worked in the UK and have (or you ought to have) paid national insurance contributions. In one case, a commissioner held that an asylum seeker who had worked in the UK was covered by the agreement with Turkey and was therefore eligible for family credit as a family benefit under that agreement.[19]

Other agreements: Israel

The EU also has various agreements with other countries. In general, these do not contain any provisions on the co-ordination of social security schemes, with the exception of the agreement with Israel.[20] This agreement is narrower in scope than those containing an agreement on equal treatment in matters of social security.

The agreement with Israel covers nationals of the EEA and Israel who are legally working in the EEA (for Israelis) or Israel (for EEA nationals) and members of their family who are legally resident.

The agreement covers benefits designed to protect against the risks of old age, invalidity and accidents at work, and benefits for survivors. The EU co-ordination rules, which should be used as an aid to interpret this agreement, also cover these, and other, risks (see p246).

However, the agreement does not go as far as either the EU co-ordination rules or the agreements that contain an equal treatment provision (see p253). Rather, it provides that:

- for Israelis, all periods of residence, insurance and employment fulfilled by a person covered by the agreement in different EEA states are totalled for the purpose of working out entitlement to the benefits covered;
- the benefits covered (except non-contributory benefits) can be exported to (for Israelis) Israel or (for EEA nationals) from Israel to the EEA.

Notes

1. Reciprocal agreements
1 s179(2) SSAA 1992
2 Art 8 EU Reg 883/04
3 Art 2 EU Reg 883/04
4 *Walder v Bestuur der Sociale Verzekeringsbank*, C-82/72 [1973] 599; *Jean-Louis Thévenon and Stadt Speyer-Sozialamt v Landesversicherungsanstalt Rheinland-Pfalz*, C-475/93 [1995] ECR I-03813
5 Art 2 EU Reg 1408/71; Art 2 EU Reg 883/04; *Galinsky v Insurance Officer*, C-99/80 [1981] 503; R(P) 1/81
6 *Rönfeldt v Bundesversicherungsanstalt für Angestellte*, C-227/89 [1991] ECR I-323; *Jean-Louis Thévenon and Stadt Speyer-Sozialamt v Landesversicherungsanstalt Rheinland-Pfalz*, C-475/93 [1995]
7 Art 3 to each of the relevant reciprocal agreements
8 Art 1 to each of the relevant reciprocal agreements
9 Art 1 to each of the relevant reciprocal agreements
10 Art 1 to each of the relevant reciprocal agreements
11 para 071393 DMG
12 DWP guidance, *Extra-statutory Payments for Claimants Moving From Northern Ireland to Great Britain*, available at: www.cpag.org.uk/content/dwp-guidance-extra-statutory-payments-esa

2. Council of Europe conventions and agreements
13 *Yesiloz v London Borough of Camden and DWP* [2009] EWCA Civ 415
14 *Szoma v SSWP* [2005] UKHL 64; [2006] 1 All ER 1, reported as R(IS) 2/06

15 R(IS)3/08

3. European Union co-operation and association agreements
16 Art 217 TFEU
17 *Sema Sürül v Bundesanstalt für Arbeit*, C-262/96 [1999] ECR I-02685; *Babahenini v Belgian State*, C-113/97 [1998] ECR I-00183
18 *Sema Sürül v Bundesanstalt für Arbeit*, C-262/96 [1999] ECR I-02685
19 CFC/2613/1997
20 *Euro-Mediterranean Agreement establishing an Association between the European Community and its Member State, of the one part, and the State of Israel, of the other part*, 20 November 1995. In force on 1 June 2000.

Part 7

Claims and getting paid

Chapter 18

· ·

Delays

This chapter covers:
1. Dealing with delays (below)
2. Waiting for a decision on a claim (p276)
3. Delays when challenging a decision (p288)
4. Delays getting paid (p292)

---

1. Dealing with delays

All benefit authorities should act promptly to process your claim, to process any challenge you make to a decision and to issue payments due to you.

Although all benefit claimants can experience delays in the administration of their benefits and tax credits, you are more likley to experience delays if you or your family member are a migrant.

If you experience a delay, in order to resolve the matter it can be helpful if you:
- can establish the reasons for the delay (see below);
- are clear at which stage the delay occurs (see p276).

The reasons for the delay

There can be many reasons for delays in benefit and tax credit administration. These are broadly due to the need for decision makers to have sufficient information, which can take time to collect, and the volume of work that decision makers have. This chapter focuses on the rules that are most relevant to migrants, but the cause of the delay in your case can be due to reasons that apply to all benefit claimants.

If you or your family member have moved to or from the UK or are not British, a delay in the administration of your benefit or tax credit can be because of the following.
- The complexity of the rules on immigration status, residence and presence, and the effect of the European Union (EU) co-ordination rules. This complexity often means that all these decisions are made by specialist decision makers within a benefit authority, and these individuals or teams often have a backlog.

- The initial benefit or tax credit claim form may not ask for all the information that the decision maker needs to be clear about the effect of the rules on immigration status, residence, presence and EU co-ordination. The decision maker therefore must write to you or to other agencies requesting further information, and this takes extra time.
- You may have difficulties obtaining and providing evidence which the decision maker has requested – eg, evidence about your immigration status. See Chapter 20 for more details on this and what you can do in this situation.
- There may be a query about whether you need or have, or have applied for, a national insurance (NI) number. See Chapter 19 for more information on NI numbers.

When the delay occurrs

What you can do to resolve a delay depends on the benefit you have claimed and also the stage at which the delay occurs. Delays can occur when you have:
- made a claim for benefit and are waiting for a decision on it (see below);
- had a decision on your entitlement and you have challenged that decision (see p288);
- had a decision on your entitlement and you are awaiting payment (see p292).

2. **Waiting for a decision on a claim**

Are you waiting for a decision on your claim?

1. If you have been waiting for a decision on your claim, what you can do depends on which benefit or tax credit you have claimed.

2. Check that your claim has been received. If it has not, if possible, provide the benefit authority with a copy of the claim and/or any evidence that was previously submitted. If the benefit authority states that it has not received your claim and you have no copy, you must submit a new claim and may be able to ask for it to be backdated. See CPAG's *Welfare Benefits and Tax Credits Handbook* for details on the backdating rules for the different benefits and tax credits.

2. If your claim has been received, but not dealt with, you should ask why. See pp277–88 for your options.

3. When trying to resolve delays, it is helpful to show the history of your previous contact. Therefore, keep a copy of any letters you send or receive, and take the name and job title of anyone you speak to on the phone and note the date.

4. In all communication with the benefit authority dealing with your claim, give your national insurance number (if you have one).

Benefits administerd by the DWP and HM Revenue and Customs

The rules about making decisions on claims for benefits and tax credits administered by the DWP or HM Revenue and Customs (HMRC) (ie, all benefits except housing benefit) do not state explicitly how long it should take to determine a claim and issue a decision.

However, the rules do say that the decision maker has a duty to decide claims for benefit,[1] and where this type of duty exists, it must be fulfilled within a reasonable time.[2]

If you think the decision maker has taken longer than a reasonable time in your case, the strength of your argument depends on:

- the volume of other claims waiting for consideration and the number of decision makers available to deal with them;[3]
- the facts of your individual case, including how long you have waited for a decision and the effect on you of your having to wait. For example, if you have no income while you wait for your claim to be decided, this is more serious for you than if the benefit, once awarded, would top up your existing income. Similarly, if you or a dependent family member has a health condition which is exacerbated by the lack of income, this may be relevant.

If there are specific reasons, such as the examples given above, which mean that the delay is making things particularly difficult for you or your family, you can suggest that it is not appropriate for your claim to be dealt with as part of a normal queuing system (whereby claims are determined in the order they are received). Tell the decision maker of any specific reasons why the delay is causing hardship for you.

If a delay continues, you could:

- request a short-term advance (certain benefits only) (see p278);
- request an interim payment of child benefit and guardian's allowance (see p281);
- make a complaint in writing (see p281);
- escalate a complaint to the Parliamentary Ombudsman (see p283);
- obtain legal advice about sending a 'letter before action' for judicial review (see p284).

You can pursue more than one of these options – eg, you can make a complaint and if this does not resolve the delay, obtain legal advice about sending a letter before action for judicial review.

While waiting for your claim to be decided, you may be able to get help from your local welfare assistance scheme (see p400).

If the delay is due to the DWP determining whether you have a right to reside for the purpose of your claim for income support (IS), income-related employment and support allowance (ESA) or (for men aged between pension credit (PC) age and men's retirement age) PC and you have a right to reside as a jobseeker, you may want to claim income-based jobseeker's allowance (JSA). Your income-based JSA claim is likely to be determined more quickly, as it is easier to establish your right to reside as a jobseeker than other residence rights that satisfy the right to reside requirement for the other benefits (see p107).

However, as the DWP computer system cannot have two claims open at once, in practice, you must request that you still want your IS (or the other benefit) claim determined, but that it should be done clerically and taken off the computer system to enable the JSA claim to be determined and put into payment. If the IS (or other benefit) is then awarded, it should be paid from the date you first claimed it. The decision to award JSA should then be revised, either because it was based on a mistake about your entitlement to IS (or other benefit) and the decision was more advantageous to you[4] or because you were awarded benefit (JSA) and then awarded another benefit (IS) for a period including the date the first benefit award (JSA) was made.[5] The IS (or other benefit) should then continue. Seek advice if you experience difficulty with this.

Short-term advances

If your claim for a benefit administered by the DWP has not been decided, or payment of your benefit is delayed, you may be able to get an advance payment of your future benefit award. This is called a 'short-term advance' and is intended to help you through a period of 'financial need' (see p279) before you receive your first (or increased) payment.

A short-term advance can be paid when (among other circumstances) you have made a claim for benefit but it is impracticable for it to be determined immediately. The power of the decision maker to make a short-term advance is discretionary – ie, s/he does not have to give you a short-term advance, but must take all the circumstances of your case into account when making her/his decision.

The decision maker can only decide to make a short-term advance if:[6]

- you have made a claim for a benefit in respect of which you can be paid a short-term advance (see p279). The only exception to this requirement is if you are not required to make a claim for benefit in order to be entitled, which only applies in very limited circumstances; *and*
- this claim has not been determined. **Note:** if there is no reason preventing the DWP from determining your claim, the decision maker should just determine the claim rather than consider a short-term advance; *and*
- you are in 'financial need' (see p279); *and*
- it appears to the decision maker likely that you will be entitled to the benefit.

You cannot get short-term advance if there is an appeal pending on the benefit on account of which the advance would otherwise be paid.[7]

You can get a short-term advance of any benefit *except*: [8]

- housing benefit (HB), although if your HB is delayed and you are a private or housing association tenant, you might be able to get a 'payment on account' (see p286);
- attendance allowance;
- disability living allowance;
- personal independence payment;
- child benefit, although you might be able to get an interim payment (see p281);
- guardian's allowance, although you might be able to get an interim payment (see p281);
- statutory sick pay, statutory maternity pay, statutory paternity pay or statutory adoption pay;
- tax credits.

Financial need

'Financial need' means that because you have not received your benefit, there is a serious risk of damage to the health or safety of you or a member of your family.

'Family' means your partner and any children for whom you or your partner are responsible – ie, for whom you or your partner could claim child benefit.[9]

Note: decision makers can also make a short-term advance of benefit if your claim has been determined and you have been awarded benefit but:[10]

- you are waiting for your first payment; *or*
- you have received your first payment, but it was for a shorter period than subsequent payments will be paid for and you are waiting for your next payment; *or*
- you have had a change of circumstances that increases your entitlement, but your benefit has not yet been increased and paid to you; *or*
- you are entitled to a payment but it is impracticable to pay all or some of it on the date on which it is due.

A short-term advance is recovered by deductions from subsequent payments of your benefit. You must be notified of your liability to have the advance recovered by deductions, and to repay any amount not recovered through deductions.[11]

There is no right of appeal against a refusal to award a short-term advance.[12] The only legal remedy is judicial review (see p284). You could contact your MP to see if s/he can help to get the decision reconsidered. If you have difficulty obtaining a short-term advance, see p280.

Note: you may be able to get help from your local welfare assistance scheme (see p400) as well as, or instead of, a short-term advance.

18

How to apply

You can request a short-term benefit advance in person or writing (by post, fax or email) to your local jobcentre or by telephoning the Jobcentre Plus contact centre. Your application should set out why you meet the criteria. You should give the relevant history of your claim, confirm that you satisfy all the conditions of entitlement, including any areas where there may be a doubt – eg, set out the basis of your right to reside (see Chapter 12) or the reason why you are not a 'person subject to immigration control' (see Chapter 7). Finally, give the reasons why you are in financial need.

The DWP aims to decide your request by the next working day and telephone you with the decision. However, before even considering your request, the DWP should first check whether it can instead simply determine your claim and issue you a payment and, if so, should telephone you to let you know.[13] If you do not have a telephone, you can provide the DWP with the number of a friend or relative and, if you cannot do that, the DWP will tell you to ring the Benefit Enquiry line after a certain time for an update on your request.

Are you having problems getting a short-term advance?

1. You may be told to seek help from your local welfare assistance scheme (see p400) or be referred to a foodbank (see p407) instead. If you consider you meet the criteria for a short-term benefit advance, you should insist on your request being passed to the decision maker to consider. The discretion to award you an advance is exercised by a decision maker, taking account of all the relevant circumstances, it is not a decision to be made by frontline staff. The system of short-term advances was introduced in April 2013, but there still appears to be some confusion among DWP staff about how the system operates.

2. The decision maker who considers your case may not be an expert on the various rules on benefits for migrants, which can be a problem because s/he can only make a short-term advance if it appears to her/him that you are likely to be entitled to benefit. It may therefore assist your application if you set out clearly how you satisfy the relevant immigration, residence and presence conditions.

3. If the reason your claim cannot be processed is because you are waiting to obtain evidence showing that you satisfy all the conditions of entitlement, it may help to summarise any other evidence that you have already submitted and explain how it is consistent with the evidence you are waiting for to show that you are entitled to the benefit. For more information on the evidence required for the immigration and residence tests, see Chapter 20.

4. The decision maker may think that you are not entitled to a short-term advance because you do not have a national insurance (NI) number. If this happens, you could point out that the guidance issued to decision makers states that, provided you can prove your identity and are complying with other requests for required evidence, a short-term benefit advance should still be considered.[14] For further information on the NI number requirement, see Chapter 19.

5. You may be told that you will be refused a short-term benefit advance because it cannot be repaid within 12 weeks from your ongoing entitlement – eg, because you have other debts that will be recovered from your benefits (such as an overpayments or a budgeting loan), or the amount of the advance, and therefore the repayments, will be large in relation to your ongoing entitlement. Although the regulations do not require you to be able repay the advance within any particular period, guidance states that the decision maker must consider whether you can repay the advance within 12 weeks when deciding whether to make a short-term advance. However, the guidance states that this period can be extended to 24 weeks in 'exceptional circumstances' where 'financial need overrides affordability', such as if you are fleeing domestic violence.[15] If you will be unable to repay your advance within 12 weeks and you think your circumstances are exceptional, you may want to refer the decision maker to this guidance.

Interim payments of child benefit and guardian's allowance

An interim payment of child benefit or guardian's allowance can be made if it appears to the HMRC that you may be entitled to benefit and:[16]

- you have not claimed correctly and it is impracticable for such a claim to be made immediately; *or*
- you have claimed correctly and all the conditions of entitlement are satisfied *except* the NI number requirement (see p299) and it is impracticable for that to be satisfied immediately; *or*
- you have claimed correctly, but it is impracticable for the claim to be dealt with immediately; *or*
- you have been awarded benefit, but it is impracticable to pay you immediately, other than by an interim payment.

Note:
- There is no right of appeal against a refusal to award you an interim payment. The only legal remedy is judicial review (see p284). You could contact your MP to see if s/he can help to get the decision reconsidered.
- An interim payment can be deducted from any later payment of the benefit and, if it is more than your actual entitlement, the overpayment can be recovered. You should be notified of this in advance.[17]
- An interim payment cannot be paid if you have an appeal pending.[18]

Making a complaint

Making a complaint when there is an ongoing problem (such as a claim that has not been decided) is quite different from making a complaint about a situation that you think should not have happened but which is no longer producing a problem – eg, if your claim has been decided, but you are unhappy it took so long. The information in this section is aimed at enabling you to use the complaints process in order to get the situation resolved (ie, to get a decision on your claim), rather than at seeking compensation or highlighting to the DWP/HMRC the hardship it has caused after a delay has been resolved.

When you make a complaint to try to resolve an ongoing delay, it is very important that you highlight in the complaint that the problem persists, that this is therefore an urgent matter and what you want to be done about it – eg, ask for your claim to be determined within X number of days.

The DWP and HMRC have different procedures for complaining.

Complaints about the DWP

If you want to complain about how a particular DWP agency has dealt with your case, you should first contact the office that is dealing with your claim. If you are unsure which office this is, contact numbers and information about the complaints procedure are provided on the DWP website.[19]

You should receive a response to your complaint within 15 days.

If you are still dissatisfied, your complaint is passed to a complaints resolution manager. This is referred to as a 'tier one' complaint. S/he should contact you by phone within 48 hours of receiving your complaint and keep you updated about its progress. Your complaint should be dealt with within 15 days.

If you remain dissatisfied, you can ask for your complaint to be passed to a more senior DWP officer. The DWP refers to this as a 'tier two' complaint. If you are still not satisfied, you can complain to the Independent Case Examiner (ICE) and you may also have grounds to make a complaint to the Ombudsman (see below).

The ICE deals with complaints about DWP agencies and its contracted providers.

A complaint can only be made to the ICE if you have already completed the complaints procedure of the particular agency concerned. This usually means that you have had a response to a tier two complaint. A complaint should be made to the ICE no later than six months after the final response from the agency you are complaining about.

The ICE first considers whether or not it can accept the complaint. If it can, it attempts to settle it by suggesting ways in which you and the agency concerned can come to an agreement. If this fails, the ICE prepares a formal report, setting out how the complaint arose and how it believes it should be settled. The ICE considers whether there has been maladministration. It cannot deal with matters of law or cases that are subject to judicial review or other legal procedures, or cases under appeal.

If you are unhappy with the way the ICE dealt with your case, first use the ICE internal complaints process. If you remain unhappy, ask your MP to consider referring your concerns to the Parliamentary and Health Service Ombudsman (see p283).

Compaints about HM Revenue and Customs

If you want to complain about how HMRC has dealt with your claim for tax credits, child benefit or guardian's allowance, first raise the complaint with the office dealing with your case, or the named contact person on the letters you have received, setting out the nature of your complaint – eg, the delay in processing information you have submitted, requesting supplementary information or evidence or in actually determining your claim. Set out the history of your claim and any telephone contact or written correspondence and say what you think HMRC has done wrong. Also include in the complaint any loss that you have incurred, or difficulty you or your family members have had as a result.

If you are not happy with the response to your complaint, you can ask for it to be passed to an HMRC complaints handler. If you are dissatisfied with her/his response, you can ask that your complaint be reviewed by another complaints handler.

HMRC's complaints procedure is set out in its factsheet, *Complaints* (C/FS), available on its website.[20]

If you are not happy with HMRC's reply, you can ask the Adjudicator's Office to look into it.

The Adjudicator only investigates a complaint if you have first exhausted the HMRC internal complaints procedure. A complaint should be made within six months of the final correspondence with HMRC.

Complaints can be made about delays, inappropriate staff behaviour, misleading advice or any other form of maladministration. The Adjudicator cannot, however, investigate disputes about matters of law. The Adjudicator can recommend that compensation be paid. HMRC has undertaken to follow the Adjudicator's recommendations in all but exceptional circumstances.[21]

Complaining to the Parliamentary Ombudsman

If you have an ongoing delay in getting a decision made on your claim for benefit, a complaint, or the threat of a complaint, to the Parliamentary and Health Service Ombudsman may result in the DWP or HMRC taking action to determine your claim. You can also make a complaint to the Ombudsman after the issue is resolved.

The role of the Ombudsman is to investigate complaints from members of the public who believe they have experienced an injustice because of maladministration by a government department.[22] 'Maladministration' means poor administration and can include avoidable delays, failure to advise about appeal rights, refusal to answer reasonable questions or respond to correspondence, and discourteousness, racist or sexist behaviour.

The Ombudsman does not usually investigate a complaint unless you have first exhausted the internal complaints procedure. However, if the decision maker is not acting on your complaint, or there are unreasonable delays, this delay may also form part of your complaint. The time limit for lodging a complaint with the Ombudsman is 12 months from the date you were notified of the matter complained about. However, a delay in bringing a complaint does not necessarily prevent a complaint being heard if there are good reasons for the delay.

A public body, such as the DWP or HMRC, is required to follow the recommendations of a complaints panel unless there are good reasons not to. If a public body has failed to do so, you may have grounds to complain to the Ombudsman and, in some circumstances, may have grounds for a judicial review.

The Parliamentary and Health Service Ombudsman deals with complaints about all central government departments. This includes the DWP, HMRC, HM Courts and Tribunals Service and any agencies carrying out functions on their behalf. In order to make a complaint, you must write to your MP, who then refers the complaint to the Ombudsman. To find out who your MP is, contact the House of Commons Information Office on 020 7219 4272 or go to http://.findyourmp.parliament.uk. The Ombudsman can only investigate complaints of maladministration and not complaints about entitlement, which should be dealt with by challenging the decision on this. The Ombudsman has powers to look at documents on your claim held by the benefit authority. You may be interviewed to check any facts. The Ombudsman can recommend financial compensation if you have been unfairly treated or experienced a loss as a result of the maladministration.

Judicial review

Judicial review is a process by which you can ask a court to look at an action (or, in the case of delay, inaction) of any public authority which affects you on the grounds that such (in)action is unlawful. If the High Court (Court of Session in Scotland) accepts that the (in)action is unlawful, it has the power to order the decision maker to determine your benefit claim (or otherwise resolve the issue).

There are many steps that must be taken before the High Court (or Court of Session) gives such a decision. Furthermore, if you do apply for judicial review about a benefit delay, it is strongly advisable *only* to do so with the help of legal advice. In particular, you risk having to pay the legal costs of the decision maker (which could run to thousands of pounds) if your challenge is unsuccessful. In order to protect against this risk, it is necessary to obtain a legal aid certificate before proceedings are issued (and this is another reason to obtain legal advice).

However, in cases of benefit delay, often a 'letter before action', in which your adviser states that judicial review action will commence unless the claim is determined by a certain date, can lead to a claim being decided promptly. The letter should be sent to the solicitor for the DWP or HMRC, together with a copy to the manager of the section responsible for dealing with your claim. Although a 'letter before action' is currently only a requirement in England and Wales, its use in Scotland can still assist in resolving delays.

There is a template for a pre-action letter (for use in England and Wales) available online.[23] The letter should include all the details required in that template.

Completing a pre-action letter

Under the section entitled 'the issue', you should include the following.

1. Set out the history of your claim for benefit – ie, which benefit you claimed and when, plus the details of all further correspondence and complaints that you have made. It is often useful to do this in the form of a chronology in date order.

2. Explain why you believe you are entitled to the benefit claimed. You should address how you meet the conditions of entitlement, including how you meet the rules about immigration status, residence or the European Union co-ordination of social security.

3. Explain that there is a legal duty to determine claims within a reasonable time (see p277 for what this means and the footnotes to that section for the legal references).

4. Explain why you believe the claim has not been determined within a reasonable time in your particular case and/or why a short-term advance should have been made. It is important to explain in as much detail as possible why you believe the DWP or HMRC has all the information needed to determine your claim, or why it should be able to obtain it. Also explain any specific reasons why the delay is causing you difficulties.

Housing benefit

The housing benefit (HB) rules state that your claim must be determined within 14 days (or as soon as reasonably practicable after that) of your submitting a valid claim and providing all the information and evidence requested and reasonably required by the local authority.[24]

What counts as 'as soon as reasonably practicable' is the same as for benefits administered by the DWP and HMRC (see p277). In addition, the fact that your home may be at risk of repossession if the rent is not paid can often be a relevant factor in determining how long it should take to make a decision.

If you experience a delay in deciding your claim for HB, you can:
- request a 'payment on account' if you are a private or housing association tenant – ie, not a council tenant (see p286);
- make a complaint in writing (see p286);
- escalate a complaint to the Local Government Ombudsman (see p287);
- obtain legal advice about sending a 'letter before action' for judicial review (see p287).

You can pursue more than one of these options – eg, you can make a complaint and if this does not resolve the delay, get legal advice about sending a 'letter before action' for judicial review.

Payments on account

The local authority must make a 'payment on account' if:[25]

- you have claimed HB as a private or housing association tenant; *and*
- it is impracticable for the local authority to make a decision on your claim within 14 days of its being made; *and*
- this is not due to your failure (without good cause) to provide the information it has requested.

A payment on account is sometimes called an 'interim payment'.

A payment on account is not discretionary. The local authority *must* pay the amount it considers 'reasonable', based on the information it has about your circumstances. If your actual entitlement is less, the local authority recovers the overpayment, or pays your arrears if your entitlement is greater.[26]

You do not need to ask the local authority to make a payment on account and you do not need to make a separate claim.[27] However, in practice, it is often necessary to write and request a payment on account, and/or make a complaint (see below), and/or write to the solicitor for the local authority and threaten judicial review (see p287) in order to get a payment.

Making a complaint

Making a complaint when there is an ongoing problem (such as an HB claim that has not been decided) is quite different from making a complaint about a situation that you think should not have happened but which is no longer producing a problem – eg, if your claim has been decided, but you are unhappy it took so long. The information in this section is aimed at enabling you to use the complaints process in order to get the situation resolved (ie, get a decision on your HB claim), rather than at seeking compensation or highlighting to the local authority the hardship it has caused after a delay has been resolved.

When you make a complaint to resolve an ongoing delay, it is very important that you highlight in the complaint that the problem persists, that this is therefore an urgent matter and what you want to be done about it – eg, ask for your claim to be determined within X number of days. In particular, you should include any relevant details of steps your landlord is taking to obtain possession of the property due to rent arrears arising from the HB delay.

Local authorities must have an effective complaints procedure, which should be made available to the public. If you are unhappy about the actions of your local authority and wish to make a complaint, you should ask for a copy of its complaints policy. If you are unable to obtain the policy or there is no formal complaints procedure, you should begin by writing to the supervisor of the person dealing with your claim, making it clear why you are dissatisfied. If you do not receive a satisfactory reply, take up the matter with someone more senior in the department and ultimately the principal officer. Send a copy of the letter to your ward councillor and to the councillor who chairs the relevant committee responsible for HB (local authority officers are always accountable to the councillors). If this does not produce results, or if the delay is causing you severe hardship, consider a complaint to the Ombudsman (see below) or obtain legal advice about a judicial review (see below).

Government departments also monitor local authorities, so you could contact your MP or write to the relevant minister.

If you want to make a complaint about an elected member of a council, you must write to the local authority. In England, the Localism Act requires all local authorities to promote and maintain high standards of conduct by elected members. However, they can choose whether or not to set up standards committees to consider complaints about the conduct of councillors. The practice may therefore vary and you should ask your local authority for its procedure for complaints against members. In Wales and Scotland, elected members of a council are subject to a code of conduct. Complaints about Scottish councillors can be made to the Commissioner for Ethical Standards in Public Life in Scotland who can refer cases to the Standards Commission for Scotland. Complaints about Welsh councillors can be made to the Public Services Ombudsman for Wales.

Complaining to the Ombudsman

If you have tried to sort out your complaint with the local authority but you are still not satisfied with the outcome, you can apply to the Local Government Ombudsman (in England), the Scottish Public Services Ombudsman (in Scotland) or the Public Services Ombudsman for Wales (in Wales). The Ombudsman can investigate any cases of maladministration by local authorities, but not matters of entitlement, which are dealt with by the First-tier Tribunal.

You can complain to the Ombudsman either in writing (including online) or by phone. The Ombudsman has powers to look at documents on your claim held by the local authority. You may be interviewed to check any facts. Straightforward cases can be dealt with in about three months. The Ombudsman can recommend financial compensation if you have been unfairly treated or experienced a loss as a result of the maladministration. A complaint may also make the authority review its procedures, which could benefit other claimants.

One outcome of your complaint may be a 'local settlement'. This is where the local authority agrees to take some action that the Ombudsman considers is a satisfactory response to your complaint and the investigation is then discontinued. If you are unhappy with the way in which the Ombudsman has dealt with your complaint, you should obtain legal advice as quickly as possible.

Judicial review

Judicial review when there is a delay in making a decision on an HB claim is similar to when there is a delay in deciding a claim for a benefit admistered by the DWP or HMRC (see p284). However, as there are different rules for how quickly a HB claim must be decided, any 'letter before action' for judicial review must refer to these. In particular, if you are a private tenant, your letter should note the rules about payments on account (see p286).

The letter should be sent to the solicitor for the local authority, together with a copy to the manager of the HB section responsible for dealing with your claim.

Note: because of the potential consequences, including costs, it is strongly advised that you obtain legal advice before initiating judicial review proceedings.

Pending test cases

The general requirement to decide your claim does not apply if there is a appeal pending against a decision of the Upper Tribunal or a court in a 'test case' that deals with issues relevant to your claim. If so, the decision maker must consider whether it is possible that the outcome of the test case would mean you would have no entitlement. If so, the decision maker can postpone making a decision on your claim (or revision or supersession request) until the test case is decided.[28] This prevents you appealing until a decision is made in the test case.

If the decision on your claim (or request for a revision or supersession) is postponed, once a decision has been made in the test case, the decision maker makes the decision in your case.[29]

If you would be entitled to benefit even if the test case were decided against you, the decision maker can make a decision.[30] This is done on the assumption that the test case has been decided in the way that is most unfavourable to you. However, this does mean that you are at least paid something while you wait for the result of the test case. Then, if the decision in the test case is in your favour, the decision maker revises her/his decision.

If you already have a decision in your favour, the decision maker can suspend payment of your benefit (see p295).

If you have already appealed to the First-tier Tribunal, see p289.

---

3. **Delays when challenging a decision**

If you have challenged a decision on your entitlement to a benefit or tax credit, there can be a delay while the:

- decision maker considers whether or not to revise (or review) the decision (see p289);
- decision maker prepares the appeal to send to the First-tier Tribunal (see p289);
- appeal is with the First-tier Tribunal waiting for a hearing date (see p289).

Note: for benefits other than housing benefit (HB), if you want to appeal to the First-tier Tribunal, in most cases you can only do so if you have first applied for a revision (or, for tax credits, a review) of the decision. The DWP and HM Revenue and Customs (HMRC) call this 'mandatory reconsideration'. You do not need to request a revision (or review) before you appeal if you were not sent a written notice of the decision that included a statement that you were required to do this. This means that, although most decisions require you to request a revision (or review) before appealing, there are some (ie, HB decisions and those for which the correct notice was not sent) that do not.

For further information on challenging decisions, see CPAG's *Welfare Benefits and Tax Credits Handbook*.

Delay in carrying out a revision

There is no express time limit in the legislation for how long it should take the decision maker to carry out a revision (or, for tax credits, a review). However, revision requests should be dealt with within a reasonable time and tax credit reviews should be carried out as soon as is 'reasonably practicable'.[31] See p277 for the factors that are relevant when determining what is reasonable. You should ensure that you highlight any specific circumstances of your case that mean it is urgent for you and therefore not appropriate for your request to be dealt with in the order in which it was received.

If a delay in conducting a revision or review continues, the options for resolving it are the same as those for resolving a delay in determining a claim and include:

- making a complaint in writing (see p281 for benefits administered by the DWP or HMRC and p286 for HB);
- escalating a complaint to the relevant Ombudsman (see p283 for benefits administered by the DWP or HMRC and p287 for HB);
- obtaining legal advice about sending a 'letter before action' for judicial review (see p284).

Note: the decision maker can postpone making a decision on your revision request if there is a 'test case' pending (see p288).

Delay while an appeal is prepared

The rules on the time in which the decision maker must send her/his appeal response to the Tribunal, and the possible solutions to delays depend on whether or not you were required to request a revision (or for tax credits, a review) before appealing.

If your appeal concerns your rights under European Union (EU) law (eg, your right to reside under EU law or the effect of the EU co-ordination rules), see also p296 for a possible argument that some payments should be paid to you while you wait for your appeal to be heard.

Delay preparing your appeal following a mandatory reconsideration

Once you have sent your appeal to HM Courts and Tribunals Service (HMCTS) you may experience a delay in its being progressed. You should first establish what stage the appeal is at. Contact HMCTS and check whether:

- your appeal has been received. You may wish to obtain proof of receipt – eg, by sending the appeal by a type of postal service that requires a signature or using the Royal Mail tracking service. Once it has been received by the Tribunal, it is responsible for ensuring that the case is dealt with 'fairly and justly', which includes 'avoiding delay so far as compatible with proper consideration of the issues';[32]
- your appeal has been sent onto the DWP or HMRC and, if so, on what date;
- the DWP/HMRC has responded (see below). A copy of this response should be sent to you and/or your representative;
- you have been sent an enquiry form or, if you have returned this, whether it has been received.

From 1 October 2014, the decision maker must send her/his response to the appeal to the First-tier Tribunal within 28 days of having received it. Before this date, decision makers were required to do so 'as soon as reasonably practicable'.[33] If the DWP/HMRC has not sent its response within 28 days, you can apply to the Tribunal to make a direction giving the DWP/HMRC a further short period in which to do so, after which time the appeal is listed and the DWP/HMRC is barred from taking further part in proceedings.[34]

If your situation is particularly urgent, you can ask the Tribunal to shorten the 28-day time limit.[35]

If the DWP/HMRC applies for a direction to extend the 28-day time limit, you should be notified of this in writing and you can then apply for a direction setting this direction aside.[36]

If you apply for a direction, you should clearly explain the consequences for you of a continuing delay and explain why it would be fair and just to determine the case more quickly than would otherwise happen.

If you request that your appeal be dealt with quickly in this way, you must also be as flexible as possible in terms of preparing your case quickly and making yourself, and any representative, available for hearings at short notice. If the Tribunal refuses to expedite your appeal, and it is arguable that this means your case is not being dealt with fairly and justly, you should get advice on whether there are grounds for judicial review (see p284).

If your appeal is delayed because of a pending 'test case', see p292.

Delay preparing your appeal without a mandatory reconsideration

The information in this section applies if your appeal is about an HB decision or a decision that did not correctly notify you that you were required to request a revision before appealing. For more information on when this applies, see CPAG's *Welfare Benefits and Tax Credits Handbook*. In these cases you send your appeal to the decision maker in the local authority, DWP or HMRC. If there is a delay in your appeal being processed, first establish what stage the appeal is at. Contact the relevant benefit authority and check whether:

- your appeal has been received; *and*
- the decision maker has written her/his response and sent it to HMCTS. A copy should also be sent to you and/or your representative.

If your appeal has been received but has not been sent to HMCTS, you should request that this is done. You can complain about the delay using the complaints procedure (see p281 for the DWP and HMRC and p286 for local authorities).

If there are special reasons why your appeal should be dealt with urgently or there has already been significant delay, you can write to the First-tier Tribunal asking it to direct the decision maker to produce the response and/or list the appeal for a hearing.[37] You should set out the history of the appeal, what you have done to try to get the matter resolved and the effect of the delay on you and your family as clearly as possible when you write to the Tribunal. You should also include all documents that you have about the decision. Bear in mind that the Tribunal expects normal procedures to be followed in the vast majority of cases but, if circumstances require, it can admit appeals directly.

Asking the First-tier Tribunal to deal with your case urgently

If you write to the First-tier Tribunal, there is a risk of a misunderstanding. The Clerk to the Tribunal (an administrative officer who processes appeals) may be confused to receive documents concerning an appeal about which the decision maker has not told the Tribunal. In order to minimise the chances of confusion, you should do the following.

1. Clearly head your letter 'Application for a Direction under Rule 6 of the Tribunal Procedure Rules' and mark it 'urgent'.

2. Explain right at the start of the letter that the papers have not been sent by the decision maker and you would like the case to be referred to a Tribunal judge to give a direction to resolve this problem.

3. Refer to the relevant caselaw.[38]

4. Clearly explain the consequences for you of a continuing delay and explain why it would be fair and just to determine the case more quickly than would otherwise happen.

5. Follow up your letter or fax with a phone call to the Tribunal to establish that it has been received and passed to a judge.

See CPAG's website for a sample letter, which you may want to adapt.[39]

If you request that your appeal be dealt with quickly in this way, you must then be as flexible as possible in terms of preparing your case quickly and making yourself, and any representative, available for hearings at short notice.

If a Tribunal judge refuses to direct the decision maker to submit her/his response to the Tribunal and to expedite the appeal, you should consider whether there are grounds for judicial review against this refusal. Depending on the particular facts, it may be arguable that a failure to give such directions has resulted in procedural impropriety because the Tribunal has failed to deal with your case fairly and justly as required.[40] You should obtain legal advice before doing this (there is a risk of costs in applying for judicial review) and you should act promptly. As with delays in processing benefit claims, a 'letter before action' for judicial review in such circumstances can often lead to the issue being resolved (in this case, the requested direction being given). In England and Wales, judicial review proceedings against action (or inaction) of the First-tier Tribunal must be started in the Upper Tribunal.[41] In Scotland, you must begin judicial review proceedings against action (or inaction) of the First-tier Tribunal by applying to the Court of Session. If certain conditions are satisfied, your case can then be transferred to the Upper Tribunal.[42]

Appeal delayed because of a pending test case

If you have appealed to the First-tier or Upper Tribunal and there is a 'test case' pending against a decision of the Upper Tribunal or a court that deals with issues raised in your case, the decision maker can serve a notice requiring the Tribunal in your appeal:[43]

- not to make a decision and to refer your case back to her/him; *or*
- to deal with your appeal by either:
  - postponing making a decision (also referred to as 'staying' your appeal) until the test case is decided; *or*
  - deciding your appeal as if the test case had been decided in the way most unfavourable to you, but only if this is in your interests. If this happens and the test case is eventually decided in your favour, the decision maker must make a new decision superseding the decision of the First-tier Tribunal or Upper Tribunal in the light of the decision in the test case.

If the decision on your appeal has been postponed, once a decision has been made in the test case, the decision is made on your appeal.

4. **Delays getting paid**

Once you have a positive decision stating that you are entitled to benefit, there may be delays in the DWP, HM Revenue and Customs (HMRC) or local authority implementing the decision and making any payments due.

It is important to check first that there is a decision in place awarding you a specified amount of benefit (see p293). If there is, unless payments can be suspended (see below), payment should be made to you as soon as reasonably practicable.[44]

If benefit is not paid promptly, you have a right to start action in the county court (England and Wales) or sheriff court (Scotland) for payment of the money owed.[45]

The decision awarding you benefit

In most cases, it is clear if there has been a decision awarding you a specified amount of benefit. However, in some cases, you may get a decision which does not award benefit but only decides one or more conditions of entitlement. For example, if you appeal to the First-tier Tribunal against the DWP's decision that it cannot pay you income support (IS) because you do not have a right to reside, the Tribunal can allow your appeal if it decides that the DWP was wrong because you do have a right to reside. However, the Tribunal's decision is not a decision awarding you benefit because it only relates to one condition of entitlement and does not decide whether you meet all the other conditions of entitlement for IS. The question of your entitlement to IS is then passed back to the DWP decision maker.

If your appeal about one condition of your entitlement is allowed and there is then a delay in a decision being made to award you benefit:

- check whether the decision maker has received notification of the Tribunal's decision;
- if the decision maker has received notification, establish what is the cause of the delay. A long time may have elapsed since your initial claim was made, and so to ensure that you have met the other conditions of entitlement since your date of claim, the decision maker may write asking you to confirm this, often by completing a claim or review form. Any further delays can be reduced if you provide the information or complete and return any forms as soon as you can;
- if you are advised that the decision maker has all the information s/he requires, but there is still a delay in deciding your claim, your options are the same as for someone who experiences a delay in getting a decision on an initial claim (see p276). You should include in any correspondence the fact that you have already had a significant wait while your appeal was determined.

Note: you only have the right to sue for benefit awarded but not paid once there is a decision actually awarding you a specified amount of benefit.

Suspension of benefit

In certain circumstances, a decision maker can suspend payment of part or all of your benefit or tax credits. In this case, you have no right to the payment (and so cannot take court action as described above). See CPAG's *Welfare Benefits and Tax*

Credits Handbook for all the circumstances in which benefit can be suspended. **Note:** the tax credit regulations use the term 'postponement' rather than 'suspension' of payment, but as HMRC uses the term 'suspension', this is used for both benefits and tax credits in this section.

There are two situations when payment of benefit or tax credits can be suspended that are most relevant to the way the immigration, residence, presence and European Union co-ordination rules operate. These are:

- because the decision maker wants more information to decide whether you continue to be entitled to benefit (see below); *and*
- while an appeal against a positive decision is pending (see p295).

Has your benefit been suspended?

1. The decision maker may be willing to continue to pay your benefit, or at least some of it, if you can show that you will experience hardship otherwise. Guidance to decision makers is clear that, in almost all decisions to suspend benefit, consideration must be given to whether hardship would result and whether this would make the suspension unacceptable. In addition, the decision to suspend your benefit can be reconsidered if the decision maker receives additional information.[46]

2. If you receive a letter telling you that your benefit has been suspended, write explaining how the suspension affects you and ask for the suspension decision to be reconsidered. In addition to hardship, there may be other arguments why your benefit should not be suspended, based on the information below.

3. You cannot appeal to the First-tier Tribunal against the decision to suspend your benefit. The only way to change the decision is to negotiate to get your benefit reinstated or to challenge the decision in the courts by judicial review (see p284).

The decision maker requires further information

You can be required to supply information or evidence if the decision maker needs this to determine whether your award of benefit should be revised or superseded.[47]

If you do not provide the information and evidence, payment of all or part of your benefit can be suspended if:[48]

- a question has arisen about your entitlement or whether a decision should be revised or superseded;[49]*or*
- you apply for a revision or supersession; *or*
- you do not provide certificates, documents, evidence or other information about the facts of your case as required.

If the decision maker wants you to provide information or evidence, s/he must notify you in writing. Within 14 days (one month for child benefit, guardian's allowance and housing benefit (HB); seven days for contribution-based jobseeker's allowance if you come under the universal credit system) of being sent the request, you must:

- supply the information or evidence.[50] You can be given more time if the decision maker is satisfied that this is necessary; *or*
- satisfy the decision maker that the information does not exist or you cannot obtain it.[51]

If the decision maker has not already done so, your benefit can be suspended if you do not provide the information or evidence within the relevant time limit.[52] Similarly, your tax credits can be suspended if you do not provide information or evidence by the date requested.[53]

The complexity of the immigration, residence, presence and European Union (EU) co-ordination rules, together with the additional information and evidence requirements these rules generate, means that if you are subject to these rules the likelihood of your benefit being suspended on the above grounds are increased. For information on some of the practical issues involved in satisfying the information and evidence requirements, see Chapter 20.

If an appeal is pending

Your benefit or tax credit can be suspended if the DWP, HMRC or local authority is appealing (or considering an appeal) against:[54]

- a decision of the First-tier Tribunal, Upper Tribunal or court to award you benefit (or to reinstate benefit); *or*
- a decision of the Upper Tribunal or court about someone else's appeal if the issue could affect your claim. For HB only, the other case must also be about a HB issue.

If the DWP, HMRC or local authority intends to request the statement of reasons for the First-tier Tribunal's decision, apply for leave to appeal or to appeal, (whichever is the first that is yet to be done), it must give you written notice. It must do this as soon as is 'reasonably practicable'.[55]

The decision maker must then take that action within the usual time limits for doing so (generally within one month in each case). If s/he does not, the suspended benefit must be paid to you.[56]

The suspended benefit must also be paid to you if the decision maker withdraws an application for leave to appeal, withdraws the appeal or is refused leave to appeal and it is not possible for her/him to renew the application.

The decision maker still has discretion not to suspend if s/he considers it would result in hardship and s/he should keep her/his decision under review so that the suspension can be lifted if your circumstances, including level of hardship experienced, changes.[57] You should therefore write to the relevant benefit authority if the suspension will cause, or is causing, you hardship.

Suspension on this ground is particularly common following appeals to the First-tier Tribunal concerning the right to reside requirement being allowed. This is due to decision makers seeking to appeal to the Upper Tribunal against the decision of the First-tier Tribunal and the large number of ongoing cases about right to reside that are in the higher courts.

If your appeal concerns your rights under EU law (eg, your right to reside under EU law or the effect of the EU co-ordination rules), see below.

If your appeal concerns European law

If the issue in your appeal concerns EU law, you may be able to argue that your benefit or tax credit should not be suspended, or that you should receive some form of interim payment. It has been established in European caselaw that national governments cannot automatically refuse requests for interim relief to individuals seeking to exercise their rights under European law. Effective judicial protection requires a national court to be able to grant interim relief necessary to ensure EU rights are respected.[58]

This argument could be used, for example, if the issue in your appeal is whether you have a right to reside in EU law (see Chapter 12) or whether you are entitled to benefit because of the EU co-ordination rules (see Chapter 16).

It may be possible to make these arguments:

- if you are waiting for your appeal to be heard by the First-tier Tribunal. You may be able to argue that you should be paid a short-term advance or that you should receive some form of interim payment while waiting for your appeal. You must request a payment outside the benefit rules from the benefit authority because its decision is that you are not entitled under these rules; *or*

- if you have won your First-tier Tribunal appeal and the decision maker suspends payment of your benefit or tax credit because s/he has appealed, or intends to appeal, to the Upper Tribunal. You may be able to argue that your benefit should not be suspended, or that you should receive some form of interim payment pending the further appeal.

Note: benefit authorities can lift the suspension on grounds of hardship.

Notes

2. Waiting for a decision on a claim

1 **WTC/CTC** s3 TCA 2002
   Other benefits s8(1)(a) SSA 1998
2 *Home Secretary v R (S)* [2007] EWCA Civ 546, para 51
3 *R v Secretary of State for Social Services and Chief Adjudication Officer ex parte Child Poverty Action Group* [1990] 2 QB 540
4 Reg 3(5)(b) SS&CS(DA) Regs
5 Reg 3(7) SS&CS(DA) Regs
6 Reg 5 SS(PAB) Regs
7 Reg 4(2) SS(PAB) Regs
8 Reg 3 SS(PAB) Regs
9 Reg 7 SS(PAB) Regs
10 Reg 6 SS(PAB) Regs
11 Reg 8 SS(PAB) Regs
12 Sch 2 para 20A SS&CS(DA) Regs
13 Guidance on short-term benefit advances available on CPAG's website at www.cpag.org.uk/stba/keyfacts, para 9
14 Guidance on short-term benefit advances available on CPAG's website at www.cpag.org.uk/stba/keyfacts, para 31
15 Guidance on short-term benefit advances available on CPAG's website at www.cpag.org.uk/stba/keyfacts, paras 5 and 7
16 Reg 22 CB&GA(Admin) Regs
17 Regs 22(3), 41 and 42 CB&GA(Admin) Regs
18 Reg 22(2) CB&GA(Admin) Regs
19 www.gov.uk/government/organisations/department-for-work-pensions/about/complaints-procedure
20 www.hmrc.gov.uk
21 For further details, see CPAG's *Tax Credits and Complaints Factsheet* at www.cpag.org.uk/content/tax-credits-and-complaints
22 s5(1)(a) Parliamentary Commissioner Act 1967
23 www.justice.gov.uk/civil/procrules_fin/contents/protocols/prot_jrv.htm
24 Reg 89 HB Regs; reg 70 HB(SPC) Regs
25 Reg 93(1) HB Regs; reg 74(1) HB(SPC) Regs

26 Reg 93(2) and (3) HB Regs ; reg 74(2) and (3) HB(SPC) Regs
27 *R v Haringey London Borough Council ex parte Azad Ayub* [1992] 25 HLR 566 (QBD)
28 **HB** Sch 7 para 16 CSPSSA 2000
   Other benefits s25 SSA 1998
29 **HB** Sch 7 para 18(2) CSPSSA 2000
   Other benefits s27(2) SSA 1998
30 **HB** Sch 7 para 16(3) and (4) CSPSSA 2000; reg 15 HB&CTB(DA) Regs
   CB/GA s25(3) and (4) SSA 1998; reg 22 CB&GA(DA) Regs
   UC/PIP/JSA&ESA under UC s25(3) and (4) SSA 1998; reg 53 UC,PIP,JSA&ESA(DA) Regs
   Other benefits s25(3) and (4) SSA 1998; reg 21 SS&CS(DA) Regs

3. Delays when challenging a decision

31 s21A(2) TCA 2002
32 r2(2)(e) TP(FT) Rules
33 r24(1)(c) TP(FT) Rules, as amended from 1 October 2014
34 rr2, 5, 6 and 8 TP(FT) Rules
35 rr5(3)(a) and 6 TP(FT) Rules
36 r6(5) TP(FT) Rules
37 R(H) 1/07; *FH v Manchester City Council (HB)* [2010] UKUT 43 (AAC)
38 R(H) 1/07; *FH v Manchester City Council (HB)* [2010] UKUT 43 (AAC)
39 www.cpag.org.uk/sites/default/files/CPAG-How-to-expedite-social-security-appeal-Aug-13.pdf
40 r2(3)(a) TP(FT) Rules
41 ss15-21 TCEA 2007 and the Direction of the Lord Chief Justice on classes of cases specified under s18(6) TCEA
42 ss20 and 21 TCEA 2007; Act of Sederunt (Transfer of Judicial Review Applications from the Court of Session) 2008, No.357; *Currie, Petitioner* [2009] CSOH 145, [2010] AACR 8; R(IB) 3/09
43 **HB** Sch 7 para 17 CSPSSA 2000
   Other benefits s26 SSA 1998

4. Delays getting paid

44 **HB** Reg 91 HB Regs; reg 72 HB(SPC) Regs
WTC/CTC Regs 8 and 9 TC(PC) Regs
Other benefits Reg 20 SS(C&P Regs

45 *Murdoch v DWP* [2010] EWHC 1988 (QB), paras 75-79; and for HB see *Jones v Waveney DC* [1999] 33 HLR 3

46 DWP, *Suspension and Termination Guide*, paras 1350, 2050-52 and 2301-02 www.gov.uk/government/uploads/ system/uploads/attachment_data/file/ 254309/STG.pdf

47 **HB** Reg 86(1) HB Regs; reg 67(1) HB(SPC) Regs
CB/GA Reg 23 CB&GA(Admin) Regs
UC/PIP/JSA&ESA under UC Reg 38(2) UC,PIP,JSA&ESA(C&P) Regs
Other benefits Reg 32(1) SS(C&P) Regs

48 **HB** Reg 13 HB&CTB(DA) Regs
CB/GA Reg 19 CB&GA(DA) Regs
UC/PIP/JSA&ESA under UC Reg 45(6) UC,PIP,JSA&ESA(DA) Regs
Other benefits Reg 17(2) SS&CS(DA) Regs

49 **HB** Reg 11(2)(a)(i) HB&CTB(DA) Regs
CB/GA Reg 18(2)(a) CB&GA(DA) Regs
UC/PIP/JSA&ESA under UC Reg 44(2)(a)(i) UC,PIP,JSA&ESA(DA) Regs
Other benefits Reg 16(3)(a) SS&CS(DA) Regs

50 **HB** Reg 13(4)(a) HB&CTB(DA) Regs
CB/GA Reg 19(2) CB&GA(DA) Regs
UC/PIP/JSA&ESA under UC Reg 45(4)(a) UC,PIP,JSA&ESA(DA) Regs
Other benefits Reg 17(4)(a) SS&CS(DA) Regs

51 **HB** Reg 13(4)(b) HB&CTB(DA) Regs
CB/GA Reg 19(2)(b) CB&GA(DA) Regs
UC/PIP/JSA&ESA under UC Reg 45(4)(b) UC,PIP,JSA&ESA(DA) Regs
Other benefits Reg 17(4)(b) SS&CS(DA) Regs

52 **HB** Reg 13(4) HB&CTB(DA) Regs
CB/GA Reg 19(5) CB&GA(DA) Regs
UC/PIP/JSA&ESA under UC Reg 45(6) UC,PIP,JSA&ESA(DA) Regs
Other benefits Reg 17(5) SS&CS(DA) Regs

53 Reg 11 TC(PC) Regs

54 **HB** Sch 7 para 13(2) CSPSSA 2000; reg 11(2)(b) HB&CTB(DA) Regs
CB/GA Reg 18(3) CB&GA(DA) Regs
WTC/CTC Reg 11 TC(PC) Regs
Other benefits s21(2)(c) and (d) SSA 1998; reg 16(3)(b) SS&CS(DA) Regs; reg 44(2)(b) and (c) UC,PIP,JSA&ESA(DA) Regs

55 **HB** Reg 11(3) HB&CTB(DA) Regs
CB/GA Reg 18(4) and (5) CB&GA(DA) Regs
Other benefits Reg 16(4) SS&CS(DA) Regs; reg 44(5) UC,PIP,JSA&ESA(DA) Regs

56 **HB** Reg 12(1)(b) HB&CTB(DA) Regs
CB/GA Reg 21 CB&GA(DA) Regs
Other benefits Reg 20(2) and (3) SS&CS(DA) Regs; reg 46(b) and (c) UC,PIP,JSA&ESA(DA) Regs

57 DWP, *Suspension and Termination Guide*, paras 2050-52 and 2354

58 *The Queen v Secretary of State for Transport ex parte Factortame and Ors*, C-213/89 [1990] ECR I-02433, para 23; *Unibet (London) Ltd and Unibet (International) Ltd v Justitiekanslern*, C-432/05 [2007] ECR I-02271, especially para 77; see also *obiter* (not binding) comments in *R (Sanneh) v SSWP and HMRC* [2013] EWHC 793 (Admin), paras 104-14

Chapter 19

National insurance numbers

This chapter covers:
1. The national insurance number requirement (below)
2. Obtaining a national insurance number (p301)
3. Common problems (p304)

This chapter covers the rules on the national insurance number requirement for benefits and tax credits and the issues that arise in satisfying this, particularly if you or a member of your family is not British.

1. The national insurance number requirement

In general, in order to be entitled to any social security benefit or tax credit, or, in England and Wales, council tax reduction (see p397), you must satisfy the national insurance (NI) number requirement.[1] This means that you and any partner included in your claim must:

- provide an NI number, together with evidence to show that it is the one allocated to you; *or*
- provide evidence or information to enable your NI number to be traced; *or*
- make an application for an NI number, accompanied with sufficient information and evidence for one to be allocated. There is no requirement for an NI number to have been allocated to you.

Certain groups of people are exempt from the requirement (see p300).

Note: the NI number is only one requirement that must be satisfied as part of making a valid claim. For general information on the main requirements, see p308. For detailed information on the requirements for each benefit and tax credit, see CPAG's *Welfare Benefits and Tax Credits Handbook*.

When the requirement applies

The NI requirement applies when you make a claim for benefit. It also applies when someone who will be included in an existing award of benefit joins your family – eg, if your partner joins you from abroad.[2]

The requirement applies to you, and also to your partner if you are claiming means-tested benefits or tax credits as a couple.[3]

This is the case, even if, for income support (IS), income-based jobseeker's allowance (JSA), or income-related employment and support allowance (ESA), you are not going to receive any extra benefit for her/him because s/he is a 'person subject to immigration control' for benefit purposes.[4]

The situation is different for pension credit (PC) because if your partner is defined as a 'person subject to immigration control', s/he is treated as not part of your household.

The situation is also different for universal credit (UC), because if your partner is defined as a 'person subject to immigration control', you are required to claim UC as a single person (although your partner's income and capital still affect your claim).

For more information about your entitlement if your partner is defined as a 'person subject to immigration control', see p71 for means-tested benefits and p73 for tax credits.

See below for when your partner does not have to satisfy the NI number requirement.

Who is exempt

You do not need to satisfy the NI number requirement:
- if you are under 16 and you are claiming disability living allowance;[5]
- for statutory maternity pay, statutory paternity pay, statutory adoption pay, statutory sick pay or a social fund payment;[6]
- for housing benefit (HB) if you live in a hostel;[7]
- for tax credits if you have a 'reasonable excuse' for failing to satisfy the requirement (see p301).[8]

If a child or qualifying young person is included in your award of IS or income-based JSA, or in your claim for HB or UC, s/he does not need to satisfy the NI number requirement.[9]

If you are the benefit claimant, your partner does not have to satisfy the NI number requirement if:[10]
- s/he is a 'person subject to immigration control' because s/he requires leave to enter or remain in the UK, but does not have it (see p56); *and*
- s/he has not previously been given an NI number; *and*
- you are claiming IS, income-based JSA, income-related ESA or PC and your partner is not entitled to that benefit her/himself, or you are claiming HB and your partner fails the 'habitual residence test' (see p98). However, in practice it is difficult to see who could satisfy the first bullet point and not satisfy this.

You are still asked for information about an NI number application for your partner, even though s/he is exempt. An NI number will be refused, but this does not prevent you from being entitled to benefits or tax credits or council tax reduction.

Note: this exemption does not apply to UC. This is because if your partner is defined as a 'person subject to immigration control' because s/he requires leave, you are required to claim UC as a single person and your partner is not required to have an NI number.

Tax credits

The NI number requirement for tax credits is as described above, including the exemption for partners who require leave but do not have it. However, the requirement does not apply if the Tax Credit Office is satisfied that you (and/or your partner if it is a joint claim) have a 'reasonable excuse' for not complying with the requirement.[11] A 'reasonable excuse' could include if you are unable to prove your identity because the Home Office has all your documents and you can show this – eg, with a letter from your solicitor.

If the decision maker decides that you have not made a valid claim because you have not satisfied the NI number requirement and you believe you had a reasonable excuse for not doing so, you can appeal against that decision.[12] In most cases, you must request a review first.

2. **Obtaining a national insurance number**

The DWP allocates all national insurance (NI) numbers.

NI numbers are allocated automatically to children shortly before their 16th birthday, but only if child benefit is being claimed for them. If child benefit was being claimed for you when you were that age, you should have an NI number. If you are under 20, you were in the UK when you turned 16 and you did not receive an NI number, you can phone the National Insurance Registrations Helpline (tel: 0300 200 3502).

If you have been allocated an NI number but do not know what it is, or if you want written confirmation of your NI number, you should complete Form CA5403 (available online) and send it to HM Revenue and Customs (HMRC). If you attend your Jobcentre Plus office with evidence of your identity, a member of staff may be able to tell you what your NI number is.

Applying for a national insurance number

If you have not been allocated an NI number, you can apply for one by contacting your local Jobcentre Plus office.

There are a number of reasons why you may need an NI number, including for employment purposes or to claim benefits or tax credits.[13]

You do not need to claim benefits in order to get an NI number, but if you want to claim a benefit or tax credit you do not need to obtain an NI number before you make your benefit or tax credit claim.

If you claim a benefit, or you apply for a supersession of an award of benefit (eg, to include your partner), when you (or s/he) do not have an NI number, the DWP, HMRC or local authority should complete Form DCI1 and send it to the NI number centre.[14] This counts as your having made an application for an NI number. It is advisable to state clearly on the form or letter that you wish to apply for an NI number, if you (or a family member for whom you are claiming benefit) do not have an NI number and you make a claim for benefit or notify the benefit authorities that your family member has joined you.

When the NI number centre receives Form DCI1, it carries out a number of checks to ensure that you do not already have an NI number. It should then contact you to arrange an interview at your local DWP office. This is generally referred to as an 'evidence of identity interview'.

You should be told what documents to take to this interview. It is important to take as many as possible that establish your identity. The DWP has produced detailed guidance on documents for staff who allocate NI numbers. In addition to general information, the guidance covers typical documents and procedure to be followed for particular groups, such as Croatian nationals (see p118) and people with leave under the 'destitute domestic violence concession' (see p34). The guidance notes, as a general point, that some documents are regarded as more secure than others. It refers to these as 'primary' evidence of identity documents and lists them as:[15]

- current passport;
- current travel document issued by any national government, including the UK;
- current identity card issued by a European Economic Area (EEA) member state or Gibraltar;
- registration certificate for an EEA national;
- certificate of registration or naturalisation as a British citizen;
- biometric residence permit;
- residence card.

If you have any of these documents, you should take them to your interview. If you do not, take any documents you do have that could help prove your identity. These could include:[16]

- an expired passport, travel document or EEA identity card;
- standard acknowledgement letter issued by the Home Office;
- application registration card issued by the Home Office to an asylum seeker;
- full driving licence;
- local authority rent book or card;
- tenancy agreement;

- council tax documents;
- life assurance/insurance policies;
- mortgage repayment documents;
- recent fuel or telephone bills in your name;
- original marriage certificate;
- original birth or adoption certificate;
- divorce or annulment papers;
- wage slip from a recent employer;
- trade union membership card;
- travel pass with photograph affixed;
- vehicle registration or insurance documents;
- work permit.

These are only some of the documents that you can use to prove your identity. If you have other documents that are not in the above list, these may also help. Photocopies of documents can be relied on to establish your identity, but you should take the originals if you have them. If not, you should explain why you do not have the original documents. For example, if some of your documents are with the Home Office, explain this and, if possible, provide proof in the form of a solicitor's letter or some other evidence. The DWP should not ask you to provide documents which you obviously do not possess.

Note: the guidance on documents lists examples of people who may not be able to provide any documentary evidence of their identity, such as people who are homeless or fleeing domestic violence, and it confirms that identity may still be verified even if you cannot provide any 'primary' identification documents. It states that in these circumstances a holistic approach should be taken and a decision made on the information provided.[17]

At the interview, you are asked to complete Form CA5400. The DWP may also ask you to complete a form allowing it to contact third parties to establish your identity.

The guidance lists some reasons why an NI number might be refused – eg, if:[18]
- you provided identity documents that are considered not genuine;
- you have been unable to prove your identity;
- you have failed to provide sufficient information;
- you failed to attend an evidence of identity interview; *or*
- you failed to respond to correspondence.

If your application for an NI number is refused, the reason should be recorded and notified to you.

You cannot appeal directly against a decision not to allocate you an NI number.[19] However, you can appeal against any decision refusing benefit because the NI number requirement is not met (see p305).

3. **Common problems**

Migrants often have problems with the national insurance (NI) number requirement (because, unlike most British citizens, they are not issued with an NI number when they turn 16). The three most common problems are:

- being told you cannot apply for benefit unless you have an NI number (see below);
- delays in benefit because of the NI number requirement (see below);
- being refused benefit on the grounds that the NI number requirement is not met (see p305).

Making a claim

If you (or your partner if s/he is included in your claim) do not have an NI number, you may be told by Jobcentre Plus, HM Revenue and Customs or the local authority that you cannot claim a benefit or tax credit. Similarly, you may find it impossible to claim online if you cannot provide an NI number.

You do not need an NI number in order to claim a benefit or tax credit, and you should not be prevented from claiming in this situation. As noted on p299, you can satisfy the NI number requirement by applying for an NI number and accompanying your application with sufficient information and evidence for the number to be allocated. Your claim for benefit should be treated as the first stage in your application for an NI number (see p301).

Have you been told you cannot apply for benefit because you do not have a national insurance number?

If you have lost entitlement because you were prevented from making a claim for benefit in this situation, there may be grounds to get a new claim backdated. If the rules for the benefit or tax credit you are claiming do not allow backdating at all or for the full period, or if the arrears do not cover the full amount lost, consider requesting compensation.

Delays

Payment of benefit can often be delayed because you (or your partner) need to apply for an NI number.

Has there been a delay?

1. First check whether you or your partner are exempt from the requirement to have an NI number (see p300).

2. If you or your partner have applied for an NI number, but there is a delay in one being allocated, request that your claim be determined, as there is no requirement for a number to be allocated (see p299). It is likely that your claim will have to be processed clerically before the NI number has been allocated, but this should not prevent payment.

3. If it is a new claim for benefit, or you are adding a partner to your claim which will result in your award increasing, you may be able to obtain a short-term advance (see p278) or, if you have made a new claim for housing benefit (HB), payments on account (see p286). If your partner is added to your existing claim and s/he does not have an NI number, your benefit may be suspended (see p293). You may be able to argue that payment should not be suspended if it is clear that the NI number requirement is likely to be met and the only factor is a question of time.

Benefit is refused

You cannot appeal directly against a decision not to allocate you an NI number. However, you can appeal against any decision refusing benefit or tax credit because the NI number requirement is not met. In most cases, except for HB, you must first request a revision or, for tax credits, a review. In the appeal (and revision request) you can argue that the NI number requirement was met.[20]

Usually, if benefit is refused because the benefit authority says the NI number requirement is not met, the issue in dispute is whether your application was accompanied by sufficient information or evidence to enable an NI number to be allocated, even if the benefit authority has not considered this point.[21] Even if you have been refused an NI number, it is possible to argue successfully that you still satisfy the NI number requirement if your application was accompanied by sufficient information or evidence to enable a number to be allocated. However, the law is unclear about whether you can satisfy the NI number requirement if you have not attended an interview,[22] or if you must have attended an interview and completed and signed Form CA5400.[23]

Have you been refused tax credits?

If the decision maker decides you have not made a valid claim for tax credits on the basis that you or your partner have been found not to satisfy the NI number requirement, you can challenge that decision. The Upper Tribunal has held that you have a right of appeal if the basis of your appeal is that your partner is exempt from the NI number requirement because s/he requires leave to enter or remain in the UK but does not have it (see p300).[24] In a subsequent case, the Upper Tribunal went further and held that there is also a right of appeal if you or your partner had a reasonable excuse for not satisfying the NI number requirement (see p301).[25] Remember that, in most cases, you must request a review before you can appeal.

Other remedies

If you are refused an NI number, you can write to your MP and ask her/him to help. Your MP can also complain to the Parliamentary and Health Service Ombudsman on your behalf. See CPAG's *Welfare Benefits and Tax Credits Handbook* for more information.

Problems with NI numbers also raise issues about race discrimination since, in practice, the NI number requirement often prejudices black and minority ethnic communities. You may therefore want to refer to the DWP's equal opportunities policy when you contact it.[26] The Equality Advisory Service may also be able to take up the issue (see Appendix 2).

Notes

1. **The national insurance number requirement**
1 s1(1A) and (1B) SSAA 1992; reg 5(4) TC(CN) Regs
2 *Leicester City Council v OA* [2009] UKUT 74 (AAC), paras 27 and 28
3 s1(1A) SSAA 1992; reg 5(4) TC(CN) Regs
4 *SSWP v Wilson* [2006] EWCA Civ 882, reported as R(H)7/06
5 Reg 1A SS(DLA) Regs
6 s1(4) SSAA 1992 and s122 SSCBA 1992
7 Reg 4(a) HB Regs; reg 4(a) HB(SPC) Regs
8 Reg 5(6) TC(CN) Regs
9 **IS** Reg 2A(a) IS Regs has continued effect in these cases due to the transitional protection in reg 1(3) SS(WTCCTC)(CA) Regs
JSA Reg 2A(a) JSA Regs has continued effect in these cases due to the transitional protection in reg 1(7) SS(WTCCTC)(CA) Regs
HB Reg 4(b) HB Regs; reg 4(b) HB(SPC) Regs
UC Reg 5 UC,PIP,JSA&ESA(C&P) Regs

10 **IS** Reg 2A IS Regs
JSA Reg 2A JSA Regs
ESA Reg 2A ESA Regs
PC Reg 1A SPC Regs
HB Reg 4(c) HB Regs; reg 4(c) HB(SPC) Regs
TC Reg 5(8) TC(CN) Regs
Bereavement benefits and retirement pensions Reg 1A(c) SS(WB&RP) Regs
11 Reg 5(6) TC(CN) Regs
12 *CI v HMRC (TC)* [2014] UKUT 0158 (AAC)

2. **Obtaining a national insurance number**
13 DWP, *Secure National Insurance Number Allocation Process Guidance*, s3 'Interviewing site', para 1
14 DWP, *Secure National Insurance Number Allocation Process Guidance*, s3 'Interviewing site', para 3; CH 4085/ 2007; HB/CTB Circular A13/2010, paras 14 and 15
15 DWP, *Secure National Insurance Number Allocation Process Guidance*, 'Documents to support a NINo application', Appendix 4
16 DWP, *Secure National Insurance Number Allocation Process Guidance*, 'Documents to support a NINo application', para 108

17 DWP, *Secure National Insurance Number Allocation Process Guidance*, 'Documents to support a NINo application', paras 13-16
18 DWP, *Secure National Insurance Number Allocation Process Guidance*, 'NINo centre process', para 198
19 CH/1231/2004

3. Common problems
20 CH/1231/2004; CH/4085/2007; *Leicester City Council v OA* [2009] UKUT 74 (AAC)
21 CH/1231/2004
22 CH/4085/2007, para 30
23 *Leicester City Council v OA* [2009] UKUT 74 (AAC), para 35
24 *ZM and AB v HMRC (TC)* [2013] UKUT 0547 (AAC)
25 *CI v HMRC (TC)* [2014] UKUT 158 (AAC)
26 The DWP's publication *Work and Welfare Strategy Directorate and Fraud, Planning and Presentation Directorate: race equality scheme* may be helpful in raising issues with the DWP.

Chapter 20

· ·

Providing evidence

This chapter covers:
1. General points about evidence (below)
2. Evidence of immigration status (p312)
3. Evidence of residence rights (p315)
4. Types of evidence (p315)

This chapter covers some of the issues that arise when you are required to provide evidence to show that you satisfy the immigration conditions (see Part 3), the residence conditions (see Part 4) or that you are covered by the European Union co-ordination rules (see Chapter 16).

---

1. **General points about evidence**

There are some issues and principles that apply to the evidence you may be asked to provide, or that you should provide, when you make a claim for a benefit or tax, or when you challenge a decision about your entitlement.

Evidence required when you make your claim

When you claim a benefit or tax credit, you must normally:
- satisfy the national insurance (NI) number requirement (see Chapter 19); *and*
- provide proof of your identity, if required (see below); *and*
- ensure your claim is valid (see p309).

To determine your claim, the decision maker needs evidence that you satisfy all the conditions of entitlement and that you are not covered by any of the exceptions that mean you are not entitled. You can be asked for evidence to show that you satisfy all the conditions of entitlement, including the immigration, residence or presence conditions, or that the European Union (EU) co-ordination rules apply to you.

Proving your identity

You may be asked to produce further documents or evidence that prove your identity. If your partner is included in your claim, even if you do not receive an amount for her/him (eg, because s/he is a 'person subject to immigration control' – see p71), you may also be asked to prove her/his identity.

There are various documents that you can provide to the benefit authorities as proof of your identity. You should not be required to supply particular documents that it is unreasonable for you to have or obtain, and you should not be refused a benefit or tax credit simply because you can not provide a particular document. For more information on providing evidence to show your entitlement to a benefit or tax credit, see below.

The DWP has produced guidance for staff who allocate NI numbers on the documents that should be accepted as proof of identity. The guidance notes that some documents are regarded as more secure than others and refers to these as 'primary' evidence of identity documents. For a list of these and other documents that could be used to prove your identity, see p301. It can be helpful to provide details of any other people who can confirm what you have stated – eg, your solicitor or other legal representative or official organisation.

Making a valid claim

To be entitled to a benefit or tax credit, you must make a valid claim. This means you must claim in the correct way and your claim must not be 'defective'. The DWP, HM Revenue and Customs or local authority should inform you if your claim is defective and must then give you the opportunity to correct the defect. If your claim is refused because it is not valid, you have a right to challenge that decision. If your claim is accepted as valid, the decision maker must make a decision on your entitlement.

What counts as a valid claim varies between the individual benefits and tax credits. What you are required to do to make your claim in the correct way is also affected by the method by which you can make your claim – ie, in writing, only on a certain form, online, and/or also by telephone. The rules for each benefit and tax credit are covered in CPAG's *Welfare Benefits and Tax Credits Handbook*.

Evidence that you are entitled

When you claim a benefit or tax credit you must generally show, on the balance of probabilities, that you meet the conditions of entitlement. If you do not meet these under the UK rules, but the EU co-ordination rules (see Chapter 16) enable you to be entitled, you must provide evidence of this.

If you have documentary evidence showing that you meet the entitlement conditions, you should always submit it. However, documentary evidence corroborates and reinforces your own evidence, given in the process of making your claim or subsequently, and your own evidence can be accepted without it being corroborated if you cannot do so. Corroborative evidence is not necessary unless there are reasons to doubt your evidence – eg, if it is self-contradictory or inherently improbable.[1]

If you are asked for a particular document that you do not have, ask why this is needed so that you have the opportunity to provide alternatives. If you cannot provide any documentary proof of a particular fact, explain why not (eg, because all your documents are with the Home Office) and, if possible, provide proof of this – eg, in a letter from your legal representative. If you consider any requests for information are unreasonable, you can complain. Seek advice if you think you have experienced discrimination – eg, from the Equality Advisory Service.[2]

Evidence that you are not excluded

Where there is an exception to entitlement that excludes you from a benefit or a tax credit to which you would otherwise be entitled (eg, because you are not habitually resident or because you are defined as a 'person subject to immigration control'), the burden of proving that this exception applies to you lies with the benefit authorities.[3]

If you have evidence that an exception to entitlement does not apply to you, you should always submit this.

If you do not provide evidence that you are not excluded from entitlement when you make your claim, the decision maker must ask you for the information and evidence required for her/him to make a decision. It is an established principle that the process of benefit adjudication is inquisitorial rather than adversarial, and it is the decision maker (or First-tier Tribunal) who knows what information is required to determine whether you are entitled to benefit or whether you are excluded from entitlement, and who must therefore ask for that information.[4]

If, after all the enquiries have been made, some relevant facts are still unknown, the question of whether an exception applies that excludes you from entitlement should be decided in your favour.[5]

If you cannot provide the evidence required to determine whether or not you are excluded, but that evidence is available to the benefit authorities, see below.

If evidence is not available to you

If your potential exclusion from benefit entitlement depends on evidence that is not available to you, but it is available to the benefit authority, the benefit authority must take the necessary steps to obtain this information. If it fails to do so and consequently it is not known whether or not you are excluded from benefit, the matter must be decided in your favour – ie, that you are not excluded.[6]

This principle is significant for migrants. For example, if the decision maker needs evidence of your immigration status and all your documents are with the Home Office, s/he must use her/his channels of communication with the Home Office and obtain the evidence.

Another area where this principle is of particular significance is if your entitlement depends on someone else's circumstances and the relevant information about these is not available to you, but is available to the benefit authority. For example, the decision maker may need evidence of your right to reside which depends on the current or past economic activity of a family member (see p152), but you cannot contact her/him or s/he will not provide you with the information you need. The family member could be a spouse from whom you have separated due to domestic violence, or a parent from whom you are estranged if you are under 21.

If this applies to you, you should provide the benefit authority with as much information as possible to enable it to trace the evidence that you cannot provide, but which could be available to the decision maker if s/he made enquiries or checked records – ask that s/he do so.

For example, if you need information on your family member's residence rights in order to know whether they give you a right of residence, it is helpful to provide the benefit authority with information on your family member's:

- name;
- date of birth;
- NI number;
- last known address;
- last known place of work;
- details of any benefit claims – eg, which benefit and when claimed.

The benefit authority is then required to take the necessary steps to trace the information, by checking records of any benefit claims or NI contributions. If it fails to do so, you cannot be excluded from benefit on the basis of not having a right to reside, as the burden of proof is on the benefit authority to show that you do not have a right to reside.

Example

Kristina is a 19-year-old Slovakian national who came to the UK last week. She came to the UK because she is due to give birth next week and wanted the support of her father, Pavol, who has been in the UK for two years. However, Pavol disapproves of Kristina's pregnancy and has said he never wants to hear from her again. Kristina is sleeping on a friend's sofa and has claimed income support (IS). If Pavol has 'worker' status, Kristina is entitled to IS as his family member – she has a right to reside as the family member of a worker and is also in a group exempt from the habitual residence test.

Kristina has her own birth certificate which names Pavol as her father and confirms his nationality. However, she cannot get evidence of Pavol's worker status from him as he will not speak to her. Kristina has heard that Pavol was made redundant two months ago and is now claiming jobseeker's allowance (JSA). Therefore, if she can provide sufficient information to the DWP for it to be able to trace Pavol's JSA claim, the DWP will be able to obtain details of his previous work from it and assess whether that work gave him worker status and whether he has retained that status while claiming JSA. The DWP holds this information and therefore must take the necessary steps to enable it to be traced. If it fails to do so, Kristina can argue that she cannot be excluded from IS on the basis of not being habitually resident as this has not been proved by the DWP.

2. Evidence of immigration status

If you are not a European Economic Area (EEA) national and you are claiming any of the benefits or tax credits listed on p63, the decision maker needs evidence of your immigration status to determine whether you are a 'person subject to immigration control' (see p55).

If you are claiming means-tested benefits or tax credits and your partner lives with you and is not an EEA national, the decision maker also needs evidence of her/his immigration status to determine whether s/he is a 'person subject to immigration control'. See p71 for the rules if your partner is a 'person subject to immigration control'.

It is rare that a decision maker needs evidence of your child's immigration status, as this does not affect whether or not you can be paid for her/him. However, if your child is the claimant (eg, for disability living allowance), the decision maker requires evidence of her/his immigration status to determine whether s/he is a 'person subject to immigration control'.

Note: if your partner or child has leave which is subject to the condition that s/he must not have 'recourse to public funds', this condition may be breached if s/he is included in your (or someone else's) claim and this could jeopardise her/his immigration status (see p57).

Further information on checking your immigration status is in Chapter 6. If you are unclear about your immigration status, you should obtain immigration advice (see Appendix 2) before making any claim for benefits or tax credits.

Problems with evidence

Problems can arise if you do not have documentary evidence or if the documents you have are unclear. The general points about evidence outlined above all apply (see p308). You should not be refused benefit because you cannot provide a particular document, and you should ask why a document is being requested so you can provide the evidence through another means. If you cannot provide a document (eg, because it is with the Home Office), it can help if you provide a letter confirming this from your legal representative, who may also be able to confirm your current immigration status and the significance of any applications you have pending.

If evidence of immigration status is not available to you but is available to the decision maker (eg, by her/his emailing the Home Office), s/he must take the necessary steps to obtain this (see p310).

Changes in immigration status

If you have time-limited leave to enter or remain, you can apply to extend your leave or apply for further leave to remain on a different basis. Provided you apply before your existing leave expires, this leave is extended until your application is decided by UK Visas and Immigration.[7] If your original leave was not subject to the condition that you do not have recourse to public funds, you were not a 'person subject to immigration control' and therefore you were entitled to all benefits and tax credits subject to the normal rules of entitlement. When your leave is extended, you must notify the benefit authorities as otherwise they may consider you to be someone whose leave has expired and therefore a 'person subject to immigration control' (see p55) and so no longer entitled to benefit.

The benefit authorities need evidence that you applied to vary your leave before your existing leave ended. If possible, you should submit documents showing when your leave was due to expire (which the benefit authorities may already have on your file), together with confirmation of the date when your application to vary that leave was submitted – eg, a letter from a legal representative who helped you with the application. Although it should not be necessary, in practice it also helps if you submit a covering letter, explaining that your previous leave is extended because your application to vary your leave was submitted before that leave expired, and therefore you continue not to be a 'person subject to immigration control' and so your benefit or tax credit entitlement continues. You should include the relevant legal references in your letter.

Note: if your application to vary your leave is refused and your leave is extended while your appeal against that refusal is pending, you may count as a 'person subject to immigration control' (see p60).

3. Evidence of residence rights

Your residence rights under European Union law can be complex and involve many steps, each requiring certain conditions to be met. It is advisable to set out your residence rights to the decision maker as clearly as possible and, wherever possible, provide evidence of every requirement. If you lack documentary evidence of one requirement, but you have provided evidence of others, it is more likely that the decision maker will accept your uncorroborated evidence on the final requirement (unless it is self-contradictory or inherently improbable – see p309).

Residence documents

The only circumstance in which you need a residence document in order to have a right to reside is if you are an 'extended family member'. In this case, you need a relevant residence document in order to be *treated as* a 'family member' of someone who can confer a right of residence on you (see p154).

For any other right to reside, you do not need a residence document because your right to reside depends on the facts of your situation. Documentation can only confirm a residence right you have and cannot give you a right to reside, even if you previously had a right to reside, but now your circumstances have changed.[8]

However, obtaining a residence document can make it easier for you to demonstrate your residence rights rather than having to provide all your evidence every time. For example, once you have acquired a permanent right of residence, it is easier to provide evidence that you have not lost this right by leaving the UK for more than two years (see p176), than, for instance, to provide weekly payslips spanning a five-year period.

You can be issued with the following residence documents.

- A **registration certificate** if you are a European Economic Area (EEA) national with a right of residence provided under the EEA Regulations.[9]
- A **residence card** if you are a non-EEA national and you have a right to reside as the family member of an EEA 'qualified person' (see p117) or an EEA national with a permanent right of residence.[10]
- A **derivative residence card** if you are an EEA national with a derivative right to reside (see p162).[11]
- A **document certifying permanent right of residence** if you are an EEA national with a permanent right of residence, or a **permanent residence card** if you are a non-EEA national with a permanent right of residence.[12]
- A **residence permit**, issued to EEA nationals and their family members before 30 April 2006. These were valid for a five-year period. From 30 April 2006, these documents should be treated as if they were the equivalent type of document issued after that date – eg, a registration certificate, a residence card or a derivative residence card.[13]
- A **family permit**, issued for entry to the UK if you are a non-EEA family member of an EEA national and do not have any of the other residence documentation.

Forms and further information, including about application fees, are available on the UK Visas and Immigration website.

4. **Types of evidence**

Certain types of evidence are of particular significance for migrants and are discussed below. Depending on your circumstances and the benefit or tax credit being claimed, this evidence may be required by all claimants to satisfy the entitlement conditions or because it affects the amount to which you are entitled. If the evidence is required by all claimants, you should not be required to submit more evidence because you are a migrant than would be required of a British person in the same circumstances.

Evidence of your nationality

The most common acceptable evidence of your nationality is a current passport, a current European Economic Area (EEA) identity card or, if you are a non-EEA national, a current travel document or biometric residence permit. However, if you cannot provide one of these, there are several other documents that the benefit authorities accept. Any of the documents the DWP considers to be 'primary' evidence of identity are acceptable (see p301), but other official documents can also be accepted. As with all evidence requirements, it helps if you can provide more than one form of evidence of your nationality.

Evidence of your relationship to someone

If your rights are based on being someone's family member or primary carer, you must provide evidence of this relationship.

Providing evidence of your relationship to someone else can be relevant if you need to show that you are covered by the European Union (EU) co-ordination rules or that you are in a group of people who can claim a benefit despite being a 'person subject to immigration control'.

It is common for evidence to be required to show that you have a right of residence as a family member of an EEA national or as the primary carer of someone who can confer residence rights on you. You can also be required to show that you are a family member of a worker or a self-employed person to be exempt from the habitual residence test (see p99). If you are a non-EEA national, you can be required to show that you are a family member of an EEA national exercising EU Treaty rights and are therefore not a 'person subject to immigration control' (see p56).

For your residence rights to be accepted, you must show that you are a family member or primary carer and that all the other requirements of that right to reside are satisfied.

For example, if you are asserting that you are a family member of a worker, you must show that:

- the person who is working is an EEA national (see above);
- the work s/he does gives her/him 'worker' status (see p319);

- if s/he has ceased to be a worker, that s/he retains worker status (see p135);
- you come within the definition of being her/his 'family member' (see p152).

If you are asserting that you are the primary carer of a worker's child in education, you must show that:
- the adult who worked is the parent of that child;
- the parent is an EEA national (see p315);
- the work the parent did gave her/him 'worker' status (see p319);
- the child was in the UK while the parent had worker status;
- the child is currently in school;
- you are her/his primary carer (see p166).

Non-European Economic Area nationals

If you are a non-EEA national and are the family member of an EEA national who confers residence rights on you, you are not a 'person subject to immigration control' (see p56).

If you entered the UK as the family member of an EEA national who is in the UK exercising her/his Treaty rights (eg, as a worker), you usually have an entry clearance document that states this. You should provide this to the benefit authorities as it is the most significant documentary evidence required. However, depending on your circumstances, the benefit authorities may also want evidence that your family member is still in the UK exercising her/his Treaty rights.

If you are a non-EEA national and are the primary carer of someone who confers a 'derivative right to reside' on you (see p162), the benefit authorities require evidence of each requirement that needs to be satisfied for you to have a right to reside. In particular, if your derivative right to reside is based on being the primary carer of a British citizen, you must show that s/he would be unable to reside anywhere in the EEA if you were required to leave (see p167).

Evidence of marriage or civil partnership

If you have been given leave to enter or remain on the basis of being a spouse or civil partner of someone, evidence of that leave is generally accepted as sufficient evidence of your relationship for the purposes of proving your entitlement to a benefit or tax credit.

Spouses and civil partners have far greater rights under EU law than partners who are not married or civil partners. Consequently, it can be important to show that someone is your spouse or civil partner – eg, when s/he can confer residence rights on you. If you need to prove that you are someone's spouse or civil partner, you must show that you are still married or in a civil partnership. If you have separated and are no longer living together or in a relationship, you are still her/his spouse or civil partner until you are finally divorced or the civil partnership is finally dissolved.[14]

A marriage or civil partnership certificate is the best evidence. If the certificate is not in English, it can be helpful also to submit an authorised translation. If obtaining a translation will cause any delay, you should ensure that you do not miss any deadlines for submitting evidence. For example, you could take the original document to a local benefit office to take an authorised copy and accompany this with a letter explaining that you are obtaining a translation.

If you do not have a marriage or civil partnership certificate, other evidence which confirms your marriage or civil partnership can be accepted. Official documents that refer to your marriage or civil partnership, as well as official correspondence confirming you live together, can all be evidence to be taken into account.

Evidence of parentage

If you have been given leave to enter or remain on the basis of being a parent or child of someone, evidence of that leave is generally accepted as sufficient evidence of your relationship for the purposes of proving your entitlement to a benefit or tax credit.

If you are showing that you are the parent or child of someone who can confer residence rights on you, it is important to show that you meet all the conditions for being defined as a 'family member'.

To be a 'family member' as a child of someone who can confer residence rights on you, you must show:
- s/he is your parent; *and*
- either you are aged under 21 or you are dependent on her/him.

To be a 'family member' as a parent of someone who can confer residence rights on you, you must show:
- you are her/his parent; *and*
- you are dependent on her/him.

A birth certificate that names you as the parent, or official DNA test results that show you as the parent, should be sufficient evidence. However, if you do not have such a document, other documents can also be accepted. If you do not have anything decisive, submit the evidence you have to back up your own evidence and ask for the decision maker to decide on the balance of probabilities (see p309).

Example
Nadifa is 18 and a Dutch national. Due to her health problems, she wants to claim income-related employment and support allowance and housing benefit (HB). She came to the UK four years ago with her mother, who is also a Dutch national, having acquired Dutch citizenship after fleeing to the Netherlands as a refugee 15 years ago. Nadifa's mother is a self-employed translator and has extensive evidence of this. However, Nadifa does not have any evidence that she is her mother's daughter. Her mother fled to the Netherlands

without any documents. Nadifa therefore submits evidence of her mother's Dutch nationality and self-employment, together with a letter setting out the relevant details of her life history and documents showing that she was given leave to remain in the Netherlands as a dependant on her mother's asylum claim, evidence that she travelled with her mother to the UK four years ago and letters from her GP and dermatologist discussing Nadifa's eczema and the likelihood of its being linked to her mother's eczema.

Note: if you are trying to show that you are someone's father or that someone is your father, until officially declared otherwise, a man is deemed to be a child's father if he was married to the child's mother at the time of the child's birth or his name was registered on the birth certificate.

Evidence of your age

Your age (or someone else's age) can affect whether or not you meet the basic conditions of entitlement to a benefit, and the amount to which you are entitled. Your age (or someone else's age) can also affect your residence rights, whether your immigration status excludes you from benefits and tax credits and/ or whether you are covered by the EU co-ordination rules. In addition, age can affect whether you (or someone else) are defined as a 'family member' or as 'dependent'.

A birth certificate, passport or identity card is usually accepted as proof of your date of birth. Other evidence that can show your date of birth includes school, medical or army records. See also the other evidence that can be accepted as proof of your identity on p301.

You may be able to show your date of birth by referring to the accepted birth dates of other relatives. For example, if you are recorded as the eldest child and your sister has been accepted as born in 1995, you must have been born before then.

If you have no record of your date of birth, it is possible for an age assessment to be carried out. However, there is no accurate scientific test that can establish a person's age and such an assessment can be disputed (see also p350).

A common problem is conflicting evidence. Your date of birth may have been wrongly recorded in your passport when it was issued – eg, because you gave the wrong date or because of an administrative error. The date in the passport may then have been used in many other official documents and it may be difficult to persuade the benefit authorities that all these dates are wrong. You should explain that all these dates come from one document and, if there is other evidence showing that date is not correct, that one document is not conclusive evidence.

While each piece of evidence must be considered, the oldest documents may be more reliable, since they were made nearer to the time of the events to which they refer.

Passports and other immigration documents are commonly recorded as '1 January' when your exact date of birth is unclear. However, if you obtain evidence of your exact date of birth later, this can be accepted.

If there is no documentary evidence, the benefit authorities should accept your own statements, unless they are contradictory or improbable (see p309).

Evidence of work

Evidence of your own or someone else's current or past employment or self-employment can be required in order to prove that you satisfy, or are exempt from, immigration or residence conditions, or that you are covered by the EU co-ordination rules. The exact evidence required depends on what you need to prove, so it is essential that you check the rules for the specific condition you are trying to satisfy or be exempt from.

Examples

Samir is a national of Algeria and is in the UK to study. He has a student visa, which gives him leave to be in the UK for the next two years, subject to the condition that he does not have recourse to public funds. Samir is therefore a 'person subject to immigration control' (see p55). He works 15 hours a week, which is permitted under the conditions of his student visa. Samir wants to claim child benefit and child tax credit (CTC) because his girlfriend's 14-year-old French son has just come to live with him while she goes to Canada for six months. Samir can claim both child benefit and CTC if he can show that he is 'lawfully working', as he will be in a group of people who can claim despite being a 'person subject to immigration control' (see p67 for child benefit and p70 for CTC). Samir needs to provide HM Revenue and Customs (HMRC) with evidence of his employment (eg, a payslip or letter from his employer), together with confirmation that his work is allowed under the conditions of his immigration leave, proof of his Algerian nationality and his student visa.

Dimitra is a Greek national who wants to claim income support (IS) and HB as she is due to have a baby in three weeks. She came to the UK six years ago and got a job after being here a month. She stayed in this job until she was made redundant last month. If Dimitra can show that she had a right to reside as a 'worker' for a continuous period of five years, she will have a permanent right to reside (see p170), which satisfies the right to reside requirement for IS and HB. Dimitra needs to provide evidence confirming that she was in an employment relationship (see p131) doing 'genuine and effective' work (see p132) for a continuous period of five years.

As with all evidence requirements, there is no definitive list of what counts as acceptable. The evidence of work is considered stronger if it has several ways of showing it relates to you – eg, if it shows your full name, your date of birth, your address, and your national insurance (NI) number, rather than just one or two of these.

Evidence of employment includes:
- a contract of employment;
- payslips;
- correspondence from your employer to you – eg, offering you the job or confirming a change in hours;
- a letter from an employer confirming your employment;
- bank statements showing wages being paid in from the employer.

If you are not actually working, you may not have ceased to have a right to reside as a 'worker' (see p134). You need to provide evidence that you are still under a contract of employment, such as a letter from your employer stating this. Alternatively, if you have ceased to be a worker, you may be able to retain your worker status and must provide evidence of the basis of this (see p135) in addition to the evidence of the worker status you had.

Evidence of self-employment includes:
- documents from HMRC confirming your registration as a self-employed person;
- evidence of paying Class 2 NI contributions;
- business accounts;
- samples of marketing;
- documents showing you have purchased the equipment needed to carry out your trade.

If you are seeking to demonstrate that you have a right to reside as a self-employed person, it should be enough to show that you have established yourself in order to undertake activity as a self-employed person (see p143).

If you are not actually working, you may not have ceased to have a right to reside as a self-employed person. You must provide evidence of all the factors that are relevant in your circumstances (see p143).

You may be able to retain your 'self-employed' status (see p144) and need to provide evidence of this in addition to the evidence of your self-employment.

If your right to reside depends on someone else being, or having been, a 'worker' or 'self-employed', but you do not have any documentary evidence of this because you cannot contact the person or s/he will not provide you with the evidence, you may be able to argue that the benefit authorities should obtain this evidence (see p310).

Croatian, A2 and A8 nationals

The additional restrictions (see p118) that currently apply to Croatian nationals and which previously applied to A2 nationals (between 1 January 2007 and 1 January 2014) and to A8 nationals (between 1 May 2004 and 1 May 2011) mean that 'workers' from these states must supply additional evidence. If you need to show that you have (or had) a right to reside as a 'worker', you must show that, at the time of working, you:

- were exempt from restrictions (see p120 for Croatian and A2 nationals and p121 for A8 nationals); *or*
- (for Croatian and A2 nationals) worked in accordance with a valid authorisation document (see p119); *or*
- (for A8 nationals) worked for an 'authorised employer' (see p119). **Note:** a registration certificate that was applied for after the first month of work is not retrospective and so is only evidence that you were working for an authorised employer from the date the certificate was issued.[15]

There are no additional restrictions and therefore no additional evidence requirements if you, or the person whose right to reside you are relying on, was self-employed.

Evidence of jobseeking

To have a right to reside as a jobseeker, you must be able to provide evidence that you are seeking employment and have a 'genuine chance of being engaged'.

These requirements are similar to the requirements to be 'actively seeking' and 'available for' work for the purposes of being entitled to jobseeker's allowance (JSA), or to satisfy the 'work search' and 'work availability' requirements for universal credit. This means that, in most cases, if the decision maker accepts that you have provided evidence to satisfy these benefit requirements, this should also be accepted as satisfying the requirements that enable you to have a right to reside as a jobseeker. For the circumstances when this might not apply, see p124.

Under European law, there is no time limit on how long you can have a right to reside as a jobseeker – it continues for as long as you can provide evidence that you are looking for work and have a genuine chance of being engaged.[16]

However, under the EEA Regulations, in order to continue to have a right to reside as a jobseeker for longer than 182 days, you must provide 'compelling' evidence that you are continuing to seek work and have a genuine chance of being engaged (see p126).

Although you can argue that you continue to have a right to reside under European law, the decision maker is likely to apply the EEA Regulations and refuse you benefit if, after 182 days, your evidence is not considered 'compelling'. You may therefore want to argue that your evidence is 'compelling', but also that, in any case, it does not need to be.

The DWP has produced guidance for JSA decision makers on what counts as 'compelling' evidence of a 'genuine chance of being engaged'. This suggests that you will be accepted as having submitted such evidence if you can show:[17]

- you have a job offer of work that will start within three months and will be 'genuine and effective'; *or*
- your circumstances have changed in a way that improves your prospects of obtaining work – eg, you have recently (the guidance suggests two months) completed vocational training or moved to an area where you are more likely to obtain work.

The guidance gives examples and discusses some other considerations. If this guidance is helpful in arguing that you should be accepted as having provided compelling evidence of having a 'genuine chance of being engaged', you should refer the decision maker to it. However, you should not be refused benefit just because your circumstances are not covered by the guidance. **Note:**

- The guidance is not legally binding. Any examples or time periods during which it is suggested your residence rights as a jobseeker can continue (such as the three- or two-month periods referred to above) are not binding requirements.
- The guidance is written for JSA decision makers and is therefore less relevant if you are claiming another benefit or tax credit, such as child benefit or CTC, on the basis of your right to reside as a jobseeker.
- The term 'compelling' is not defined in the EEA Regulations and so it should have its ordinary, everyday meaning.
- The requirement in the EEA Regulations for your evidence to be 'compelling' after 182 days is not a requirement in European law, and provided you submit evidence that you are continuing to submit evidence and have a genuine chance of being engaged, you continue to have a right to reside as a jobseeker.

Although it is arguable that you should not be required to alter the quality of your evidence after a particular time period, the longer you have been a jobseeker without obtaining work, the more likely it is that the decision maker will try to argue that this shows that you do not, in fact, have a genuine chance of getting work. To avoid this or to challenge a decision that you are not entitled to benefit because you do not have a right of residence as a jobseeker, you need evidence to demonstrate that you have a genuine chance of being engaged, despite the long period of unemployment. This can include evidence of your:

- work history in the UK;
- work history in other countries;
- qualifications;
- voluntary work;
- having recently completed a course on obtaining work as part of the Work Programme;

- having broadened the type of work you are looking for or the hours of work you are able to do;
- having arranged for adequate childcare to enable you to attend interviews and take up employment;
- improved English language skills.

Notes

1. General points about evidence
1 R(SB)33/85, para 14
2 www.equalityadvisoryservice.com
3 R(IS) 6/96, para 15; see also *Kerr v Department for Social Development (Northern Ireland)* [2004] UKHL 23, paras 61-69
4 *R v Medical Appeal Tribunal (North Midland Region) ex parte Hubble* [1958] 2 QB 228; *Kerr v Department for Social Development (Northern Ireland)* [2004] UKHL 23, paras 61-62
5 *Kerr v Department for Social Development (Northern Ireland)* [2004] UKHL 23, paras 61-69
6 *Kerr v Department for Social Development (Northern Ireland)* [2004] UKHL 23, paras 61-69

2. Evidence of immigration status
7 s3C(2)(a) IA 1971

3. Evidence of residence rights
8 *SSWP v Dias*, C-325/09 [2011] ECR I006387; *EM and KN v SSWP* [2009] UKUT 44 (AAC)
9 Reg 16 I(EEA) Regs
10 Reg 17 I(EEA) Regs
11 Reg 18A I(EEA) Regs
12 Reg 18 I(EEA) Regs
13 Reg 31(2) and Sch 4 para 2 I(EEA) Regs

4. Types of evidence
14 *Diatta v Land Berlin*, C-267/83 [1985] ECR 567
15 *SSWP v ZA* [2009] UKUT 294 (AAC); *Szpak v SSWP* [2013] EWCA Civ 46

16 *The Queen v Immigration Appeal Tribunal ex parte Gustaff Desiderius Antonissen*, C-292/89 [1991] ECR I-00745, para 21
17 Memo DMG 15/14, paras 14-15

Part 8

Support for asylum seekers

Chapter 21

Support for asylum seekers

This chapter covers:

1. Introduction

Types of support for asylum seekers

There are three main types of government support for people who have made an application for asylum in the UK:

- **asylum support** (Section 95 support) for the period until a final decision on an asylum application is made;[1]
- **temporary** (often called **emergency**) **support**, available to asylum seekers waiting for an asylum support decision;[2]
- **Section 4 support** (previously known as **hard cases support**), available to failed asylum seekers and other migrants who meet certain criteria.[3]

Note: the phrase 'asylum support' is sometimes used to refer to all three types of support. This can be confusing and, therefore, in this chapter 'asylum support' is used only when referring to support provided until a final decision is made on an asylum application.

Background to the system of support

Before 5 February 1996, asylum seekers without funds received income support, at the urgent cases rate of 90 per cent, and housing benefit. Those without accommodation and in 'priority need' were entitled to local authority housing under the homelessness legislation. In February 1996, the government decided that providing benefits was a factor that attracted asylum seekers to the UK. Access to state benefits was removed from many asylum seekers, who therefore sought the safety-net provisions from local authorities, relying in particular on s21 of the National Assistance Act 1948 and also ss17 and 20 of the Children Act 1989.

From 6 December 1999, the Immigration and Asylum Act 1999 restricted the ability of asylum seekers and other migrants to access support from local authorities. These restrictions have been extended, so they now apply to the following local authority support: [4]

- ss21 and 29 of the National Assistance Act 1948;
- s2 of the Chronically Sick and Disabled Persons Act 1970;
- s21 and Schedule 8 of the National Health Service Act 1977;
- ss17, 23C, 24A and 24B of the Children Act 1989;
- s2 of the Local Government Act 2000;
- s1 of the Localism Act 2011.

Note: the exclusions do not prevent a local authority from providing support under the above provisions to a child,[5] or if failing to do so would result in a breach of a person's human rights (see p347).[6]

The Immigration and Asylum Act 1999 also retained the general exclusion of asylum seekers and others from most state benefits and other welfare provisions on the basis that they are 'persons subject to immigration control' (see p55).[7] Instead, asylum seekers whose applications are outstanding are provided with accommodation and support directly by the Home Office, under s95 of the Act (often called **Section 95 support** or **asylum support**).

Until early 2005, failed asylum seekers could only receive 'hard cases support' under s4 of the Immigration and Asylum Act 1999, provided entirely at the Home Office's discretion. On 31 March 2005, regulations were introduced, specifying entitlement to support under this section (known as **Section 4 support**) for certain failed asylum seekers and their dependants (see p336).[8] If your application has been refused, accommodation and support may be provided under s4 of the Act, but with strict eligibility criteria.

This system, introduced in April 2000, remains the current system of asylum support and is now managed by the Home Office.

Home Office agencies

Since the Immigration and Asylum Act 1999 came into force, the role of providing accommodation and support to asylum seekers has passed between several different Home Office agencies. Until April 2006, the support scheme for asylum seekers and failed asylum seekers was administered by the National Asylum Support Service (NASS). In April 2006, NASS ceased to exist and its role was taken over by the Border and Immigration Agency (BIA). On 7 April 2008, the UK Border

Agency (UKBA) was formed, taking over the support role of the BIA, as well as the immigration and asylum functions of the Immigration and Nationality Department. The UKBA was abolished on 26 March 2013 and all of its functions were returned to the Home Office. Asylum support applications are therefore now dealt with by the Home Office.

Despite this, you may find that advisers and even officials still refer to asylum support as 'NASS' or 'UKBA' support.

All new applications for asylum made after April 2007 are dealt with by the Home Office under the 'new asylum model' (known as NAM) and are allocated to a regional 'caseowner'. Your caseowner is responsible for all issues concerning you until you are granted refugee status or some other permission to remain, or you leave the UK. Thus, the caseowner is also responsible for deciding whether or not you should receive asylum support.

A separate part of the Home Office, the Older Live Cases Unit, deals with issues relating to people who made their original application for asylum before 1 April 2007. Until July 2011, these cases were dealt with by the Case Resolution Directorate, and then by the Case Assurance and Audit Unit. The Older Live Cases Unit deals with your asylum claim, appeals, further representations and all support matters until you obtain permission to remain or you leave the UK. It is based in Liverpool.

Asylum Help

Asylum Help is a national confidential and impartial advice service for asylum seekers, funded by the Home Office and provided by the charity Migrant Help. It can help you make your application for support and give general advice about the asylum process. For contact details and a list of other organisations that provide advice services to asylum seekers, see Appendix 2.

2. **Who is entitled to asylum support**

You are entitled to asylum support (Section 95 support) if:[9]
- you are an asylum seeker or a dependant of an asylum seeker; *and*
- you are destitute or likely to become destitute; *and*
- unless you made your application before 8 January 2003, you have made your application for asylum 'as soon as reasonably practicable' after you entered the UK.[10]

See p335 for who is entitled to temporary support. The criteria are similar, but you must be destitute, not simply likely to become destitute.

Who is an asylum seeker for support purposes

For the purposes of asylum support, you are an asylum seeker if:[11]
- you are over 18 years; *and*
- you have made an application for asylum; *and*
- your application has been recorded by the Secretary of State (see below); *and*
- the application has not yet been determined (see p331).

Your asylum application may be made either under the 1951 Refugee Convention (see p12) or under Article 3 of the European Convention on Human Rights. If you have made a different type of application, such as under Article 8 of the European Convention on Human Rights or an application for indefinite leave to remain (see p23) and you have not also made an asylum or Article 3 application, you cannot claim asylum support. You may be eligible for local authority support or, if you are on temporary admission or applying for bail, for Section 4 support (see p344). For further details on asylum applications, see p30.

When an asylum application is recorded

The 'recording' of an asylum application is not a process clearly defined by Home Office rules, nor the regulations. It appears that this could be a simple statement or action by the Secretary of State, acting through the Home Office, in recognition that an application for asylum has been made.

In 2012, the Home Office introduced a new procedure for making an asylum application. Previously, people could claim asylum by attending the Asylum Screening Unit (ASU) in person and their application was 'recorded' on the same day. Now, you must first make an appointment to attend the ASU by calling a dedicated phone line. Your application is not treated by the Home Office as recorded until you attend a screening interview, which could be weeks, or even months, later. The Home Office says it tries to prioritise 'vulnerable' asylum seekers and those who have no accommodation, but it is not clear how this is assessed.

It could be argued that an application should be treated as recorded from the date you phone to book an appointment. If you are destitute, this means you should be eligible for asylum support immediately, rather than having to wait for your screening interview at the ASU. However, the issue may need to be settled by a legal challenge.

A fresh application (ie, a subsequent claim) from a failed asylum seeker who has exhausted her/his appeal rights is not recorded until the Home Office accepts that the representations constitute a fresh claim – ie, they are significantly different to the material considered in the first asylum application.[12] While you are waiting for your further representations to be considered, you may be eligible for Section 4 support (see p336).

When an asylum application is determined

An asylum application remains undetermined during the time allowed for any appeal to be made and during any appeal lodged within that time (or any appeal accepted out of time) to the First-tier Tribunal (Immigration and Asylum Chamber), or a further appeal. However, an asylum application is not considered undetermined while a judicial review is outstanding.

For support purposes, you continue to be treated as an asylum seeker for 28 days after:[13]

- your application for asylum is granted; *or*
- you are granted leave to remain; *or*
- your asylum appeal is allowed.

Alternatively, you continue to be an asylum seeker for 21 days after your asylum application has been refused by the Home Office or, if there is an appeal, for 21 days after that appeal is finally dismissed.

Families with children

If you have a dependent child when your application for asylum is determined, you continue to be treated as an asylum seeker for support purposes until her/his 18th birthday, provided s/he remains in the UK.[14] **Note:** this only applies if you had a dependent child under 18 years old in the UK when you were still an asylum seeker for support purposes.

The asylum support adjudicators (as the appeal tribunal was called at that time) dismissed an appeal by an asylum seeker who had a dependent child with her in the UK, but was not claiming asylum support at the relevant time.[15] This decision relied on the word 'continuing' in s94(5) of the Immigration and Asylum Act 1999 which says, 'he is to be treated (for the purposes of this Part) as continuing to be an asylum-seeker'. This interpretation, however, is challengeable as it can be argued that the word 'continuing' means that someone continues to be an asylum seeker for support purposes, not that there must be some pre-existing support that will be continued. If you are refused support on this basis, you should appeal.

This provision does not apply if your children were born after your asylum application was refused and you had exhausted all your rights of appeal. In this case, you cease to be an asylum seeker for support purposes and are no longer eligible for asylum support. However, you and your children may be eligible for Section 4 support (see p336) or for support under the Children Act 1989 (see p347).

The Home Office has the power to withdraw asylum support from failed asylum-seeker families who, in its opinion, have not taken steps to leave the UK voluntarily.[16] This means that you are expected to demonstrate that you are taking steps to arrange your departure from the UK to return home. **Note:** this power was piloted across the UK in 2005, but has not been adopted as general practice. If the Home Office decides to withdraw your support because it says that you are not taking steps to leave the UK with your family, you can appeal against this decision to the First-tier Tribunal (Asylum Support) (see Chapter 24).

Who is a dependant for support purposes

Support is provided to asylum seekers and their dependants, so long as they are destitute. You are a 'dependant' of an asylum seeker if you are:[17]

- her/his spouse or civil partner;
- a child aged under 18 years of the asylum seeker or her/his spouse/civil partner and you are dependent on her/him;
- a child aged under 18 years of the close family of the asylum seeker/spouse/ civil partner (you do not have to be dependent on her/him);
- a child aged under 18 years and you have lived in the asylum seeker's household for six out of the last 12 months, or since birth;
- now over 18 years old, but you were under 18 and fell within one of the above categories when the asylum support application was made or when you entered the UK;
- a close family member, or someone who has lived with the asylum seeker for six out of the last 12 months (or since birth), and you are disabled and in need of care and attention from a member of the household;
- her/his partner and you were living with her/him as an unmarried couple for at least two of the three years before the application for support or before entering the UK;[18]
- a member of the household who was previously receiving support under s17 of the Children Act 1989 immediately before 6 December 1999;
- someone who lodges a claim with the Home Office to remain on the basis of being her/his dependant.

The definition of destitute

You are considered destitute if:[19]

- you do not have adequate accommodation or any means of obtaining it (whether or not your other essential living needs are met); *or*
- you have adequate accommodation or the means of obtaining it, but cannot meet your other essential living needs.

When you make an application for asylum support, you are regarded as destitute if there is a likelihood of destitution within 14 days.[20] If you already receive asylum support, you continue to be regarded as destitute if there is a likelihood of destitution within 56 days.

See Chapter 22 for what income and assets are taken into account when deciding whether or not you are destitute.

3. **Who is excluded from asylum support**

Even if you meet the definition of a person eligible for asylum support, you can be excluded from getting support if:[21]
- you are not excluded from getting social security benefits because of your immigration status (see p64);
- you are not being treated as an asylum seeker or the dependant of an asylum seeker (see below) for immigration purposes;
- you apply for support as part of a group and every person is excluded under either of the above.

You can also be excluded if you did not claim asylum 'as soon as reasonably practicable' on entering the UK.[22] **Note:** this only applies to asylum seekers without dependent children.

There is no statutory definition of the term 'as soon as reasonably practicable' and this led to substantial numbers of in-country asylum seekers (ie, people who did not claim asylum at the port of entry, but only after they had entered UK) being refused support, and subsequent judicial review cases in the High Court when the rule was first implemented. The Home Office has since issued a policy, stating that any claim made within three days of arrival is treated as made 'as soon as reasonably practicable'.[23]

Asylum support should not be withheld if a refusal of support would be in breach of a person's human rights.[24] There have been many legal challenges on this issue, the result of which is that asylum support should only be withheld from people who have an alternative source of support.[25]

Dependants of asylum seekers

If you make an application for asylum support for yourself as a dependant of an asylum seeker, you cannot get asylum support if the Home Office does not treat you as her/his dependant for immigration purposes.[26]

There is a difference between people who are treated as dependants of asylum seekers for asylum support purposes (see p332)[27] and those whom the Home Office generally treats as dependent on an asylum claim. The spouse and minor children of an asylum seeker who accompany her/him to the UK are considered to be dependants of the asylum claim unless they apply in their own right.[28] A dependent child who reaches 18 before a decision is made on the application continues to be treated as a dependant pending the decision and during any appeal. The Home Office also has discretion to treat other relatives and those who do not arrive at the same time as the principal applicant as dependants, provided there has not yet been a decision on the asylum application.

Other exclusions

The following people are excluded from asylum support (and also excluded from local authority support – see p347):[29]

- people with refugee status granted by a European Economic Area (EEA) state and their dependants;[30]
- EEA nationals and their dependants.[31]

Note: a child cannot be excluded from support, nor can someone if the provision of support is necessary to avoid a breach of human rights.[32]

4. When asylum support can be suspended or discontinued

If you have been granted support, the Home Office has the power to discontinue or suspend it in certain circumstances.[33] **Note:** a 'power' means a discretion which the Home Office must exercise lawfully. Support can be suspended or discontinued if:

- the Home Office has reason to believe that you or your dependant have committed a serious breach of the rules of the accommodation, if accommodated in 'collective accommodation' – eg, a hostel or shared house.[34] Each accommodation provider is likely to have a set of 'house rules', which every person must follow – eg, to be respectful of other residents and not to make any noise late at night;
- the Home Office has reason to believe that you or your dependant have committed an act of seriously violent behaviour;[35]
- you or your dependant have committed a criminal offence under Part VI of the Immigration and Asylum Act 1999.[36] This includes making a false claim to get support and failing to report a change of circumstances to the Home Office – eg, a change in your financial resources;
- you fail within five working days to provide the Home Office with information about an application for, or receipt of, support;[37]
- you fail without reasonable excuse to attend an interview relating to your dependant's support;[38]
- you fail within 10 working days to provide information about your dependant's asylum application;[39]
- the Home Office has reason to believe that you or your dependant have concealed financial resources and unduly benefited from asylum support;[40]
- you or your dependant fail to comply with reporting requirements;[41]
- the Home Office has reason to believe that you or your dependant have made, or you attempted to make, a second application for asylum before the first application is determined;[42]

- there are 'reasonable grounds' to suspect that you have abandoned your 'authorised address' (see p367) without first informing the Home Office or without its permission.[43] Even if you have only asked the Home Office for financial support and not accommodation (eg, because a friend has offered to let you stay with her/him), you must inform it of your address for support purposes and this becomes your authorised address. You must tell the Home Office if you need to leave this address, and you are not allowed to leave the address for more than 14 days.

Your asylum support can only be suspended or discontinued if you are already being supported by the Home Office.[44] Suspension is temporary and is used when the Home Office requires time or more information to decide whether to discontinue your support – ie, to terminate it entirely. If it is satisfied that there has been a breach of conditions, it must take into account the extent of the breach when deciding whether or not to continue to provide support. **Note:** even if the grounds for suspension or discontinuation are established, you can still retain your entitlement to support if you can show that you are destitute and require support to avoid a breach of your human rights.

If you apply for support again after it has been discontinued, the Home Office may refuse to consider your application if:[45]

- there has been no 'material change in circumstances' since the original decision to suspend or discontinue the support. This means a change of any of the circumstances which you must notify to the Home Office (see p360);[46] *and*
- there are no exceptional circumstances that justify considering your application. New evidence that you are destitute would be a basis for making a new application.

If the Home Office decides to consider your application for support in these circumstances, it may still refuse support.[47]

A decision to refuse or stop asylum support can be appealed to the First-tier Tribunal (Asylum Support) (see Chapter 24).

5. **Temporary asylum support**

While the Home Office considers your application for asylum support, it can provide a temporary form of support to you or your dependant(s).[48] This is commonly called 'emergency support'.

Temporary asylum support can be provided if it appears that you *may* be destitute at the time of the application – ie, even if there is some uncertainty.[49] The definition of 'destitution' is the same way as for ordinary asylum support (see p355),[50] except that temporary support cannot be provided solely on the basis that you are likely to become destitute within 14 days.[51]

Temporary support may be provided subject to conditions, which must be given in writing. It can only be provided until the Home Office decides whether or not asylum support is to be provided. If the Home Office refuses asylum support, temporary support ends at the same time.

There is no right of appeal to the First-tier Tribunal (Asylum Support) (see p378) against a refusal or withdrawal of temporary support.[52] The only method of challenging such a decision is by judicial review proceedings.

Who is excluded from temporary support

You are excluded from temporary support if:[53]
- you are not excluded from getting social security benefits because of your immigration status (see p64);
- you apply as a dependant, but you are not being treated as a dependant of an asylum seeker for immigration purposes;
- you apply as part of a group and every person in the group is excluded under either of the above provisions.

---

6. **Who is entitled to Section 4 support**

If you are a failed asylum seeker who has reached the end of the appeal process and exhausted any appeal rights, you are generally not entitled to support from the Home Office; it expects you to return to your country of origin. If you are unable to leave the UK, you may be able to claim support under s4 of the Immigration and Asylum Act 1999. This is known as 'Section 4 support' (formerly, as 'hard cases support').

To get Section 4 support you must:
- be destitute (see below); *and*
- meet one of the five criteria for support (see p337).[54]

The Home Office can also provide Section 4 support to people who are temporarily admitted to the UK or on bail from immigration detention, regardless of whether they have claimed asylum (see p344).[55]

The definition of destitute

The definition of 'destitute' is the same as for asylum support (see p332).[56] If you apply for Section 4 support within 21 days of your asylum support ending, the Home Office automatically accepts that you are destitute. However, if you have not recently had asylum support, the Home Office usually insists that the onus is on you to prove that you are now destitute, and requires detailed information on how you have survived without social security benefits and how your situation has now changed to leave you destitute. In these circumstances, the Home Office asks you to provide evidence, such as letters from friends, family and charities, explaining what support they have given you in the past and why that cannot continue.

If this evidence cannot be obtained, you must tell the Home Office (and the First-tier Tribunal in any appeal) why this is the case – eg, the friendship may have now deteriorated because you have overstayed your welcome.

It is also important to remember the test of destitution as it is set out in the regulations on p332. If you are an asylum seeker or failed asylum seeker who has relied on friends and relatives, you may still have been destitute within the regulations, even while receiving that help – eg, you may have spent nights sleeping on various friends' floors without a key to gain access, and walking the streets during the day, or have had no money and/or little food. In this situation, you have been destitute under the regulations throughout this period as you have not had adequate accommodation and/or have been unable to meet your essential living needs. When applying for Section 4 support in these circumstances, it is important to give full details about what support has been made available in the past.

Criteria for support

As well as being destitute, to qualify for Section 4 support, you must also prove that you fall into one of the following situations.

You are taking all reasonable steps to leave the UK

You must be taking all reasonable steps to leave the UK or place yourself in a position in which you are able to leave the UK, including, if relevant, applying for a travel document.[57] The Home Office funds a voluntary return programme through the charity Refugee Action called 'Choices'. Initially, signing up for voluntary return with Choices is usually regarded as sufficient to satisfy this requirement.[58] However, you must then show that you have diligently pursued the aim of leaving the UK. This includes regularly contacting Refugee Action Choices to check the progress of what is being done to help you leave. You are also expected to continue with attempts to get travel documents – eg, by visiting your embassy. The Home Office reviews such cases every six weeks or so after granting Section 4 support and asks you for documentary proof of what you have done. It is advisable to keep a diary of the steps you take. It is also important to keep copies of all letters and emails, and notes of telephone calls and visits to, for example, Refugee Action Choices and your embassy.

If you apply for support on these grounds, Home Office policy is to provide support for a maximum of three months. It is the Home Office's view that a three-month period of support is sufficient for most people to be able to arrange their departure from the UK.[59] Section 4 support only continues in exceptional circumstances if the initial claim to Choices for assisted voluntary return is not successful within three months of its being made. This policy may not be lawful as it does not reflect the test in the regulations, which refers to whether a failed asylum seeker 'is' taking all reasonable steps to leave the UK. Thus, the question is what steps you are currently taking and not solely what have you done in the past. If you are refused support on this basis, you should appeal to the First-tier Tribunal (Asylum Support) (see Chapter 24).

Section 4 support is often withdrawn on the grounds that someone has not taken *all* reasonable steps. It could be argued that the Home Office's view on this is often unrealistic, bearing in mind that applicants are destitute, desperate and may speak little English. However, on appeal, the First-tier Tribunal (Asylum Support) may take the view that, if any reasonable step can be identified that you have not taken, even if you did not previously think of it, you have not satisfied the requirement and will be refused support. Each case should be considered on its own merits.

Note: at the time of writing, Choices is currently unable to return anyone to Syria, Palestine and South and Central Somalia. It is also unable to return anyone who does not have a valid travel document to Iran, Congo Brazzaville, Eritrea, Kuwait and Togo. If you are from one of these countries, you can still apply for voluntary return, but your application will be withdrawn after three months. Bear in mind that you can only apply for voluntary return twice. It is a good idea to contact the Home Office to ask what steps can be taken to obtain a travel document and how it can assist with your return. Check Refugee Action Choices website for updates (see Appendix 2).[60]

You are unable to leave the UK because of illness or a disability

This means you are unable to travel (ie, to make a single journey from the UK to your country of origin) because of 'a physical impediment' or other medical reason.[61]

If you apply for support on this ground, you must submit a completed medical declaration (available from www.gov.uk/asylum-support/how-to-claim) to the Home Office. Arguably, a letter containing the same information on headed paper should be sufficient, but it is advisable to use the form if possible.

The medical declaration must be completed by your GP, consultant or psychiatrist and must state that you are unable to leave the UK because of your medical condition. Your GP may charge a fee for this service, in which case the money can be recovered from the Home Office. A refugee advice agency, such as the Red Cross, may be able to help you pay the fee upfront.

The medical declaration or letter should explain your medical problems, and it is crucial that it states that these problems mean that you unable to travel. The test is not whether you should be allowed to stay in the UK – eg, because there is no medical treatment available in your own country or because it would be preferable for you to remain in the UK to continue a course of treatment.

When asking the medical professional to complete the declaration, you should point out the method of travel (eg, by plane) and how many hours it will take to travel to, and wait at, the UK international airport, as well as the number of hours to travel by air to your country of origin and home area. When deciding whether to grant Section 4 support, the Home Office does not consider your doctor's opinion that you should be allowed to stay in the UK – eg, on compassionate grounds or to get treatment for medical problems. Indeed, if your doctor says this, the Home Office might discount the report, believing that s/he has applied the wrong test.

The Home Office accepts that a woman cannot travel during the period of 'around' six weeks before the expected date of giving birth and six weeks after the birth.[62] With your Section 4 application form, you must provide medical documentation (usually Form MATB1 issued by your GP or midwife) to confirm the pregnancy and expected date of birth, or the birth certificate. The Home Office recognises that a woman may be unable to travel for a longer period if there are particular medical problems with the pregnancy. To establish this, you must provide further medical evidence. In any event, according to the NHS, 'the length of a normal pregnancy varies between about 37 and 42 weeks', although the expected delivery date is 'calculated at 40 weeks from the first day of your last period'.[63] However, only 5 per cent of babies are born on their due date. This means that, in practice, a substantial number of babies are born up to three weeks before the expected due date. The First-tier Tribunal (Asylum Support) has accepted this as evidence of the need to provide support earlier than six weeks before the expected date of delivery.

You are unable to leave the UK because there is no viable route of return

To qualify for support under this ground, the Secretary of State must have made a declaration that, in her/his opinion, there is no viable route to a particular country.[64]

At the time of writing, there is no country to which this applies. Irrespective of your personal circumstances, therefore, you will not succeed in claiming support under this criterion unless, by the time of your application, the Secretary of State has made a declaration that there is no safe route. In January 2005, the Secretary of State did say there was no viable route to Iraq, but then withdrew the statement six months later.[65] If your application under this ground is refused, you might be able to argue that this is a breach of your human rights (see p340).

You have applied for judicial review

You must have lodged with the court an application for judicial review to challenge a decision refusing your application for asylum and, in England and Wales, you must have been granted permission to proceed (or leave to proceed in

Northern Ireland).[66] Simply lodging a judicial review application at court in Scotland is sufficient as there is no permission/leave stage.

If you have lodged an application in England and Wales and are waiting for the court to consider whether to grant permission, you are likely to be able to receive support to avoid a breach of your human rights (see below).

Section 4 support is necessary to avoid a breach of human rights

You qualify for Section 4 support if you can show that the provision of accommodation is necessary to avoid a breach of human rights.[67] The courts have said that denying support to asylum seekers whose claims are outstanding, in the context in which they are not allowed to work and would be faced with street homelessness, constitutes 'inhuman and degrading treatment'.[68] This is prohibited under Article 3 of the European Convention on Human Rights. Separating a family by denying some members support could also breach Article 8, which protects private and family life.[69]

If you are a failed asylum seeker, you must also show that it is not reasonable for you to leave the UK. The arguments you may be able to rely on include:

- you have lodged fresh representations with the Home Office (see below);
- you have made an 'out of time' appeal to the First-tier Tribunal (Immigration and Asylum Chamber) (see p342);
- you have applied for a judicial review challenging a refusal of leave, or you have sent a letter threatening proceedings (see p342);
- you have an outstanding application to the European Court of Human Rights (see p342);
- you have no safe route of return (see p343);
- other human rights arguments (see p343).

You have lodged fresh representations with the Home Office

This is the most usual situation in which a failed asylum seeker is given support to avoid a breach of her/his human rights. You must show that:

- you have made a further application to the Home Office to remain in the UK (see p37). The application is usually by way of 'fresh representations' (sometimes called fresh submissions) that you want the Home Office to accept as a fresh asylum claim. It can, however, include an application under Article 8 (see p33);
- this application is still outstanding – eg, the Home Office has not yet decided whether it amounts to a fresh asylum claim;
- it would be a breach of your human rights (under either Article 3 or Article 8) to require you to leave the UK until that application is decided by the Home Office and to refuse you support in the meantime.

The High Court has stated that Section 4 support should be provided in the above circumstances.[70]

Since October 2009, if you want to make further submissions, you must visit the Home Office in person and hand them in. If you applied for asylum under the 'new asylum model' (ie, after 5 March 2007), you must visit your local reporting centre. If your case is being dealt with by the Older Live Cases Unit (ie, if you claimed asylum before 5 March 2007), you must book an appointment and travel in person to the Further Submissions Unit (FSU) in Liverpool (see Appendix 3), unless you are too unwell to do so, in which case representations may be made by fax.

The First-tier Tribunal has granted support on human rights grounds if someone has prepared fresh representations and has an appointment to attend the FSU and submit them on a future date and, in exceptional cases, if further submissions are still being prepared.[71] This is because the applicant has done all that s/he reasonably can to submit the fresh representations. However, the approach of judges varies and some may refuse support unless the representations have been submitted in person.

Even if the representations have been submitted, the Home Office can refuse Section 4 support under this ground if: [72]

- the fresh claim or representations contain no detail whatsoever – eg, if you write to the Home Office stating that you are still fearful of returning to your country of origin, but do not give any further information or simply state that you will send new information later; *or*
- the evidence or arguments that you have submitted as part of your fresh claim have already been seen and rejected by the Home Office or rejected on appeal and they do not rely on any change in the law since the previous refusal.

Once the Home Office has looked at any fresh representations, you are informed in writing whether they have been accepted as a new asylum application. If so, a fresh asylum application is recorded. At this point, you become an asylum seeker again and should reapply for asylum support under Section 95 (see p329). If your representations are not accepted as an asylum application, your Section 4 support is withdrawn unless you can prove that you meet one of the other criteria for support.

Note: the Home Office used to have a policy of delaying making a decision on a Section 4 application for at least 15 working days to allow the caseowner (see p329) time to consider the further submissions. The High Court ruled that this policy was unlawful, because it led to a 'significant risk' that Article 3 of the European Convention on Human Rights would be breached if applicants were left destitute while waiting for a decision.[73] The Home Office amended its policy to comply with the ruling. According to the new instructions:[74]

- the caseowner must make every effort to consider the further submissions at the same time as considering the Section 4 application;
- the decision about support should not be delayed because of administrative or other problems in assessing the merits of the further submissions;

- 'as a general rule', caseowners must make a decision on support applications made on the basis of further submissions within five working days;
- if the application is a higher priority, the caseowner must make 'every reasonable effort' to decide the application within two working days;
- there is a non-exhaustive list of cases requiring extra prioritisation, including people who are street homeless, families with minors, people who are disabled, elderly or pregnant, and potential victims of torture and trafficking;
- caseowners must 'check that the further submissions are not clearly abusive, manifestly unfounded or repetitious'.

You have made an 'out of time' appeal to the First-tier Tribunal

If you want to appeal against the refusal of your asylum application but the time for appealing has expired, you must ask the First-tier Tribunal (Immigration and Asylum Chamber) for permission for your 'out of time' appeal to proceed. In these circumstances, the Home Office and the First-tier Tribunal (Asylum Support) usually grants Section 4 support, considering that it would be a breach of your human rights to expect you to leave the UK in the meantime.

If you appeal within the prescribed time limits, you are still considered to be an asylum seeker and so you may still be eligible for asylum support under Section 95 (see p329). If the First-tier Tribunal (Immigration and Asylum Chamber) gives you permission to appeal out of time, you become an asylum seeker again and are eligible for Section 95 support (and, at that stage, no longer eligible for Section 4 support).

You have issued or threatened judicial review proceedings on an asylum matter

If your further submissions are rejected, you can challenge this by judicial review. In England and Wales, you are not eligible for support under this ground unless you have been granted permission by the High Court.[75] This can take some time. In the meantime, you may be eligible for support to avoid a breach of your human rights.

A ruling by the High Court in 2009 held that the criteria may also be satisfied if you have an outstanding letter threatening judicial review proceedings or if you have issued judicial review proceedings in the High Court.[76] You must show that your case is not 'entirely without merit'.

You have made an application to the European Court of Human Rights

Failed asylum seekers who have exhausted their appeal rights in the UK, but who claim that their removal would lead to a breach of their human rights, can apply to the European Court of Human Rights in Strasbourg for an order preventing their imminent removal (called a Rule 39 order).

If this applies to you and you are waiting for a decision from the European Court and you are destitute, you may be eligible for Section 4 support. In a decision in 2011, a judge in the First-tier Tribunal (Asylum Support) laid down criteria for deciding when support should be granted.[77] You must show that:

- your application to the European Court 'has some merit'. This includes showing that it is 'fully reasoned and individuated'. The level of detail required depends on the case;
- you exhausted all remedies in the UK before applying to the European Court, including making a fresh application for asylum and challenging any refusal by judicial review. However, there is no need to have applied for a remedy if it was 'bound to fail'. So, for example, if you have been refused legal aid for a judicial review because of existing UK caselaw, you may still satisfy this ground;
- you have 'raised the prospect of imminent risk on return'. This is usually satisfied if you have applied for a Rule 39 order.

Note: this decision is not binding on other judges in the First-tier Tribunal (Asylum Support), but is persuasive.

You have no safe route of return

In the case *M Ahmed v Asylum Support Adjudicator and the Secretary of State*, Mr Ahmed argued that there was no safe route for him to return to his home in Iraq and, therefore, he could not leave the UK and so should be given Section 4 support to avoid a breach of his human rights.[78] The High Court ruled that he did not have sufficient evidence to establish that the route back to his home was so dangerous that it would be a breach of his human rights to require him to leave the UK. The Secretary of State, however, agreed that there may be cases in which this argument could succeed and the judge agreed that such an argument might well succeed if there were sufficient evidence to support it. However, the Home Office (or the First-tier Tribunal (Asylum Support)) would be entitled to conclude that the risks to an applicant of a return journey would have been considered when the asylum application was refused, and so s/he would have to show that circumstances had since changed. The issue may need to be tested again in the light of the deteriorating situation in Iraq and Syria.

Other human rights arguments

Many cases depend on their own particular facts. For example, it might be a breach of your human rights under Article 8 of the European Convention of Human Rights to expect you to leave the UK when you have a partner and/or child who has British nationality who is settled in the UK.

On one occasion, the First-tier Tribunal (Asylum Support) decided that a failed asylum seeker could not be expected to leave the UK while on probation, and subjected to reporting requirements and medical tests because of drug offences. Leaving the UK would have meant that he could not comply with the probation order made by the court. In this particular case, the applicant would have been street homeless in the UK, which would have constituted a breach of Article 3 because, as with most asylum seekers and failed asylum seekers, he was not entitled to work to support himself.

Section 4 support for people on bail or temporary admission

If you are on bail from immigration detention, or you are currently detained and intend to seek bail, you can apply for accommodation and support from the Home Office under s4(1)(c) of the Immigration and Asylum Act 1999 (see p362).[79] You do not need to be an asylum seeker or a failed asylum seeker, but the Home Office refuses support if it does not consider that you are destitute. If support is refused, you can appeal to the First-tier Tribunal (Asylum Support) (see Chapter 24).

In addition, Home Office has broad powers to provide accommodation and support to anyone on temporary admission or release.[80] Temporary admission is usually granted to people subject to immigration control who are not detained but do not have leave to remain. If this applies to you, you will have been given a form (called an IS96), which usually includes reporting requirements (see p14). This power is potentially very broad, because there is no need for you to be an asylum seeker or failed asylum seeker as defined in the legislation.

In 2013, the Home Office published guidance on when this power will be used.[81]

- Support is not provided to asylum seekers or to failed asylum seekers. They should apply for Section 95 or Section 4 support instead.
- Support may be provided to unaccompanied asylum-seeking children who have reached the age of 18, but whose asylum application was determined before their 18th birthday. This is to close a loophole whereby such people do not fit within the definition of an asylum seeker or failed asylum seeker. You must show that you are destitute, that you meet the conditions for Section 4 support and that you are not eligible for support from your local authority.
- Applications are only considered from people in other immigration categories (eg, overstayers who have never made a claim for asylum) 'in truly exceptional circumstances'. You must show that you are destitute and that support is required to avoid a breach of human rights, which generally means that it is not reasonable for you to leave the country. The guidance states that this will not be the case if you have an outstanding application for leave to remain under Article 8 or based on long residence. However, whether or not human rights are likely to be breached depends on the facts of the individual case and, if necessary, the First-tier Tribunal may need to decide.

The First-tier Tribunal has granted support under Section 4(1)(a) to the following destitute people on temporary admission who had never claimed asylum:

- a 21-year-old man who arrived in the UK aged 15 claiming he was a British citizen. He had been waiting for seven years for the Home Office to decide his case;[82]
- a man with severe mental health problems who had been certified by his doctor as unable to travel and who had applied for leave to remain outside the Immigration Rules;[83]
- a 43-year-old homeless man who had applied for voluntary return and was waiting for a travel document so that he could return to India.[84]

7. **When Section 4 support can be suspended or discontinued**

Certain people are excluded from Section 4 support. They are the same people who are excluded from asylum support under Section 95 (see p333).

However, when Section 4 support can be suspended or discontinued is different.

When support can be suspended

The Home Office has no power to suspend Section 4 support. This may have been an oversight in drafting the regulations or it may have been thought that, as the nature of the support is in theory temporary, it can simply be terminated.

When support can be discontinued

The Home Office may discontinue your support if it believes that you are no longer eligible – eg, because you are not taking all reasonable steps to leave the UK or an application for judicial review has failed.

The Home Office's policy is to review Section 4 support:[85]
- two weeks after it is granted on the basis that you are taking all reasonable steps to leave the UK and you have indicated on the application that you intend to apply for assisted voluntary return through Refugee Action Choices (see p337);
- six weeks after you have applied for assisted voluntary return and every six weeks thereafter;
- six weeks after the birth of a baby if you have received support on the basis of late pregnancy or birth of a baby (the Home Office accepts that a woman cannot travel six weeks before or six weeks after giving birth);
- at the end of the period estimated by the Home Office medical adviser, or your doctor, as the period within which you should recover sufficiently from an illness or disability that has prevented you from travelling earlier.

Before discontinuing support, the Home Office should send you a review letter, asking you to provide reasons why support should not be withdrawn. If you do not provide a satisfactory response justifying why it should continue, the Home Office then sends a further letter terminating support. You can appeal against the decision (see Chapter 24).

If you have breached the conditions of support

Section 4 support can be granted subject to certain conditions. The conditions must be given to you in writing and must involve:[86]
- specified standards of behaviour; *or*
- a reporting requirement; *or*
- a requirement:
  - to reside at an authorised address; *or*
  - if absent from an authorised address without the Home Office's permission, to ensure that the absence is for no more than seven consecutive days and nights or for no more than a total of 14 days and nights in any six-month period; *or*
- specified steps to facilitate your departure from the UK.

If the Home Office believes you have breached a condition of your Section 4 support, it must write to you, giving details of the alleged breach, explaining the consequences and inviting you to provide an explanation. It is important to respond promptly, otherwise your support will be withdrawn. The Home Office's policy gives some examples of how it treats certain breaches and when it considers it appropriate to terminate support.

In some cases, the Home Office has simply terminated support, alleging a breach of a condition without first inviting comments from the recipient – eg, where it appeared that a reporting requirement had not been complied with, but this had not been communicated to the individual concerned. If this occurs, you should appeal immediately, as the appeal time limit is very short (see p378). You could also telephone the Home Office immediately to get your support reinstated to allow time for a response. If this is not successful, you should also make a complaint, pointing out the Home Office's stated policy of inviting comments before withdrawing support.

A refusal or termination of Section 4 support can be appealed to the First-tier Tribunal (Asylum Support) (see p377).

The best interests of children

The Home Office has a duty to ensure that all its decisions take into account the need to safeguard and promote the welfare of children.[87] It has an internal policy of not discontinuing Section 4 support to families with children unless:[88]
- they are assessed as no longer destitute; *or*
- they have left the UK; *or*

- they are now in receipt of alternative support and Section 4 support is no longer required; *or*
- there has been a serious breach of the conditions of support.

Home Office policy is also to signpost families to social services departments and not to discontinue support until the local authority has assessed whether they are eligible for support under the Children Act 1989 (see p349).

8. **Support from your local authority**

You may be eligible for support from your local authority if you have care needs or if there is a child in your family.

Note: this is a complex area of law and beyond the scope of this *Handbook*. What follows is a brief description of the support available under the National Assistance Act 1948 and the Children Act 1989, as it relates to asylum seekers and failed asylum seekers. If you believe that you may be entitled to support from your local authority, you should get expert advice from a community care adviser.

Local authority support is not listed as a 'public fund' in the Immigration Rules. Therefore, if you have been granted leave to remain subject to the condition that you do not have 'recourse to public funds' (see p25), you are not excluded from claiming support from your local authority during periods of destitution, provided you have care needs.

Who is excluded from support

You are not eligible for local authority support if you come into an excluded group, unless to exclude you would be a breach of human rights (see p348). You are excluded if:[89]

- you have, or you are the dependant of someone who has, been granted refugee status by another European Economic Area (EEA) state;
- you are, or you are the dependant of someone who is, an EEA national;
- you are, or you are the dependant of someone who is, a failed asylum seeker who has not complied with removal directions;
- you are not currently an asylum seeker and you are in the UK unlawfully – ie, in breach of immigration laws. **Note:** if you are a failed asylum seeker, you are in the UK lawfully if you originally applied for asylum on your arrival (ie, at the port of entry) and you have abided by the terms of your temporary admission. You may be unlawfully present (and therefore excluded from community care support) if you only applied for asylum later (ie, 'in-country') or after any leave you had expired;
- you are a failed asylum seeker with children, you are treated as an asylum seeker for support purposes, and the Secretary of State has stated that you have

failed, without reasonable excuse, to take reasonable steps to leave, or place yourself in a position to leave, the UK (called 'Section 9 cases'). **Note:** although the Home Office has retained the right to apply this exclusion, it is rarely used.

The above exclusions do not apply to children, or where support is necessary to avoid a breach of human rights.[90] There are various situations in which support may be necessary to avoid a breach. In particular, failed asylum seekers and other migrants who are unlawfully in the UK, but who have made a fresh application for asylum or for permission to remain in the UK on human rights grounds, may be able to argue that a local authority should provide support in order to avoid a breach of their human rights while their further submissions are outstanding. However, the submissions must not be manifestly unfounded, or merely repeat grounds you have previously made.[91]

Community care support

If you need care and attention (see below), you may qualify for accommodation and support from your local authority social services department under s21 of the National Assistance Act 1948.[92]

If you are entitled to support under s21 of the National Assistance Act, the fact that you are receiving, or may be eligible for, asylum support or Section 4 support from the Home Office must be ignored by the local authority when deciding whether or not to provide community care support and at what level.[93]

A need for care and attention

To be eligible for community care support, you must have a need for care and attention, which can only be met by the provision of accommodation.[94] The need must arise from:

- age;
- physical or mental illness;
- disability; *or*
- some other reason.

Note: 'destitution' alone is not enough (see p349).

Pregnant women and breastfeeding mothers who are in need of care and attention can apply for community care support, but the local authority has a discretion whether or not to provide it. The High Court considered this issue in 2008 and decided that pregnant and breastfeeding asylum seekers should be supported by the Home Office, not local authority social services departments, unless there are particular difficulties that give rise to the need for care and attention.[95]

The relevant test is not the presence of a serious illness, but whether there is a need to be 'looked after'.[96] Furthermore, the need for care and attention must not be 'available otherwise than by the provision of accommodation'. The Supreme

Court has suggested that this means that the care and attention must be 'accommodation related' or of a sort that is normally provided in the home or which is effectively useless if you have no home.[97]

> **'Destitution plus'**
>
> If you are a 'person subject to immigration control' (see p55), which includes asylum seekers and failed asylum seekers on temporary admission, your need for care and attention must not arise solely from being destitute or from the anticipated effects of being destitute.[98] In other words, you cannot get community care support if the only reason you need looking after is because you are destitute. There must be some additional reason why you need to be looked after. This test has become known as the **'destitution plus'** test.

How to apply

The usual community care process is followed. The social services department carries out an assessment and, on the basis of this, decides whether or not to provide a service to meet an unmet need under s21 of the National Assistance Act 1948.

Social services departments must carry out a needs assessment of anyone over 18 who comes to their attention who may be in need of community care services.[99] Strictly, it is not necessary to make a written application, but apart from very straightforward cases (eg, an application from an older person for a bus pass), a community care assessment will need to be in writing in order to reflect adequately your situation.

The social services department in the area where you 'reside' is responsible for assessing you. Many asylum seekers and failed asylum seekers do not 'reside' in any particular area.[100] In these situations, the department that covers the area where you happen to be on the day or where you spent the previous night is responsible. There are special procedures that local authorities must follow to resolve arguments between themselves about who must assess and provide any community care support. In the meantime, assessments must be carried out and appropriate support must be provided.

Support under the Children Act

Local authorities have a duty to safeguard and promote the welfare of children who are 'in need' in the area.[101] If you are destitute and have children, you may therefore be eligible for accommodation or support from your local authority under the Children Act 1989 (in Scotland, the Children (Scotland) Act 1995). A child who is destitute is generally considered to be 'in need', but a child can also be in need if s/he is disabled, or if s/he is unlikely to achieve or maintain a reasonable standard of health or development without the provision of services by a local authority.[102]

Although the duty is to support the child, it extends to supporting parents or other family members if this is in the child's best interests.[103]

If you request accommodation under the Children Act for yourself and your children, some local authorities may suggest that a breach of human rights can be avoided by providing accommodation for the child only and not you, the parent. This is often unlawful. If this happens, you should obtain expert advice from a community care adviser or lawyer as it may be possible to challenge the local authority's decision by judicial review.

Asylum seekers

If you are eligible for asylum support (see p329), you and your dependants are excluded from help under the Children Act 1989.[104] However, if you or your children cannot claim asylum support (eg, because you have breached the conditions of support), you may be eligible for Children Act support. **Note:** you cannot be entitled to asylum support if you are aged under 18. Therefore, if you are an unaccompanied asylum seeker under 18, you are not excluded from Children Act support (see below). When you turn 18, the local authority may have a duty to continue to provide you with support.[105]

Failed asylum seekers

The parents of a child (although not the child her/himself) who are failed asylum seekers unlawfully in the UK are excluded from local authority support, unless support is necessary to avoid a breach of human rights. Support may be necessary to avoid a breach if you are destitute and you have an arguable application for leave to remain on human rights grounds which is outstanding.[106]

The fact that you may be eligible for Section 4 support (see p336) does not exclude you from claiming Children Act support.[107] This is because Section 4 is a 'residual power' and any duty to support under the Children Act should come first. Despite this, some local authorities still refuse support on this basis. If this happens, you should seek expert advice as it may be possible to challenge the local authority's refusal by judicial review.

Unaccompanied asylum-seeking children

Children under the age of 18 years who arrive in the UK alone and claim asylum (often referred to as 'unaccompanied minors') are the responsibility of the local authority to support under the Children Act.

Unaccompanied asylum-seeker children tend to be dispersed around the country, rather than assisted in the areas in which the UK ports and airports are situated. The local authority in the new area should then make arrangements for suitable accommodation, which can include foster care.

If you have already been supported by a local authority as an unaccompanied minor, it may continue to have a duty to provide you with support when you turn 18 under the Children (Leaving Care) Act 2000.[108] This allows for a needs assessment and potential support up to the age of 21, or 24 if you continue in education.

There may be a dispute about your age. If you claim asylum as an unaccompanied minor, the Home Office should refer you to social services for support unless it strongly believes that you are over 18 years old. If the social services department has any doubt about your age, it can carry out an age assessment.[109] Specialist refugee organisations, such as the Refugee Council, can assist if your age has been, or could be, disputed (see Appendix 2).

Notes

1. Introduction
1 s95 IAA 1999
2 s98 IAA 1999
3 s4 IAA 1999
4 Sch 3 para 1 NIAA 2002
5 Sch 3 para 2 NIAA 2002
6 Sch 3 para 3 NIAA 2002
7 s115(9) IAA 1999
8 IA(POAFAS) Regs; see also www.gov.uk/immigration-operational-guidance/asylum-policy

2. Who is entitled to asylum support
9 ss94(1) and 95(1) and Sch 9 paras 1-3 IAA 1999; regs 2(1) and 3 AS Regs
10 s55 NIAA 2002
11 ss94(1) and 95(1) and Sch 9 para 1(1)(2) IAA 1999; reg 3(1) AS Regs
12 para 353 IR
13 s94(3) IAA 1999; regs 2 and 2A AS Regs
14 s95(4) IAA 1999
15 ASA/02/02/1877
16 s9 AI(TC)A 2004
17 s94(1) IAA 1999; reg 2 (4) AS Regs
18 R (Chen) v Secretary of State for the Home Department [2012] EWHC 2531 (Admin)
19 s95(3) IAA 1999
20 Reg 7 AS Regs

3. Who is excluded from asylum support
21 s95(2) IAA 1999; reg 4 AS Regs
22 s55 NIAA 2002
23 Home Office, Asylum Support Policy Bulletin 75, para 3.5

24 s55 IAA 1999
25 R (Limbuela and others (Shelter intervener)) v Secretary of State for the Home Department [2005] UKHL 66
26 Reg 4(4)(c) AS Regs
27 Reg 2(4) AS Regs
28 para 349 IR
29 Sch 3 NIAA 2002
30 Sch 3 para 4 NIAA 2002
31 Sch 3 para 5 NIAA 2002
32 Sch 3 paras 2 and 3 NIAA 2002

4. When asylum support can be suspended or discontinued
33 Reg 20(1) AS Regs provides that support 'may' be suspended or discontinued.
34 Reg 20(1)(a) AS Regs
35 Reg 20(1)(b) AS Regs
36 Reg 20(1)(c) AS Regs
37 Reg 20(1)(e) AS Regs
38 Reg 20(1)(f) AS Regs
39 Reg 20(1)(g) AS Regs
40 Reg 20(1)(h) AS Regs
41 Reg 20(1)(i) AS Regs
42 Reg 20(1)(j) AS Regs
43 Reg 20(1)(d) AS Regs

44 See the wording of reg 20(1) AS Regs, which refers to support for a 'supported person' or her/his dependants. Such a person is defined as an asylum seeker or the dependant of an asylum seeker who has applied for support and for whom asylum support has been provided (s94(1) IAA 1999), and indeed the regulation refers to the 'suspension' or 'discontinuation' of the existing support, which presupposes the current provision of that support.
45 Reg 21(1) AS Regs; Home Office, *Asylum Support Policy Bulletin* 84
46 Reg 21(1)(c) and (2) AS Regs, with reference to reg 15 AS Regs
47 Reg 21(3) AS Regs

5. Temporary asylum support
48 s98 IAA 1999
49 s98(1) IAA 1999; Home Office, *Asylum Support Policy Bulletin* 73
50 s98(3) IAA 1999, applying s95(11)
51 As compared with the position relating to asylum support under s95(1) IAA 1999.
52 This is because s103 IAA 1999, which deals with appeals, does not refer to s98 support.
53 Reg 4(8)(9) AS Regs

6. Who is entitled to Section 4 support
54 Reg 3(1)(a) IA(POAFAS) Regs
55 s4(1)(a) IAA 1999
56 These are listed in reg 3(2)(a-e) IA(POAFAS) Regs
57 Reg 3(1)(b) and (2)(a) IA(POAFAS) Regs; ASA 06/03/12859
58 The assisted voluntary return package is often referred to as AVR or VAARP (voluntary assisted returns and reintegration programme).
59 Incorporated into Home Office policy instructions 'Section 4 support: instruction' and 'Section 4 review: instruction', available at www.gov.uk/government/collections/asylum-support-asylum-instructions
60 www.choices-avr.org.uk/countries_of_return/countries_where_choices_are_unable_to_assist_with_assisted_voluntary_return
61 Reg 3(1)(b) and (2)(b) IA(POAFAS) Regs; *R (SSHD) v ASA and Osman, Yillah, Ahmad and Musemwa (interested parties)* [2006] EWHC 1248

62 Home Office policy instruction 'Section 4 support: instruction', available at www.gov.uk/government/collections/asylum-support-asylum-instructions
63 *NHS Choices: pregnancy*, available at www.nhs.uk
64 Reg 3(1)(b) and (2)(c) IA(POAFAS) Regs
65 *R (Rasul) v ASA* [2006] EWHC 435; ASA 06/03/12859
66 Reg 3(1)(b) and (2)(d) IA(POAFAS) Regs
67 Regs 3(1)(b) and (2)(e) IA(POAFAS) Regs
68 *R (Limbuela and others (Shelter intervener)) v Secretary of State for the Home Department* [2005] UKHL 66
69 *Clue v Birmingham City Council* [2010] EWCA Civ 460
70 *R (Nigatu) v Secretary of State for the Home Department* [2004] EWHC 1806 (Admin), para 20
71 See, for example, AS/14/06/31490, 11 June 2014
72 Reg 3(2)(e) IA(POAFAS) Regs
73 *R (MK and AH) v Secretary of State for the Home Department* [2012] EWHC 1896
74 Home Office policy instruction 'Section 4 support: instruction', para 11.1, available at www.gov.uk/government/collections/asylum-support-asylum-instructions
75 Reg 3(2)(d) IA(POAFAS) Regs
76 *R (NS) v First-tier Tribunal* [2009] EWHC 3819 (Admin)
77 AS/11/06/26857, 18 August 2011
78 *M Ahmed v Asylum Support Adjudicator and the Secretary of State* [2008] EWHC 2282 (Admin), judgment given 2 October 2008
79 s4(1)(c) IAA 1999
80 s4(1)(a) and (b) IAA 1999
81 Home Office policy instruction 'Section 4 support: instruction', available at www.gov.uk/government/collections/asylum-support-asylum-instructions
82 AS/11/09/27448, 30 September 2011
83 AS/11/11/76787, 22 November 2011
84 AS/11/12/27777, 12 January 2012

7. When Section 4 support can be suspended or discontinued
85 Home Office policy instructions 'Section 4 support: instruction' and 'Section 4 review: instruction', available at www.gov.uk/government/collections/asylum-support-asylum-instructions
86 Reg 6 IA(POAFAS) Regs
87 s55 Borders, Citizenship and Immigration Act 2009

88 Home Office policy instruction 'Section 4 review: instruction', available at www.gov.uk/government/collections/asylum-support-asylum-instructions

8. Support from your local authority

89 Sch 3 NIAA 2002
90 Sch 3 para 2 NIAA 2002
91 *R (AW) v Croydon London Borough Council* [2005] EWHC 2950; *Birmingham City Council v Clue* [2010] EWCA Civ 460
92 'Accommodation' under s21 NAA 1948 is defined as including 'board and other services, amenities and requisites provided in connection with the accommodation' except where the local authority deems unnecessary.
93 *R (Westminster) v NASS* [2002] UKHL 38; *R (AW) v Croydon London Borough Council* [2005] EWHC 2950
94 s21 NAA 1948; *SL v Westminster City Council* [2013] UKSC 27
95 *R (Gnezele) v Leeds City Council* [2007] EWHC 3275 (Admin)
96 *R (M) v Slough Borough Council* [2008] UKHL 52
97 *SL v London Borough of Westminster* [2013] UKSC 27
98 s21(1A) NAA 1948
99 s47(1) National Health Services and Community Care Act 1990; s55 in Scotland
100 s24 NAA 1948
101 s17 CA 1989; s22 C(S)A 1995
102 s17(10) CA 1989
103 s17(3) CA 1989; s22(3) C(S)A 1995
104 s122 IAA 1999
105 Home Office policy instruction, 'Transition at age 18: instruction', available at www.gov.uk/government/publications/transition-at-age-18-instruction
106 *Birmingham City Council v Clue* [2010] EWCA Civ 460
107 *Birmingham City Council v Clue* [2010] EWCA Civ 460
108 *R (SO) v London Borough of Barking and Dagenham* [2010] EWCA Civ 1101; Home Office policy instruction, 'Transition at age 18: instruction', available at www.gov.uk/government/publications/transition-at-age-18-instruction
109 *R (C) (on the application of) v London Borough of Merton* [2005] EWHC 1753 (Admin)

Chapter 22

· ·

Applications

This chapter covers:

---

1. **Applying for asylum support**

If you are either an asylum seeker or a dependant of an asylum seeker for support purposes, you can apply for asylum support from the Home Office.[1] The application can be for you alone or for yourself and your dependants.[2] As with social security benefits, you must use a particular form to apply for asylum support.[3] At the time of writing, this is the ASF1 application form.

The application form is available from Migrant Help (see p329) and from the government website (www.gov.uk/asylum-support/how-to-claim). Even if the application is for both yourself and your dependants, you only need to complete one form. If you wish to obtain support as a dependant of a person who is already being supported by the Home Office, you do not need to complete the application form again – the Home Office considers providing additional support for you if notified of your existence in writing.[4] However, it is advisable to complete a separate application form, as you then appear to have the right of appeal against any subsequent refusal, which may not be so clear if the asylum seeker simply notifies the Home Office that s/he has been joined by a dependant.[5]

Migrant Help can help you complete the form and submit it to the Home Office. It is strongly advised to get assistance from Migrant Help or a local advice agency if you can. You must complete the form in full and in English.[6] There are detailed notes accompanying the application form, which give further information about the application procedure and guidance on how to complete the form.

The form asks for details of the stage your asylum application has reached, the kind of support you need, your current accommodation, any other kind of support you receive (including support from friends or relatives, details of cash, savings, investments or other property you own, any employment you have and state benefits you receive, both for yourself and your dependants), and details of any disabilities or special needs you have. You must send documents to confirm the information you give.

The form can be completed electronically but, at the time of writing, there is no electronic means of submission, so it must be printed before being sent. For your application to be considered as soon as possible, the form can be faxed to the Home Office (Migrant Help will do this for you); otherwise it can be posted.[7]

The Home Office may ask you for further information on any of the details contained in the application form.[8]

2. **Making a decision on your application**

Deciding whether you are destitute

If you apply for support for yourself, the Home Office must be satisfied that you are 'destitute'. If you apply for support for yourself and your dependants, it decides whether the group as a whole is destitute.[9]

'Destitute' includes if you are 'likely to become destitute within 14 days'.[10] You are destitute if either:[11]

- you do not have 'adequate accommodation' (see p356), or any means of getting adequate accommodation; *or*
- you cannot meet your essential living needs (see p358), even if you do have adequate accommodation.

The Home Office must follow rules that set out what is and what is not relevant in deciding these questions. These apply when you make an application for support and at any stage if there is a question of whether support should continue.

When considering whether you are destitute, the Home Office must take into account any of the following that are available to you or to any of your dependants:[12]

- any income you have, or which you may reasonably be expected to have;
- any other support that is available, or which may reasonably be expected to be available, to you;
- any of the following assets that are available to you, or which might reasonably be expected to be available to you:
  - cash;
  - savings;
  - investments;
  - land;
  - vehicles;
  - goods for trade or business.

This might include support from friends and relatives in the UK or from voluntary sector organisations. Land may include property, such as a house and other outbuildings. Investments include business investments, income bonds, life assurance policies, pension schemes, stocks and shares, and unit trusts (but not jewellery[13]).

The Home Office may provide you with support on a limited basis to allow you time to sell items of property – eg, six months if it is a house. The Home Office treats the money received from the sale as cash or savings and takes it into account when deciding whether or not to provide support. If you do not consider it reasonable that you should have to sell your property, give your reasons for this when you send in your application form.[14]

When deciding whether you are destitute, the Home Office must ignore any:
- assets you or your dependants have that are not listed on p355;[15]
- Home Office support or temporary support that you or your dependants currently have or with which you may be provided.[16]

The Home Office has confirmed that it ignores items of personal clothing, bedding, and medical or optical items – eg, wheelchairs.[17] Although jewellery is excluded, you should disclose any items of jewellery or watches belonging to you or your dependants that are worth over £1,000 at the current market value in your application for support, and inform the Home Office immediately if any of these items are subsequently sold and for how much.[18] The money you receive as a result of the sale may be taken into account.

Adequate accommodation

If you are applying for support but you have some form of accommodation, the Home Office must decide whether or not this is 'adequate'. Similarly, if you are already being financially supported by the Home Office but your accommodation is not being provided (as previously you did not require it), you can ask the Home Office for accommodation. In this case, the Home Office must consider whether your current accommodation is adequate or whether it should provide you with accommodation in addition to financial support. The Home Office must take into account whether:[19]
- it is 'reasonable' for you to continue to occupy the accommodation;
- you can afford to pay for the accommodation;
- you can gain entry to the accommodation;
- if the accommodation is a houseboat, a caravan or some other moveable structure that can be lived in, whether there is somewhere you can place it and have permission to live in it;
- you can live in the accommodation with your dependants;
- you or your dependants are likely to experience harassment, threats or violence if you continue to live in the accommodation.

Accommodation may be considered inadequate, for example, if you are staying with a friend and sleeping on her/his floor, or if you cannot gain entry to it during the day, or if it is unsuitable for you because of your health needs or a physical disability.

If you have told the Home Office that you want to stay in your current accommodation and only want financial assistance, the factors listed above are not taken into account when deciding whether you are destitute, except for the question of whether you can afford the accommodation.[20]

Is it reasonable for you to continue to occupy the accommodation?

The Home Office must consider whether it is 'reasonable' for you to continue to occupy the accommodation.[21] In considering this, it may take into account the general housing circumstances in the district[22] of the local government housing authority in which the accommodation is situated.[23] So if your accommodation is worse or more overcrowded than other accommodation generally found in the area in which you live, it may not be reasonable for you to continue to live there.

Can you afford to pay for the accommodation?

The Home Office must consider whether you can afford to pay for your existing accommodation.[24] It must take into account:[25]

- any income or assets (see p355), other than from Home Office support or temporary support, available to you or any of your dependants, or which might be expected to be available;
- the costs of living in the accommodation;
- your other reasonable living expenses.

Do you have access to the accommodation?

Circumstances in which you would be considered not to have access to your accommodation include if you have been illegally evicted from the accommodation, or squatters have unlawfully moved in.

Is there harassment, threats or violence?

The Home Office must consider whether it is 'probable' that your continued occupation of the accommodation will lead to domestic violence against you or any of your dependants.[26] The domestic violence must be:[27]

- from a person who is, or who has been, a 'close family member'; *and*
- in the form of either actual violence, or threats of violence that are likely to be carried out.

There is no definition of 'close family member'. Depending on the circumstances, it may cover a married or unmarried partner and ex-partner, those to whom you have a blood relationship, in-laws, relatives of your partner and others who live (or have lived) in your household. **Note:** the family member does not have to live with you.[28] You may fear that because your address is known to her/him, your continued occupation of that accommodation is likely to lead to domestic violence.

Although the asylum support rules only expressly refer to domestic violence, it is arguable that other forms of violence or threats which you have received from anyone not normally associated with you are also relevant when deciding whether your current accommodation is adequate. This may be in the form of racial harassment or attacks,[29] sexual abuse or harassment, and harassment because of your religion or for other reasons.

Your essential living needs

When deciding whether you can meet your essential living needs,[30] certain items are not treated as essential. When deciding whether you are destitute, your inability to provide any of the following items for yourself is not relevant:[31]

- the cost of sending or receiving faxes, photocopying or buying or using computer facilities;
- travelling expenses;
- toys and entertainment expenses.

Although the above expenses cannot be taken into account at this stage, if you are found to be destitute, they can be relevant if the Home Office must consider the expenses incurred in connection with your asylum application or if your case is exceptional (see p369).

Although the rules exclude travel costs, the regulations exempt from this exclusion the cost of your initial journey from the place in the UK where you happen to be to the accommodation being provided for you by the Home Office, or to alternative accommodation where you intend to live, the address of which you have given to the Home Office.[32] This is normally the accommodation in which you must live as a condition of your temporary admission to the UK (see p14). Although the rules do not expressly state that these journeys must be taken into account when considering whether you are destitute, the fact that they are exempt from being excluded indicates that the Home Office should take them into account and, if you do not have the means to pay for this travel, should provide support in order for you to travel to your accommodation.

If you have another need that is not referred to in these rules, it does not necessarily mean that it is an 'essential living need'.[33] The Home Office must decide whether the need is essential, taking into account your individual circumstances.

Clothing

When deciding whether you can meet your essential living needs in terms of clothing, the Home Office cannot take into account your personal preferences.[34] This rule is designed to prevent complaints based on your inability to provide particular clothing that is more expensive than that which is reasonably required – eg, particularly fashionable clothes or designer wear. However, the Home Office can take into account your individual circumstances when deciding whether you can meet your clothing requirements, including:[35]

* whether you can afford to provide clothes for yourself that are suitable for the different weather conditions in the UK;
* whether you have sufficient changes of clothes required for cleanliness; *and*
* whether you have clothes that are suitable for any particular health or other individual needs that you have.

Decisions

Although the Home Office is not required to make a decision on your application for support within any particular time limit, the government intends that it should do so within two working days of receiving your application. However, this target is often missed. If no decision has been made within seven days of making an application, the Home Office should write to you, explaining why there is a delay.[36]

You must respond to any enquiry from the Home Office about your application within five working days. It does not consider your application if you do not complete the form properly or accurately, or if you fail to provide any evidence requested without a reasonable excuse within this period.[37]

While you are waiting for a decision on your application, you should be provided with temporary support.[38] This is provided through the one-stop service, currently run by Migrant Help, and paid for by the Home Office (see p329).

If the Home Office decides to provide you with support, it informs you in writing that your application has been accepted and about the package of support you will receive. Although the Home Office is not required to give you reasons for its decision, the government intention is to give you a written explanation if you are refused all support. The Home Office also gives you details about how you can appeal.[39]

Conditions attached to the support

The Home Office may provide you with support, subject to certain conditions.[40] The regulations do not contain examples of these, but they must be reasonable. The conditions might include, for example, that the accommodation is not sub-let or that noise is kept to a reasonable level in the interests of neighbours, or that you must live at the address the Home Office has provided and inform it of any changes in your circumstances. The conditions must be in writing[41] and given to the person who is being supported.[42]

The Home Office may take into account any previous breach of conditions when deciding whether or not to provide you with support, whether to continue to provide support, and in deciding the level or kind of support to be provided.[43]

Dispersal

The Home Office's general policy is to provide support and accommodation outside London.[44] Under this 'dispersal' policy, most people who are entitled to support are provided with accommodation outside London and the south east of England, unless they can show a strong reason for staying where they currently live – eg, if a child is about to take her/his GCSEs or A levels or a young person is care leaver. It is generally very difficult to succeed in arguing against dispersal (see p367).

Health benefits

If your application for asylum support is accepted, the Home Office should also issue you with a certificate (HC2), enabling you to get free NHS prescriptions, dental treatment, sight tests and wigs. You may also be able to get vouchers towards the cost of glasses and contact lenses. The HC2 certificate itself tells you how to use it and what you can use it for. If you have already paid for any of the above items or for travel to and from hospital for NHS treatment, you may be able to claim the money back.

Change of circumstances

If you are provided with support, you must notify the Home Office of certain relevant changes in your circumstances.[45] These are if you (or any of your dependants):[46]

- are joined in the UK by a dependant;
- receive or obtain access to any money or savings, investments, land, cars or other vehicles, or goods for the purposes of trade or other business, which you have not previously declared;
- become employed or unemployed;
- change your name;
- get married or divorced;
- begin living with another person as if you were married to her/him, or if you separate from a spouse or from a person with whom you have been living as if you were married;
- become pregnant or have a child;
- leave school;
- begin to share your accommodation with another person;
- move to a different address or otherwise leave your accommodation;
- go into hospital;
- go into to prison or some other form of custody;
- leave the UK;
- die.

If there is a relevant change of circumstances, a decision may be made to change the nature or level of the existing support, or to provide or withdraw support for different individuals.

Eviction from accommodation

The usual law on security of tenure does not apply to Home Office accommodation.[47] Tenancies or licences created when Home Office support is provided can come to an end when asylum support is terminated – ie, if:[48]
- your asylum support is suspended or discontinued (see p334) because:
  - there has been a breach of the conditions or a criminal offence;
  - you have concealed financial resources;
  - you have been absent from the address without permission;
  - you have ceased to reside at the address;
- your application for asylum has been determined;
- you are no longer destitute;
- you move to be supported in other accommodation.

In any of the above circumstances, any tenancy or licence is terminated at the end of the period (minimum of seven days) specified in a 'notice to quit' given to you.[49]

Further applications for support

If you are refused support, in most cases you can make a further application at any time and this must be considered by the Home Office. The exception to this is if your support is suspended or terminated because of a breach of its conditions.[50] In this case, the Home Office has the discretion not to accept a new application from you unless there has been a 'material change of circumstances' (see p335)[51] or if there are 'exceptional circumstances'. **Note:** the Home Office has discretion and so a change of circumstances is not always necessary.

3. **Applying for Section 4 support**

The procedure for applying for Section 4 support is very similar to applying for asylum support under s95 of the Immigration and Asylum Act 1999 (see p354). You use the same Form ASF1, which can be obtained from Migrant Help or the government website (www.gov.uk/asylum-support/how-to-claim).

It is crucial to submit all the necessary information and documentation with your application form. If you supply insufficient or ambiguous information, your application will be rejected or the Home Office will write to you requesting more information, which delays the provision of support. There is no interim or emergency support available under Section 4.

The Home Office previously had a target of making a decision on a Section 4 application within two days. In October 2009, this target was removed for people applying for support on the basis that they had submitted a fresh asylum claim. Home Office caseworkers were instructed to delay considering an application for Section 4 support for 15 working days in order to first make a decision on the fresh asylum claim/further submissions. The High Court has found this blanket instruction to be unlawful because it involves a significant risk that human rights will be breached.[52] The Home Office has revised its policy instruction to comply with this judgment. The policy is now to make all decisions on applications for Section 4 support based on further submissions within five working days and, for priority applicants, within two working days.

However, you may still experience significant administrative delays in decision making. Although the Home Office should provide support as soon as your eligibility is established, there are routine delays. Home Office policy is to give accommodation providers five to nine days in which to provide accommodation, but this often takes longer.

Section 4 support for people applying for bail or temporary admission

If you are detained (or were detained) under the Immigration Acts and want to apply for support and an address for bail or temporary admission (see p344), the application form is a very simple four-page form. This is because the destitution test and other detailed criteria do not apply. If you are currently detained by the immigration authorities and have applied to be released or intend to apply for bail, you apply for an accommodation address and support in the expectation of your release.[53] The form should be marked 'Priority A' (as you are detained) and faxed to the Home Office.

If you have already been given temporary admission (see p14), there is no specific application form to use to apply for Section 4 support. You should choose one of the other application forms to complete, but make it clear in a covering letter that you are requesting support under Section 4(1)(a). It appears that, in order for the Secretary of State to use her/his discretion under this section, you must be destitute, and so it may be more convenient to complete Form ASF1 as it includes sections on destitution.

How your application is dealt with

Regional Home Office teams deal with Section 4 applications (see p329). People who applied for asylum before 5 March 2007 are allocated caseowners in regional teams. If you applied for asylum before 5 March 2007 and do not have a caseowner (or are not sure whether you have a caseowner), you should submit your support application to the Section 4 team at the Older Live Cases Unit.

When the Home Office has decided that you should receive Section 4 support and has made the necessary arrangements with an accommodation provider, you are notified of the travel arrangements to the dispersal area (see p367).

Notes

1. Applying for asylum support

1 Reg 3(1) AS Regs
2 Reg 3(2) AS Regs
3 Reg 3(3) AS Regs
4 Reg 3(6) AS Regs
5 See wording of s103 IAA 1999
6 Reg 3(3) AS Regs. See also Form ASF1 on the www.gov.uk website.
7 Form ASF1 guidance notes
8 Reg 3(5) AS Regs

2. Making a decision on your application

9 s95(4) IAA 1999; reg 5(1) AS Regs
10 Reg 7 AS Regs
11 s95(3) IAA 1999
12 s95(5) and (7) IAA 1999; reg 6(4)-(5) AS Regs
13 Form ASF1 guidance notes, 'Cash, savings and assets'
14 Form ASF1 guidance notes, 'Property'
15 Reg 6(6) AS Regs
16 Reg 6(3) AS Regs
17 Home Office policy instruction 'Assessing Destitution: instruction', available at www.gov.uk/government/collections/asylum-support-asylum-instructions
18 Form ASF1 guidance notes, 'Jewellery'
19 s95(5)(a) IAA 1999; reg 8(1)(a)-(b) and (3) AS Regs
20 Reg 8 (2) AS Regs
21 Reg 8(3)(a) AS Regs
22 Reg 8(6)(b) AS Regs. 'District' for these purposes has the same meaning as in s217(3) Housing Act 1996.
23 Reg 8(4) AS Regs
24 Reg 8(3)(b) AS Regs
25 Reg 8(5)(a)-(c) AS Regs
26 Reg 8(3)(g) AS Regs
27 Reg 8(6)(a) AS Regs; Home Office, *Asylum Support Policy Bulletin* 70
28 Although Form ASF1 guidance notes ask for information about people who 'normally stay with you as members of your family'.
29 See Home Office, *Asylum Support Policy Bulletin* 81
30 s95(7)-(8) IAA 1999
31 Reg 9(3)(4) AS Regs
32 Reg 9(5) AS Regs
33 Reg 9(6) AS Regs
34 s95(7)(b) IAA1999; reg 9(1)(2) AS Regs
35 Reg 9(2) AS Regs
36 Form ASF1 guidance notes, 'How Long Will an Application Take'
37 s57 NIAA 2002; reg 3(5A-5B) AS Regs; see also Home Office, *Asylum Support Policy Bulletin* 79
38 s98 IAA 1999
39 Form ASF1 guidance notes, 'What Happens Next?'
40 s95(9) IAA 1999
41 s95(10) IAA 1999
42 s95(11) IAA 1999
43 Reg 19 AS Regs
44 Home Office, *Asylum Support Policy Bulletin* 31
45 Reg 15(1) AS Regs
46 Reg 15(2) AS Regs
47 They are 'excluded tenancies' under s3A (7A) Protection from Eviction Act 1977.
48 Reg 22(2) AS Regs
49 Reg 22(1) AS Regs
50 Reg 21(1) AS Regs
51 Regs 15 and 21(2) AS Regs

3. Applying for Section 4 support

52 *MK and AH (Refugee Action Intervening) v Secretary of State for the Home Department* [2012] EWHC 1896 (Admin)
53 This is the case even though s4(1) refers to an individual who has already been released.

Chapter 23

Payment and accommodation

This chapter covers:
1. Asylum support (below)
2. Contributions and recovery (p370)
3. Section 4 support (p372)

1. Asylum support

If you are a supported asylum seeker, you can be provided with:[1]
- support for your and your dependants' essential living needs;
- accommodation that is adequate for your and your dependants' needs;
- expenses, other than legal expenses, in connection with your asylum application;
- expenses that you or your dependants have in attending bail hearings if you or your dependants are detained for immigration purposes;
- education, English language lessons, sporting or other developmental activities;[2]
- if your circumstances are exceptional, any other form of support that the Home Office thinks is necessary.[3]

Note: the Home Office can disregard any preference you or your dependants have as to how the asylum support is provided or arranged.[4]

When deciding what support to give you, the Home Office takes into account any income, support or assets (see p355) that you or your dependants have, or might reasonably be available to you.[5]

The Home Office may also take into account whether you have complied with any conditions attached to your support (see p334).[6] For example, if you have deliberately damaged any property provided to you, it may take this into account when deciding what further support to provide.[7] The meaning of 'compliance with conditions' is the same as for the purpose of excluding you from support entirely (see p334).[8] When deciding whether to change the level of your support on this basis and, if so, by how much, the Home Office must take into account how serious or trivial the breach of your conditions was.[9] In practice, however, we do not know of any incident where the Home Office has reduced the level of financial support because of a person's past conduct (as opposed to suspending and/or terminating it completely – see p334). Furthermore, in view of the low level of asylum financial support, it is doubtful that it could be reduced without constituting degrading treatment and risking a breach of Article 3 of the European Convention on Human Rights or the European Union (EU) Directive on the reception of asylum seekers. The latter sets out minimum standards for the reception of asylum seekers and is binding on EU member states. It should therefore be considered if you are challenging a refusal of, or the inadequacy of, asylum support.

Support for your essential living needs

If the Home Office decides you need support for your essential living needs, the general rule is that you are provided with cash on a weekly basis.[10]

Amount of support

The weekly amount of support provided from June 2013 is set out in the table below.[11] If your application includes someone in more than one of the categories listed, the amounts are added together to work out the total amount of weekly support.[12] For example, if a couple apply for support for themselves and their 14-year-old daughter, the total value of their support would be £125.48.

Weekly amount	
Couple	£72.52
Lone parent aged 18 or over	£43.94
Single person:	
– aged 25 or over who was granted support and reached 25 before 5 October 2009	£42.62
– aged 18 or over	£36.62
– 16/17-year-old	£39.80
– under 16-year-old	£52.96

There are additional payments of:[13]
- £3 a week for pregnant women;
- £5 a week for babies under one;
- £3 a week for children between the ages of one and three.

The amounts in the above table are reduced if the Home Office provides you with accommodation as part of your support and some provision for your essential living needs is included with it.[14] For example, if you are being provided with bed and breakfast accommodation, the amount of support on p365 is reduced by an amount corresponding to the cost of your breakfasts.

The standard rates of support used to be based on the equivalent of 70 per cent of the applicable amount of income support (IS), without any premiums, to which an adult would otherwise be entitled if s/he qualified for IS and had no other income. See CPAG'S *Welfare Benefits and Tax Credits Handbook* for more details.

The standard weekly rates of asylum support are fixed each year by regulations, which usually take effect from around the beginning of April. Initially, the rates were increased in April every year, but from April 2011 the rates were frozen, meaning a cut in real terms over several years.

In 2013, the charity Refugee Action brought a judicial review challenge against the Home Secretary's decision to freeze the rate of asylum support. The challenge was upheld by the High Court in April 2014, which ruled that the Home Secretary had acted irrationally and failed to take all relevant factors into account, in accordance with her duties under the EU Reception Directive and the Immigration and Asylum Act 1999 to provide for asylum seekers' essential living needs.[15] On 9 August 2014, the Home Secretary reconsidered the level of support in the light of this judgment, but decided it should remain unchanged. This may be subject to further legal challenge.

You collect your financial support on a weekly basis from your local post office using your application registration card. If it is necessary and as a temporary measure, you may be issued with emergency support tokens, which are delivered to your address.

Maternity payment

You may be eligible for a one-off maternity payment of £300.[16] You must apply in writing between one month before the expected birth and two weeks after, enclosing evidence – eg, a birth certificate, Form MAT B1 from your GP or some other original formal evidence. A payment can also be made if you are a supported parent or a parent applying for support and you have a child under three months old who was born outside the UK. It is important to make this application in time. If it is made late it is likely to be refused. The Home Office policy bulletin that allows maternity payments does not say whether or not it is possible to make a late claim, but it may be worth trying if you can give good reasons for the delay.

Backdating support

There is often a delay between applying for support and getting paid. This can be serious if you are without support in the meantime. With social security benefits, regulations normally stipulate the start date of the particular benefit. This is not the case with asylum support as there are no rules in the legislation identifying the date from when support must be provided. It is, therefore, unclear whether you are entitled to support from, for example, the date the Home Office receives your application or the date it makes a decision.

In the absence of legislation stating otherwise, it is arguable that support should be payable from the date the Home Office receives a full and valid claim – ie, an application that shows that you are destitute and eligible for support. This should be the case, no matter what delays are caused by the Home Office or the appeal procedure.

In practice, the Home Office usually only awards support from the date it makes the original decision.

In its *Policy Bulletin* 80 and *Asylum Process Guidance*, the Home Office recognises that awards of Section 95 asylum support should be backdated if there is a delay on the part of the Home Office and the applicant has not caused it.[17] However, these policies relate to missed payments of support after a favourable decision on eligibility has already been made. They do not relate to delays by the Home Office in processing the initial application for support and before a favourable decision has been made.

These written policies also recognise that the First-tier Tribunal (Asylum Support) has the power to award backdated support. See p388 for details.

Accommodation

The majority of applications for asylum and asylum support are made in the south east of England. The Home Office has a strict policy of 'dispersal'.[18] This means that, apart from a few exceptions, the accommodation and support it provides are outside London and south east England.

The Home Office does not own and provide accommodation itself. It makes arrangements with private contractors and local authorities, which provide the support and accommodation throughout the UK.[19] These arrangements, which include transport, are a crucial part of the dispersal scheme.

When deciding the location and nature of the accommodation you are given, the Home Office must consider:[20]

- the fact that you are only being provided with accommodation on a temporary basis until your application for asylum has been dealt with (including any period during which you are appealing);
- the fact that it is desirable to provide accommodation for asylum seekers in areas where there is a good supply of accommodation – eg, outside London, as it is the government's view that there is an acute shortage of accommodation in the London area.[21]

The Home Office does not take into account your preferences on:

- the area in which you would like the accommodation to be located;[22]
- the nature of the accommodation to be provided;[23]
- the nature and standard of the fixtures and fittings in the accommodation.[24]

However, the Home Office may still take into account your individual circumstances if they relate to your accommodation needs.[25] These include:[26]

- your ethnic group and/or religion. Ethnicity is taken into account, although it does not usually prevent dispersal since the Home Office considers asylum dispersal accommodation to be located in areas where there is either an already established ethnic minority community or where one can be sustained.[27] Your freedom to practice religion is also taken into account and, if you can demonstrate that you should be allocated accommodation in an area because it is the only place you can worship, this may be accepted. However, if others of the same religion have been dispersed, the Home Office is likely to consider it possible that you can practise your religion with others in the dispersal area;
- any special dietary needs you or your dependants may have;
- your or your dependants' medical or psychological condition, any disabilities you have and any treatment you are receiving for these.

The Home Office should delay dispersal on medical grounds, pending further medical advice if:[28]

- you are HIV positive or have tuberculosis;
- you have severe mental health problems;
- you are pregnant and four weeks from your expected due date, or you have experienced complications, or you have medical advice against travel, or you are a new mother whose baby is less than four weeks old. You are not expected to travel for longer than four hours to your dispersal accommodation at any point during your pregnancy;
- you are receiving ongoing treatment which is only available in the area where you currently live or which would be hard to replicate elsewhere;
- you are booked to receive invasive surgery within a month, or you are recovering from an operation, or surgery has been booked to take place in more than a month's time but any delay would have an adverse impact on your health;
- delaying dispersal is necessary to arrange continuity of care – eg, if you are undergoing kidney dialysis;
- an infectious and notifiable disease is present or suspected;
- you have been referred to or admitted to secondary care services due to acute need.

The list is not exhaustive, so the Home Office may consider delaying dispersal in other circumstances.

The Home Office did have a policy not to disperse people who were patients of Freedom from Torture (formerly the Medical Foundation for the Care of Victims of Torture) and the Helen Bamber Foundation.[29] However, this policy document has been withdrawn from the Home Office website and its status is currently uncertain.

Note: the Home Office must apply the criteria on p368 when deciding how and where support should be provided, even though a private contractor or local authority makes the actual arrangements.

Expenses in connection with your asylum application

The Home Office may meet some of the expenses connected to your asylum application.[30] These do not include 'legal' expenses – eg, the costs of paying your lawyer to prepare your case and represent you.

Eligible expenses include the cost of preparing and copying documents and travelling to Home Office interviews[31] and may include the cost of:
- sending letters and faxes in order to obtain further evidence;
- medical reports and expert reports on your country of origin;
- your travel expenses (or those of your witnesses) to attend your appeal;
- medical or other examinations in connection with your application.

Note: although the cost of faxes, computer facilities, photocopying and travel expenses are excluded[32] from being 'essential living needs' for the purpose of deciding whether or not you are 'destitute' (see p358),[33] these expenses can be met when providing support.

There is no prescribed way of claiming these expenses (except travel expenses) from the Home Office.[34] In practice, the difficulties and bureaucratic nature of dealing with the Home Office often make the process of claiming overwhelming and uneconomic. In addition, the Home Office is aware that funding from the Legal Aid Agency is available to pay for assessments and reports to support your asylum application.

Although not paid as asylum support, the cost of your fares incurred in travelling to comply with any immigration reporting requirements can be reclaimed from the Home Office if you live more than three miles from the reporting centre.[35] You must claim these at the reporting centre. It is only possible to claim the travel costs for attending your next reporting date (ie, in advance), not the costs already incurred. Some reporting centres are very strict in applying the wording of the guidance. This says that the test is a three-mile 'radius', interpreted as the straight-line distance between the reporting centre and your accommodation, not whether the distance that you must travel is over three miles. The Home Office has, however, been pressed to interpret the guidance more sensibly. The cost of fares can be reclaimed by anyone who has to report. It is not necessary to be in receipt of asylum support.

Services

If you are receiving asylum support, the Home Office may provide the following services:[36]
- education, including English language lessons;
- sporting or other developmental activities.

The Home Office has the power to provide these services, but it is not under a duty to do so. In addition, the services may only be provided in order to 'maintain good order' among supported asylum seekers.[37] This does not mean that 'good order' must have broken down before these services are provided. However, the Home Office must, at least, be able to anticipate that 'good order' is less likely to be maintained without the stimulation of education, language lessons and developmental activities, and general access to, and integration into, the wider community.

2. Contributions and recovery

Contributions to support

When deciding what level of support to give you as a destitute asylum seeker, the Home Office must take into account any income, support and assets that are available (or might reasonably be expected to be available) to you (see p355).[38] However, if you have income and/or assets, it can decide that you should make a contribution to the cost of your support rather than reducing the level of support provided.[39] If this is the case, you are notified of the amount and you must make payments directly to the Home Office.[40] If you are required to make a contribution, the Home Office may also make it a condition of your support that you pay your contributions promptly.[41] In practice, however, we are not aware of any such contributions ever having been required.

Recovery of support

There are four circumstances in which you may be required to repay your asylum support. **Note:** there is no equivalent process of recovery for Section 4 support.

The Home Office may require you to repay your asylum support if:

- you had assets at the time of your application for support that you can now convert into money (see p371). This only applies to asylum support (under Section 95) not to temporary support (under Section 98);[42]
- you have been overpaid support as a result of an error (see p371).[43] This applies to both asylum support (under Section 95) and temporary support (under Section 98);[44]
- you have misrepresented or failed to disclose a 'material fact (see p371). This applies to both asylum support (under Section 95) and temporary support (under Section 98);[45]
- it transpires that you were not destitute.[46]

In addition, the Home Office may try to recover any asylum support provided to you from a person who has sponsored your stay in the UK (see p371).[47]

The Home Office can recover the support through deductions from your existing asylum support[48] or through the civil courts as though it were a debt.[49] Temporary support can only be recovered through the civil courts and not through deductions.[50] In both cases, the Home Office has discretion to waive recovery, even if the relevant conditions are met.[51]

Convertible assets

Apart from any overpayments, the Home Office can require you to repay the value of any asylum support if, at the time of your application for asylum support, you had assets (eg, savings, investments, property or shares) either in the UK or elsewhere that you could not convert into money that is available to you, but you now can (even if you have not done so). [52]

The Home Office cannot require you to repay more than either:[53]

- the total monetary value of all the support provided to you up to the date that it asks you to make a repayment; *or, if it is a lesser amount*
- the total monetary value of the assets which you had at the time of the application for support and which you have since been able to convert into money.

Overpayments of support as a result of an error

The Home Office may require you to repay any temporary support or asylum support that has been provided to you as a result of an 'error' by the Home Office.[54] Unlike recovery of overpayments of most social security benefits, you do not need to have been responsible for the overpayment in any way.

The Home Office may recover the support from you whether or not you are still being supported.[55] It cannot recover more than the total monetary value of the support provided to you as a result of its mistake.[56]

Misrepresentation and failure to disclose

If the Home Office believes that you have received support as a result of a misrepresentation or failure to disclose a material fact, it may apply to a county court (or, in Scotland, the sheriff court) for an order to require the person who made the misrepresentation, or who was responsible for the failure to disclose to repay the support.[57] This means that recovery is possible from people other than you or your dependants. The total amount that the court can order the person to repay is the monetary value of the support paid as a result of the misrepresentation or failure to disclose, which would not have been provided had there not been that misrepresentation or failure to disclose.[58]

Recovery from a sponsor

Support may be recovered from a sponsor of someone who receives asylum support.[59] A **'sponsor'** is a person who has given a written undertaking under the Immigration Rules to be responsible for the maintenance and accommodation of someone seeking to enter or remain in the UK (see p26).[60] This form of recovery is intended to deal with the situation in which someone obtains admission to the UK under a sponsorship agreement in a non-asylum capacity and then seeks to remain in the UK as a refugee and becomes entitled to asylum support during the process. The sponsor is only liable to make payments for the period during which the undertaking was in effect.[61] S/he should not, therefore, be liable for payments for any period of leave given subsequent to the original leave for which the undertaking was given, unless a further undertaking was also given. The sponsor is not liable for payments during any period of residence without leave.

In order to recover, the Home Office must apply to a magistrates' court (or, in Scotland, the sheriff court) for an order. The court may order the sponsor to make weekly payments to the Home Office of an amount which the court thinks is appropriate, taking into account all the circumstances of the case and, in particular, the sponsor's own income.[62] The weekly sum must not be more than the weekly value of the support being provided to the asylum seeker.[63] The court can order that payments be made to cover any period before the time the Home Office applied to the court, but if it does so, it must take into account the sponsor's income during the period concerned rather than her/his current income.[64] The order can be enforced in the same way as a maintenance order.[65]

3. **Section 4 support**

Section 4 support is provided as a package of accommodation and a pre-paid payment card which can be used to obtain food and goods in certain shops. The payment card is often called an 'azure card' because of its colour. The card is held by the failed asylum seeker and credited on a weekly basis with the Section 4 support due.

No cash is paid to you at any stage. Even if additional services are provided (see p373), they are made available by vouchers or the payment card.

Unlike asylum support under Section 95, there are no specific provisions to reduce the value of any support provided under Section 4, to require you to make contributions, or to recover the value of Section 4 support if it has been provided to someone who is not entitled to it.

The value of the payment card

The financial element of Section 4 support is not fixed in the legislation, but is decided by the Secretary of State for the Home Department. When the Section 4 support regulations were made in 2005, the value of the vouchers was set at £35 per individual – ie, for each adult and child. This was even lower than the rate of asylum support under Section 95. This amount has only been increased once since 2005 – in early 2010 it was raised to £35.39 for each member of the household.

If you are a single person, you cannot carry over more than £5 a week on your payment card. Families can carry over their balance, in recognition that they may need to save for particular items. However, if too much balance is accrued, the Home Office may query the family's destitution.[66]

Note: the High Court ruling in April 2014 overturning the Home Secretary's decision to freeze asylum support (see p366) does not apply to Section 4 support.[67] However, it may be arguable that refused asylum seekers who have made a fresh asylum application are covered by the European Union Reception Directive[68] and therefore the rate of Section 4 support should also be reconsidered.

Additional support

There has been severe criticism of the very low level of financial support provide under Section 4 and, in order to comply with a European Directive, the government introduced additional Section 4 support in 2007.[69] This additional support can be claimed by failed asylum seekers (and/or their dependants) in prescribed circumstances. **Note:** this additional support is not provided automatically. You must submit a claim to the Home Office. There is no statutory application form and so, in theory, you could make an oral application. However, the Home Office has issued a particular form, which it requires you to use, and you will find it difficult to persuade the Home Office to provide extra support without using this.[70] An application form for extra support is also included with the new ASF1 application form (see p354).

You can claim additional support:[71]

- for the costs of travel to receive healthcare treatment where a 'qualifying journey' is necessary. A **'qualifying journey'** is a single journey of at least three miles, or of any distance if:
  - you or your child are unable, or virtually unable, to walk up to three miles because of a physical impediment or for some other reason; *or*
  - you have at least one dependant aged under five years; *or*
- for the costs of travel to register a birth;
- to obtain a child's full birth certificate;
- if you are age 18 or over, for telephone calls and letters (ie, stationery and postage) about medical treatment or care and to communicate with:
  - the Home Office;
  - a 'qualified person' – ie, a solicitor, barrister or authorised immigration adviser;
  - a court or tribunal;
  - a voluntary sector partner;
  - a Citizens Advice Bureau;
  - a local authority;
  - an immigration officer;
  - the Secretary of State;
- if you are pregnant (up to £3 a week);

- if have a child under one year (up to £5 a week);
- if have a child between one and five years (up to £3 a week);
- for clothing for a child under 16 years old (up to £5 a week);
- for exceptional specific needs. The Home Office must be satisfied that there is an exceptional need (which may not be met by the above) for travel, telephone calls, stationery and postage, or essential living needs.

There is also a one-off additional payment for pregnant women and new mothers under Section 4, similar to the maternity payment that can be made under Section 95 (see p366). The amount is £250 (£500 if twins) and it is provided as a credit on your payment card. You should apply on the Home Office form 'Provision of Services or Facilities for Section 4 Service Users', with a MAT B1 certificate or birth certificate. You must apply between eight weeks before the expected due date and six weeks after the birth.

Many failed asylum seekers and others in receipt of Section 4 support are required to sign at an immigration reporting centre each week and may be able to reclaim their travel costs (see p14).

Accommodation

If you have friends or family who can provide you with accommodation, but who cannot support you, the Home Office cannot provide you with the financial element of Section 4 unless you occupy Home Office accommodation.[72] You must therefore take up the offer of Home Office accommodation in order to receive payment card credits. In this way, the Section 4 system is fundamentally different to the asylum support system provided under Section 95, in which cash alone can be claimed and provided.

This situation can cause severe hardship and can seem absurd. You may have friends who can provide you with accommodation, companionship and social, psychological and moral support which may be crucial to you and, in this case, it would be substantially less expensive for the government simply to provide you with the payment card without accommodation. You may therefore be left with the stark choice of living with your friends but remaining destitute (with the risk that your friends may then refuse to accommodate you), or being dispersed – possibly far from your friends to a place where you know no one and, if you are a single person, where you may have to share a room with strangers.

The Home Office has split adults (ie, over 18 years old) from their families in this way when they have had separate asylum applications.[73] It is therefore important that you obtain advice from your immigration lawyer on the inclusion of a family member in the asylum claim of another as a dependant.

In the case *R (Kiana and Musgrove) v Secretary of State for the Home Department* in 2010, the High Court found that a refusal to provide support to a refused asylum seeker in a way that allowed him to continue to live with his British partner and child did not breach their right to family life under Article 8 of the European Convention on Human Rights.[74] In this case, the Home Office stated that it would make 'every effort' to house the applicant within a 'reasonable walking distance' of close family members. If you are dispersed to accommodation that is a long distance from your family, you may still be able to challenge the dispersal by judicial review.

Notes

1. Asylum support

1 s96(1) IAA 1999
2 Sch 8 para 4 IAA 1999; reg 14 AS Regs
3 s96(2) IAA 1999
4 s97(7) IAA 1999
5 Reg 12(3) AS Regs
6 Reg 19(1) AS Regs
7 Vandalism is the example given in the IAA 1999 Explanatory Notes, para 284
8 s95(9)-(11) IAA 1999
9 This is because reg 19(1) allows the Secretary of State to take into account the 'extent' to which conditions have been complied with.
10 Reg 10(1)(2) AS Regs
11 Reg 10(2) AS Regs; The Asylum Support (Amendment) (No.2) Regulations 2009, No.1388
12 Further definitions are contained in reg 10(3)(4) AS Regs
13 Reg 10A AS Regs, introduced by The Asylum Support (Amendment) Regulations 2003, No.241; see also Home Office, *Asylum Support Policy Bulletin 78*
14 Reg 10(5) AS Regs
15 *R (Refugee Action) v Secretary of State for the Home Department* [2014] EWHC 1033 (Admin)
16 Home Office, *Asylum Support Policy Bulletin 37*
17 This would be made under s96(2) IAA as an exceptional payment. See Home Office policy instruction, 'Backpayments of Asylum Support', available at www.gov.uk/government/collections/asylum-support-asylum-instructions
18 Home Office, *Asylum Support Policy Bulletin 31*
19 ss94(2) and 99-100 IAA 1999
20 s97(1)(a) IAA 1999
21 IAA 1999, Explanatory Notes, para 303
22 s97(2)(a) IAA 1999
23 Reg 13(2)(a) AS Regs
24 Reg 13(2)(b) AS Regs
25 Reg 13(2) AS Regs
26 Home Office, *Asylum Support Policy Bulletin 31*
27 Home Office, *Asylum Support Policy Bulletin 31*
28 Home Office policy instruction, 'Healthcare needs and pregnancy dispersal: instruction', available at www.gov.uk/government/collections/asylum-support-asylum-instructions
29 Home Office, *Asylum Support Policy Bulletin 19*
30 s96(1)(c) IAA 1999
31 Expressly included in IAA 1999, Explanatory Notes, para 300
32 s95(8) IAA 1999; reg 9(4) AS Regs, but see also s97(5)(6) IAA 1999, which treats such expenses as essential living needs for the specific purposes of limiting the amount of overall expenditure incurred by the Secretary of State to any particular person.
33 s95(3) IAA 1999
34 Home Office, *Asylum Support Policy Bulletin 28*

35 Home Office policy instruction, 'Enforcement Instructions and Guidance', Chapter 22, para 22a.3.3, available at www.gov.uk/government/collections/enforcement-instructions-and-guidance
36 Sch 8 para 4 IAA 1999; reg 14 AS Regs
37 Reg 14(1) AS Regs

2. **Contributions and recovery**

38 Reg 12(3) AS Regs
39 Reg 16(2) AS Regs
40 Reg 16(3) AS Regs
41 Reg 16(4) AS Regs. Conditions may generally be imposed under s95(9)-(12) IAA 1999
42 Reg 17 AS Regs
43 s114 IAA 1999
44 s114(1) IAA 1999
45 ss112 and 114(1) IAA 1999
46 Reg 17A AS Regs
47 s113 IAA 1999
48 Regs 17(4) and 18 AS Regs
49 s114(3) and Sch 8 para 11(2)(a) IAA 1999
50 This is because, despite the general wording of reg 18 AS Regs, s114(4) IAA 1999 only enables the regulations to provide for recovery from support provided under s95, not s98, IAA 1999.
51 Note the word 'may' in s114(2) IAA 1999 and reg 17(2) AS Regs. In particular, in the case of the latter, it is also clear that the Home Office has discretion to recover less than the amount which is, in fact, recoverable. See reg 17(3) AS Regs.
52 Sch 8 para 11 IAA 1999; reg 17(1) AS Regs. Note that it is unclear whether the Home Office can require a person who is no longer being supported to repay the value of the support. There is no equivalent wording in para 11 or reg 17 to that effect in s114(2) IAA 1999, which expressly refers to both those who are, and those who have ceased to be, supported persons for the purposes of recovery as result of Home Office errors.
53 Reg 17(2)(3)(5) AS Regs
54 s114(1) IAA 1999; see Home Office, *Asylum Support Policy Bulletin* 67
55 s114(2) IAA 1999
56 s114(2) IAA 1999
57 s112 IAA 1999
58 s112(2)(3) IAA 1999
59 s113 IAA 1999
60 s113(1)(a) IAA 1999
61 s113(1)(b) IAA 1999
62 s113(3) IAA 1999
63 s113(4) IAA 1999
64 s113(5) IAA 1999
65 s113(6) IAA 1999

3. **Section 4 support**

66 For further information about payment card conditions, see www.gov.uk/government/uploads/system/uploads/attachment_data/file/258358/vouchers.pdf
67 *R (Refugee Action) v Secretary of State for the Home Department* [2014] EWHC 1033 (Admin)
68 *R (ZO (Somalia) and others) v Secretary of State for the Home Department* [2010] UKSC 36
69 The Immigration and Asylum (Provision of Services or Facilities to Failed Asylum Seekers) Regulations 2007, No.3627
70 The form should be available from Migrant Help and can also be downloaded from www.gov.uk/government/publications/application-for-section-4-extra-services-or-facilities
71 Home Office policy instruction, 'Section 4: additional services or facilities under the 2007 regulations', available at *www.gov.uk/government/uploads/system/uploads/attachment_data/file/333049/Section_4_Additional_Services.pdf*
72 *R (Kiana and Musgrove) v Secretary of State for the Home Department* [2010] EWHC 1002 (Admin); *MK v Secretary of State for the Home Department* [2011] All ER(D) 158 (CA); s4(1) and (2) IAA 1999
73 However see Home Office, *Asylum Support Policy Bulletin* 83
74 *R (Kiana and Musgrove) v Secretary of State for the Home Department* [2010] EWHC 1002 (Admin)

Chapter 24

···

Appeals

This chapter covers:
1. Introduction (below)
2. The right to appeal (p378)
3. How to appeal (p378)
4. Decisions the First-tier Tribunal can make (p387)

---

1. **Introduction**

If you are dissatisfied with a decision made by the Home Office about asylum support or Section 4 support, you may be able to appeal to the First-tier Tribunal (Asylum Support).

Before 3 November 2008, appeals were made to the Asylum Support Tribunal in Croydon. On 3 November 2008, a new unified tribunal system was created, consisting of a First-tier Tribunal and an Upper Tribunal. The appeal functions of most existing tribunals in the UK were transferred to this new structure and assigned to 'chambers' according to subject matter. The Asylum Support Tribunal became the First-tier Tribunal (Asylum Support), which is part of the Social Entitlement Chamber. Since September 2009, it sits in East London.

Although the Upper Tribunal deals with appeals from some tribunals, this is not the case with appeals from the First-tier Tribunal (Asylum Support). Thus, a decision of the First-tier Tribunal can only be legally challenged by judicial review. This was previously the case with the Asylum Support Tribunal. The First-tier Tribunal (Asylum Support) does have a very limited power to 'set aside' some of it own decisions (see p389).

The Tribunal Procedure (First-tier Tribunal) (Social Entitlement Chamber) Rules 2008 (referred to as the 'tribunal rules' in this chapter) contain the rules for appeals in the Social Entitlement Chamber.[1] Most of these are common to all tribunals in the Social Entitlement Chamber, but a few refer solely to the First-tier Tribunal (Asylum Support).

In all asylum support appeals, a single judge considers the appeal and makes the decisions. Tribunal judges have no power to make an order relating to the parties' costs, so even if you lose your appeal, you cannot be ordered to pay any legal costs to the Home Office or to the First-tier Tribunal.

Note: in this chapter we refer to the First-tier Tribunal (Asylum Support) as the First-tier Tribunal.

2. **The right to appeal**

The circumstances in which you have the right to appeal to the First-tier Tribunal are limited. You can only appeal if you have been refused support by the Home Office or your support has been stopped – ie:[2]

- you have applied for asylum support under Section 95 or Section 4 and it has been refused; *or*
- your support under Section 95 has been stopped for a reason other than because you have ceased to be an asylum seeker (unless the Home Office has made a mistake and you are still an asylum seeker);[3] *or*
- your support under Section 4 is stopped for any reason.

Any other Home Office decision about your asylum support (such as the level of support or the place of dispersal) or *any* decision about temporary support can only be challenged by judicial review. In addition, it is not possible to appeal a decision refusing you support if the reason for the refusal is that:

- you failed to provide complete or accurate information in connection with your application;[4] *or*
- you failed to co-operate with enquiries made in respect of the support application;[5] *or*
- you did not make your application for asylum as soon as reasonably possible.[6]

These decisions must be challenged by judicial review, although the Home Office reconsiders an application if missing information is later provided.

3. **How to appeal**

Time limits

The tribunal rules set out a timetable for appeals to the First-tier Tribunal, a summary of which is set out on p379.[7]

Day	Event
Day one	Notice of appealable decision is received by you.
Day four (latest)	Notice of appeal must be received by the First-tier Tribunal. Delivery of a notice of appeal at any time up to midnight on the relevant day is sufficient. If not lodged in time, you must apply for an extension of time (see p382).
Day four or day five	First-tier Tribunal faxes notice of appeal to the Home Office.
Day seven (latest)	Home Office sends its response and documentation to the First-tier Tribunal by fax/hand, and to you by first-class post or by hand.
Day seven or thereafter 'with the minimum of delay'	First-tier Tribunal judge decides whether to hold an oral hearing and: – if no oral hearing is to be held, determines the appeal and sends a notice of the decision and a statement of reasons for the decision to you and the Home Office; *or* – fixes the hearing date for the oral hearing, giving both parties one to five days' notice. It is likely that, at the same time, directions are given. If the judge believes the appeal should be 'struck out' (eg, if the First-tier Tribunal does not have jurisdiction), s/he must give you an opportunity to make representations. It is likely that a hearing date is arranged to consider striking out and the full hearing follows immediately if the appeal is not struck out.
Day nine or thereafter 'with the minimum of delay'	Oral hearing held. The First-tier Tribunal judge notifies the decision to you and the Home Office at the end of the hearing or, if not present, sends a decision notice.
Within three days after an oral hearing	First-tier Tribunal judge sends a statement of reasons for the decision to you and the Home Office.

Appeals to the First-tier Tribunal should be processed with the minimum of delay.[8] Before November 2008 under the previous rules, an appeal had to be listed for hearing within eight days of the Asylum Support Tribunal receiving the appeal notice. Since this date, however, there is no fixed time within which the hearing must take place. As asylum seekers are arguing that they are destitute and so require support immediately (and bearing in mind that if support has been refused, no interim support pending an appeal is available), the First-tier Tribunal usually lists oral hearings close to the previous timescale because of the requirement to have minimum delay and to avoid any breach of human rights under Article 3 (prohibition of inhumane and degrading treatment) of the European Convention on Human Rights.

All notices or documents must be sent to the First-tier Tribunal by post, fax or given by hand unless it agrees otherwise – eg, if it agrees to receive information by email.[9]

If a time limit expires on a non-working day (Saturday, Sunday and bank holidays), it is treated as expiring on the next working day.[10]

Representation

You may be represented throughout the appeal procedure by a representative of your choice. S/he does not have to be legally qualified.[11] If you are represented, the name and address of your representative must be given in writing to the First-tier Tribunal.[12] This can be done by including the details in the appeal notice (see below). An adviser should *not* state that s/he is your representative if s/he is simply helping you to complete and submit the appeal form and perhaps acting as a mail box for you. In these circumstances, s/he should write on the form that this is the limit of her/his involvement.

It is generally understood that 'representation' implies an ongoing responsibility for the prompt conduct of all stages of the appeal including:

- securing and preparing all available relevant evidence and submitting it to the First-tier Tribunal;
- dealing with all correspondence with the First-tier Tribunal and the Home Office;
- responding in writing to the directions given by the First-tier Tribunal;
- advising you on each of these steps and at every stage;
- representing you or arranging for a legal adviser to represent you at the First-tier Tribunal;
- advising you on the outcome of the appeal and on any steps to be taken – eg, to secure support if the appeal has been successful or any further challenge (eg, by judicial review) if the appeal was unsuccessful.

If you state that you have a representative, the First-tier Tribunal must give her/his details to the Home Office. Any documents that the Home Office is required to serve must be served on the representative (and need not be served on you).[13] Anyone else who accompanies you to the appeal hearing cannot assist in presenting your case without the First-tier Tribunal's approval.[14]

Advice through legal aid may be available in asylum support cases if you are at risk of homelessness, but it is not available for representation in First-tier Tribunal hearings.[15] **Note:** at the time of writing, the Ministry of Justice was consulting on removing access to legal aid for anyone who has not been 'lawfully resident' in the UK for at least one year, with exemptions for asylum seekers and newly recognised refugees, but not for failed asylum seekers.

The Asylum Support Appeals Project (ASAP) aims to attend the First-tier Tribunal, Monday to Friday, to provide free representation and advice to as many people as possible (see Appendix 2). This service is provided by volunteer solicitors and barristers. The Tribunal judge might not allow ASAP to represent you, however, if the notice of appeal says that you are 'represented' by solicitors in the appeal, even if they never intended to attend the hearing.

Notice of appeal

If the Home Office refuses your application for support or terminates your support, it gives you a written decision with reasons. It also informs you in the decision letter whether you have a right of appeal and, if so, provides an appeal form. You can also get an appeal form from the First-tier Tribunal website at www.justice.gov.uk/forms/hmcts/asylum-support. The notice of appeal must be on this prescribed form.[16]

The Home Office does not always get this right. So if you want to appeal, but the Home Office says you do not have the right to appeal, you should seek legal advice immediately.

The notice of appeal must be completed in English or in Welsh.[17]

You must state the grounds for your appeal (ie, why you disagree with the Home Office's decision) and include a copy of the decision you are appealing against. If the appeal notice does not include all the necessary information and/or is not accompanied by the written Home Office decision, the First-tier Tribunal does not accept it and any later attempt to appeal may be out of time.

If you have any further information or evidence which relates to your application for support or your appeal, you should (if possible) send copies of the relevant documents to the First-Tier Tribunal with the notice of appeal.[18] However, you should not delay submitting your appeal in order to get any further evidence – this can be faxed to the First-tier Tribunal later. It is very important that you provide the First-Tier Tribunal with any evidence that proves you are entitled to support. For example, if the Home Office does not accept that you are destitute, you may have to provide letters from someone who has been providing you with support, but who cannot continue to do so, or from a voluntary agency who knows your situation.

The notice of appeal asks whether you want to attend or be represented at an oral hearing or whether you are content for the appeal to be decided on the papers submitted to the First-Tier Tribunal. An appeal can be decided on the papers without a hearing if both sides consent and the First-tier Tribunal believes it can make a decision without a hearing.[19] Even if you ask for a paper appeal without an oral hearing, the First-Tier Tribunal may still hold an oral hearing if there are issues to be explored that are raised, but not explained, in the papers (see p384). It is usually advisable to attend the hearing in person (the Home Office arranges and pays your fares and overnight accommodation in London for you, your dependants and any witnesses if necessary – see p384). The First-tier Tribunal judge is likely to understand your appeal much better if you are present to explain your situation. In 'mixed households' (ie, if your partner is a British national or has leave to remain and is in receipt of state benefits), it is usually important for her/him to attend the appeal in order to be able to give full details of her/his benefits (with documentary evidence) and to explain why s/he cannot support you.

If you might find it difficult to travel to the hearing (eg, because of medical problems, pregnancy or lack of childcare), you can request for it to be heard by videolink. If the Tribunal approves, you attend the hearing from a court in your local area, with a video line linking you to the Tribunal in London, where the interpreter, Home Office representative and judge attend.

In the notice of appeal you must also state whether you will need an interpreter at the hearing and, if so, in what language and dialect. If you have any difficulties with the English language you should ask for an interpreter. If required, an interpreter is supplied by HM Courts and Tribunals Service.

Once you have completed the appeal form, you[20] (or your representative[21]) must sign it.

You must send your notice of appeal to the First-Tier Tribunal so that it is received by it within three days after the day on which you received the notice of the decision.[22] If you receive the Home Office's decision letter more than two days after the date it was written, it is advisable to state in your appeal the date on which you received it to show that you are not (or not fully) responsible for any delay. You can submit it to the First-tier Tribunal by fax – the number is on the appeal form.

Extending the time limits

If you do not appeal in time, you should ask the First-Tier Tribunal in the notice of appeal to extend the time limit.[23] You should explain why you could not appeal earlier – eg, if you were ill and incapable of dealing with your affairs at the time you received the notice, or you needed advice. The First-tier Tribunal judges recognise that the usual time limit to appeal is very short, and an extension of a two or three days, or longer, is often granted, especially for destitute people who may not speak English and may be relying for advice on an advice agency that is only open during certain hours. As with all decisions, the judge must consider your application fairly and justly, including why you (or your representative) could not comply with the time limit.

If the First-tier Tribunal refuses to extend the time limit, your only alternative is to seek a judicial review of the Home Office decision and/or of the decision of the First-tier Tribunal to refuse to give you more time.[24]

Striking out an appeal

The First-tier Tribunal has the power to decide that your appeal cannot continue, even before a hearing takes place. This is called 'striking out' your appeal. The First-tier Tribunal must strike out your appeal if it does not have jurisdiction to decide the matter – eg, it cannot consider an appeal about how much money the Home Office should pay you each week in asylum support.[25] The First-tier Tribunal may also strike out your appeal without a hearing if it considers your case has no reasonable prospect of success.[26]

In either case, before striking out your appeal, the First-tier Tribunal must give you the opportunity to make representations. It may direct you to make these in writing by a certain deadline, following which a decision is made by the judge 'on the papers'. Alternatively, the Tribunal may fix a date for you and the Home Office to attend to make any representations and, if the appeal is not struck out, the appeal then proceeds to a full hearing on the same day.

Response from the Home Office

On the same day as the First-tier Tribunal receives your notice of appeal or, if not reasonably practicable, as soon as possible on the next day, it must fax to the Home Office a copy of your notice of appeal and any supporting documents that you sent with your appeal form.[27]

By the third day after the notice of appeal is received by the First-tier Tribunal, the Home Office must ensure that the First-tier Tribunal receives:[28]

- a statement saying whether or not the Home Office opposes the appeal;
- a copy of the decision letter refusing or withdrawing support;
- any other evidence that the Home Office took into account when refusing you support;
- any other grounds and reasons for the decision that have not been included in the decision letter;
- copies of all documents the Home Office has that are relevant to the case.

At the same time, the Home Office must provide you (or your representative) with a copy of all the above information and documents.[29]

This is commonly referred to as the Tribunal 'bundle'. It is important that you receive a copy of the bundle before the hearing so that you are aware of all the evidence in the appeal. If you or your representative have not received the bundle on time, you should alert the Tribunal and/or contact the Home Office.

The hearing

Paper hearings

After it receives the Home Office's response, the First-tier Tribunal judge must consider all the documents and decide whether it is necessary to hold an oral hearing, or whether the appeal can be determined simply by considering the papers. The First-tier Tribunal can only decide the appeal without a hearing if both parties agree, but it can decide that an oral hearing is necessary even if you ask for a paper appeal.

You may have stated on the notice of appeal form that you did not want an oral hearing, but may not have been aware of all of the information or evidence relied on by the Home Office until after you lodged your appeal – eg, new papers might subsequently be disclosed to you by the Home Office or the First-tier Tribunal. If, having seen any new material, you change your mind and decide that you want an oral hearing in order to make direct representations to the First-tier Tribunal, you should notify the Tribunal as soon as possible by fax or telephone. The judge must then take this into account when deciding whether to grant an oral hearing. If you want to make written representations to the First-tier Tribunal about this further evidence, you should do so as soon as possible.

Decisions

In all cases, the First-tier Tribunal must make a decision with minimum delay.[30] If no oral hearing is required, the First-tier Tribunal judge proceeds to decide the appeal. S/he must send a copy of the decision notice, together with the written statement of reasons for the decision, to both parties on the same day as the appeal is decided.[31]

Oral hearings

Hearing date

If an oral hearing is necessary, the First-tier Tribunal must promptly inform the parties of the time and date. Since 3 November 2008, there has been no set time within which the First-tier Tribunal must hear an appeal. Nevertheless, because of the desperate situation of many destitute asylum seekers, it is likely that the hearing will take place within 11 days or so of the First-tier Tribunal receiving the notice of appeal.

Directions

When sending out the notice of a hearing date, the First-tier Tribunal usually also sends 'directions' to both you and the Home Office – eg, to produce further evidence.[32] This may include evidence of your destitution, medical evidence or copies of a previous asylum determination. If possible, these documents should be faxed to the First-tier Tribunal before the hearing. Even if you do not have the time and opportunity to fax them, you should take the relevant documents to the appeal hearing. It is very important to comply with any directions, because if you do not, the First-tier Tribunal may not have all the evidence needed to make a decision on your appeal. If an agency or solicitor has helped you complete the appeal form, the directions may be sent to her/him, so it is important to keep in close and regular contact to check that the directions have been received and whether the adviser/solicitor can help you respond.

Further evidence

If you decide that you want to submit more evidence in support of your appeal which you did not send with your notice of appeal, you may still send it to the First-tier Tribunal to be considered. In particular, you may wish to rely on evidence which shows a change in your circumstances after the date of the Home Office decision or which has only now come into your possession. You should send this evidence to the First-tier Tribunal judge before the time for her/him to determine the appeal. You should do this immediately and by fax if possible, especially if no oral hearing is to be held, as the First-tier Tribunal will determine the appeal very quickly.

You should also send a copy of this further evidence to the Home Office.[33] Although the tribunal rules no longer require you to do so, the First-tier Tribunal judge will want to ensure that the Home Office has seen the further evidence. There is even the (very unlikely) risk that the judge will refuse to allow evidence that is provided late and which has not been seen by the Home Office.[34]

In any event, you should take copies of all the appeal papers, including your evidence and the Home Office's documents and any new evidence, to the appeal hearing as you may need to refer to them. You should also ensure, at the start of the hearing, that none of the papers have gone astray and that the judge has all your evidence.

The Home Office can also send further evidence to the First-tier Tribunal before the appeal is determined. It is likely that the Home Office and/or the First-tier Tribunal will send copies to you (or your representative) or, if there is not sufficient time, provide you with copies at the hearing. In any event, you must be provided with copies of any documents on which the Home Office intends to rely at the hearing and you must have time to consider them.

Travel to the hearing

You are usually sent tickets for your travel to and from the First-tier Tribunal, and overnight accommodation is arranged and paid for by the Home Office if you live some distance away.[35] If tickets are not sent, a travel warrant can be requested from the Home Office travel bureau.[36] The Home Office should also provide tickets for dependants and witnesses, if requested.

The hearing

In principle, oral hearings before the First-tier Tribunal take place in public, but it is extremely rare for the public to attend.[37] The First-tier Tribunal judge can decide that a hearing, or part of it, should be in private and can exclude anyone who is likely to cause a disruption or defeat the purpose of the hearing. In practice, judges politely check who is in the hearing room in order to ensure that there is no one present who may intimidate you or otherwise hinder a fair hearing. If, for any reason, you think that someone should be excluded from the hearing, you should tell the First-tier Tribunal either before or at the start of the hearing.

As there are no rules setting out the procedure which must be adopted at the oral hearing, this is decided by the First-tier Tribunal judge.[38] S/he should explain the procedure to you at the outset. There are no strict rules on evidence, and so hearsay and letters from third parties can be considered. You can provide oral evidence, call any witnesses to give oral evidence in support of your case and question any Home Office witnesses. You or your representative must also have the opportunity of directly addressing the First-tier Tribunal about the decision it should make and commenting on all of the evidence, documentary or oral. If witnesses are called, they may be required to give their evidence under oath or affirmation.[39]

If you have any evidence which has not been presented to the Home Office or to the First-tier Tribunal before the appeal, you should take it to the hearing. If either you or the Home Office attend the hearing with further evidence which has not previously been provided, the other party must be given the opportunity to photocopy and look at it in order to comment on it before the hearing proceeds. The judge has the power to exclude evidence that was not provided in the time allowed by an earlier direction given by the First-tier Tribunal. This is very unlikely to happen if you have acted as promptly as can be expected – the power to exclude evidence is more likely to be applied to the Home Office, which has experience and resources, and should be expected to respect the First-tier Tribunal's directions.

If possible, take notes of what is said at the hearing. It is usual for the judge to make her/his own written record. If you later want to challenge the decision by judicial review, you can request a copy of this.

If you do not arrive at the hearing in time, it may go ahead without you (or in the absence of a Home Office representative) if the judge:[40]

- is satisfied that you/the Home Office have been notified of the hearing or that reasonable steps have been taken to notify you/the Home Office of the hearing; *and*
- considers that it is in the interests of justice to proceed.

Decisions

At the end of the hearing, the judge must tell you and the Home Office representative the decision that has been reached.[41] The judge may retire for a period in order to consider the decision before telling you the outcome.

The judge must give reasons for her/his decision in writing. S/he must provide both parties with a 'decision notice' (ie, without reasons) at the end of the hearing.[42] This simply states whether the appeal has been allowed, dismissed or remitted (see p387). The notice is also sent on the same day to any party (ie, you or the Home Office) who was not present at the hearing of the appeal. In addition, whether or not you were at the hearing, the judge must send a statement containing the reasons for her/his decision to both parties within three working days of the hearing.[43]

4. **Decisions the First-tier Tribunal can make**

When deciding the appeal, the First-tier Tribunal judge can:[44]

- substitute her/his own decision for the decision made by the Home Office and thus allow the appeal, meaning you are entitled to support; *or*
- dismiss the appeal, so that the decision of the Home Office stands; *or*
- require the Home Office to reconsider the matter. The First-tier Tribunal calls this 'remitting' the appeal (see below).

The effect of remitting a decision is to set aside the decision of the Home Office. This requires the Home Office to reconsider and come to a new decision on whether you should be provided with support. This puts you back into the position you were in before the decision was made. So if you had been receiving support and the Home Office's decision to withdraw your support is remitted by the First-tier Tribunal, the Home Office must immediately reinstate the support until it comes to a new decision. If you were previously without support and are appealing the Home Office's decision to refuse your application, a First-tier Tribunal decision to remit that refusal decision leaves you in your previous position of being without support, at least until the Home Office comes to a new decision.[45]

Cases come before the First-tier Tribunal in which people are not sure of their immigration status or it has changed since an appeal has been lodged. It may become apparent at the hearing that you have applied for the wrong form of support – eg, the Tribunal may find that you are eligible for Section 95 support as an asylum seeker, although you have applied for support under Section 4 as a failed asylum seeker. Previously, the practice of the Tribunal in such cases was to dismiss the appeal, suggesting that you reapply on the correct form. However, in 2011, the Home Office introduced a combined form for Section 95 and Section 4 support, called the ASF1 (see p354). Since then, some judges have been willing to grant Section 95 support where eligibility is clear, even though the person also filled in the sections relating to Section 4 support, and vice versa.

First-tier Tribunal judges decide issues of fact on a balance of probabilities. This simply means deciding which facts in your case are more likely than not to be true. In appeals against a *refusal* of an application for support, it is up to you to prove, on a balance of probabilities, that you are entitled to support and meet the relevant criteria. If you are appealing a decision to *withdraw* support, it is up to the Home Office to establish, on the balance of probabilities, that the support should be terminated.

Under the previous tribunal rules for the Asylum Support Tribunal (see p377), when reaching a decision, the Tribunal was specifically able to take into account any change of circumstances that took place between the date on which the decision of the Home Office was made and the date of the determination of the appeal.[46] This has remained the practice of the First-tier Tribunal, even though it is not expressly provided for in the rules.

A decision on an appeal by the First-tier Tribunal is legally binding and, if the appeal is allowed, the Home Office is obliged to provide support on that day.

If your appeal is successful, you may be left with a difficult choice. The Home Office offers 'emergency' accommodation situated in south east London while you wait to be allocated 'dispersal' accommodation elsewhere in the UK. This emergency accommodation can be requested from the Home Office representative at the hearing or, if the Home Office did not attend your hearing, you can ask the Tribunal clerk to put you in contact with the representative on duty that day. The accommodation is offered on condition that you stay there on the night of your appeal. If you are then allocated accommodation in a different part of the UK to where you were previously living, the Home Office does not provide travel costs to allow you to go back and collect any belongings.

Alternatively, after the hearing, you can return to the town in which you were living, using the return ticket provided by the Home Office. The Home Office should then contact you directly, or through your advice agency, to arrange your accommodation. This usually takes several days to arrange, in some cases even longer, during which time you may be left homeless. You are given travel tickets to get to your new accommodation. This option is therefore more appropriate if you need to collect belongings and you have somewhere to stay in the short term.

This arrangement is clearly unsatisfactory, particularly if you are street homeless but have left belongings (eg, medication) in the town where you were sleeping. If there is any delay by the Home Office in providing Section 4 or Section 95 support immediately after a successful appeal, it is acting unlawfully and should be challenged in judicial review proceedings.

Backdating support

There are two situations in which you may you may want to ask the First-tier Tribunal to backdate support if your appeal is successful. These are if:

- the Home Office has granted support, but its decision was delayed and it has refused to backdate the support to the date of your claim; or
- the First-tier Tribunal allows an appeal against a refusal of support.

The Home Office refuses to backdate support

It is generally presumed that a refusal by the Home Office to provide backdated support cannot be appealed to the First-tier Tribunal (and we are not aware of any such appeal having been made). This may be because you can only appeal against:[47]

- a decision that you do not qualify for support; or
- a decision to withdraw support.

It is accepted that this does not allow for an appeal against the actual amount of an award. However, this does not mean that you cannot appeal against the date used to calculate the commencement of support. If an appeal to the First-tier Tribunal is not possible on this point, it would mean that any decision granting support but refusing (or restricting) backdating could only be challenged by judicial review proceedings, which are cumbersome and relatively expensive in an individual case.

However, there is a good argument that a decision by the Home Office not to pay backdated support is, in fact, a decision that 'the applicant does not qualify for support' for the relevant period and so falls within the appeal jurisdiction of the First-tier Tribunal. Thus, it appears that an appeal could be made to the First-tier Tribunal to decide the date from which you qualify for support.

The First-tier Tribunal has allowed an appeal

It is extremely rare for the First-tier Tribunal to state in its decision that a successful appellant should receive support backdated to before the hearing. However, this is because backdated support is rarely asked for.

Section 103(5) of the Immigration and Asylum Act 1999 specifies the powers of the First-tier Tribunal judge and states that s/he may substitute her/his decision for the decision against which the appeal is brought. This means that the judge has the same decision-making powers as the Home Office had in arriving at the original decision. So if the Home Office can backdate an award, a First-tier Tribunal judge can award backdated support.

It is therefore hoped that more requests will be made to the First-tier Tribunal for backdated support – ie, to state in its decision that the date from when the successful appellant qualifies for support is the day the Home Office received a full and valid application for support.

Note: it is not possible ask for a backdated award of Section 4 support, because support is provided 'in kind' – ie, through the azure payment card.

After the hearing

There is no right of appeal against the decision of the First-tier Tribunal. If you are dissatisfied with the decision, in limited circumstances you can ask the Tribunal to set it aside (see below).[48] Otherwise, the only way of challenging the decision is by judicial review.

Setting aside a decision

The First-tier Tribunal can only set aside its own decision and make a new decision (or set aside and remake part of a decision) if:[49]

- it was a decision 'disposing of the proceedings' – ie, a final decision or a decision to strike out the appeal; *and*
  - a document relating to the proceedings was not sent or was not received at an appropriate time by either party or her/his representative; *or*

- a document relating to the proceedings was not sent to the First-tier Tribunal at an appropriate time; *or*
- a party or representative was not present at a hearing; *or*
- there has been some other procedural irregularity in the proceedings; *and*
- the First-tier Tribunal considers that it is in the interests of justice to do so.

You cannot, therefore ask the First-tier Tribunal to set aside a decision simply because you do not agree with it. Remember that, even if one of these conditions does apply, the First-tier Tribunal may still decide that it is not in the interests of justice to set aside the decision. For example, even if you did not receive a relevant document at the appropriate time, it may still consider that this did not make any difference to the decision that was eventually made, and so it is not in the interests of justice to set it aside.

If you wish to apply to set aside a decision, your application must be in writing and received by the First-tier Tribunal no later than one month after the date on which it sent the decision to you.[50]

Judicial review

Judicial review is consideration by a judge in the High Court of the lawfulness of a decision of a public body, including a decision of the First-tier Tribunal. There must be an error in law for a judicial review application to succeed – it is not enough that you do not agree with the decision the judge made (unless you can clearly show that no reasonable tribunal could have come to that decision). To be successful in judicial review proceedings, you will need help from a solicitor, as it is a very legalistic procedure.

An application for judicial review must be made promptly and, in any event, within three months of the decision complained of. It must be in writing, laying out the facts and legal arguments, and be accompanied by copies of all relevant documents.

You must get the permission of a High Court judge to take judicial review proceedings. A judge looks at the papers you lodge to see if there is an arguable point of law and, if not, refuses you permission to proceed. In any event, a judge has a discretion to refuse you permission (or to reject your case at the full hearing) if s/he does not think an order should be made. If you think judicial review might be appropriate in your case, you should immediately seek legal advice.

Decision to remit

If the First-tier Tribunal decides to remit the matter (see p387) and the Home Office then makes a new decision refusing you support, you may appeal again to the First-tier Tribunal against the new decision.

Making a new application for support

Following an unsuccessful appeal, the Home Office cannot consider any further application for support from you, whether under Section 4 or Section 95, unless it is satisfied that there has been a 'material change' of circumstances between the time of the appeal and the new application. A 'material change' is defined and includes a long list of events – eg, if you change your address or separate from your partner. However, if you are destitute and believe that your application or appeal may now be successful, you should reapply. The Home Office and Tribunal will want to see evidence that your situation has got worse since the last decision.

Withdrawing the appeal

If, at any stage before the hearing, you decide you do not wish to carry on with your appeal, you can give written notice of withdrawal.[51] If the withdrawal is made on the day of the hearing, the consent of the judge is required. The rules do not specify the effect of serving this notice, but it is clear that if *you* withdraw your appeal, the proceedings come to an end because they were instigated by, and based on, your notice of appeal.

If the Home Office wants to withdraw the appeal, the procedure differs, depending on when the notice is delivered. If the Home Office serves a notice of withdrawal before 12 noon on the day before the hearing, the First-tier Tribunal treats this as concluding the appeal proceedings, leaving the Home Office to make a fresh decision. There is no guarantee that the new decision will be to grant support. This may mean that you must appeal again to the First tier Tribunal against a new decision letter, further delaying the final decision on whether you are eligible for support. If this happens, consider making a complaint to the Home Office. It may also be possible to challenge this approach by judicial review.

If the withdrawal is made after 12 noon on the day before the hearing, the Home Office must make its application in the hearing itself. The judge only consents to the withdrawal if:[52]

* the Home Office confirms in writing that the decision under appeal is being withdrawn and you are to be granted support immediately; *or*
* the Home Office serves you with a copy of a fresh decision letter, and you or your representative agree that the hearing can proceed on the basis of this new decision; *or*
* both parties agree to adjourn the proceedings (for no longer than 14 days) and the Home Office confirms in writing that you will be provided with support in the meantime.

Notes

1. Introduction
1 TP(FT) Rules

2. The right to appeal
2 s103(1)-(3) IAA 1999
3 s103(2) IAA 1999. Note that the legislation provides a right of appeal where a decision is made to stop providing support 'before that support would otherwise have come to an end'. The wording is ambiguous, but the intention is to allow a right of appeal in any case where support is terminated before the asylum seeker has ceased to be an asylum seeker for support purposes. See IAA 1999, Explanatory Notes, para 317.
4 s57 NIAA 2002
5 s57 NIAA 2002
6 s55 NIAA 2002

3. How to appeal
7 rr22(2)(a) and (7)(a), 24(1)(a), 29, 33 and 34 TP(FT) Rules
8 s104(3) IAA 1999 requires the appeal regulations to provide for this.
9 r13(1) TP(FT) Rules
10 r12(2) and (3) TP(FT) Rules
11 r11(1) TP(FT) Rules. Note also that asylum support law is not immigration law and so an adviser does not have to be registered with the Office of the Immigration Services Commissioner.
12 r11(2) TP(FT) Rules
13 r11(6a) TP(FT) Rules
14 r11(7) TP(FT) Rules
15 Sch 1 Part 1, para 31 Legal Aid, Sentencing and Punishment of Offenders Act 2012
16 Practice Direction, Social Entitlement Chamber, First-tier Tribunal Asylum Support Cases, 30 October 2008
17 r22(3) TP(FT) Rules
18 The standard appeal form itself indicates this.
19 r27(1) TP(FT) Rules
20 r22(3) TP(FT) Rules
21 r11(5) TP(FT) Rules
22 r22(2)(a) TP(FT) Rules
23 rr5(3)(a) and 22(6) TP(FT) Rules

24 Note that, in judicial review proceedings, the court may refuse to interfere with the decision you wish to challenge if you have failed to exercise a right of appeal.
25 r8(2) TP(FT) Rules
26 r8(3) TP(FT) Rules
27 r22(7)(a) TP(FT) Rules
28 r24(2) and (4) TP(FT) Rules
29 r24(5) TP(FT) Rules
30 s104(3) IAA 1999
31 s103(4) IAA 1999; r34(1)(b) TP(FT) Rules
32 r15 TP(FT) Rules
33 This used to be the case under r8(1)(2) ASA(P) Rules
34 r15(2)(b)(1) TP(FT) Rules
35 Since late 2008, in response to representations made by the ASAP, the Home Office has agreed that the overnight accommodation includes an evening meal on arrival in south London the night before, and breakfast and a packed lunch for the return journey.
36 s103(9) IAA 1999; Home Office, *Asylum Support Policy Bulletin* 28
37 r30(1) TP(FT) Rules
38 TP(FT) Rules
39 r15(3) TP(FT) Rules
40 r31 TP(FT) Rules
41 r33 TP(FT) Rules
42 r33(2)(a) TP(FT) Rules
43 s103(4) IAA 1999; r34(1)(a) TP(FT) Rules

3. Decisions the First-Tier Tribunal can make
44 s103(3) IAA 1999
45 In an application for Section 95 support you could, in theory, receive temporary support under s98 IAA 1999 until a new decision is made.
46 r10(2) ASA(P) Rules
47 s103(1) and (2) IAA 1999

48 Some other tribunals have the power to review their own decisions under r40 TP(FT) Rules, but the First-tier Tribunal is expressly excluded from doing so by r40(1). If an application is made to the First-tier Tribunal to review one of its own decisions, it can instead treat the application as a request for the decision to be set aside: r41 TP(FT) Rules

49 r37(1) TP(FT) Rules

50 r37(3) TP(FT) Rules

51 r17(1) TP(FT) Rules

52 Home Office, *Asylum Support Policy Bulletin* 23

Part 9

Other sources of help

Chapter 25

....

Other sources of help

This chapter covers:

This *Handbook* is primarily concerned with migrants' entitlement to social security benefits, tax credits and asylum support. However, you may also be entitled to other financial help.

---

1. **Council tax reduction**

If you need help to pay council tax, you might be able to get a reduction under your local authority's council tax reduction scheme. **Note:** a council tax reduction is *not* a social security benefit or a tax credit, and how the scheme operates depends on where you live.

In:[1]

- England and Wales, local authorities may devise their own local schemes, which must meet minimum requirements. If a local authority does not set up its own scheme, a default scheme applies. Check with your local authority whether it has its own local scheme or whether the default scheme applies;
- Scotland, there is a national scheme, administered by local authorities.

The regulations for all the schemes are in CPAG's *Housing Benefit and Council Tax Reduction Legislation* and a short overview is also provided in CPAG's *Welfare Benefits and Tax Credits Handbook*.

The regulations on the minimum requirements, the default schemes in England and Wales and the national scheme in Scotland contain immigration and residence rules. To be entitled to council tax reduction you must:

- not be defined as a 'person subject to immigration control' (see below); *and*
- be habitually resident in, including having a right to reside in, the common travel area (see below), unless you are in an exempt group.

There are also rules that exclude you from council tax reduction if you are absent from the property. The first 13 weeks of a temporary absence that does not exceed 52 weeks (or up to 52 weeks in limited circumstances) are disregarded.[2]

People subject to immigration control

You are not entitled to council tax reduction if you are defined as a 'person subject to immigration control' (see p55).[3] There are no exemptions from this exclusion.

Council tax reduction is defined as a public fund under the Immigration Rules.[4] If your leave to enter or remain in the UK is subject to a 'no recourse to public funds' condition, you are defined as a 'person subject to immigration control' (see p57) and are therefore excluded from claiming council tax reduction. In addition, you should avoid being included in someone else's claim because if s/he receives a larger council tax reduction because of your presence, this breaches your 'no recourse to public funds condition' and could affect your right to remain in the UK (see p22).[5]

Asylum support counts as income for the purposes of council tax reduction, except if you are defined as a 'pensioner'.[6]

If you apply for council tax reduction in England and Wales, you, and anyone included in your application, must satisfy a national insurance (NI) number requirement that is similar to the requirement for benefits (see p299).[7] However, this does not apply to:[8]

- a child or young person; *or*
- a person who:
  - is defined as a 'person subject to immigration control' because s/he requires leave but does not have it (see p56); *and*
  - has not previously had an NI number; *and*
  - is not habitually resident. **Note:** this is always likely to apply if you satisfy the first point as you do not have a right to reside.

Residence requirements

You are not entitled to council tax reduction unless you are:[9]
- habitually resident in, and you have a right to reside in, the 'common travel area' – ie, the UK, Ireland, Channel Islands and the Isle of Man; *or*
- exempt (see below).

You are exempt from the habitual residence test for council tax reduction if you:[10]
- are a European Economic Area (EEA) national and are a 'worker' (see p129), including if you retain this status (see p135);

- are an EEA national and are a self-employed person (see p141), including if you retain this status (see p144);
- are the family member (see p151) (other than an 'extended family member', except in Scotland) of someone in either of the above two groups;
- are an EEA national with a permanent right of residence acquired in less than five years (the main groups cover certain former workers or self-employed people who have retired or are permanently incapacitated – see p174) or you are the family member of such a person;
- are a refugee;
- have humanitarian protection;
- have limited leave granted outside the Immigration Rules following the refusal of your asylum application (see p35);
- have been deported, expelled or otherwise legally removed from another country to the UK and you are not a 'person subject to immigration control' (see p55);
- (England and Wales only) are a Crown servant or member of HM Forces posted overseas and immediately prior to your posting you were habitually resident in the UK.

If you are *not* in one of the above exempt groups, you need to be accepted as 'habitually resident in fact' (see p102) and have a right to reside (see p107).

Any right to reside satisfies this requirement, except the initial right of residence that EEA nationals have for the first three months (see p122) or as the family member of such a person. See Chapter 12 for who has a right to reside.

If you are not accepted as 'habitually resident in fact' and/or you do not have a right to reside, you are defined as a person 'treated as not being in Great Britain' and not entitled to council tax reduction.

In Scotland, provided you are not someone who is 'treated as not being in Great Britain', you can be treated as being present in Great Britain when you are abroad in your capacity as (or accompanying your partner in her/his capacity as) an aircraft worker, mariner, continental shelf worker, crown servant or member of HM Forces.[11] You can also be treated as being present in Great Britain during certain temporary absences for up to one, two or six months.[12]

Note: local authorities cannot require you to have resided in that local authority area for a set period of time before you can be entitled to council tax reduction.[13]

---

2. Local welfare assistance schemes

Help may be available under local welfare assistance schemes set up by your local authority (in England) or by the devolved administrations (in Wales and Scotland). The DWP may refer to this as 'local welfare provision'.

Depending on your local authority and your circumstances, you may qualify if you need help – eg:

- with immediate short-term needs in a crisis – eg, if you do not have sufficient resources, or you need help with expenses in an emergency or as a result of a disaster, such as a fire or flood in your home;
- to establish yourself in the community following a stay in institutional or residential accommodation, or to help you remain in the community;
- to set up a home in the community as part of a planned resettlement programme;
- to ease exceptional pressure on your family;
- to enable you to care for a prisoner or young offender on temporary release;
- with certain travel expenses – eg, to visit someone in hospital, to attend a funeral, to ease a domestic crisis, to visit a child living with her/his other parent or to move to suitable accommodation.

In England, the local scheme is entirely at your local authority's discretion. Check with your local authority to find out what help is available, whether you qualify and how to apply.

In Wales, the Discretionary Assistance Fund for Walse offers emergency assistance grants. It links with credit unions to provide loans for those who are not eligible for a grant.

In Scotland, the Scottish Welfare Fund provides community care grants and crisis grants. These are administered by local authorities, following the Scottish government's guidance, but with some local discretion.

See www.cpag.org.uk/lwas for details of the scheme in your area.

Note: assistance from a local welfare assistance scheme does not count as a 'public fund' under the Immigration Rules.[14] If you have leave to enter or remain in the UK which is subject to a condition that you do not have recourse to public funds (see p25), you have not breached this condition if you receive any assistance from one of these schemes.

---

3. Healthy Start food and vitamins

If you qualify for Healthy Start food and vitamins, you get free vitamins as well as vouchers that can be used to buy specified types of food.

Healthy Start food

If you qualify for Healthy Start food (see below), you:[15]
- get fixed-value vouchers (worth £3.10 each in 2014/15) that can be exchanged for Healthy Start food at registered food outlets; *or*
- you are paid an amount equal to the value of the vouchers to which you are entitled, if there is no registered food outlet within a reasonable distance of your home.

Healthy Start food

'**Healthy Start food**' means liquid cow's milk and cow's milk-based infant formula, fresh or frozen fruit and vegetables including loose, pre-packed, whole, sliced, chopped or mixed fruit or vegetables (but not fruit or vegetables to which fat, salt, sugar, flavouring or any other ingredients have been added).[16]

Who can claim Healthy Start food

You qualify for Healthy Start food vouchers:[17]
- if you are pregnant and have been for more than 10 weeks, and you are:
  - 18 or over and are entitled to (or are a member of the family of someone who is entitled to) a 'qualifying benefit' (see p402); *or*
  - under 18 (whether or not you are entitled to a qualifying benefit), unless you are defined as a 'person subject to immigration control' (see p55); *or*
- if you are a mother who has 'parental responsibility' for a child and:
  - you are 18 or over and either your child is under one or it is less than a year since her/his expected date of birth. This means you can continue to qualify for vouchers for a period after your child is one – ie, if s/he was born prematurely. You must be entitled to (or be a member of the family of someone who is entitled to) a qualifying benefit other than income-related employment and support allowance (ESA); *or*
  - it is less than four months since your baby's expected date of birth and you have not yet notified Healthy Start that s/he was born. You must have been getting a qualifying benefit before your baby was born. This allows your entitlement to vouchers to continue until you notify the birth. Once you do, you can then qualify under the rule above (if you are 18 or over). **Note:** as long as you provided the notification within the four-month period, you can also get extra vouchers for your child from her/his date of birth. If you qualify for vouchers for more than one child under this rule (eg, you have twins), you get a voucher for each. If you do not have parental responsibility but would otherwise qualify for vouchers, your child qualifies instead of you;
- for a child under four who is a member of your family. You or a member of the family must be entitled to a qualifying benefit (see p402) other than income-related ESA.

In practical terms, this means that each week you get one voucher for each of your children aged between one and four, two vouchers for each child under one (or within one year of her/his expected date of birth), plus one voucher if you are pregnant.

Definitions

The **'qualifying benefits'** are income support, income-based jobseeker's allowance and income-related ESA (in some cases). Child tax credit (CTC) is also a qualifying benefit (provided that gross income for CTC purposes does not exceed £16,190 in 2014/15 and there is no entitlement to working tax credit (WTC), other than during the four-week WTC run-on period). **Note:** it is understood that universal credit was to be a qualifying benefit from some point in October 2013, but there was to be an earnings threshold. At the time of writing, the rules had not yet been amended.

'Parental responsibility' means parental responsibility as defined in s3(1) of the Children Act 1989 (in England or Wales) or s1(1) of the Children (Scotland) Act 1995 (in Scotland).[18]

'Family' means a person and her/his partner and any child or qualifying young person who is a member of her/his household and for whom s/he or her/his partner counts as responsible.[19] So for example, if you are not entitled to a qualifying benefit, but are included in your mother's or father's claim for one of these, you can qualify for Healthy Start food vouchers.

Claims

You must make an initial claim for Healthy Start food vouchers in writing, and must provide specified information and evidence.[20] You can:

- complete the form in the Healthy Start leaflet (HS01), available from midwives, health visitors, maternity clinics and some doctors' surgeries or from 0845 607 6823;
- download a form or complete it online and print it off at www.healthystart.nhs.uk;
- email yourself a form from www.healthystart.nhs.uk.

The form must be countersigned by a health professional (eg, a midwife or health visitor) who certifies when your baby is due (if you are pregnant) and that you have been given appropriate advice about healthy eating and breastfeeding. If you are under 16, your claim must also be signed by your parent or carer. Send the completed form to: Healthy Start Issuing Unit, Freepost RRTR-SYAE-JKCR, PO Box 1067, Warrington WA55 1EG.

If you are getting Healthy Start food vouchers while you are pregnant and then inform Healthy Start of your baby's birth by telephone while s/he is under four months old, you can get extra vouchers for her/him from her/his date of birth.[21] You may need to make a claim for CTC for her/him (or add her/him to your existing claim) to ensure that you continue to get the vouchers.

If you do not get vouchers to which you think you are entitled, or have any other problems with these, contact the Healthy Start helpline on 0845 607 6823.

Healthy Start vitamins

If you qualify for Healthy Start food vouchers, you also qualify for Healthy Start vitamins.[22] Mothers and pregnant women are entitled to 56 vitamin tablets, and children under four to 10 millilitres of vitamin drops, every eight weeks. Ask your local health professional what the local arrangements are for getting your free vitamins.

You do not have to make a separate claim for Healthy Start vitamins; you are sent Healthy Start vitamin coupons with your Healthy Start food vouchers. However, you must show evidence to the vitamin supplier that you are entitled (ie, the letter to which your most recent Healthy Start vouchers were attached) and, if requested, proof of your child's age.[23]

4. Education benefits

Financial help is available from your local authority if you are in school or are a student, or if you have children in school or college.

Free school lunches

Children are entitled to free school lunches if their families receive:[24]
- income support (IS), income-based jobseeker's allowance or income-related employment and support allowance (ESA);
- child tax credit (CTC) and have annual taxable income of £16,190 (in Scotland, £16,010) or less. However, this does not apply if the family is entitled to working tax credit (WTC) unless:
  - this is during the four-week 'WTC run-on' period (see CPAG's *Welfare Benefits and Tax Credits Handbook* for when this applies); *or*
  - in Scotland only, the WTC award is based on annual taxable income of £6,420 or less – ie, the family gets maximum WTC;
- universal credit (UC);
- in England and Wales only, guarantee credit of pension credit (PC). PC claimants in Scotland may qualify if they receive CTC, as above.

Also entitled are:
- 16–18-year-olds receiving the above benefits or tax credits in their own right;
- asylum seekers in receipt of asylum support (see p329).[25]

Note: free school lunches are provided to all primary school children in reception, and years one and two in England from September 2014 and in Scotland from January 2015.

School transport and school clothes

Local authorities must provide free transport to school for pupils aged five to 16 if it is considered necessary to enable that pupil to get to the 'nearest suitable school'. This applies if s/he lives more than a set distance from that school. However, if there is no safe walking route, a pupil must be given free transport no matter how far away s/he lives from the nearest suitable school. Free school transport must also be be provided to pupils with special educational needs and to those whose parents are on a low income – ie, if they receive a benefit that would qualify them for free school lunches or the maximum rate of WTC.

Local authorities can give grants for school uniforms and other school clothes. Each authority determines its own eligibility rules. Some school governing bodies or parents' associations also provide help with school clothing.

Education maintenance allowance and 16 to 19 bursaries

Education maintenance allowance is a means-tested payment for young people aged 16 to 19 from Wales and Scotland who stay on in further education. Payments are made directly to the young person and are conditional on regular course attendance. The young person receives a weekly allowance during term time. The amount depends on the household income. For further details, see www.emascotland.com or www.studentfinancewales.co.uk.

16 to 19 bursaries are payments for young people aged 16 to 19 who stay on in further education or training in England. These are available through the school, college or training provider. Certain young people in need (eg, young people in care, care leavers, young people who get IS or UC, or who get ESA and either disability living allowance or personal independence payment) can get the maximum bursary. Discretionary bursaries are available to those in financial difficulty. See www.gov.uk/1619-bursary-fund for further information.

Neither payment counts as income for any benefits or tax credits the parent may be getting. They are also not affected by any income the young person has from part-time work.

Note: if you are a student, to find out what help is available to finance your studies contact your local authority or college or university, or see www.gov.uk/student-finance. Also see CPAG's *Student Support and Benefits Handbook* and *Benefits for Students in Scotland Handbook*.

5. Free milk for children

Children under five are entitled to 189–200 millilitres of free milk on each day they are looked after for two hours or more:[26]
- by a registered childminder or daycare provider; *or*

- in a school, playcentre or workplace nursery which is exempt from registration; *or*
- in local authority daycare.

Children under one are allowed fresh or dried milk.

---

6. **Community care support from the local authority**

You may be able to get accommodation and other support from your local authority or NHS primary care trust under one of several legislative provisions, which are often collectively referred to as community care support. Some of these provisions have restrictions and exclusions that affect certain groups of migrants, but there are also exceptions to these rules that can, depending on your circumstances, mean you may still access support.

This *Handbook* does not cover the community care support that is available for migrants, but see p347 for more information on community care support for asylum seekers.

Community care law is complex and community care support is often misunderstood and poorly administered by local authorities and other providers. You are strongly recommended to obtain specialist advice before applying to your local authority for support and, in all cases, if you want to challenge a refusal of support.

Support under the National Assistance Act 1948

Under s21 of the National Assistance Act 1948, local authorities can provide accommodation, and other support in connection with it, to someone who has a need for care and attention. However, if you are defined as a 'person subject to immigration control' (see p55), you are excluded if your need for care and attention is solely as a result of being destitute. This means that, even if you are also destitute, there must be another reason for your needing the support – eg, because of your age, disability, or physical or mental health problem. For more information about this exclusion, see p348.

Other groups of migrants are also specifically excluded from support under the Act, but there are exceptions (see p348).

See p347 for more information on support from your local authority if you have claimed asylum.

Other types of support

There are a number of other types of community care support that may be available from local authority social services departments or from NHS primary care trusts. The type of support available depends on your individual circumstances. The support available may be just services, but could include accommodation – eg, if you have been detained, admitted or transferred to hospital under various sections of the Mental Health Act 1983, you are now no longer detained and you leave hospital, the clinical commissioning group, primary care trust or local health board and the local social services department have joint duties to provide you with aftercare services, which can include accommodation. A summary of the different community care provisions is in the *Disability Rights Handbook* published annually by Disability Rights UK.

7. Support under the Children Act 1989

Local authorities have a duty to safeguard and promote the welfare of children who are 'in need' in their area.[27] If you are destitute and have children, you may therefore be eligible for accommodation or support from your local authority under the Children Act 1989 (in Scotland, the Children (Scotland) Act 1995). A child who is destitute is generally considered to be 'in need', but a child can also be in need if s/he is disabled, or if s/he is unlikely to achieve or maintain a reasonable standard of health or development without the provision of services by a local authority.[28] Although the duty is to support the child, it extends to supporting parents or other family members if this is in the child's best interests.[29] There are some exclusions from Children Act support that affect some groups of migrants, but there are also exceptions.

The provision of support can be complex and is often misunderstood and poorly administered by local authorities. You are strongly recommended to obtain specialist advice before applying to your local authority for support and, in all cases, if you want to challenge a refusal of support or an offer to only accommodate your child and not you as well.

This *Handbook* does not cover support for migrants under the Children Act. However, see p349 for more information if you are an asylum seeker.

8. Other financial help

Other financial help is available, to which you may be entitled, especially if you are on a low income, have children, are an older person, or have an illness, disability or other special needs.

See the *Disability Rights Handbook*, published by Disability Rights UK, for help if you have care needs.

Food banks

If you are experiencing severe financial hardship (eg, caused by debt or benefit delays), you may be able to get vouchers for food which can be redeemed at a food bank. One voucher can be exchanged for three days' food. Vouchers are available from frontline care professionals, such as doctors, health visitors, social workers and advice workers. Jobcentre Plus staff may also give out vouchers. Further information and details of where there are food banks is available at www.trusselltrust.org.

You may be able to get help with food or meals through local community groups which are part of the FareShare network. Further information is available at www.fareshare.org.uk.

Repairs, improvements and energy efficiency

Your local authority may be able to provide you with a grant to help with the cost of improving your home. The main types of grant available are:
- home improvement grants; *and*
- disabled facilities grants.

You may also be able to get:
- assistance from a home improvement agency (a local not-for-profit organisation) to repair, improve, maintain or adapt your home, sometimes called 'care and repair' or 'staying put' schemes, or with small repairs, safety checks and odd jobs from a handyperson service. For information see, in England, www.foundations.uk.com, in Wales, www.careandrepair.org.uk and in Scotland, www.careandrepairscotland.co.uk;
- a grant for help with insulation and other energy efficiency measures in your home. Help with fuel bills may also be available. Different schemes operate in England, Wales and Scotland. For further information, contact the Energy Saving Advice Service on 0300 123 1234 (calls charged at standard national rates) or at www.energysavingtrust.org.uk. For more details, see CPAG's *Fuel Rights Handbook*.

Special funds for sick or disabled people

A range of help is available for people with an illness or disability to assist with things like paying for care services in their own home, equipment, holidays, furniture and transport needs, and for people with haemophilia or HIV contracted via haemophilia treatment. Grants are also available for practical support to help people do their jobs – eg, to pay for specialist equipment and travel. For more information, see the *Disability Rights Handbook*, published by Disability Rights UK.

Payments for former members of the armed forces

If you are a former member of the UK armed forces, or your spouse or civil partner died while in service, you may be able to claim under the one of the various schemes administered by the Ministry of Defence. The benefits and lump-sum payments include pensions, disablement benefits and compensation payments. Your entitlement depends on your circumstances, including the dates of service and, where relevant, the degree and effect of any disablement or ill health and the final salary. Further details are available from Veterans UK.[30]

Charities

There are many charities that provide various types of help to people in need. Your local authority social services department or local advice centre may know of appropriate charities that could assist you, or you can consult publications, such as *A Guide to Grants for Individuals in Need* and the *Charities Digest*, in your local library. The organisation turn2us has a website (www.turn2us.org.uk) with an A–Z of charities that can provide financial help. In many cases, applications for support can be made directly from the website.

Notes

1. **Council tax reduction**
   1 **E** CTRS(DS)E Regs; CTRS(PR)E Regs
      W CTRS(DS)W Regs; CTRSPR(W) Regs
      S CTR(S) Regs; CTR(SPC)S Regs
   2 **E** Sch para 19 CTRS(DS)E Regs; Sch 1 para 5 CTRS(PR)E Regs
      W Reg 24 CTRSPR(W) Regs; Sch para 17 CTRS(DS)W Regs
      S Reg 15 CTR(SPC)S Regs; reg 15 CTR(S) Regs
   3 **E** Sch para 22 CTRS(DS)E Regs; reg 13 CTRS(PR)E Regs
      W Reg 27 CTRSPR(W) Regs; Sch para 20 CTRS(DS)W Regs
      S Reg 19 CTR(SPC)S Regs; reg 19 CTR(S) Regs
   4 para 6 IR
   5 para 6A IR
   6 **S** Reg 39(11) CTR(S) Regs
      W Sch para 51(10) CTRS(DS)W Regs
      E Sch paras 3 and 54(10) CTRS(DS)E Regs

   7 **E** Sch para 113 CTRS(DS)E Regs; reg 7 CTRS(PR)E Regs
      W Sch 13 para 5 CTRSPR(W) Regs; Sch para 111 CTRS(DS)W Regs
   8 **E** Sch para 113(3) CTRS(DS)E Regs; Sch 8 para 7 CTRS(PR)E Regs
      W Sch 13 para 5(3) CTRSPR(W) Regs; Sch para 111(3) CTRS(DS)W Regs
   9 **E** Sch para 21 CTRS(DS)E Regs; reg 12 CTRS(PR)E Regs
      W Reg 26 CTRSPR(W) Regs; Sch para 19 CTRS(DS)W Regs
      S Reg 16 CTR(SPC)S Regs; reg 16 CTR(S) Regs
   10 **E** Sch para 21 CTRS(DS)E Regs; reg 12 CTRS(PR)E Regs
      W Reg 26 CTRSPR(W) Regs; Sch para 19 CTRS(DS)W Regs
      S Reg 16 CTR(SPC)S Regs; reg 16 CTR(S) Regs
   11 Reg 17 CTR(SPC)S Regs; reg 17 CTR(S) Regs

12 Reg 18 CTR(SPC)S Regs; reg 18 CTR(S)
Regs
13 *(AA and others) v Sandwell Metropolitan
Borough Council*, CO/633/2014

2. Local welfare assistance schemes
14 para 6 IR

3. Healthy Start food and vitamins
15 Regs 5(2) and 8 HSS&WF(A) Regs
16 Regs 2(1) and 5(1) and Sch 3
HSS&WF(A) Regs; HSS(DHSF)(W) Regs
17 Reg 3 HSS&WF(A) Regs
18 Reg 2(1) HSS&WF(A) Regs
19 Reg 2(1) HSS&WF(A) Regs
20 Reg 4 and Sch 2 HSS&WF(A) Regs
21 Reg 4(2) HSS&WF(A) Regs
22 Reg 3 HSS&WF(A) Regs
23 Reg 8A HSS&WF(A) Regs

4. Education benefits
24 **E** s512ZB Education Act 1996; The
Education (Free School
Lunches)(Prescribed Tax
Credits)(England) Order 2003, No.383
W s512ZB Education Act 1996; The
Education (Free School
Lunches)(Prescribed Tax Credits)(Wales)
Order 2003, No.879 (W.110)
S s53(3) Education (Scotland) Act 1980;
The Education (School Lunches)
(Scotland) Regulations 2009, No.178
25 Provided under Part VI of IAA 1999

5. Free milk for children
26 Reg 18 WF Regs

7. Support under the Children Act 1989
27 s17 CA 1989; s22 C(S)A 1995
28 s17(10) CA 1989
29 s17(3) CA 1989; s22(3) C(S)A 1995

8. Other financial help
30 www.veterans-uk.info

Appendices

Appendix 1

Glossary of terms

A2 national. A national of the European Union member states Romania and Bulgaria.

A8 national. A national of the European Union member states Czech Republic, Estonia, Hungary, Latvia, Lithuania, Poland, Slovakia and Slovenia.

Absent. Not physically in the UK; the alternative to present.

Accession states. The newer members of the European Union: Croatia, the A2 states and the A8 states.

Administrative removal. A legal mechanism used to remove foreign nationals who have entered the UK illegally, including by deception, or to remove those who have breached the conditions of their leave, including overstaying.

Applicable amount. The maximum amount of benefit set by the government, taking account of certain factors such as age and whether someone is single or part of a couple.

Application registration card. The form of identification for those who have claimed asylum, replacing the standard acknowledgement letter.

Association agreement. A treaty signed between the European Union and a country outside the European Union, giving reciprocal rights and obligations.

Asylum. Leave to enter or remain in the UK as a refugee, given under the Refugee Convention or Article 3 of the European Convention on Human Rights (including protection under the Refugee Qualification Directive).

Asylum seeker. A person who has applied for asylum and whose application has yet to be decided, or whose appeal against a refusal of an asylum application remains outstanding.

Asylum support. Support given to asylum seekers while they wait for a final decision on their asylum application. **Temporary** (or **emergency**) **support** is also available to asylum seekers waiting for an asylum support decision.

Azure card. A credit card-type card given to failed asylum seekers in receipt of Section 4 asylum support. It is credited by the Home Office and then used by the holder to make purchases at designated shops.

Certificate of entitlement. A certificate of entitlement to the right of abode demonstrates that a person has the right of abode – ie, the right to travel freely to and from the UK. British citizens have the right of abode and can demonstrate this by producing their passports. A few Commonwealth nationals also have the right of abode and can obtain a certificate of entitlement, endorsed in their own national passport, to demonstrate this.

Common travel area. The UK, Ireland, Isle of Man and the Channel Islands.

Commonwealth countries. Antigua and Barbuda, Australia, Bahamas, Bangladesh, Barbados, Belize, Botswana, Brunei Darussalam, Cameroon, Canada, Cyprus, Dominica, Fiji Islands, Gambia, Ghana, Grenada, Guyana, India, Jamaica, Kenya, Kiribati, Lesotho, Malawi, Malaysia, Maldives, Malta, Mauritius, Mozambique, Namibia, Nauru, New Zealand, Nigeria, Pakistan, Papua New Guinea, Samoa, Seychelles, Sierra Leone, Singapore, Solomon Islands, South Africa, Sri Lanka, St Kitts and Nevis, St Lucia, St Vincent and the Grenadines, Swaziland, Tanzania, Tonga, Trinidad and Tobago, Tuvalu, Uganda, Vanuatu, Zambia.

Competent state. The European Economic Area country responsible for paying your benefit and to which you are liable to pay natioanl insurance contributions.

Court of Justice of the European Union. The European Union institution that ensures that European Union law is observed by member states. It sits in Luxembourg. Previously known as the **European Court of Justice**.

Deportation. A legal mechanism used to remove a foreign national on the recommendation of a criminal court following her/his conviction for a criminal offence, or if the Home Secretary has decided that a person's presence in the UK is 'not conducive to the public good'. If an order has been signed to deport a foreign national, s/he may not return unless and until the order has been revoked.

Derivative right to reside. The term given to certain residence rights that are derived from someone else.

Destitute. For asylum support purposes, someone who does not have access to adequate accommodation or who cannot meet her/his essential living needs.

Destitute domestic violence concession. A provision under which people who have leave on the basis of a relationship, but which has broken down as a result of domestic violence, can be granted three months' leave in which to apply for indefinite leave to remain.

Discretionary leave. Permission to enter or remain in the UK given to a person outside the Immigration Rules or to someone who is refused asylum but who cannot be removed under another Article of the European Convention on Human Rights or for other humanitarian reasons.

Enforcement. A term used to refer to any of the different ways in which a person can be forced to leave the UK for immigration reasons – ie, having been refused entry at a port, having been declared an illegal entrant, or having been notified that s/he is someone who is liable for administrative removal, or who is being deported.

Entry clearance officer. An official at a British post overseas who deals with immigration applications made to that post.

European Community. The European Union was previously known as the European Community and before that the European Economic Community. In this *Handbook*, the legislation of all three is referred to as European Union law.

European Convention on Human Rights. An international instrument agreed by the Council of Europe. The rights guaranteed by it have now largely been incorporated into UK law by the Human Rights Act 1998.

European Convention on Social and Medical Assistance. An agreement signed by all the European Economic Area states, plus Turkey, requiring the ratifying states to provide assistance in cash and kind to nationals of other ratifying states who are lawfully present in their territory and who are without sufficient resources on the same conditions as their own nationals.

European Economic Area. Covers all European Union states plus Iceland, Liechtenstein and Norway. European Economic Area nationals have free movement within these and all European Union member states. From 1 June 2002, the right to free movement also applies to Switzerland.

European Social Charter. The 1961 Council of Europe Social Charter, signed by all the European Economic Area countries, plus Macedonia and Turkey.

European Union. Austria, Belgium, Bulgaria, Croatia, Cyprus, Czech Republic, Denmark, Estonia, Finland, France, Germany, Greece, Hungary, Ireland, Italy, Latvia, Lithuania, Luxembourg, Malta, Netherlands, Poland, Portugal, Romania, Slovakia, Slovenia, Spain, Sweden and the UK (including Gibraltar).

European Union/European Economic Area national. The term used in this *Handbook* to describe citizens of European Union member states/European Economic Area countries.

Exceptional leave. A form of leave to remain granted outside the Immigration Rules that has now been replaced with humanitarian protection and discretionary leave for those seeking asylum.

First-tier Tribunal (Asylum Support). The tribunal that decides appeals against the refusal or termination of asylum support or Section 4 support. Currently, it sits in East London, but deals with all support appeals.

First-tier Tribunal (Immigration and Asylum Chamber). The tribunal that hears and determines appeals against decisions made by the Secretary of State for the Home Department about asylum, immigration and nationality.

First-tier Tribunal (Social Entitlement Chamber). The tribunal that hears and determines appeals against decisions made by the Department for Work and Pensions and local authorities about benefit entitlement.

Habitual residence. The type of residence someone must have (unless s/he is exempt) to get income support, income-based jobseeker's allowance, income-related employment and support allowance, housing benefit, pension credit, universal credit, attendance allowance, disability living allowance, carer's allowance and personal independence payment. The term 'habitually resident' is not defined in the benefit regulations and is determined by looking at all the person's circumstances.

Home Office. The government department responsible for asylum, immigration and nationality issues.

Humanitarian protection. Permission to enter or remain in the UK given to a person who needs to be protected from harm, but whose case does not fit the criteria for refugee status.

Illegal entrant. A person who immigration officials decide has entered the UK in breach of the immigration laws. This could be by deception or clandestinely.

Immigration judge. A person who determines appeals in the First-tier Tribunal (Immigration and Asylum Chamber) or Upper Tribunal (Immigration and Asylum Chamber).

Immigration officer. An official, usually stationed at a British port of entry, who decides whether to grant or refuse leave to enter. Immigration officers also have responsibility for enforcing immigration control.

Immigration Rules. Rules made by the Home Secretary, setting out the requirements for granting or refusing entry clearance, leave to enter and leave to remain to people applying in the different categories.

Indefinite leave. Permission to enter or remain that has no time limit.

Integration loan. An interest-free loan made to assist people who have recently been given refugee status or humanitarian protection integrate into UK society.

Lawfully working. Depending on the context, this can mean working with the permission of the Home Office or, for accession state nationals, working in accordance with any employment restrictions that apply.

Limited leave. Permission to enter or remain that is given for a certain period of time only. Also referred to as 'time-limted leave'.

Maintenance undertaking. A written undertaking given by someone under the Immigration Rules to be responsible for the maintenance and accommodation of another person who is applying to come to or stay in the UK.

Ordinarily resident. A residence requirement for several benefits and tax credits. A person is ordinarily resident where s/he has her/his home that s/he has adopted for a settled purpose and where s/he lives for the time being.

Past presence test. A requirement for some benefits to have been present in Great Britain or the UK for a period of time before the date of claim.

Person from abroad. A social security definition that refers to a person who has failed the habitual residence test for the purposes of income support, income-based jobseeker's allowance, income-related employment and support allowance or housing benefit.

Person subject to immigration control. A person in one of four specific groups of non-European Economic Area nationals who are excluded from entitlement to most social security benefits and whose entitlement to support under the National Assistance Act 1948 is restricted.

Points-based system. The system of controlling migration to the UK from outside the European Union for economic purposes or studies.

Present. Physically in the UK; the alternative to absent.

Public funds. These are defined in the Immigration Rules as: housing provided by local authorities, either for homeless people or allocated from its housing register; attendance allowance; carer's allowance; child benefit; child tax credit; council tax benefit; council tax reduction; disability living allowance; income-related employment and support allowance; housing benefit; income support; income-based jobseeker's allowance; pension credit; personal independence payment; severe disablement allowance; social fund payments; working tax credit; and universal credit.

Reciprocal agreement. A bilateral agreement made between the UK and another country, with the purpose of protecting benefit entitlement for people moving between the two.

Refugee. A person who satisfies the definition of someone who needs international protection under Article 1A(2) of the 1951 Convention Relating to the Status of Refugees.

Refugee Convention. The 1951 United Nations Convention Relating to the Status of Refugees, a multilateral treaty defining who is a refugee and setting out the rights of people who are granted asylum.

Removal. The final procedure for sending a person refused entry, or who is being treated as an illegal entrant, or who is subject to the administrative removal or deportation process, away from the UK.

Resident. A requirement of a Category D retirement pension and a necessary part of ordinary residence and habitual residence. Residence is more than presence and is usually where you have your home for the time being.

Restricted leave. Leave to remain given outside the Immigration Rules to someone who is excluded from refugee or humanitarian protection leave but who cannot be removed from the UK for human rights reasons. Replaced discretionary leave.

Right of abode. The right to enter, remain, leave and return freely to the UK without needing to obtain leave from the immigration authorities. All British citizens, and some Commonwealth nationals, have the right of abode.

Right to reside. A residence requirement for entitlement to some benefits and tax credits. For child benefit and child tax credit, a person must have a right to reside in the UK, and to satisfy the habitual residence test for means-tested benefits s/he must have a right to reside in the common travel area. The right to reside depends on someone's nationality, immigration status and whether s/he has rights under European Union law.

Secretary of State for the Home Department (the Home Secretary). The government minister with primary responsibility for decisions made by the Home Office on immigration, asylum and nationality.

Section 4 support. Support available from the Home Office in limited circumstances for some people whose claim for asylum has been refused and for people released from immigration detention or granted temporary admission.

Settlement/settled status. Defined in immigration law as being ordinarily resident in the UK without any restrictions on the time the person is able to remain here. Those with indefinite leave are generally accepted as being settled in the UK.

Sponsor. The person (usually a relative) with whom someone is applying to join or remain with in the UK, and/or a person who is to be responsible for the applicant's maintenance and accommodation in the UK.

Stateless person. Someone who is not considered a national by any country.

Subject to immigration control. Often used to refer to those who need leave to enter or remain in the UK – and this is the definition given in the Asylum and Immigration Act 1996. However, the Immigration and Asylum Act 1999 gives a different, narrower, definition, which is used to exclude people from non-contributory benefits and certain services provided by local authorities' social services departments. This *Handbook* uses the term as it is defined in the 1999 Act.

Temporary admission. A temporary licence given to people to be in the UK while they are waiting for a decision to be made on their immigration status or while they are waiting to be removed from the UK. The alternative to temporary admission is detention.

Third country. Usually used to refer to a country to which the Home Office wishes to send an asylum seeker for her/his application for asylum to be considered, other than the country of which s/he is a national, rather than in the UK.

The United Kingdom. Comprises England, Wales, Scotland and Northern Ireland. The Channel Islands of Jersey and Guernsey, and the Isle of Man are Crown dependencies and not part of the UK.

UK Visas and Immigration. The Home Office department that deals with immigration control.

Unmarried partners. A term used in the Immigration Rules to refer to couples (heterosexual or same-sex) who have been together for two or more years, who are in a relationship 'akin to marriage' and who cannot marry according to the law – eg, because they are of the same sex or one of them is already married. The Immigration Rules give unmarried partners some rights to enter and remain in the UK if one partner is settled in the UK or has limited leave to enter or remain here.

Upper Tribunal (Immigration and Asylum Chamber). The tribunal that hears and determines appeals against determinations made by the First-tier Tribunal (Immigration and Asylum Chamber) and most immigration-related applications for judicial review.

Upper Tribunal (Social Entitlement Chamber). The tribunal that hears and determines appeals against decisions made by the First-tier Tribunal (Social Entitlement Chamber) about benefit entitlement.

Visa national. A person who must obtain entry clearance before travelling to the UK for most purposes, unless s/he is a person with indefinite leave returning within two years or returning within a period of earlier leave granted for more than six months. For a list of countries covered, see Appendix 1 to the Immigration Rules.

Work permit. A document issued by UK Visas and Immigration to employers, allowing them to employ a named individual in a particular job.

Appendix 2

Information and advice

Immigration and asylum

If you need help with an immigration problem, you should obtain advice from your local law centre, a solicitor specialising in immigration work or one of the agencies listed below.

Afro-Asian Advisory Service

53 Addington Square
London SE5 7LB
Tel: 020 7701 0141
www.aaas.org.uk
Advice line: 0845 618 5385 (Mon – Fri 2–5pm)

Provides a specialist legal service, free of charge.

AIRE Centre (Advice on Individual Rights in Europe)

3rd Floor
17 Red Lion Square
London WC1R 4QH
Tel: 020 7831 4276
info@airecentre.org
www.airecentre.org

Promotes awareness of European legal rights and assists people to assert these.

Asylum Aid

Club Union House
253–254 Upper Street
London N1 1RY
Tel: 020 7354 9631
info@asylumaid.org.uk
www.asylumaid.org.uk
Advice line: 020 7354 9264 (Tues 1–4pm)

Law Centres Network

Floor 1, Tavis House
1-6 Tavistock Square
London WC1H 9NA
Tel: 020 3637 1330
info@lawcentres.org.uk
www.lawcentres.org.uk

Does not give advice, but can provide details of your nearest law centre.

Asylum Help

English (or any other language) 0808 8000 630
Albanian 0808 800 0620
Amharic 0808 800 0622
Arabic 0808 800 0624
Bengali 0808 800 0626
Chinese Mandarin 0808 800 0628
Farsi 0808 800 0632
French 0808 800 0634
Punjabi 0808 800 0636
Pushto 0808 800 0638
Somali 0808 800 0640
Tamil 0808 800 0642
Tigrinya 0808 800 0644
Urdu 0808 800 0646
Vietnamese 0808 800 0648
http://.asylumhelpuk.org

Provides confidential advice and information for asylum seekers about the asylum process and applying for accommodation and support.

Asylum Support Appeals Project (ASAP)

Ground Floor
Anchorage House
2 Clove Crescent
East India Dock
London E14 2BE
Tel: 020 3716 0284
Advice line (advisers only): 020 3716 0283 (Mon, Wed and Fri 2pm–4pm)
www.asaproject.org

British Red Cross
44 Moorfields
London EC2Y 9AL
Tel: 0844 871 11 11
information@redcross.org.uk
www.redcross.org.uk

Provides support for refugees and vulnerable migrants in specific areas across the UK.

Civil Legal Advice
Tel: 0345 345 4345
www.gov.uk/civil-legal-advice

Includes access to a directory of legal aid suppliers.

Greater Manchester Immigration Aid Unit
1 Delaunays Road
Crumpsall Green
Manchester M8 4QS
Tel: 0161 740 7722
http://gmiau.org

Provides free, confidential immigration and asylum legal advice and representation to people in the local community.

Immigration Law Practitioners' Association
Lindsey House
40–42 Charterhouse Street
London EC1M 6JN
Tel: 020 7251 8383
info@ilpa.org.uk
www.ilpa.org.uk

A professional association aiming to promote and improve advice and representation in immigration, nationality and asylum law.

Joint Council for the Welfare of Immigrants
115 Old Street
London EC1V 9RT
Tel: 020 7251 8708
info@jcwi.org.uk
www.jcwi.org.uk

Migrant Help

Charlton House
Dour Street
Dover CT16 1AT
Tel: 01304 203 977
mhl@migranthelpline.org
www.migranthelp.org

Delivers support and advice services to migrants in the UK.

Refugee Action

Victoria Charity Centre
11 Belgrave Road
London SW1V 1RB
Tel: 020 7952 1511
www.refugee-action.org.uk

Choices: Assisted Voluntary Return Service

www.choices-arr.org.uk
Tel: 0808 800 0007

Refugee Council

PO Box 68614
London E15 9DQ
Tel: 020 7346 6700
www.refugeecouncil.org.uk

Scottish Refugee Council

5 Cadogan Square
Glasgow G2 7PH
Tel: 0141 248 9799
info@scottishrefugeecouncil.org.uk
www.scottishrefugeecouncil.org.uk

Welsh Refugee Council

120-122 Broadway
Cardiff CF24 1NJ
Tel: 02920 489 800
info@welshrefugeecouncil.org.uk
www.welshrefugeecouncil.org.uk

Social security

Independent advice and representation

It is often difficult for unsupported individuals to get a positive response from the Department for Work and Pensions, local authority or HM Revenue and Customs (HMRC). It can help if you obtain advice about your entitlement and how you can demonstrate this. If you can get good quality assistance from an adviser who will take on your case, this is even more helpful, particularly if you need to challenge a decision.

If you want advice or help with a benefit problem, the following agencies may be able to assist.

- Citizens Advice Bureaux (CABx) and other local advice centres provide information and advice about benefits and may be able to represent you. You can find out where your local CAB is from the Citizens Advice website at www.citizensadvice.org.uk (England and Wales) or www.cas.org.uk (Scotland).
- Law centres can often help in a similar way to CABx and advice centres. You can find your nearest law centre at www.lawcentres.org.uk.
- Local authority welfare rights workers provide a service in many areas and some arrange advice sessions and take-up campaigns locally.
- Local organisations for particular groups of claimants may offer help – eg, unemployed centres, pensioners' groups and centres for disabled people.
- Claimants' unions give advice in some areas.
- Some social workers help with benefit problems, especially if they are already working with you on another problem.
- Solicitors can give some free legal advice. This does not cover the cost of representation at an appeal hearing, but can cover the cost of preparing written submissions and obtaining evidence, such as medical reports. However, solicitors do not always have a good working knowledge of the benefit rules and you may need to shop around until you find one who does.
- Civil Legal Advice (tel: 0845 345 4345 or www.gov.uk/civil-legal-advice). Note, however, that help with welfare benefits is limited to appeals in the Upper Tribunal and higher courts.

Advice from CPAG

Unfortunately, CPAG is unable to deal with enquiries directly from members of the public, but if you are an adviser you can phone or email for help with advising your client.

Advisers in England, Wales and Northern Ireland can call from 10am to 12pm and from 2pm to 4pm (Monday to Friday) on 020 7833 4627. Email advice is now limited to possible judicial review cases and enquiries that are specifically about child benefit, tax credits or other HMRC-administered benefits. Our email address is advice@cpag.org.uk.

Organisations based in Scotland can contact CPAG in Scotland at Unit 9, Ladywell, 94 Duke Street, Glasgow G4 0UW or email advice@cpagscotland.org.uk. A phone line is open for advisers in Scotland from 10am to 4pm (Monday to Thursday) and from 10am to 12pm (Friday) on 0141 552 0552.

For more information, see www.cpag.org.uk/advisers.

Human rights

Information, advice and support on discrimination and human rights issues, and the relevant law.

Equality Advisory Service
Freepost FPN4431
Tel: 0808 800 0082
Textphone: 0808 800 0084
www.equalityadvisoryservice.com

Appendix 3

Useful addresses

Immigration and asylum
UK Visas and Immigration
Lunar House
40 Wellesley Road
Croydon CR9 2BY
www.gov.uk/government/organisations/uk-visas-and-immigration

UK Visas and Immigration Contact Centre
Tel: 0300 123 2241
Textphone: 0800 389 8289

Asylum Customer Contact Centre
Tel: 0300 123 2235
For asylum applications submitted before 5 March 2007: 0151 213 4288

Enquiries from European citizens
Tel: 0300 123 2253

Sponsorship, Employer and Education Helpline
Tel: 0300 123 4699
BusinessHelpDesk@homeoffice.gsi.gov.uk

Citizenship and nationality
Tel: 0300 123 2253
NationalityEnquiries@homeoffice.gsi.gov.uk
www.gov.uk/contact-ukvi/british-citizenship-and-nationality

Passport Office
4th Floor
Peel Building
2 Marsham Street
London SW1P 4DF
Tel: 0300 222 0000
www.gov.uk/government/organisations/hm-passport-office

Independent Chief Inspector of Borders and Immigration
5th Floor
Globe House
89 Eccleston Square
London SW1V 1PN
chiefinspector@icinspector.gsi.gov.uk

First-tier Tribunal and Upper Tribunal (Immigration and Asylum Chamber)
PO Box 6987
Leceister LE1 6ZX
Tel: 0300 123 1711
Textphone: 0300 123 1264
www.justice.gov.uk/contacts/hmcts/tribunals/immigration-asylum
Note: these are not the contact details you must use when appealing.

First-tier Tribunal (Asylum Support)
2nd Floor
Anchorage House
2 Clove Crescent
East India Dock
London E14 2BE
Freephone: 0800 389 7913 (for those who need to discuss their appeal or the appeal process)
www.gov.uk/asylum-support

Office of the Immigration Services Commissioner
5th Floor
21 Bloomsbury Street
London WC1B 3HF
Tel: 020 7211 1500
info@oisc.gov.uk
http://oisc.homeoffice.gov.uk

Solicitors Regulation Authority
The Cube
199 Wharfside Street
Birmingham B1 1RN
Tel: 0370 606 2555
www.sra.org.uk

Legal Ombudsman

PO Box 6806
Wolverhampton WV1 9WJ
Tel: 0300 555 0333
Minicom: 0300 555 1777
enquiries@legalombudsman.org.uk
www.legalombudsman.org.uk

For complaints about lawyers.

European Commission Representation in the UK

Europe House
32 Smith Square
London SW1 P 3EU
Tel: 020 7973 1992
www.ec.europa.eu/unitedkingdom

Social security

HM Courts and Tribunals Service

Tribunal areas

Birmingham
Administrative Support Centre
PO Box 14620
Birmingham B16 6FR
Tel: 0300 123 1142
Birmingham@hmcts.gsi.gov.uk

Cardiff
Eastgate House
Newport Road
Hoel Casnewydd
Cardiff CF24 0YP
Tel: 0300 123 1142
SSCSA-Cardiff@hmcts.gsi.gov.uk

Glasgow
Wellington House
134–136 Wellington Street
Glasgow G2 2XL
Tel: 0141 354 8400
SSCSA-Glasgow@hmcts.gsi.gov.uk

Leeds
York House
York Place
Leeds LS1 2ED
Tel: 0300 123 1142
SSCSA-Leeds@hmcts.gsi.gov.uk

Liverpool
36 Dale Street
Liverpool L2 5UZ
Tel: 0300 123 1142
SSCSA-Liverpool@hmcts.gsi.gov.uk

Newcastle
Manor View House
Kings Manor
Newcastle upon Tyne NE1 6PA
Tel: 0300 123 1142
SSCSA-Newcastle@hmcts.gsi.gov.uk

Sutton
Copthall House
9 The Pavement
Grove Road
Sutton SM1 1DA
Tel: 0300 123 1142
SSCSA-Sutton@hmcts.gsi.gov.uk

First-Tier Tribunal (Tax)
HM Courts and Tribunals Service
Third Floor
Temple Court
35 Bull Street
Birmingham B4 6EQ
Tel: 0845 223 8080
www.justice.gov.uk/tribunals/tax
taxappeals@tribunals.gsi.gov.uk

The Upper Tribunal (Administrative Appeals Chamber)

England
5th Floor Rolls Building
7 Rolls Buildings
Fetter Lane
London EC4A 1NL
Tel: 020 7071 5662
www.justice.gov.uk/tribunals/aa
adminappeals@hmcts.gsi.gov.uk

Scotland
George House
126 George Street
Edinburgh EH2 4HH
Tel: 0131 271 4310
utaacmailbox@Scotland.gsi.gov.uk

Northern Ireland
Bedford House
16–22 Bedford Street
Belfast BT2 7FD
Tel: 028 9072 4883

Wales
Civil Justice Centre
2 Park Street
Cardiff CF10 1ET
Tel: 02920 662257

The Upper Tribunal (Tax and Chancery Chamber)

England and Wales
45 Bedford Square
London WC1B 3DN
Tel: 020 7612 9700
financeandtaxappeals@tribunals.gsi.gov.uk

Scotland
George House
126 George Street
Edinburgh EH2 4HH

Department for Work and Pensions
Caxton House
Tothill Street
London SW1H 9NA
www.gov.uk/dwp

Department for Work and Pensions (Office of the Solicitor)
DWP Litigation Division
Caxton House
Tothill Street
London SW1H 9NA

Department for Work and Pensions (Overseas Healthcare)
Room TC001
Tyneview Park
Newcastle upon Tyne NE98 1BA
Tel: 0191 218 1999

Disability and Carers Service

Attendance Allowance Unit
Warbreck House
Warbreck Hill
Blackpool FY2 0YE
Tel: 0345 605 6055
Textphone: 0845 604 5312
attendance.allowanceenquiries@dwp.gsi.gov.uk
www.gov.uk/attendance-allowance

Disability Living Allowance Unit
Claimants aged 16 years and over:
Warbreck House
Warbreck Hill
Blackpool FY2 0YE
Tel: 0345 712 3456
Textphone: 0345 722 4433
dcpu.customer-services@dwp.gsi.gov.uk

Claimants aged under 16 years:
Disability Benefits Centre 4
Post Handling Site B
Wolverhampton WV99 1BY
Tel: 0345 712 3456
Textphone: 03457 22 44 33
midlands-dbc-customer-services@dwp.gsi.gov.uk
www.gov.uk/dla-disability-living-allowance-benefit

Personal Independence Payment Unit
New claims
Post Handling Site B
Wolverhampton WV99 1AH
Claims: 0800 917 2222 (textphone 0800 917 7777)
Helpline: 0345 850 3322 (textphone 0345 601 6677)
www.gov.uk/pip

Carer's Allowance Unit
Palatine House
Lancaster Road
Preston PR1 1HB
Tel: 0345 608 4321
Textphone: 0345 604 5312
cau.customer-services@dwp.gsi.gov.uk
www.gov.uk/carers-allowance

Exporting benefits overseas
Exportability Team
Room B201
Pension, Disability and Carers Service
Warbreck House
Warbreck Hill Road
Blackpool FY2 0YE
Tel: 01253 331 044
exportability.team@dwp.gsi.gov.uk

Jobcentre Plus (income support, jobseeker's allowance, employment and support allowance and incapacity benefit)

New benefit claims
Tel: 0800 055 6688
Tel: 0800 012 1888 (Welsh speakers)
Textphone: 0800 023 4888
www.gov.uk/contact-jobcentre-plus

Enquiries about ongoing claims
Tel: 0345 608 8545
Tel: 0345 600 3018 (Welsh speakers)
Textphone: 0345 608 8551
www.gov.uk/contact-jobcentre-plus

Contacting your local jobcentre
Tel: 0345 604 3719
Tel: 0345 604 4248 (Welsh speakers)
Textphone: 0345 608 8551
www.gov.uk/contact-jobcentre-plus

The Pension Service
Tel: 0800 731 7898 (new claims)
Textphone: 0800 731 7339
Tel: 0345 606 0265 (enquiries or to report a change of circumstances)
Textphone: 0345 606 0285
www.gov.uk/contact-pension-service

Winter fuel payments
Winter Fuel Payment Centre
Mail Handling Site A
Wolverhampton WV98 1LR
Tel: 0845 915 1515
Textphone: 0845 606 0285
www.gov.uk/winter-fuel-payment

International Pension Centre
The Pension Service 11
Mail Handling Site A
Wolverhampton WV98 1LW
Tel: 0191 218 7777
Textphone: 0191 218 7280
trp.internationalqueries@gsi.gov.uk
www.gov.uk/international-pension-centre

HM Revenue and Customs (tax credits)

Tax Credit Office
Preston PR1 4AT
www.gov.uk/child-tax-credit
www.gov.uk/working-tax-credit

Tax Credit Helpline
Tel: 0345 300 3900
Textphone: 0345 300 3909
Advice line for advisers and intermediaries: 0345 300 3946

HM Revenue and Customs (child benefit and guardian's allowance)

Child benefit
Child Benefit Office
PO Box 1
Newcastle upon Tyne NE88 1AA
Tel: 0300 200 3100
Textphone: 0300 200 3103
Advice line for advisers and intermediaries: 0300 200 3102
www.gov.uk/child-benefit

Guardian's allowance
PO Box 1
Newcastle upon Tyne NE88 1AA
Tel: 0300 200 3101
Textphone: 0300 200 3103
www.gov.uk/guardians-allowance

HM Revenue and Customs (Office of the Solicitor)
South West Wing
Bush House
Strand
London WC2B 4RD

HM Revenue and Customs (national insurance)
National Insurance Contributions Office
Benton Park View
Newcastle upon Tyne NE98 1ZZ
Tel: 0300 200 3500
www.hmrc.gov.uk/ni

HM Revenue and Customs (Statutory Payments Disputes Team)
Room BP2301
Benton Park View
Longbenton
Newcastle upon Tyne NE98 1YS
Tel: 0191 225 5221

NHS Business Services Authority (help with health costs)
Tel: 0300 330 1343 (low income scheme)
Tel: 0300 330 1341 (medical and maternity exemption certificates)
Tel: 0300 330 1347 (NHS tax credit exemption certificates)
www.nhsbsa.nhs.uk/healthcosts

. . . .

Local Government Ombudsman

England
PO Box 4771
Coventry CV4 0EH
Tel: 0300 061 0614
www.lgo.org.uk

Scottish Public Services Ombudsman
4 Melville Street
Edinburgh EH3 7NS
Tel: 0800 377 7330
www.spso.org.uk

Public Services Ombudsman for Wales
1 Ffordd yr Hen Gae
Pencoed CF35 5LJ
Tel: 0300 790 0203
www.ombudsman-wales.org.uk

The Parliamentary and Health Service Ombudsman

Millbank Tower
Millbank
London SW1P 4QP
Tel: 0345 015 4033
phso.enquiries@ombudsman.org.uk
www.ombudsman.org.uk

The Adjudicator

Judy Clements
Adjudicator's Office
PO Box 10280
Nottingham NG2 9PF
Tel: 0300 057 1111
www.adjudicatorsoffice.gov.uk

Independent Case Examiner

The Independent Case Examiner
PO Box 209
Bootle L20 7WA
Tel: 0345 606 0777
ice@dwp.gsi.gov.uk
www.ind-case-exam.org.uk

Judicial Conduct Investigations Office
81–82 Queens Building
Royal Courts of Justice
Strand
London WC2A 2LL
Tel: 020 7073 4719
www.gov.uk/complain-judge-magistrate-tribunal-coroner

Standards Commission for Scotland
Room T2.21 Scottish Parliament
Edinburgh EH99 1SP
Tel: 0131 348 6666
enquiries@standardscommission.org.uk
www.standardscommissionscotland.org.uk

Commissioner for Ethical Standards in Public Life in Scotland
39 Drumsheugh Gardens
Edinburgh EH3 7SW
Tel: 0300 011 0550
info@ethicalstandards.org.uk
To make a complaint: investigations@ethicalstandards.org.uk
www.publicstandardscommissioner.org.uk

Appendix 4

Useful publications

Immigration, nationality and asylum

JCWI immigration, Nationality and Refugee Law Handbook
(6th edition), JCWI, 2006

Macdonald's Immigration Law and Practice
(9th edition), I Macdonald and R Toal, forthcoming

Immigration Law Handbook
(8th edition), M Phelan and J Gillespie, Oxford University Press, 2013

Fransman's British Nationality Law
(3rd edition), Bloomsbury Professional, 2011

Support for Asylum Seekers and Other Migrants
(3rd edition), S Willman and S Knafler, Legal Action Group, 2009

Best Practice Guide to Asylum and Human Rights Appeals
M Henderson and A Pickup, ILPA, 2012

Blackstones's Guide to the Human Rights Act 1998
J Wadham, H Mountfield, E Prochaska amd C Brown (eds), Oxford University
Press, 2011

Free Movement of Persons in the Enlarged European Union
N Rogers, R Scannell and J Walsh, Sweet and Maxwell, 2012

Children

*Working with Children and Young People Subject to Immigration Control: guidelines for
best practice*
H Crawley, ILPA, 2012, www.ilpa.org.uk/pages/publications.html

Children in Need: local authority support for children and families
(3rd edition), I Wise QC and others, Legal Action Group, forthcoming

Resources Guide for Practitioners Working With Refugee Children
(4th edition), S Gillan, A Harvey and S Myerscough, ILPA, 2014, www.ilpa.org.uk/
pages/publications.html

Working With Migrant Children: community care law for immigration lawyers
A Hundt and Z Yazdani, ILPA, 2012, www.ilpa.org.uk/pages/publications.html

Separated Children and Legal Aid Provision
S Valdez, ILPA, 2012, www.ilpa.org.uk/pages/publications.html

Resources Guide for Practitioners Working With Refugee Children
(3rd edition), A Harvey, ILPA, 2012, www.ilpa.org.uk/pages/publications.html

Working With Refugee Children: current issues in best practice
(2nd edition), S Bolton and others, ILPA, 2012, www.ilpa.org.uk/pages/
publications.html

Social security legislation

The Law Relating to Social Security
All the legislation but without any commentary. Known as the 'Blue Book'.
Available at http://lawvolumes.dwp.gov.uk (it is expected that this will transfer
to www.gov.uk sometime in 2014).

Social Security Legislation, Volume I: Non-Means-Tested Benefits, D Bonner, I Hooker
and R White (Sweet & Maxwell)
Legislation with commentary. 2014/15 edition (October 2014): £104 for the main
volume.

*Social Security Legislation, Volume II: Income Support, Jobseeker's Allowance and the
Social Fund*, J Mesher, P Wood, R Poynter, N Wikeley and D Bonner (Sweet &
Maxwell)
Legislation with commentary. 2014/15 edition (October 2014): £104 for the main
volume.

*Social Security Legislation, Volume III: Administration, Adjudication and the European
Dimension*, M Rowland and R White (Sweet & Maxwell)
Legislation with commentary. 2014/15 edition (October 2014): £104 for the main
volume.

*Social Security Legislation, Volume IV: Tax Credits and HMRC-Administered Social
Security Benefits*, N Wikeley and D Williams (Sweet & Maxwell)
Legislation with commentary. 2014/15 edition (October 2014): £104 for the main
volume.

Social Security Legislation, Volume V: Universal Credit, P Wood, R Poynter and N Wikeley (Sweet & Maxwell)
Legislation with commentary. 2014/15 edition (October 2014): £104 for the main volume.

Social Security Legislation – updating supplement to Volumes I – V, (Sweet & Maxwell)
The spring 2015 update to the 2014/15 main volumes: £66.

CPAG's Housing Benefit and Council Tax Reduction Legislation, L Findlay, R Poynter, S Wright, C George and M Williams (CPAG)
Legislation with detailed commentary. 2014/15 (27th edition, winter 2014): £109 including Supplement. The 26th edition (2013/14) is still available, £107 per set.

Social security official guidance

Decision Makers' Guide
Available at www.gov.uk/government/collections/decision-makers-guide-staff-guide.

Advice for Decision Making: staff guide
Available at www.gov.uk/government/publications/advice-for-decision-making-staff-guide.

Housing Benefit Guidance Manual
Available at www.gov.uk/government/collections/housing-benefit-claims-processing-and-good-practice-for-local-authority-staff.

Tax Credits Technical Manual
Available at www.hmrc.gov.uk/manuals.

Budgeting Loan Guide
Available at www.gov.uk/government/publications/budgeting-loan-guide-for-decision-makers-reviewing-officers-and-further-reviewing-officers.

Leaflets

The DWP publishes many leaflets available free from your local DWP or Jobcentre Plus office. To order large numbers of leaflets, or receive information about new leaflets, contact iON Contact Centre, One City West, Gelderd Road, Leeds LS12 6NT, tel: 0845 850 0475, email: ion-pass@xerox.com. www.gov.uk/government/collections/dwp-leaflets-and-how-to-order-them. Leaflets on housing benefit are available from your local council.

Periodicals

Welfare Rights Bulletin (CPAG, bi-monthly)
Covers developments in social security law, including Upper Tribunal decisions. The annual subscription is £35 but it is sent automatically to CPAG Rights members (more information at www.cpag.org.uk/membership).

Articles on social security and immigration can also be found in *Legal Action* (Legal Action Group), *The Adviser* (Citizens Advice) and the *Journal of Social Security Law* (Sweet & Maxwell).

Other social security publications

CPAG's Welfare Benefits and Tax Credits Online
Includes the full text of the *Welfare Benefits and Tax Credits Handbook* updated throughout the year. Annual subscription £55 + VAT per user (bulk discounts available). More information at www.cpag.org.uk/bookshop.

Universal Credit: what you need to know
£11 (2nd edition, July 2013)

Personal Independence Payment: what you need to know
£12 (1st edition, September 2013)

Winning Your Benefit Appeal: what you need to know
£12 (1st edition, December 2013)

Guide to Housing Benefit 2014-17
£35 (May 2014)

Help with Housing Costs: universal credit and council tax rebates 2014/15
£35 (1st edition, May 2014)

Disability Rights Handbook 2014/15
£32.50 (May 2014)

Tribunal Practice and Procedure
£55 (3rd edition, autumn 2014)

For CPAG publications and most other publications, contact:
CPAG, 94 White Lion Street, London N1 9PF, tel: 020 7837 7979, email: bookorders@cpag.org.uk. Order forms are available at www.cpag.org.uk/bookshop. Postage and packing: free for online subscriptions and orders up to £10 in value; for order value £10.01–£100 add a flat rate charge of £3.99; for order value £100.01–£400 add £6.99; for order value £400+ add £10.99.

Appendix 5

Reciprocal agreements

Benefits covered in conventions with European Economic Area member states

State	Retirement pension	Bereavement benefits	Guardian's allowance	Incapacity benefit (short-term)	Incapacity benefit (long-term)	Jobseeker's allowance	Maternity allowance	Disablement benefit	Industrial injuries benefits	Child benefit	Attendance allowance	Carer's allowance
Austria	✓	✓	✓	✓	✓	✓	✓	✓	✓	✓	-	-
Belgium	✓	✓	✓	✓	✓	✓	✓	✓	✓	✓	-	-
Croatia	✓	✓	-	✓	✓	✓	✓	✓	✓	✓	-	-
Cyprus	✓	✓	✓	✓	✓	✓	✓	✓	✓	-	-	-
Denmark	-	✓	✓	✓	✓	✓	✓	✓	✓	✓	✓	-
Finland	✓	✓	-	✓	✓	✓	✓	✓	✓	✓	-	-
France	✓	✓	-	✓	✓	✓	✓	✓	✓	✓	-	-
Germany	-	✓	✓	✓	✓	✓	✓	✓	✓	✓	✓	-
Iceland	✓	✓	✓	✓	✓	✓	-	✓	✓	✓	-	-
Ireland	✓	✓	✓	✓	✓	✓	✓	✓	✓	-	-	-
Italy	✓	✓	✓	✓	✓	✓	✓	✓	✓	-	-	-
Luxembourg	✓	✓	✓	✓	✓	-	✓	✓	✓	-	-	-
Malta	✓	✓	✓	✓	✓	✓	-	✓	✓	-	-	-
Netherlands	✓	✓	✓	✓	✓	✓	✓	✓	✓	-	-	-
Norway	✓	✓	✓	✓	✓	✓	✓	✓	✓	✓	✓	-
Portugal	✓	✓	✓	✓	✓	✓	✓	✓	✓	✓	-	-
Spain	✓	✓	✓	✓	✓	✓	✓	✓	✓	✓	-	-
Slovenia	✓	✓	-	✓	✓	✓	✓	✓	✓	✓	-	-
Sweden	✓	✓	✓	✓	✓	✓	✓	✓	✓	✓	-	-

There is no agreement with Greece or Liechtenstein. The agreement with Gibraltar provides that, except for child benefit, the UK and Gibraltar are treated as separate European Economic Area countries.

Although Northern Ireland is part of the UK, there is an agreement between Great Britain and Northern Ireland. This is because benefits in Northern Ireland and Great Britain are separate and administered under different social security legislation.

Benefits covered in conventions with non-European Economic Area member states

State	Retirement pension	Bereavement benefits	Guardian's allowance	Incapacity benefit (short-term)	Incapacity benefit (long-term)	Jobseeker's allowance	Maternity allowance	Disablement benefit	Industrial injuries benefits	Child benefit	Attendance allowance	Disability living allowance	Carer's allowance
Barbados	✓	✓	✓	✓	✓	-	✓	✓	✓	✓	-	-	-
Bermuda	✓	✓	-	-	-	-	-	✓	✓	-	-	-	-
Bosnia-Herzegovina	✓	✓	-	✓	✓	✓	✓	✓	✓	✓	-	-	✓
Canada	✓	-	-	-	-	✓	-	-	-	✓	-	-	-
Guernsey	✓	✓	✓	✓	✓	✓	✓	✓	✓	✓	✓	✓	-
Isle of Man	✓	✓	✓	✓	✓	✓	✓	✓	✓	✓	✓	✓	✓
Israel	✓	✓	✓	✓	✓	-	✓	✓	✓	✓	-	-	-
Jamaica	✓	✓	✓	-	✓	-	-	✓	✓	-	-	-	-
Jersey	✓	✓	✓	✓	✓	-	✓	✓	✓	✓	✓	✓	-
Kosovo	✓	✓	-	✓	✓	✓	✓	✓	✓	✓	-	-	-
Macedonia	✓	✓	-	✓	✓	✓	✓	✓	✓	✓	-	-	-
Mauritius	✓	✓	✓	-	-	-	-	✓	✓	✓	-	-	-
Montenegro	✓	✓	-	✓	✓	✓	✓	✓	✓	✓	-	-	-
New Zealand	✓	✓	✓	✓	-	✓	-	-	-	✓	-	-	-
Philippines	✓	✓	-	-	-	-	-	✓	✓	-	-	-	-
Serbia	✓	✓	-	✓	✓	✓	✓	✓	✓	✓	-	-	-
Switzerland	✓	✓	✓	✓	✓	-	-	✓	✓	✓	-	-	-
Turkey	✓	✓	✓	✓	✓	-	✓	✓	✓	✓	-	-	-
USA	✓	✓	✓	✓	✓	-	-	-	-	-	-	-	-

Appendix 6

Passport stamps and other endorsements

Figure 1: UK passport

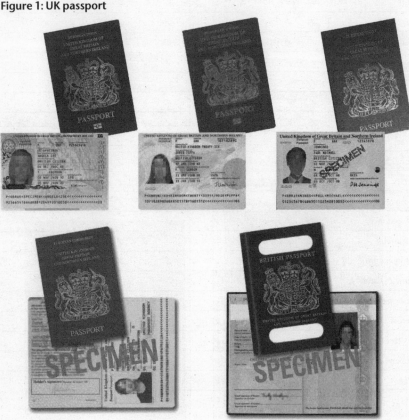

Figure 2: Certificate or document certifying permanent residence

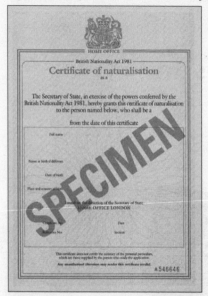

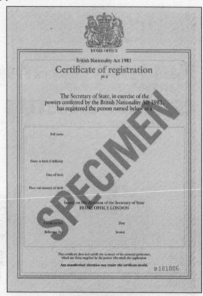

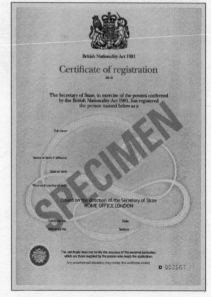

Figure 3: Certificate of entitlement to the right of above

Figure 4: Immigration status document

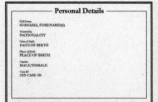

Figure 5: Biometric residence permit

The card's design is set by European Union (EU) regulation. It is a standard credit card size (86mm x 54mm) and will look similar to identity cards issued by other EU countries. The card is made from polycarbonate plastic and contains a chip to make it more secure against forgery and abuse.

1. Holder's digital image
2. Holder's name
3. Valid until – the date the card expires. This date is at the end of the time the holder is allowed to stay; or five or 10 years if the holder has been given permission to settle in the United Kingdom (known as indefinite leave to remain)
4. Place and date of issue – this is the UK followed by the date the card was issued
5. Type of permit – this is the immigration category the holder is in (for example, STUDENT)
6. Remarks – these are the immigration entitlements for the length of the holder's stay, and may continue on the back of the card
7. ZU1234567 – unique card number
8. Holder's signature

9. Biometric chip
10. Holder's gender
11. Holder's date and place of birth
12. Holder's nationality
13. Remarks – this is a continuation of immigration entitlements for the length of time of the holder's stay (see 6 above)
14. Machine readable zone (MRZ) – this area allows information printed on the card to be read quickly by machine

Figure 6: Registration certificate or document certifying permanent residence

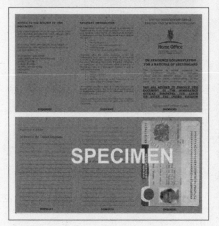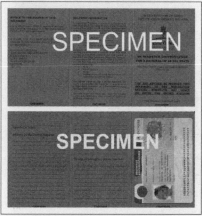

Figure 7: Residence card (including an accession residence card or a derivative residence card) issued by the Home Office to a non-European Economic Area national who is a family member of a national of a European Economic Area country or Switzerland or who has a derivative right of residence

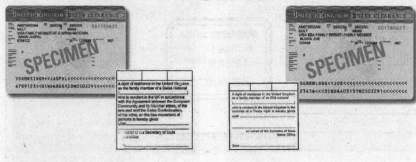

Figure 8: (clockwise from top left) Historic ink stamp endorsements, application registration card, visa vignettes and residence permit vignette

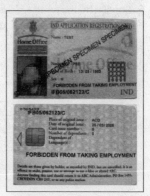

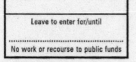

Figure 9: Entry clearance vignette

Figure 10: Date stamp on entry clearance vignette

Figure 11: Refugee Convention travel document

Figure 12: Notice of liability for removal

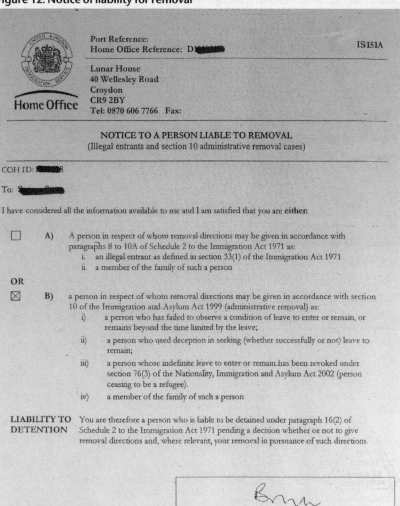

Port Reference:
Home Office Reference: D1████

IS151A

Lunar House
40 Wellesley Road
Croydon
CR9 2BY
Tel: 0870 606 7766   Fax:

Home Office

NOTICE TO A PERSON LIABLE TO REMOVAL
(Illegal entrants and section 10 administrative removal cases)

COH ID: ████

To: ████

I have considered all the information available to me and I am satisfied that you are **either:**

☐   A)   A person in respect of whom removal directions may be given in accordance with paragraphs 8 to 10A of Schedule 2 to the Immigration Act 1971 as:
    i.   an illegal entrant as defined in section 33(1) of the Immigration Act 1971
    ii.   a member of the family of such a person

OR

☒   B)   a person in respect of whom removal directions may be given in accordance with section 10 of the Immigration and Asylum Act 1999 (administrative removal) as:
    i)   a person who has failed to observe a condition of leave to enter or remain, or remains beyond the time limited by the leave;
    ii)   a person who used deception in seeking (whether successfully or not) leave to remain;
    iii)   a person whose indefinite leave to enter or remain has been revoked under section 76(3) of the Nationality, Immigration and Asylum Act 2002 (person ceasing to be a refugee).
    iv)   a member of the family of such a person

LIABILITY TO DETENTION   You are therefore a person who is liable to be detained under paragraph 16(2) of Schedule 2 to the Immigration Act 1971 pending a decision whether or not to give removal directions and, where relevant, your removal in pursuance of such directions.

Date: ●December 2006

On behalf of the Secretary of State

Important notice for persons detained under the Immigration Act 1971.

You may on request have one person known to you or who is likely to take an interest in your welfare informed at public expense as soon as practicable of your whereabouts.

IS151A 04/06

Figure 13: Notice of temporary admission

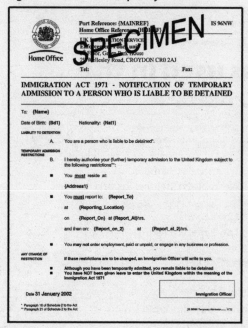

Figure 14: Embarkation stamp (not currently in use)

Appendix 7

Abbreviations used in the notes

AAC	Administrative Appeals Chamber
AACR	Administrative Appeals Chamber Reports
AC	Appeal Cases
All ER	All England Law Reports
All ER(D)	All England Law Reports (Digest)
Art(s)	Article(s)
CA	Court of Appeal
Ch	chapter
Civ	Civil Division
CJEU	Court of Justice of the European Union
Crim App R	Criminal Appeal Reports
CSOH	Court of Session, Outer House
Dir	Directive
ECJ	European Court of Justice
ECR	European Court Reports
EEA	European Economic Area
EFTACR	European Free Trade Association Court Reports
EU	European Union
EULR	European Union Law Reports
EWCA	England and Wales Court of Appeal
EWHC	England and Wales High Court
FLR	Family Law Reports
HC	High Court
HL	House of Lords
HLR	Housing Law Reports
IAC	Immigration and Asylum Chamber
Imm AR	Immigration Appeal Reports
INLR	Immigration and Nationality Law Reports
NICA	Northern Ireland Court of Appeal
NICom	Northern Ireland Commissioner
para(s)	paragraphs(s)

PC	Privy Council
QB	Queen's Bench Reports
QBD	Queen's Bench Division
r(r)	rule(s)
Reg(s)	regulation(s)
s(s)	section(s)
Sch(s)	Schedule(s)
SLT	Scots Law Times
SSAC	Social Security Advisory Committee
UKAIT	United Kingdom Asylum and Immigration Tribunal
UKHL	United Kingdom House of Lords
UKIAT	United Kingdom Immigration Appeal Tribunal
UKSC	United Kingdom Supreme Court
UKUT	United Kingdom Upper Tribunal
WLR	Weekly Law Reports

Acts of Parliament

AI(TC)A 2004	Asylum and Immigration (Treatment of Claimants, etc) Act 2004
BNA 1981	British Nationality Act 1981
CA 1989	Children Act 1989
C(S)A 1995	Children (Scotland) Act 1995
CSPSSA 2000	Child Support, Pensions and Social Security Act 2000
IA 1971	Immigration Act 1971
IA 1978	Immigration Act 1978
IA 1988	Immigration Act 1988
IA 2014	Immigration Act 2014
IAA 1999	Immigration and Asylum Act 1999
JSA 1995	Jobseekers Act 1995
NAA 1948	National Assistance Act 1948
NIAA 2002	Nationality, Immigration and Asylum Act 2002
SPCA 2002	State Pension Credit Act 2002
SSA 1975	Social Security Act 1975
SSA 1998	Social Security Act 1998
SSAA 1992	Social Security Administration Act 1992
SSCBA 1992	Social Security Contributions and Benefits Act 1992
TCA 2002	Tax Credits Act 2002
TCEA 2007	Tribunals, Courts and Enforcement Act 2007
WRA 2007	Welfare Reform Act 2007
WRA 2012	Welfare Reform Act 2012

Regulations and other statutory instruments

Each set of regulations has a statutory instrument (SI) number and date. You ask for them by giving their date and number.

A(IWA) Regs	The Accession (Immigration and Worker Authorisation) Regulations 2006 No.3317
A(IWR) Regs	The Accession (Immigration and Worker Registration) Regulations 2004 No.1219
AC(IWA) Regs	The Accession of Croatia (Immigration and Worker Authorisation) Regulations 2013 No.1460
AS Regs	The Asylum Support Regulations 2000 No.704
ASA(P) Rules	The Asylum Support Appeals (Procedure) Rules 2000 No.541
CB Regs	The Child Benefit (General) Regulations 2006 No.223
CB&GA(AA) Regs	The Child Benefit and Guardian's Allowance (Administrative Arrangements) Regulations 2003 No.494
CB&GA(Admin) Regs	The Child Benefit and Guardian's Allowance (Administration) Regulations 2003 No.492
CB&GA(DA) Regs	The Child Benefit and Guardian's Allowance (Decisions and Appeals) Regulations 2003 No.916
CTC Regs	The Child Tax Credit Regulations 2002 No.2007
CTR(S) Regs	The Council Tax Reduction (Scotland) Regulations 2012 No.303
CTR(SPC)S Regs	The Council Tax Reduction (State Pension Credit) (Scotland) Regulations 2012 No.319
CTRS(DS)E Regs	The Council Tax Reduction Schemes (Default Scheme) (England) Regulations 2012 No.2886
CTRS(DS)W Regs	The Council Tax Reduction Schemes (Default Scheme) (Wales) Regulations 2012 No.3145 (W.317)
CTRS(PR)E Regs	The Council Tax Reduction Schemes (Prescribed Requirements) (England) Regulations 2012 No.2885
CTRSPR(W) Regs	The Council Tax Reduction Schemes and Prescribed Requirements (Wales) Regulations 2012 No.3144 (W.316)
ESA Regs	The Employment and Support Allowance Regulations 2008 No.794
ESA(TP)(EA) Regs	The Employment and Support Allowance (Transitional Provisions, Housing Benefit and Council Tax Benefit) (Existing Awards) (No.2) Regulations 2010 No.1907
GA(Gen) Regs	The Guardian's Allowance (General) Regulations 2003 No.495

HB Regs	The Housing Benefit Regulations 2006 No.213
HB(HR)A Regs	The Housing Benefit (Habitual Residence) Amendment Regulations 2014 No.539
HB(SPC) Regs	The Housing Benefit (Persons who have attained the qualifying age for state pension credit) Regulations 2006 No.214
HB&CTB(DA) Regs	The Housing Benefit and Council Tax Benefit (Decisions and Appeals) Regulations 2001 No.1002
HSS(DHSF)(W) Regs	The Healthy Start Scheme (Description of Healthy Start Food) (Wales) Regulations 2006 No.3108
HSS&WF(A) Regs	The Healthy Start Scheme and Welfare Food (Amendment) Regulations 2005 No.3262
IA(POAFAS) Regs	The Immigration and Asylum (Provision of Accommodation to Failed Asylum-Seekers) Regulations 2005 No.930
I(EEA) Regs	The Immigration (European Economic Area) Regulations 2006 No.1003
I(EEA)A Regs 2012	The Immigration (European Economic Area) (Amendment) Regulations 2012 No.1547
I(EEA)A Regs 2013	The Immigration (European Economic Area)(Amendment) (No.2) Regulations 2013 No.3032
I(EEA)A Regs 2014	The Immigration (European Economic Area) (Amendment) Regulations 2014 No.1451
I(LER)O	The Immigration (Leave to Enter and Remain) Order 2000 No.1161
ILRFO Regs	The Integration Loans for Refugees and Others Regulations 2007 No.1598
IS Regs	The Income Support (General) Regulations 1987 No.1967
JSA Regs	The Jobseeker's Allowance Regulations 1996 No.207
JSA Regs 2013	The Jobseeker's Allowance Regulations 2013 No.378
JSA(HR)A Regs	The Jobseeker's Allowance (Habitual Residence) Amendment Regulations 2013 No.3196
SFM&FE Regs	The Social Fund Maternity and Funeral Expenses (General) Regulations 2005 No.3061
SFWFP Regs	The Social Fund Winter Fuel Payment Regulations 2000 No.729
SMP Regs	The Statutory Maternity Pay (General) Regulations 1986 No.1960
SMP(PAM) Regs	The Statutory Maternity Pay (Persons Abroad and Mariners) Regulations 1987 No.418
SPC Regs	The State Pension Credit Regulations 2002 No.1792

SPPSAP(G) Regs	The Statutory Paternity Pay and Statutory Adoption Pay (General) Regulations 2002 No.2822
SPPSAP(PAM) Regs	The Statutory Paternity Pay and Statutory Adoption Pay (Persons Abroad and Mariners) Regulations 2002 No.2821
SS(AA) Regs	The Social Security (Attendance Allowance) Regulations 1991 No.2740
SS(C&P) Regs	The Social Security (Claims and Payments) Regulations 1987 No.1968
SS(DLA) Regs	The Social Security (Disability Living Allowance) Regulations 1991 No.2890
SS(DLA,AA&CA)(A) Regs	The Social Security (Disability Living Allowance, Attendance Allowance and Carer's Allowance) (Amendment) Regulations 2013 No.389
SS(HR)A Regs	The Social Security (Habitual Residence) Amendment Regulations 2004 No.1232
SS(IA)CA Regs	The Social Security (Immigration and Asylum) Consequential Amendments Regulations 2000 No.636
SS(IB) Regs	The Social Security (Incapacity Benefit) Regulations 1994 No.2946
SS(IB-ID) Regs	The Social Security (Incapacity Benefit – Increases for Dependants) Regulations 1994 No.2945
SS(ICA) Regs	The Social Security (Invalid Care Allowance) Regulations 1976 No.409
SS(II)(AB) Regs	The Social Security (Industrial Injuries) (Airmen's Benefits) Regulations 1975 No.469
SS(II)(MB) Regs	The Social Security (Industrial Injuries) (Mariners' Benefits) Regulations 1975 No.470
SS(IIPD) Regs	The Social Security (Industrial Injuries) (Prescribed Diseases) Regulations 1985 No.967
SS(NIRA) Regs	The Social Security (Northern Ireland Reciprocal Arrangements) Regulations 1976 No.1003
SS(PA)A Regs	The Social Security (Persons from Abroad) Amendment Regulations 2006 No.2528
SS(PAB) Regs	The Social Security (Payments on Account of Benefit) Regulations 2013 No.383
SS(PFA)MA Regs	The Social Security (Persons From Abroad) Miscellaneous Amendment Regulations 1996 No.30
SS(PIP) Regs	The Social Security (Personal Independence Payment) Regulations 2013 No. 377
SS(WB&RP) Regs	The Social Security (Widow's Benefit and Retirement Pensions) Regulations 1979 No.642

SS(WTCCTC)(CA) Regs	The Social Security (Working Tax Credit and Child Tax Credit)(Consequential Amendments) Regulations 2003 No.455
SSB(Dep) Regs	The Social Security Benefit (Dependency) Regulations 1977 No.343
SSB(PA) Regs	The Social Security Benefit (Persons Abroad) Regulations 1975 No.563
SSB(PRT) Regs	The Social Security Benefit (Persons Residing Together) Regulations 1977 No.956
SS&CS(DA) Regs	The Social Security and Child Support (Decisions and Appeals) Regulations 1999 No.991
SSP Regs	The Statutory Sick Pay (General) Regulations 1982 No.894
SSP(MAPA) Regs	The Statutory Sick Pay (Mariners, Airmen and Persons Abroad) Regulations 1982 No.1349
TC(CN) Regs	The Tax Credits (Claims and Notifications) Regulations 2002 No.2014
TC(Imm) Regs	The Tax Credits (Immigration) Regulations 2003 No.653
TC(PC) Regs	The Tax Credits (Payment by the Commissioners) Regulations 2002 No. 2173
TC(R) Regs	The Tax Credits (Residence) Regulations 2003 No.654
TP(FT) Rules	The Tribunal Procedure (First-tier Tribunal)(Social Entitlement Chamber) Rules 2008 No.2685
UC Regs	The Universal Credit Regulations 2013 No. 376
UC(TP) Regs	The Universal Credit (Transitional Provisions) Regulations 2013 No. 386
UC,PIP,JSA&ESA (C&P) Regs	The Universal Credit, Personal Independence Payment, Jobseeker's Allowance and Employment and Support Allowance (Claims and Payments) Regulations 2013 No.380
UC,PIP,JSA&ESA(DA) Regs	The Universal Credit, Personal Independence Payment, Jobseeker's Allowance and Employment and Support Allowance (Decisions and Appeals) regulations 2013 No. 381
WF Regs	The Welfare Food Regulations 1996 No.1434
WTC(EMR) Regs	The Working Tax Credit (Entitlement and Maximum Rate) Regulations 2002 No. 2005

Other information

ADM	*Advice for Decision Making*
API	Asylum Policy Instructions
ASGN	Asylum Support Guidance Notes
DMG	*Decision Makers' Guide*
GM	*Housing Benefit/Council Tax Benefit Guidance Manual*
IDI	Immigration Directorate Instructions
IR	Immigration Rules
TCCCM	*Tax Credits Claimant Compliance Manual*
TCM	*Tax Credits Manual*
TCTM	*Tax Credits Technical Manual*

References like CIS/142/1990 and R(IS) 1/07 are to commissioners' decisions.
References like CH/426/2008 [2009] UKUT 34 (AAC) are references to decisions of the Upper Tribunal.
References like ASA/02/02/1877 are references to decisions of the First-tier Tribunal (Asylum Support).

Index

working tax credit
    abroad 231
    EU co-ordination rules 199, 233
    NI number 301, 305
    partner subject to immigration control 73
    person subject to immigration control 68
    refugees 77
    residence rules 198
workseekers
    see: jobseekers

Y
young people
    family members of EEA nationals 153

BECOME A MEMBER OF CHILD POVERTY ACTION GROUP

Over 2,000 organisations and individuals are members of Child Poverty Action Group. Please join us today to support our work, and to benefit from regular updates and member discounts.

Supporting membership – is a great way to contribute to our work and stay in touch with our campaign to end child poverty in the UK. You'll receive our members' magazine *Poverty* three times a year, along with monthly e-news and campaign updates.

Cost: £32 per year, or £13 for unwaged/students.

Rights membership – keep up-to-date with benefit changes and receive:

5% off all public training courses

A free *Welfare Benefits and Tax Credits Handbook* worth £46

A year's free subscription to our *Welfare Rights Bulletin* worth £35, sent to you six times a year. This is compulsory reading for welfare rights advisers and anyone needing to keep up to date with benefit changes. It includes essential caselaw summaries and provides updates to the *Handbook*

Pre-publication discounts on our main *Handbook*, as well as legislation volumes on social security, housing benefit and child support

Poverty **magazine** three times a year and monthly e-news.

You'll save at least £15 on publications right away, in addition to savings on legislation volumes and training.

Cost: £66 per year.

Rights online membership – similar to Rights membership above, but you will receive a one-year subscription to our online *Handbook* instead of a print copy.

Cost: £75 per year.

Find out more about our membership packages at: **www.cpag.org.uk/membership** or email: **membership@cpag.org.uk**

Child Poverty Action Group is a charity registered in England and Wales (registration number 294841) and in Scotland (SC039339). Company limited by guarantee and registered in England (registration number 1993854) Registered office: 94 White Lion Street, London N1 9PF. VAT No: 690 808117

CHILD POVERTY ACTION GROUP

DO YOU BELIEVE IN OUR WORK AND WANT TO MAKE A DIFFERENCE TO THE LIVES OF CHILDREN LIVING IN POVERTY IN THE UK?

Here are five easy ways you can help:

1 Take on a challenge or host your own event

Are you looking for a new sporting challenge, or have a brilliant idea for supporting CPAG via an event at your workplace, college or club? We would love to hear from you! Visit **www.cpag.org.uk/challenge-events** or email **fundraising@cpag.org.uk** to receive a free information pack.

2 Make a regular gift

Making a small donation to CPAG each month is the perfect way to show your support. Regular gifts are especially valuable as they enable us to plan ahead. Visit: **www.cpag.org.uk/donate-now** to download a standing order form.

3 Connect with us

Sign up to our email *News from CPAG* to find out about our latest campaigns, or follow us on Facebook or Twitter to keep up to date with our latest news and debates. **www.cpag.org.uk/signup/campaigns**.

4 Become a CPAG member

CPAG has membership packages to suit all interests, with plenty of fantastic benefits included. Please visit **www.cpag.org.uk/membership** or contact **membership@cpag.org.uk** for an information pack.

5 Ask your college or workplace to help

The CPAG fundraising team has lots of brilliant ideas to support your college or workplace in their fundraising. We would be enormously grateful if you would consider choosing CPAG as your charity beneficiary this year. Please contact Emily on **(0207) 812 5217** for an informal chat.